P9-DFI-441

# REIMAGINING INDIANS

*Native Americans through Anglo Eyes, 1880–1940*

Sherry L. Smith

2000

OXFORD
UNIVERSITY PRESS

Oxford New York
Athens Auckland Bangkok Bogotá Bombay Buenos Aires
Calcutta Cape Town Dar es Salaam Delhi Florence Hong Kong
Instanbul Karachi Kuala Lumpur Madras Madrid Melbourne
Mexico City Nairobi Paris Shanghai Singapore Taipei Tokyo Toronto

and associated companies in
Berlin Ibadan



Published by Oxford University Press, Inc.
198 Madison Avenue, New York, New York 10016

Oxford is a registered trademark of Oxford University Press.



Library of Congess Cataloging-in-Publication Data
Smith, Sherry Lynn.
Reimagining Indians : native Americans through Anglo eyes,
1880–1940 / Sherry L. Smith
p. cm.
Includes bibliographical references and index.
ISBN 0-19-513635-7
1. American literature—20th century—History and criticism. 2. American literature—19th century—History and criticism. 3. Indians in literature. 4. Literature and history—United States—History—20th century. 5. Literature and history—United States—History—19th century. 6. Indians of North America—Government relations.
I. Title.
PS173.I6 S55 2000
810.9'897—dc21 99-059096

1 3 5 7 9 8 6 4 2

Printed in the United States of America
on acid-free paper

For Bob

# ACKNOWLEDGMENTS

THE DUNE COUNTRY OF Northwest Indiana was the geography of my childhood. It was also, as it turns out, the inspiration for this book, although I did not realize that until I was well into the project. My family had a summer cabin on the shores of Lake Michigan. One of our neighbors was a man named Roy Hawkinson, a son of Swedish immigrants, born and raised in eastern South Dakota at the end of the nineteenth century. He migrated to Chicago where he sold rare books and spent his summers in the Indiana Dunes, but he never forgot his western boyhood and the Indians who lived on a nearby reservation. He decorated his Duneland cabin with drums and headdresses, pipes and blankets, all meant to evoke the people and the place he loved. On special occasions he dressed in Indian clothing, sang songs, and danced. He gave me and my entire family "Indian names." He was the grandfather I never had.

I now know that Roy Hawkinson was an "Indian hobbyist," one of those midcentury people who demonstrated an intense interest in Indians and attempted to recreate their dance, songs, and craftwork. He ignited in me an interest in the American West, Indian cultures, and, unconsciously, the importance of both to American culture and identity. I did not make the link between my childhood and this work, however, until the day I was sitting in the University of Montana Mansfield Library reading the correspondence of Frank Bird Linderman, a collector of Indian tales and writer of Indian "autobiography." There, to my surprise, I found a fan letter written by my friend Roy Hawkinson. I recognized the signature. I could hear his voice. At that moment I understood this book was more than an intellectual exercise. It was an effort to understand an important element of my life. Thank you, Roy, for enriching my childhood and inspiring my work.

Many others have contributed along the way. I owe a great debt to historians Paul Hutton, Patricia Nelson Limerick, Martin Ridge, Lewis O. Saum, and Richard White who liked my ideas and helped convinced others to support my research. The Huntington Library provided a Mellon Fellowship for a semester of research. The interest and support of Martin Ridge, Peter Blodgett, and informal conversations with other fellows, including Kathy Morrissey and Esther Lanigan, made the Huntington an ideal place to begin. A Frederick Beinecke Fellowship in Western Americana funded a one-month stay at Yale's Beinecke Library, and I greatly appreciated George Miles' and Howard Lamar's attentions to my work. The University of Texas, El Paso, provided several research grants including two University Research Institute grants and a Faculty Development grant which made possible travel to research libraries. The National Endowment for the Humanities supported this book through a Travel to Collections grant, a Summer Stipend grant, and a Fellowship for College Teachers. All were important, but the last was especially crucial to completing it.

Historians' works are inevitably dependent upon the expertise of librarians. I am most appreciative of the help provided by George Miles, Patricia Willis, and the staff of the Beinecke Library during my New Haven sojourn, as well as Richard Buchen's willingness to scour the Southwest Museum's Braun Library collections in search of relevant materials. Peter Blodgett and the Huntington Library staff were equally dedicated. Princeton University librarian Alfred Bush found relevant materials as did the staffs of the Montana State Historical Society; the Bancroft Library, University of California; Mansfield Library, University of Montana; Library of Congress; and the Sterling Library, Yale University. I appreciate the willingness of all these libraries, as well as the heirs of Frank Bird Linderman, to permit me to quote from materials and reproduce photographs from their collections. *The Pacific Northwest Quarterly* granted permission to reprint portions of two chapters that first appeared in that journal and Houghton Mifflin to reprint lines from Charles Fletcher Lummis's "Man-Who-Yawns" and "Santiago Narango" which appeared in *A Bronco Pegasus*.

I researched and wrote this book while teaching at the University of Texas, El Paso, where my colleagues proved to be sources of intellectual stimulation, professional encouragement, and inspiration. The core group of our Friday afternoon "seminars": Cheryl and Charles Martin, Sandy McGee Deutsch, Carl and Margaret Jackson, Kenton and Marlee Clymer, Chuck and Gloria Ambler, Ron and Merrie Weber, Ninon and the late Ellery Schalk created a climate of both genuine collegiality and long-lasting friendship. I am also appreciative of the interest of other historian friends, especially Michael Cassity, Mary Murphy, Joseph Jastrzembski, and Marly and Dan Merrill, who gave encouragement, asked questions about this project . . . and then listened. Dave Emmons first brought Frank Bird Linderman to my attention and Sandy McGee Deutsch did the same regarding Anna Ickes. The careful reading and editing by Oxford University Press's Thomas LeBien, Susan Ferber, and their anonymous reviewers improved the book considerably.

My family, including my brother, Brian Smith, and my sister, Reverend Barbara SilverSmith, continues to sustain me in my work and life. Atwood Smith, my father, takes pride in his children's academic and professional accomplishments, but those achievements are possible only because of the educational opportunities he and my mother, the late Adeline Behnke Smith, provided. More than that, they instilled in us a love of books, history, and, of course, provided the Indiana Dunes experience and the opportunity to know someone like Roy Hawkinson.

Finally, my husband and fellow historian, Robert Righter, has been a constant source of intellectual and emotional support. He encouraged this project from beginning to end, accompanied me on research trips, listened, prodded me to dig deeper, read various drafts, and gently suggested ways to approximate his own felicitous, clean writing style in my prose. But the greatest gift he has given me is a model of how to live a full life: one that engages in serious work, such as writing history, but one that also makes time for enjoying life—urging me occasionally, for example, to put aside books and float down the Snake River in his raft. These are just some of the reasons that I have dedicated this book to him.

# CONTENTS

# Reimagining Indians

# 1

# INTRODUCTION

A FEW YEARS AGO, I attended a slide-illustrated lecture on "Blackfeet Sacred Geography" presented by a member of the Blackfeet tribe. As lights lowered in the room and views of magnificent Montana and Alberta landscapes lit up the screen, Curly Bear Wagner described the events that made these places sacred. He explained where and how the Beaver Bundle came to the Blackfeet. He talked about Scarface and the Sun Dance. While Wagner displayed pictures of the sacred places, seemingly unchanged over the years, and related his peoples' connection to them, my mind drifted to Walter McClintock who, exactly one hundred years before Wagner's lecture, walked into a Blackfeet camp and found his life's calling.

McClintock was one of those turn-of-the-century types who concluded the Blackfeet, and other Indians, could not survive in the twentieth century. So, he set about filling notebooks with Indian stories, legends, and descriptions of ceremonies. He spent several years photographing the Blackfeet of Montana and Canada in various poses. In time, McClintock put together his own lantern-slide-illustrated lectures and went on the road, regaling audiences with stories of how the Blackfeet acquired the Beaver Bundle and tales of Scarface and the Sun Dance. He believed that without such efforts as his, all traces of Blackfeet culture would disappear forever.

Now, at the cusp of the twenty-first century, the Blackfeet are still here. They produce their own lectures and send their own representatives to explain who they are and how they came to be. Now we know that McClintock's prophecy, shared by so many of his generation, proved wrong, and that culture is not nearly so fragile or brittle an entity as once believed. Blackfeet culture survives in living, vital, and sometimes altered forms from those McClintock chronicled, because Blackfeet survive. The same holds true for other Native Americans. Credit for the perpetuation of Indian cultures goes to those tribal members who served as storehouses of memory and traditions and to families who, according to one historian, "continued to insulate individual Indians from alien cultures and provide a source of history and identity." For many years, in fact, the dominant culture's rejection and alienation actually served to foster Indian pride and dignity.[1]

Indian cultural survivals exist, however, in the context of an Anglo-dominated culture, and non-Indians have a role in this story too. Beginning in the late nineteenth century, some whites joined Indians' "war on homogeneity," and McClintock proved a perhaps unwitting recruit in the battle.[2] He perceived beauty and value in Blackfeet culture. He shaped his observations into books and, in the company of other writers, scholars, and artists working in the American West from the 1880s through the 1930s, produced a rich trove of materials that slowly, gradually, but undeniably nudged Anglo-Americans into reconsidering not only their view of Indians, but also Indians' place in this country . . . and in the future. This book examines some of those writers.

The twentieth century has witnessed a significant shift in Anglo-Americans' perceptions of Indians and the value of their cultures. One hundred years ago, when the nation's Indian population was at its nadir and forced assimilation seemed the most logical policy, the majority of Americans assumed the extinction of Indian cultures.[3] Today, not only has that assumption disappeared, but also now many non-Indians *celebrate* the persistence of diverse Indian cultures within the boundaries of the United States. Some even demonstrate an eagerness to embrace an Indian identity for themselves as increasing numbers of Americans claim Native American ancestry. Never before in American history have people been so eager to identify themselves genetically with American Indians.[4]

Alterations in federal Indian policy accompanied changing attitudes. Between the 1790s and the early twentieth century, conquest, acquisition of Indian land, and a cultural program of forced acculturation predominated. By the 1920s and 1930s, however, Indian policy "movers and shakers" began to reconsider the wisdom of past policies, particularly forced acculturation. Doubts became convictions by the Indian New Deal when, in 1934, Congress and Indian Commissioner John Collier scrapped assimilation and promoted cultural preservation. To be sure, this proved controversial not only among non-Indians but among some Indians too, particularly those who had accepted the means and ends of acculturation. Moreover, the changes Collier instituted, arguably deemed revolutionary, did not go unchallenged, and by the late 1940s and 1950s, the termination policy reversed the trend back to assimilation. By the middle of the twentieth century, however, Americans witnessed a resurgence in not only numbers, but also pride, self-awareness, and political and cultural assertiveness of Indians. Since the 1960s, themes of the Indian New Deal such as cultural persistence and pluralism reasserted themselves and evolved further into calls for greater self-determination and tribal sovereignty.[5]

How did this metamorphosis in attitude and action happen? The answer is complex, but we know the transformation was gradual. For centuries, conquest and corresponding assumptions about superior European civilization and inferior Indian savagery predominated. Throughout Indians continued to assert their worth and perpetuate their cultures. Such persistence proved crucial for a number of reasons, not the least of which was self-preservation. In addition, when ethnology and anthropology emerged in the nineteenth century, these Indian cultures attracted scholars' attention. As the latter scurried to record languages, practices, customs, and religious beliefs, they accorded respect for the cultures they wrote about. In time, they also promulgated new concepts of culture itself, rejecting social evolutionary hierarchies or racial models and replacing them with concepts of cultural relativism.[6]

Furthermore, popular writers such as Walter McClintock, George Bird Grinnell, and Mabel Dodge Luhan joined the academically trained anthropologists in giving Indians a fresh look. Some of these popularizers meant to do nothing more than capture for posterity a presumably fading portrait of Indian life in America. Some sought to find *themselves* through immersion in an alien yet attractive culture. Some sought to shatter stereotypes and replace them with complicated, humanized images of vibrant people and cultures. Taken altogether, their works transcended the personal and proved both culturally and politically consequential.

For approximately fifty years, the period roughly between the Dawes Act of 1887 and the Indian Reorganization Act of 1934, these writers produced books for popular audiences that offered new ways to conceptualize Indian people, alternatives to the images that had transfixed Americans for centuries. Simply put, these writers asserted Indians' humanity, artistry, community, and spirituality. Sometimes they lamented Indians' supposed demise. Sometimes they celebrated Indians' cultural resiliency and tenacity and insisted that Indians' cultural perpetuation would benefit all Americans. In the process they helped lay the cultural and intellectual groundwork not only for the Indian New Deal but also for deeper and more fundamental change in popular conceptions of Indians. In revealing their own doubts and misgivings about the superiority of European-American culture, they provided a more conducive climate for Indian cultural survivals in a world indisputably dominated by Anglo-Americans and encouraged notions of cultural pluralism among a greater number of people.

Essentially, these writers represent one group of non-Indians competing for the right, in the late nineteenth and early twentieth centuries, to construct identities for Indians. Lawyers, judges, journalists, educators, assimilationists, professional anthropologists, and this more amorphous collection of popularizers of ethnography, essayists, and poets who produced works about Indians for general rather than scholarly audiences joined the chorus.[7] All contested the right to speak on behalf of Indians, to define them and their place in the twentieth century, and to influence the political agenda regarding federal Indian policy. In doing so, they partook of a habit long ingrained in the American mind. To identify and articulate the meaning of Indianness had preoccupied non-Indians since the turn of the sixteenth century. From that point on, Europeans who visited American shores and those who chose to stay, contemplated "Indian" and used those deliberations not only to define Native Americans but also themselves. In short, the place of Indian in the American national imagination is a long-standing one.[8]

Of course, definitions changed over time. In the early years of the Republic some attempted to incorporate Indians into the national family, as part of a "consensual union of virtuous citizens."[9] Formation of a national identity seemed, in fact, to require coming to terms with Indians' precedence and presence. But such efforts kept colliding with history, with the reality that bloody conquest rested at the heart of the nation's relationships with Indians. The latter's status, rights, land, and livelihood was continually challenged, compromised, and often destroyed. The disconnect between political ideals and mendacious practices did not go unnoticed. Some even expressed fear that the nation's treatment of Indians meant capitalism and competitive individualism could not sustain America's moral values and sense of community. Most concluded that the fault rested ultimately with inferior Indians who had only two choices: assimilate or disappear.

By the conclusion of the nineteenth century, however, assumptions of Indian inferiority were undergoing serious revision just as doubts about capitalism, competitive individualism, and materialism grew—at least in some camps. Consensus was always a rare phenomenon in American thought, but turn-of-the-century contestants over the meaning of Indianness seemed particularly splintered. They also appeared more intent on scoring points against one another in their own debates than in defining Indians.[10] Perhaps once physical conquest was complete, the interpretive possibilities for the usable Indian opened up. The variety and heterogeneity of these various voices should not be completely surprising, however. American culture rarely offers a consistent central message but rather reveals patterns of meaning across the genres and among different people. Even when patterns emerge, we need to understand they include inconsistencies and tensions revealing inevitable cultural complexity.[11] At any given time no one discourse represents all opinions or attitudes.

In unraveling the cacophony of voices speaking about Indians at the turn of the century, historians have given most attention to political activists who advocated assimilation and to professional anthropologists.[12] In the post-Civil War years, assimilationists assumed that Indians, while culturally inferior, had the capacity for civilization and thus could be assimilated. Couching notions about Indians in the tenets of social evolutionary theory, they believed that Indians were capable of "progress" and that incorporating Indians into American society would be accomplished in a reasonably short time. They frowned on anything that impeded Indian progress toward civilization, whether it be living on reservations, practicing Indian religions, or participating in Wild West Shows. The latter, they believed, glorified a "savage past" and reinforced negative stereotypes, particularly regrettable since these shows often provided the only encounter many Americans and Europeans had with Indian people.[13] Though they could not forbid Indians from finding employment in such shows, assimilationists could exercise control over other aspects of their lives. They focused their energies on providing opportunities for ownership of private property, citizenship, and education, preferably at off-reservation boarding schools. The Dawes Act, which divided tribal lands into individual or family homesteads and then conferred citizenship upon allottees, was the legislative culmination of this philosophy.

By the 1890s, however, total assimilationists' optimism began to fade, replaced by growing disenchantment over Indians' capacity for progress. As a darker, more racist, more pessimistic view gained adherents, Indians found themselves now defined as permanently peripheral, destined to economic dependence and political impotence.[14] Conceptions of racial determinism eclipsed notions of social evolution as racial formalists argued Indians were biologically inferior, lacking both powers of reason and creativity. Destined to fall behind, they would eventually disappear altogether. Land allotment, citizenship, and education would not transform Indians after all, and so policymakers modified their approach accordingly. Land cessions accelerated, as did loss of Indian control of property through leasing and sale of allotments. The focus of Indian education turned increasingly toward vocational training for menial jobs. Indians found their citizenship rights drastically eroded, sometimes in the name of protecting Indians from exploitation (limiting the sale of alcohol), sometimes representing clear-cut discrimination on the basis of race (eliminating voting rights).[15]

Yet such ideas did not constitute the sum total of Anglo-American thought. A cluster of ideas associated with the professionalization of anthropology simultaneously arose. Rejecting both social evolution and racial formalism, anthropologists such as Franz Boas developed a concept of culture that included notions of relativism, pluralism, and functionalism. They stressed the diversity of cultures and abandoned the long-established practice of associating culture (singular) with civilization (Western or European). They advanced the integrative wholeness of all cultures.[16] Repudiating the imperialist, universalizing tendencies rooted in the French Enlightenment, this new concept provided a way of understanding human diversity. In the process, anthropologists discarded the tendency to rank all tribal societies as inferior to European ones. They appreciated Native American cultures in all their variety and strove to understand Indians and their achievements on Indians' terms.[17]

Popularizers, the subject of this book, joined in this debate but did not display the theoretical sophistication of their academic counterparts or take a consistent point of view. Espousing at times the rhetoric of assimilationists and at other times that of cultural pluralists, these writers proved much less systematic, cohesive, and intellectually constant than either anthropologists or assimilationists. They were, until the 1920s, more certain about the failures of current policy than alternatives to it. But they expressed growing doubts about the wisdom of forced acculturation and shared a profound interest in Indian cultures and a commitment not only to writing about, but also celebrating, them.

In the process, they also engaged in a conversation with, and about, modernity. To a degree, they shared the modernist inclination to shatter nineteenth-century conventions regarding cultural classifications and notions about race.[18] They demonstrated movement toward pluralism in thought, tolerance, and the assertion of all cultures' value. Simultaneously, they articulated a growing unease with the consequences of American industrialization, urbanization, and immigration. American life was undergoing tremendous transformation and they found in Indians, or more precisely Indianness, a refuge from the world they inhabited but wanted to flee. In reading the popularizers' works, one realizes that these people engaged with their times, rather than evade them; attempted to alter aspects of modern American life they found distasteful, rather than simply escape them. If they intended their works as windows into Indian worlds, they also served as mirrors into their own, presenting refracted images of their longings, desires, and sometimes neuroses. This is not to ignore the fact that some, particularly Grinnell and Frank Linderman and to a lesser extent Charles Fletcher Lummis and Walter McClintock, gathered and published substantial information about Indians. But in their works, too, concerns about contemporary American life seep in and rest just below the surface.

Their views of Indians, then, serve as vehicles for analyzing American culture in an era of great social and political upheaval. Their texts, many of which appear to be simple and uncomplicated, speak to a number of complex cultural themes as America entered the industrial age. Many of the works, for instance, are drenched in antimodernism. On the verge of a new century, some thoughtful, articulate Americans expressed doubts about industrial, capitalist society's "modern ethic of instrumental rationality that desanctified the outer world of nature and the inner world of self." These antimodernists worried about modernity's overemphasis on individualism, materialism, and worship of science and technology. To them, the new world seemed spiritually sterile and morally impotent. To counter these developments and recover some sense of transcendent meaning in a desanctified world, antimodernists—particularly those from Northeastern middle and upper classes who exercised considerable cultural power—looked for alternatives and found them in Oriental and medieval religious beliefs, preindustrial arts and crafts, and so-called primitive cultures.[19]

They also found them in American Indians, although historian Jackson Lears fails to acknowledge this important strain of antimodernism rooted in the West. Just as Henry Adams found transcendent meaning in Chartres Cathedral, Mabel Dodge Luhan found it in the Taos Pueblo. The antimodernists' quest for models of the simple life, the strenuous life, or the life of religious and spiritual meaning could take a Northeastern bourgeois across the Atlantic Ocean—or across the Mississippi River. Yearning for the authentic, the natural, the real could draw one to Asia—or to Arizona. Whether it was a fascination with the supposedly childlike and innocent aspects of premodern cultures, an enchantment with European folk and fairy tales, an attraction to the archaic warrior ideal, or an interest in visionary experiences, all of these impulses normally associated with antimodernists' off-shore gazes had their domestic counterparts in books about Indians. The writers examined here provide, then, a western corollary to earlier views of antimodernism which focused too myopically on the Northeast and Europe.[20]

Like the antimodernists of Boston, New York, and Philadelphia, and simple lifers from across the land, writers drawn to the West's Indians, expressed concerns over the present and anxiety about the future. Such impulses were partly inspired by nostalgia for a real or imagined past, partly by revulsion over the present, and partly by fear of the future. What they believed they saw in Indians' lives—mystery, beauty, spirituality, artistry, and community—appealed to them precisely because of its apparent divergence from Anglo-American emphases on possessive individualism, conformity, rationality, scientific determinism, materialism, and corruption. In turning to Indians, they offered a very American, though not uniquely North American, alternative.[21]

Of course, they did not agree completely on what ailed the modern world. One of the most important movements to emerge from the modernist revolution was feminism, and some of the men examined here found feminism deeply disconcerting. Frank Linderman positively despaired over women in politics. George Bird Grinnell shared this concern. Moreover, Grinnell's and Charles Fletcher Lummis's anxieties about the effeminacy of postfrontier urban life help explain the former's fascination with Plains Indians' hunting and warfare and the latter's fixation on masculinity and virility. Mary Austin, on the other hand, embraced feminism. An inability to elude completely her culture's limitations on women shaped her life and career as well as that of Anna Ickes and, to a lesser extent, Mabel Dodge Luhan. They challenged such restrictions. Not surprisingly, regardless of their views on gender or feminism, all found examples in Indians' worlds to support their positions.[22] The same holds true for other contemporary issues and themes—nativism, anarchism, progressivism, and primitivism—that find their ways into these authors' writing on Indians. The turmoil of the modern world led them to seek solace among Indians, but "Indians" did not provide one consistent blueprint on how to negotiate troubled times.

While antimodernism explains much about these writers, they can also, ironically, be labeled "ethnographic modernists" because they shared the turn-of-the-century compulsion to place Indians, and other so-called marginal people, into a historical and ethnographic space defined by the Western imagination. That meant, among other things, that Indians' destiny limited them to static, "traditional" pasts. In an increasingly complicated world dominated by capitalism and industry, these "endangered authenticities" supposedly had few options. Not only did anthropologists and the popularizers chronicled here assume a stagnant or static position for Indians, but they also assumed for themselves the authority to define the essential elements and boundaries of Indian cultures. They exhibited great confidence in their abilities to define a group's identity and authenticity because they operated in an intellectual climate where cultural difference was believed to be a "stable, exotic otherness."[23]

Recently, these ideas have come under attack and their hold over anthropologists and intellectuals is in decline. Yet for much of the twentieth century, what historian James Clifford called these "habits of mind and systems of value" predominated. The Western inclination to assume the power to define certain groups as exotic, to relegate them to a supposedly traditional past, and to see them as purer than "the diluted inventions of a syncretic present" remain powerful.[24] Charles Erskine Scott Wood, Frank Linderman, Mary Austin, Mabel Dodge Luhan, and others in this book shared these assumptions and, through their works, reinforced them. Nowhere is this clearer than in their almost universal dismissal of, if not downright hostility toward, Indians who attended off-reservation boarding schools and then returned to their reservations. They viewed these returning students as tainted by their experiences with the broader culture, as people who had lost their authenticity and consequently their ability to teach the dominant culture anything useful.

If they did not view all Indians as equally authentic, they did move toward the idea—in keeping with the concept of cultural relativism—that Indians and their cultures were not inferior to those of Europeans. Several went on to insist upon the universality of man. In the hands of non-Indian writers, the implications of this idea could cut several ways. It helped undermine commitment to notions of Anglo or European superiority and the concomitant policy of forced assimilation. It could also reinforce, perhaps unintentionally or unconsciously, racism. The correlations between notions of equality, universality, and racism have been elucidated by Sally Price, who defined the "Universality Principle" as a Western concept that emphasizes a "planetwide closeness with the flavor of Unity, Equality, and Brotherly Love."[25] This "Family of Man" ideology promotes toleration, benevolence, and compassion. It allows for an enlightened awareness and appreciation of cultural diversity and difference, but it is usually the Westerners who issue the invitations to join in the Brotherhood. They are the ones who initiate this generous, affectionate gesture. Meanwhile, the recipients of the invitation, particularly the "primitive artists" among them, are often relegated to categories such as simple, direct, and elemental.

These ideas, which Price attributed first to nineteenth-century anthropologists and then to twentieth-century Western artists and critics—and I would add people who wrote popular works about Indians in the early decades of this century—have become widely accepted as common knowledge. Just as ethnographic modernism has come under attack in some quarters, so too has the notion of primitive people as pure and innocent.[26] But such widely held beliefs do not die easily, and the authors examined here helped establish and reinforce them in the minds of their readers. Their works illuminate the popular roots of such common twentieth-century notions, and they reveal the potential for racism and ethnocentrism, even among those who believe themselves well-meaning and beyond such impulses.

This is a story, then, that speaks to broad themes of American cultural history. The writers examined here represent national rather than regional developments. Certainly, none of them were "western" in any simply defined way. All hailed originally from the East, Midwest, or England. Their formative years and their educations all took place far from desert stretches, the Rocky Mountains, Indian pueblos, or reservations. They came to the West only as adults. True, most of these writers lived much of their adult lives in the West and sometimes saw themselves as spokesmen and women for the region. The West's landscapes, and its Indian inhabitants in particular, profoundly impacted these chroniclers, for it was the one region in the nation where Indians still maintained a significant, distinctive cultural and physical presence. Military conquest notwithstanding, Indians continued to live in cohesive, though constantly threatened, communities in the West. This was especially true of the Pueblos and other Southwestern tribes who inspired so much commentary. Nevertheless, these writers' misgivings about the state of modern, American civilization derived from eastern experiences; only their "solution," turning to Indians, derived from western ones.

That said, the question remains: Where are Indians in all this? What roles did they play, if any, in the production of these works, and what value did the results have, if any, to Native Americans? To a certain extent, popularizers consciously attempted to integrate Indian people and voices into their works. And some Native Americans willingly participated in all aspects and all levels of this on-going conversation about themselves and their cultures. Certainly, they maintained their own internal set of identifiers. Their cultural life and validity required no outsiders' verification or articulation. At the same time, many Indians understood that they existed in a world which inevitably included European-Americans and that their self-definition could not exist without some interaction with the latter.[27] Just as American cultural identity entailed some relationship to Indianness, so too did Indian identity at least partially stem from the inescapable presence of Anglo-Americans.

Native Americans involved themselves in the discourse about Indians, then, because they understood the connection between knowledge, ideas, and truth, on the one hand, and agency, power, and practice, on the other. They attempted both to shape ideas and exercise social power despite their limited access to political power. Moreover, Indians did not agree on either what constituted the truth about themselves and their cultures, or on the proper goals of policy. And so, different individuals joined the conversation with different sectors of the dominant culture. Some supported the assimilationists' stance, though not the increasingly racist aspects of it. Many cooperated with anthropologists, advancing a more sophisticated understanding of their cultures and simultaneously the cause of cultural pluralism. Native Americans also played prominent roles in the production of popular works. Here, in fact, they took on their most pronounced, even public, roles. A few coauthored autobiographies. Others allowed Anglo writers to ghostwrite them. Yet others appeared prominently in the texts as informants. Every writer represented in these pages depended on Indian informants, men and women who chose to talk with them, tell stories around campfires, share their experiences, serve as intermediaries, interpret, and provide access to people and situations that helped enlighten them. Indians, after all, were the keepers of the information, cultural ways, rituals, and spiritual values that so attracted Anglo observers. Without Indian cooperation there would have been no stories to tell. To be sure, professional anthropologists and ethnologists relied on informants, but in their works, they often remained hidden, obscured in the language of an academic "science." The popularizers were more forthcoming about the collaboration.

The Indian participants in the production of "popular" knowledge naturally brought motives and perspectives distinctive from those of their white collaborators. First, as already noted, they provided an "insider's" point of view, thus offering crucial access to information as well as other informants. At the same time, the goal of humanizing Indians and combating stereotypes would prove more personally compelling to the Indian collaborators. Indians inevitably suffered the most direct and painful consequences of conquest and racism. And they encountered greater challenges in asserting their voices. Access to publishers and readers proved especially elusive for Native American writers in the early twentieth century.[28] Of course, a handful of Indian authors did break through the publishing barrier. Charles Eastman, Gertrude Bonnin or Zit-kala-sa, and Francis LaFlesche were among the most prominent Indian writers who published autobiographies. This important group of Indian intellectuals has attracted increasing attention and deserves more.[29] It is significant that Anglo popularizers steadfastly ignored Indian writers, as well as activists, who belonged to organizations such as the Society of American Indians. They preferred the supposedly more authentic, less tainted Indians of the reservation.

As a result, the efforts of those Native Americans engaged in the reimagining process examined here proved more circuitous and less direct than those of Eastman, Bonnin, and LaFlesche. Most often these Indian collaborators neither sought out white people nor initiated the encounters. Neither did they necessarily know how the information they shared would be shaped into texts that might distort or offend.[30] But once faced with the Anglos' presence, they decided to engage. Why did they cooperate? Motives ranged from a belief that rapid change dictated the necessity of preserving vestiges of their past, to hopes of gaining a political ally, setting the record straight, consciously trying to assert and define their place in the modern world, or receiving pay. The use to which some of these writers put Indians' knowledge, sacred or otherwise, no doubt caused some informants to regret their participation and others to determine never to do so again.[31]

Sometimes authors highlighted Indian informants' names and identities. Frank Linderman's "autobiographies" of the Crow, Pretty-shield, and Plenty Coups, provide one example. Mabel Dodge Luhan made it abundantly clear that Tony Lujan provided her a primary conduit into Taos Pueblo life, and Walter McClintock identified Brings-Down-the-Sun and Mad Wolf or Siyeh as his sources. Others did not reveal their Indian collaborators' identities. George Bird Grinnell's published pieces usually provided no clue about the people or the situations that informed his work. Whatever the degree of public recognition afforded Indians, however, it is clear the collaborations were not between equals. Clearly, the production of this knowledge involved power relations wherein the non-Indians held the balance. Not only did they have the English language skills, but they also had greater access to publishers and, by consequence, the hearts and minds of the American reading public. In addition, they had potentially greater access to political power, which Indians understood and sometimes attempted to manipulate. All the Anglo-American authors, perhaps not surprisingly, failed to acknowledge these power dynamics, let alone differentials.

These authors and most "western" ethnographers, whether professional or popular, never doubted their authority to speak for "natives." It was a time when Indians were just beginning to gain the education, language, skills, and publishing connections that would allow them more direct access to non-Indian readers. It was a time when Indians were just beginning to assert their right to speak for themselves. Moreover, it was a time when many intellectuals believed that all distinctive ways of life were destined to dissolve into the "modern"; and no one imagined these distinctive ways would reassert themselves. Today, according to Clifford, the "time is past when privileged authorities could routinely 'give voice' (or history) to others without fear of contradiction." We live in a time when "self and other, culture and its interpreters appear less confident entities."[32] The authors examined here exhibited no such anxieties. They exuded great confidence about their abilities to serve as purveyors of truth about Indians.

To be sure, as Clifford has noted, it is nearly impossible to know what happened in these ethnographic encounters. While all ethnographies are "textual constructions" and thus "complex, negotiated, historically contingent truth specific to certain relations of textual production," it remains difficult to ascertain the nature of those negotiations or to measure just how much power Indians had in shaping those constructions.[33] One can search, usually futilely, in Grinnell's field notebooks for clues. Frank Linderman's letters offer some insight into the techniques he used to interview Pretty-shield. But for the most part, the Indians' viewpoints are elusive. How did they understand and influence the research process? To what extent did the final texts reflect Indian concerns, emphases, interests, understandings, and purposes? One can never answer such questions definitively, but whenever possible I have incorporated Indian collaborators' points of view and perspectives into this story. It is certain that Indians consistently used—or tried to use—their relationships with these writers to advance particular interests or concerns, whether it be ridding themselves of a corrupt agent or advancing broader goals. Furthermore, some of these authors' works retain value to Native Americans today. Curly Bear Wagner, for instance, acknowledged that Grinnell's Blackfeet notebooks contain much valuable information. Walter McClintock's and George Wharton James's photographs have great worth to scholars and Indian descendants alike. Certainly, other Indians find the fruits of "salvage ethnography"—old texts of myths, linguistic samples, lore—still have a place in their history and tribal literature.[34] Ultimately, however, Anglos retained the dominant position in this discourse. They shaped the "data" informants provided into the texts that audiences consumed. That is why the Anglo writers remain the primary focus of this study.

I have selected a representative, but not exhaustive, group of non-Indian popularizers, nonacademic writers whose works provide geographical breadth across the West and chronological sweep from the 1880s through the 1930s.[35] Charles Erskine Scott Wood, George Bird Grinnell, Walter McClintock, and Frank Bird Linderman wrote about Indians of the Pacific Northwest, Alaska, the Northern Rockies, and the Great Plains. Charles Fletcher Lummis, George Wharton James, Anna Ickes, Mary Austin, and Mabel Dodge Luhan turned their attention to Native Americans of California and the Southwest. The fact that they represent geographical diversity and, at least, two distinctive generations indicates how widespread and long-lasting this reimagining process was. They often knew one another, corresponded, and understood they shared an interest in Indians, though it would be an overstatement to claim they represent a school of thought. Some were more prominent in their lifetimes than others. Some wrote extensively about Indians, others only sporadically. Some spent considerable time among Indian people, others very little. Some were men, others women. They represented wide swings on the political spectrum, from C.E.S. Wood's radical anarchism to Frank Linderman's right-wing nativism, from Grinnell's close relationship with Republican politicians to Luhan's connection with Democratic ones. Yet all shared a deep interest in and commitment to telling the "truth" about Indians, and all intended the majority of their works for general audiences, rather than scholarly ones. What fame some maintain to this day rests on their role as interpreter of Native Americans for the general reader.[36]

These writers wished to shape Americans' views of the Indian cultures in their midst. They all insisted on a nuanced, sympathetic, and humane vision that went well beyond the limits of earlier centuries' expressions of noble savagery. To acknowledge that they often failed to grasp the complexities of Indian peoples; that they often failed to transcend their own ethnocentric and even racist assumptions; and that early twenty-first century Indian and Anglo readers might find their works sentimental, romantic, and simple-minded does nothing to negate their cultural power. These writers worked autonomously and articulated no shared sense of purpose. Certainly, none of these figures individually or single-handedly moved Americans to reconsider either their collective assessment of Indians or their place in American society. Nor did any of them necessarily expect to shape or reconfigure the contours of federal Indian policy.

It is not their individual efforts, then, but rather the cumulative, collective effect and force of all these writers' utterances about Indians that helped to gradually, subtly, bit-by-bit bring about substantive change in attitude, understanding, and eventually policy. Astoundingly simple messages such as Indians are human beings, Indians have families that love one another, and Indians carry on lives of religious beauty and deep spirituality served to counter deeply held notions that Indians were more bestial than human, had little sense of connection to family or home, and were pagans. Decade after decade, writer after writer, these simple messages found expression until, finally, they had so eroded nineteenth-century assumptions that there was finally acknowledgment of Indians' essential humanity, the value of their cultures, and the possibility of their having a future in the twentieth century.

Certainly, the seeds of such perceptions had been sown long before. The concept of noble savagery contained the kernels of such potential reassessments. What is different in these writers' works is the absence of savagery and nobility. The message now was: Indians are more like you and me than either noble or savage would suggest. In this way these works cohere with the complicated, turn-of-the-century story regarding the emergence of cultural pluralism. The figures in this book contributed to this development, even if they were not always consciously doing so. Many of them shared anthropologists' inclinations toward cultural relativism and pluralism and perhaps proved equally influential, for they addressed their books and articles to different—broader, more extensive audiences—than did the scholars.

This issue of influence, of course, is an important yet slippery one. Did these writers play a key role in reorienting public attitudes, and even policy, away from assimilation and toward cultural acceptance and toleration? And, if so, how does one measure, let alone prove, it? Does the historian count the number of books each author published or sold? How can we know if consumers ever read the books, how they read them, if they ever found themselves influenced, shaped, or changed by them, or if they were even conscious of such potential change? Historian Lawrence Levine has argued that audiences are not mindless consumers but active participants in the creation of popular culture. Alas he provides no model for how to discern audiences' roles in shaping culture or in being shaped by it.[37] In the end, cultural historians usually assert influence rather than document it. Still, this remarkable group of articulate people, publishing a constant stream of books about Indians that affirmed their humanity and celebrated their cultures—when viewed cumulatively and when understood to represent a significant collective voice of this period—is difficult to ignore. To deny their importance seems greater folly than to affirm it.

If one looks to lobbying and legislation as the political expression of culture, though, a pattern of influence can be more clearly discerned. The decades covered in this book coincide with a period of the most heavy-handed forced acculturation. The Dawes Act of 1887 instituted the break-up of reservations and made allotment, usually in the form of 160 acre homesteads, mandatory for many tribal members. Off-reservation boarding schools became increasingly popular among policymakers, who sometimes forcibly removed children from home and family to attend them. On-reservation suppression of Indian religions and dances paralleled this educational initiative. Some agents feared religious practices encouraged resistance to federal policy; others viewed them as pagan. What is notable about the writers examined here is their almost universal disagreement with the major policy initiatives of the day. Allotment, boarding schools, and suppression of religion and dance all came under attack. Furthermore, they not only criticized these policies in print, but also utilized the power of their pens and political connections to remedy the greatest abuses of the government. Often encouraged to engage in political wrangling on behalf of Indians, *by Indians*, the majority of these writers engaged at some level. And the sum total of their efforts was to undermine, if not completely reverse, the most deleterious aspects of forced acculturation.

Significant rethinking of fundamental policy goals did not materialize, however, until the 1920s. It came primarily out of the Southwest, inspired by efforts to protect Pueblos' land and water. Opposition to the Bursum Bill, which attempted to deprive the Pueblos of property and water rights, politically mobilized writers from across the West, including many examined here. They also supported John Collier's 1934 Indian Reorganization Act, which is both the political expression and the legislative climax of the cultural developments that this book tracks. Actually, some of the writers featured here played a central and direct role in helping construct the intellectual, cultural, and political foundation for this legislation. Charles Fletcher Lummis, Mabel Dodge Luhan, Mary Austin, and Anna Ickes all knew and helped shape Commissioner John Collier's view of Indians and Indian cultures.[38] C.E.S. Wood and Frank Linderman lived outside Collier's orbit, but when the time came, they threw their support behind his efforts at federal reform. George Bird Grinnell and Walter McClintock, on the other hand, did not know Collier or anticipate his assumptions about Indians or Indian policy. Still, even Grinnell and McClintock helped erode certainty about Anglo-American superiority and, consequently, commitment to a policy designed to destroy Indians' ways of life. If they did not offer a blueprint for completely redesigning policy, they certainly raised doubts about the assumptions underlying contemporary approaches. If they did not trumpet the advantages of cultural pluralism, they certainly sounded notes of doubt about ethnocentrism.

For too long historians have interpreted the Indian New Deal primarily as the work of John Collier. According to one historian, Collier was "the individual most responsible for shaping alternatives" to the Dawes Act. According to another, behind the dramatic policy change of the 1930s "stood one man, the clearest symbol of the end of the old and the beginning of the new—John Collier."[39] To begin and end with Collier is to ignore the much more complicated story of the many men and women, Indians and Anglos, scholars and popularizers, whose published works and public actions contributed to significant policy change. It also oversimplifies the process by which change takes place, at least in American politics, which is more often than not evolutionary, rather than revolutionary; moving in fits and starts.

In pushing for Indian policy reform, however bumpily, these writers take on additional national significance and diverge from other antimodernists. People such as Linderman, Lummis, Ickes, Austin, and Luhan found ways to translate their abstract ideas about Indians into action. Whereas Lears argues that Northeastern antimodernists ultimately failed in their quest for a life of meaning because they had no ethical or religious commitments which transcended the self, the Indian enthusiast antimodernists did transcend self, break through old patterns, and help institute meaningful change. By presenting Indian people and cultures through a positive prism, they helped break down the assimilationist-acculturationist hold on American imaginations and cleared the way for a more pluralistic view. The legislative expression of these impulses, particularly the Indian New Deal, rejected a hierarchical understanding of cultures; challenged a long-standing, single-minded policy emphasis on possessive individualism; and replaced it with a celebration of cooperation and group culture. This, in turn, led to tangible change for some tribes, including expansion and reconsolidation of reservation land bases; the end of government suppression of religious and other cultural practices; revitilization of Indians arts and crafts; and in some cases, establishment of tribal councils to exercise a greater degree of power over their lives, though surely falling short of complete sovereignty. The Depression, that remarkable social and economic crisis which called into question many aspects of American culture, offered a golden opportunity for such a turn-about. Antimodern Indian enthusiasts or "western" simple-lifers were primed to take advantage of it.[40] These voices out of the West helped forge a way to transport innovative ideas about Indians from the realm of the imagination to that of the reservation.

I have organized the book by taking up these writers individually. In part, this reflects the idiosyncratic nature of their works. Each found his or her way to Native Americans through a unique, distinctive route. While I believe they shared much in their conceptions of Indians and critiques of American culture and modernity, separate analysis demonstrates how wide-ranging was the Anglo-American impulse to reimagine Indians. I begin with several men, born at mid-nineteenth century, who first encountered Indians in the Pacific Northwest and Northern Plains before conquest was complete. I end with several women, born a generation later, who arrived in the Southwest, several centuries after the Pueblos had come to terms with their own conquest by Europeans. The chapters follow a geographical arc starting in the Pacific Northwest and moving out to the Northern Rockies, the Plains, California, and the Southwest. They are also organized chronologically, starting with C.E.S. Wood's earliest published works which appeared in the 1880s and ending with Mabel Dodge Luhan's books of the 1930s.

Furthermore, I have arranged the writers into thematic cohorts. Wood,

Grinnell, and McClintock came West and into Indians' orbits somewhat accidentally with the army or a thirst for adventure bringing about the initial acquaintance. Wood's sharp critiques of American life and flirtations with anarchism notwithstanding, all three represent Progressive responses to Indians. Lummis's, Linderman's, and James's entrance into the West and its wonders was more purposeful, conscious, and focused. They became regional interpreters who more vigorously critiqued American and particularly Eastern culture, more rigorously questioned Indian policy, and pushed for more significant reform. Austin, Ickes, and Luhan make up the third group, a generation distinctive from the first in age and orientation. Their misgivings about modern America were more pronounced and their cultural critiques and reconceptions of Indian policy more radical. They helped bring to fruition Collier's Indian New Deal.

Threaded throughout the three cohorts is the gradual development of a relativist appreciation of Indian cultures; a shared appreciation for individualism and self-expression (particularly their own), on the one hand, and a celebration of community on the other; and a growing inclination to turn cultural critique and aesthetic appreciation into political activism and reform. Finally, they were all products of their time—and shapers of ours.

Interestingly, all of these writers' works remain in print and continue to shape peoples' views of Indians. After Curly Bear Wagner finished his lecture on Blackfeet Sacred Geography, which he presented in a museum, I wandered into the gift shop and bookstore. There I discovered many of these writers' works on display—an impressive number of them recently reissued in colorful, bright, new paperback versions. Wood's, McClintock's, Lummis's, James's, Linderman's, Austin's, Luhan's, and Grinnell's works can all be readily found in libraries and bookstores across the country, poised to influence readers and shape images of Indians into the twenty-first century. Who *were* these people? What drew them to Indians as subjects of their work? Why did Indians cooperate with them? What views did they present of Indians and, in the process, what did they reveal about themselves? What long-term impact did they have politically and culturally? The time has come to take a serious look at them.

# Part I

# Eastern Adventurers

# 2

# FROM ENEMY TO INSPIRATION

## *Charles Erskine Scott Wood and the Meaning of Indians*

IN 1875, LIEUTENANT CHARLES ERSKINE SCOTT WOOD, a freshly minted graduate of the United States Military Academy, set off for the West. He carried with him the trappings of a soldier, but the soul of a poet. That Wood landed in the Indian-fighting army was his father's doing. William Maxwell Wood, surgeon general of the United States Navy, had secured a West Point appointment for his son. But the imaginative, artistic young man did not enjoy the regimentation of military life, and his academic record proved mediocre for Erskine and his father were often at odds. Wood believed his father's military demeanor made him a "despot" within the family, later claiming that the "joyless tyranny in which we were brought up made a lasting impression on me." For his part, the father declared Erskine "a perfect Indian."[1] From earliest childhood, then, Erskine juxtaposed the army and the Indian, with the military representing regimentation, despotism, and tyranny, and the Indian, resistance to such things.

Although he did not realize it in the mid-1870s, Wood was about to embark on an experience that would build on his childhood definition of "Indian" and shape his life. For the remainder of that very long life, which included careers as a soldier, corporate lawyer, and poet, Indians played a role. Whether enemy or inspiration, they helped formulate Wood's political and poetic point of view. Indians became exemplary foils for his brand of social criticism and prototypes for his view of alternative ways to live.

Wood's introduction to Indians, then, originated in the nineteenth-century story of conquest. But from the start he brought to the encounter a distinctive sensibility, one that set him apart from most of his fellow army officers and that would place him squarely in the company of those early twentieth-century types simultaneously drawn to elements of modernity but repelled by others. Wood, a reluctant warrior, welcomed the opportunity to become intimately acquainted with Indian men and women over the decade he spent in his nation's infantry. Attracted to them, enamored with what he saw as their simpler but more poetic lives, Wood formed friendships with native people. In later years, as he worked and reworked these experiences with Indians into prose and poetry, he reformulated the fundamental meaning of "Indian" from object of conquest to tool of social criticism and object of emulation.

C.E.S. Wood's experiences with Indian people, however, remained limited. He did not systematically study them or live among them for long periods of time, as other writers did. After he left the army and took up law in Portland, Oregon (where he completed many of his writings on Indians), his interactions with them became even more tenuous. The Indians of Wood's works, then, are mostly romanticized, abstract, primitivist projections of Wood's yearnings. They mirror his soul rather than the Nez Perces', Shoshones', or Chilkats'. He was more interested in expressing himself than in explaining them. Indians, in the end, became the raw material out of which C.E.S. Wood fashioned a vision of life founded on beauty, simplicity, truth, and Nature. And yet, in his insistence on the attractions of "Indian ways," and in contrasting them to the ugliness and depravity of the society that attempted to destroy them, Wood anticipated a major impulse of the twentieth century. He, like other, later modernists found in Indianness salvation, both personal and social, during troubled times. Charles Erskine Scott Wood was among the first to set the new terms many Anglo-Americans would eventually accept regarding the meaning and value of Indians in the modern world.

Born on the shores of Lake Erie in 1852, Wood's childhood games focused more often on playing pirates than cowboys and Indians. Although he chafed at his father's harsh discipline, he also admitted that the senior Wood loved books and saw to it that his children encountered great literature at an early age. This became one of the father's more beneficial legacies. By the time of the Civil War, surgeon Wood moved his family to the outskirts of Baltimore, where Erskine enjoyed the Maryland woods and attended Baltimore schools. At age eighteen, Wood reluctantly accepted the West Point appointment his father arranged. At the military academy, Wood's rebellious nature found fertile grounds, although never to the point of expulsion. He managed to pass his mathematics and engineering courses, excel in military drawing, and, in 1874, graduated in the middle of his class.[2]

Wood's lackluster academic performance resulted in a commission, in 1875, to the Twenty-First Infantry, stationed at remote Fort Bidwell in northeast California. He had hoped for a more glamorous assignment with the Seventh Cavalry, but when he tried to exchange this post for one in Custer's Cavalry, the adjutant general refused the request. Later, Wood claimed this decision saved his life, since over two hundred of Custer's men died the following year on the banks of the Little Bighorn River. Meanwhile, the infantry appointment proved surprisingly advantageous. It afforded the dashing young officer the opportunity to befriend, rather than fight, Indian people. At Fort Bidwell, his unusual, even intimate, relationships with Indians began.

Given the profound impact these early encounters with Indians had upon

Wood, they deserve some attention. He befriended, for instance, a Paiute named Debe. Wood hunted with him and even stayed in his home where, he later remembered, "we all turned in . . . like a happy family. That should be the way if Indians were treated properly." In fact, Wood had a standing invitation from Debe to visit or hunt with him.[3] Such opportunities provided respite from an assignment Wood otherwise found desolate and solitary. Prospects brightened, however, with new orders to pack for Fort Vancouver, Washington Territory, which, in contrast to Bidwell, seemed "the very midst of civilization." During the march from California through eastern Oregon, Wood encountered the Harney Desert for the first time. He discovered, "It was all tremendously beautiful, breathtaking. That desert was as if it were the whole world. The sky above was a million worlds. It was enough to impress the most calloused heart."[4] Wood found, in the midst of that desert, the core of meaningful existence.

The young lieutenant tucked away the memory of that place's poetic potential, for a future day. At Fort Vancouver, Wood again became bored with military life and, anxious for escape as well as adventure, jumped at the chance to go to Alaska as a military escort for Charles Taylor, a mountain climber from Chicago. When the sailing schooner Taylor had chartered for the trip proved unavailable, Taylor and Wood hired a large Haida war canoe. The Indian owner acted as steersman, assisted by four oarsmen and an interpreter who spoke a smattering of Russian and English. Wood told Taylor they would have to "do as the Indians do—subsist from the sea—and so we set forth." They paddled up to Cape Fairweather and successfully scaled Mount Fairweather but did not reach their other goal, the top of Mt. St. Elias. At the end of the adventure, they returned to Sitka where Wood was not yet ready to go back to Fort Vancouver.[5]

Inspired by the blank map of Alaska, he applied for a three-year leave of absence to explore the interior. Though Wood left no contemporary record of this period, he wrote about it later in life. While waiting for a response from the army, he decided to explore the source of some rich ore samples two prospectors had shown him. Caught in a furious storm amidst calving icebergs, the little group took refuge in an Indian village at the head of an icy bay. Finding the village chief's son ill, Wood ministered some quinine pills and powder and, in return, the grateful headman offered Wood's group his hospitality. He also introduced Wood to his niece. She was "young, plump, good looking (as the round faced Thlinkit [*sic*] Indian are -good looking after their fashion)" and when she offered to share her quarters with the young lieutenant, he accepted. "I was then 25 and wore sky-blue army trousers," Wood romantically recalled, when "the 'princess' after the simple frank fashion of her sex among her people made love to me." Comfortable midst the bear skins, seal and fox furs, Wood remained with her until the "storm was well over."[6]

The lieutenant told the woman, who remained nameless in his accounts, that he hoped to ascend the Chilkat River to its source and cross the divide to

*In 1877, Lieutenant Charles Erskine Scott Wood fought in the Nez Perce War but found himself attracted to the Indian enemy. Later in life he sent his son to live with Chief Joseph for several summers. Reproduced by permission of The Huntington Library, San Marino, California.*

the Yukon, but that he understood her uncle would kill anyone who attempted this. She offered to take Wood herself, using her own slaves and canoes, and then to bring him "safely back to live with her." She would take no other soldiers, Wood went on, "because her uncle tho' he would have no objection to me as her lover—certainly would be restive and suspicious of an armed band and we might all be wiped out except herself." In her "princessly, autocratic executive" way, she guaranteed the success of Wood's endeavor and so, he returned to Sitka to pick up supplies for the adventure. The woman promised to wait for him and, in his absence, prepare for their journey.[7]

As it turned out, Wood never saw her again. When he reached Sitka, he received mixed messages. The government granted his three-year leave of absence, but Wood also learned that his regiment had been ordered into the field against the Nez Perces. Believing his primary duty rested with his regiment in combat, he left immediately for Fort Vancouver. "[H]onestly to this day," Wood wrote nearly fifty years after the event, "it is one of my regrets that the Nez Perces War sudden and unexpected made me break my word to this girl and add one more example to the long list of mans [*sic*] and white mans perfidy."[8] To be sure, Wood intended to use this woman in order to expedite his explorations. It is clear this relationship satisfied his sexual desire. Wood claimed that she initiated their relationship and that, in the context of her own culture, her actions were perfectly acceptable. Certainly, he wanted to convey the impression that neither she nor others in the village perceived her as his victim. The fact that he never returned, nor relayed a message explaining his whereabouts, might have changed that, however. His apparently genuine regret may be linked to concern that his apparent desertion left the impression it was merely an exploitive liaison, after all.

Of course, Wood presented this relationship in language that is hopelessly stereotypical. Indian princess imagery typified most army officers' discussions of friendships and intimacies with Indian women. In some cases, such language masked the more sordid aspects of these encounters, particularly those occurring in the context of war and rape. In other situations, men of limited literary skills or imagination relied on such language to convey relationships of genuine affection and mutual respect. Wood's presentation of his affair implied the latter, although his usual literary proficiency failed him here. Furthermore, because Wood left no contemporary record of this relationship, it is difficult to know how regretful he was at age twenty-five. Most likely, the significance of the event grew over the years and Wood's remorse deepened. However he behaved or whatever he felt as a young man, in later years he understood that she deserved better treatment.[9]

Wood's relationship with the woman, as well as his friendship with Debe, undoubtedly affected his feelings about fighting Indians. Unlike most officers of the Indian fighting army, Wood had several exceptional opportunities to get to know Indians personally by the time he actually met Indians in combat. How could he see them as faceless enemies? How could he forget their friendship, affection, perhaps even love?

His diary from the 1877 Nez Perce War, indeed, discloses a man who did not relish the prospect of war with anyone, including Indians. As he sailed by Port Townsend on his way back from Alaska, Wood noted in his diary, "cheering remarks from citizens of Go in and kill 'em all boys. Dont spare the bloody savages. Confound these cusses,—wish they were going to fight them instead of standing on a wharf and pat[ting] us on the back." As his ship steamed by the Dalles on the Columbia River, Wood noticed some Indians who waved to the soldiers as they passed by, but he was uncertain if they were encouraging the soldiers to kill—or be killed. "Hard to tell which they prefer."[10]

As he neared the theater of war, Wood's mood darkened. Part of his anxiety stemmed from natural concerns about his own safety. His diary revealed not only Wood's psychological state as he neared battle, but also his emerging poetic sensibilities:

> *fearing the field, peculiar nervous feeling of going to death, shrinking from the exposure.most desire to be out of the expedition. old soldiers the same way. Each fight more dreaded than the last. The desire to investigate immortality, thoughts on death, inability to change the mode and tenor of life and thought . . . each one's expectation that* he *will escape.*[11]

A few days later, when he helped bury the dead after the Battle of White Bird Canyon, that chore brought him face to face with the horrors of war. The stench of blackened and mutilated bodies, "death in ghastly forms, strewn on every side," made an imprint on Wood's sensitive soul. In camp afterward, the men sang, told stories, swore, feigned carefree demeanors, and joked about their own fate. Each sat down, in anticipation of the next battle, to pen last messages to wives, mothers, and sweethearts. The tension brought on by "Rain—eternal rain," as well as fear of Indian attack, led Wood to scrawl in his journal: "nervous eagerness for the fight . . . desire to be at the front. All thoughts of the future vanishing . . . only want a crack at an Indian and feel no disposition to show any quarter."[12]

That this was only momentary animosity was apparent several weeks later when Wood, guarding some Nez Perce prisoners, now sympathized with them. He wrote, "musings on the unhappy people and the fate before them, thoughts on the Indian as a human being, a man and brother." Coming in the wake of his participation in the Battle of Clearwater, such sentiments indicate that Wood's experience with Indian people in California and Alaska *had* left their mark. He could not forget the "enemy" was also "a man and a brother." In addition, Wood reflected on the morality of the war as he listened to the "woes and troubles of the innocent captives."[13]

Later, after the long chase across Idaho and Montana, Wood witnessed Chief Joseph surrendering his rifle to Oliver O. Howard and Nelson Miles at the Bear Paw Mountains. Some scholars attribute much of the now-famous

Chief Joseph "Surrender Speech," with its poetic phrasing: "From where the sun now stands I will fight no more forever," to Wood rather than Chief Joseph.[14] It is richly ironic that the words of this Indian resistor, so well known to twentieth-century sympathizers, possibly came from an enemy, an army officer, a military man, a conqueror. To the very end of his life, however, Wood insisted the words were Joseph's.[15]

Whoever the true author of the surrender speech, there is no doubt that Wood sought out Joseph. The two men exchanged saddles. Over the years the bond strengthened. Eventually Wood twice sent his oldest son, Erskine, to live with Joseph for several months.[16] The Nez Perce War, then, rather than altering Wood's views of Indians as men and brothers, reinforced them and provided him with another opportunity to form a friendship, this time lasting, with an Indian person. The Nez Perce War also offered an outlet for Wood's creative and literary impulses, perhaps in the surrender speech and certainly in his various newspaper accounts of the war, which represent his first published works on Indians. Finally, it provided Wood with a cache of material for his increasingly critical view of American government, society, and culture.

After the war, however, Wood continued to wear the army uniform and carry out his duties in the West, apparently without publicly questioning authority, policy, or his personal role in it. It is noteworthy that none of his other army duties brought out the same compassion for Indians that the Nez Perce War engendered. Neither letters nor diary entries from the remainder of the 1870s reflect a man troubled by his nation's treatment of Indians.[17] It was only in later years, when Wood took up the law and his political proclivities became more pronounced and well defined, that he returned to the Indian Wars and systematically began to reinterpret their meaning, developing his themes of injustice and perfidy, and becoming more radical over time.

Finally, in the early 1880s, Wood resigned from the military career he had never embraced. He later maintained that he left because he was bitterly opposed to Indian Bureau corruption, which deprived Indians of their rightful appropriations, writing that when "we were ordered out to fight them, I felt I was supporting an unworthy cause." But his primary motivation for resigning was personal. While serving as Howard's adjutant at West Point, Wood received permission to attend Columbia University Law School. According to his son, Wood resigned his commission in 1884, a year after his graduation, thus breaking "away from the rigidity and restraints and barrenness of army life" to begin practicing law in Portland, Oregon.[18]

For the next thirty-four years, C.E.S. Wood practiced maritime and corporate law, raised a family of five children, and honed his personal brand of philosophical anarchism. While, on the surface, Wood led a life of apparent conventionality, he resisted a completely traditional bourgeois existence. A complex man of tremendous appetites, vitality, warmth, personal charisma, and charm, Wood moved easily among all levels of Portland society. He counted businessmen, artists, lawyers, poets, politicians, and labor organizers among his friends and acquaintances. He secured himself a place in respectable, sophisticated circles while simultaneously seeking out the rebellious and bohemian elements. In his dress and appearance he affected the latter image. "With his curly hair, his wide-set, luminous eyes, a soft, broad-brimmed Stetson, and a flaring, black military cape to turn the Oregon rain," his biographers wrote, "he made a commanding and dramatic figure."[19]

Politically, he defined himself as an anarchist, celebrating individual freedom and scorning inhibitions which suppressed it. He counted Emma Goldman, Clarence Darrow, and Lincoln Steffens among his friends. He became increasingly radical, growing convinced "that too often in the clash between property and human rights the latter were sacrificed." Theory was one thing, his practice of law another. In his legal career, Wood often took up on behalf of the rich, the propertied, the privately owned utility companies, shipping interests, railroads, and banks. "Lawyer Wood," according to historian Edwin Bingham, "continued to earn his living by representing exemplars of the system against which he inveighed."[20]

Certainly Wood's law career provided a comfortable living for his family that explains, at least in part, his willingness to continue. But his heart was not in it. To handle the growing abyss between family obligations and professional demands, on the one hand, and his personal inclinations toward poetry and radical political causes on the other, he separated his life into distinctive spheres, physically and mentally. He maintained an office in Portland's Chamber of Commerce Building, away from his law office, where he wrote poetry and essays. He also compartmentalized his mental commitments, using free moments during business trips to write in his journal and work on poems. If he embraced some elements of modern life in the industrial age, he also attempted to separate himself—literally and psychologically—from others. If railroad cars, smoke-filled conference rooms, and lawyering represented one aspect of his life, nature, Indians, poetry, and artistry represented the other.

No sooner did Wood settle in Portland than he began urging Olin Warner, an artist and sculptor friend from his law school days in New York City, to come out west and study Indian life. Like Mabel Dodge Luhan, Wood's first inclination was to invite others to the West to see his vision of Indians and then articulate it for others. Wood sent Warner a pair of Indian moccasins, some buckskin, and a stream of letters about the artistic potential to be found among the natives of the Pacific Northwest. Warner was tempted, writing that he "might be doing a good thing for Art by using the Indians before they are extinct or ruined by civilization." When Warner finally came to Portland in 1891, he crafted a set of medallions of Indian leaders, several of which ended up in the New York Metropolitan Museum. Warner allowed Wood to use photographs of the medallions as illustrations for an 1893 article the latter published in *Century Magazine* and promised to return west "[to] show that the Indians have never been done."[21] Before Warner could return, however, he was struck and killed by a drunken cabman in New York City.

Warner's death devastated Wood, not the least because it represented what Wood so feared for himself: the end of life before he had experienced it freely and completely, before he had developed and expressed his creative potential. Fear of sharing Warner's fate acutely depressed Wood, who filled his diary with musings on death's inevitability. "My thoughts seem morbidly now to dwell on Death," he admitted. Most appalling to Wood was the extinction of individual existence, personal thought, and knowledge. He longed for immortality, writing, death "makes life seem such a struggle, so sad, so unsatisfying."[22]

What antidote did Wood offer to offset such dismal views of life? Several options occurred to him: delight in the pleasure of the senses while one can; or dive into Nature, as the Indians did. "I am sensuous," Wood claimed in Whitmanesque fashion, "I am a man—I have senses    I love to pleasure them. I know not if I will ever have any other joy. I am *sensuous*." Wood engaged his senses in food, wine, art, and affairs with women, but he also believed the senses should be gratified through contact with the natural world and he found in Indians models of how to proceed. On a January evening in 1893, while traveling on a train through Colorado, Wood noted that night was falling on the desert. "But you can't feel it in a Pullman car," he wrote, "you must lie on your back on our 'mother the earth' as old *Too houl-houl-sole* used to say: smelling the pungent sage brush in the cold night air—feeling you are alone with God and Life and Death and all the mysteries."[23] Several months later, while in Olympia, Washington, working on behalf of his Tobacco Trust clients, Wood despaired over the work, over corrupt politics ("this rotten old gourd"), and over "how curiously non original this age is in everything but the hard practical spheres of mechanics and science." He added: "We seem to have utterly lost the powers of the imagination." In classic antimodern form Wood lamented that the American emphasis on theory, logic, rationality, and scientific deduction killed creativity, inspiration, and originality. The remedy he offered was direct contact with Nature and Nature's people. "The North American Indians are still imaginative and poetical," he maintained, adding "my good friends of Portland do not understand why I want to plunge Erskine [his son] into that atmosphere of Nature which mentally and as I maintain morally is as fresh as the scent of the fir woods."[24]

C.E.S. Wood, then, sent *his* son not to West Point but to the Nez Perce, his former enemy, to be trained, not in army regimentation, but in Nature's rhythms. In this way, Wood was able to bridge the gap between army and Indian, between a life of monotony and freedom, shallowness and substance, methodical routine and limitless imagination, modernity and antimodernity. Certainly, Wood was not one to reenact his life through his son, but in this instance the soldier's son, whom Joseph adopted, became the "perfect Indian," the very thing that Wood's father had accused Wood of being. In joining Joseph's family, young Erskine made the transformation from soldier to Indian complete. It represented C.E.S. Wood's effort to cleanse his own family of what he found "rotten" about his own age and culture through the powers of Nature, poetry, and Indians.

*During his years as a Portland, Oregon, attorney, Wood often turned to Indians for inspiration in his poetry and his politics. Reproduced by permission of Special Collections Division, University of Washington Libraries, Negative No. U.W. #3991.*

Wood had partially plunged into that atmosphere as a young army officer, but career and family obligations limited his ability to complete the immersion. Yet, in later years, he returned to his favorite haunts, with sons in tow, to reconnect with Nature and gather inspiration for one of the major themes of his prose and poetry: the "comparison between Nature in her largesse, freedom and beauty, and man in his poverty, enslavement, and ugliness."[25] One finds in the early poems and journal entries from these trips the musings that would eventually emerge full-blown in his best published piece, *The Poet in the Desert*. For example, during an 1898 hunting excursion with sons Erskine, Max, and Berwick, they retraced his Nez Perce War steps, twenty-one years past. Memories crowded in as they passed the spot on the Camas Prairie, where "poor little Raines was killed in 1877," and White Bird Canyon, where Wood recalled finding the ground covered with men in army blue "in all sorts of fantastic positions and rotting back to earth fly blown and with a stench I sometimes smell in my dreams."[26]

Wood wrote some rather pedestrian verse during this trip, significant not for its artistry but for what it reveals about how he chose to interpret his military past, revisiting battles with Indians and rewriting their "endings." In "The Trooper," Wood related a tale of a soldier wounded during a fight with an unnamed tribe. As he lay on the ground an Indian woman approached:

Shell Flower she crouched beside me
She with red beneath her cheek
She knew no word to speak
But like a panther wide eyed
She watched me bloody, weak.

His Indian enemies took the soldier captive and he awaited "the hell to come." But then Shell Flower, Pocahontas style, came to his rescue, cutting the bonds that imprisoned him. Into the night they ran—together.

Three days we lay in the tules
Where cries the great curlew
And above us the wild ducks flew
And I kissed her like mad all over
As a lover ought to do.

For three days they laughed and learned one another's language and the soldier concludes:

I am sick of belts and chevrons
What is it all to me
Who am one of the tribe of the free
I am sick of taps and quarters
I am sick of reveille
By the God that made the desert
There is something in my veins
That is kin to the great wide plains
And the winds that blow across them.[27]

In this poetic rendering of Indian warfare, Wood's soldier becomes the vanquished, redeemed through the love of an Indian woman. Not only does she literally save his life, but she also provides him an opportunity to become his true self, "one of the tribe of the free." In this rendition, Indians are the winners both in battle and in life. They offer freedom from the rigidity of military existence and tender love to those willing to accept it.

The following year, Wood returned to the same places. Again his sons hunted while Wood mostly composed romantic verse. He set one of his untitled pieces in the Nevada Desert. Once again he featured an Indian woman, who this time pleaded with her soldier-lover not to desert her:

Don't you leave me for I love you
You are all I have you know
Don't you leave me for the trumpets and
    the troops so bright and blue
Don't you go with them across the sagebrush plains
Don't you leave me for I love you
You are all I have you know
Don't you leave me for that marching column blue—

So I put upon my saddle
    both my carbine and my sword
And I doffed my chevroned jacket bright and blue

And I bade old grey go follow
And I broke my soldier's word
For I didn't know what else a man could do.[28]

Here Wood repeated the motif of a soldier forsaking military life for the love of an Indian woman. Unlike the real C.E.S. Wood who did not break his "soldier's word" but rather left his Indian lover to fight in the Nez Perce War, this fictional trooper made the opposite choice. An Indian's love, at least in poetry, proved more compelling than soldierly duty. In literature, if not life, love triumphed over war.

Not all the verse Wood composed in 1899 focused on such romantic themes. Another prominent topic was antiwar sentiment, inspired by the Spanish-American War and its aftermath. In a poem about the so-called Philippine Insurrection, he urged the Filipinos:

Ye fight for home and liberty
As we did long ago . . .

We want your land and by your hap
We are the better blood . . .

Your doom is sealed. As ye no alms
But play as brave men play.
These glorious isles of fern and palms
Must own the white man's sway . . .[29]

Taking a swipe at the white man's right to rule, Wood clearly meant to challenge those who wedded whiteness with civilization, race with manliness, morality with force.[30] The Filipinos' position was the virtuous one, yet, he believed, the white man's determination, greed, and raw power would overwhelm them and ultimately prevail.

Nor did Wood see this as something new. Americans' appetite for overseas expansion had a domestic origin. "Private Stiles" featured a soldier who while struggling to understand the purpose of the Philippines conflict, compared it to the Battle of Wounded Knee and other Indian fighting:

I'm a thinking Jim I'm thinkin of
these Philipina [*sic*] chaps
Be they rebels be they niggers be they what?
How comes our job to kill them
We kin kill em like a breeze
But what's the beggars done for to be shot?

I kin tumble to the scrimmage
With old Big Foot and his ghosts
They are right here all among us raisin hell
But to go a rakin over to them hot and steaming lands
For to plug a nig is more'n I can tell.[31]

Even a lowly private could see the immorality of fighting the Filipinos. As to the morality of fighting Indians, Private Stiles had fewer doubts. At least they lived "right here" and were "raisin hell," but what had the Filipinos done to warrant warfare against them? For Wood, however, American overseas military ventures were an extension of a long-standing, malign, destructive Indian policy. Imperialism was not a new departure but rather a continuation of centuries-old impulses.

By the time Wood composed these poems, he had already begun to express such thoughts publicly, in prose rather than poetry. In fact, Wood's first publications were essays, several of which he published in *Century Magazine*, one of the nation's most influential periodicals. "Among the Thlinkits in Alaska" was a fairly standard nineteenth-century, army-inspired travel account chock full of negative stereotypes of native people. He described various Alaskan natives as drunken, haughty, and savage. He portrayed the men he hired to paddle their Haida war canoe as "stolidly smoking the tobacco we had given them" while resting "with bovine contentment." The article included a Lewis and Clarklike checklist of Alaska's resource possibilities and discussed the Chilkat version of slavery, the Thlinkit love of money ("there seems to be no hurt to a Thlinkit's honor that money or goods will not heal"), and the power Alaskan Indian women wielded in family and financial matters. He made no mention of the woman with whom he supposedly lived, noting only that when a stranger of rank arrived, a village chief often presented the newcomer with a wife from his own household. "In morals," Wood claimed with a Puritanlike propensity he would later discard, "the Alaskans are much inferior to most Indian tribes of the plains."[32] Nowhere in this article does the reader find the sensitive man who years later expressed regret over his treatment of an Indian woman or outrage over his government's policy toward native people. Still, the article incorporated a respectful synopsis of a Thlinkit legend, a theme he later returned to in his *Book of Tales*, and some attractive characterizations of Alaskan Indians, noting their gentle treatment of children and generous hospitality toward strangers.

Two years later, Wood's article on Chief Joseph for *Century* conveyed a more positive image of Indians. In fact, the opening sentence which declared Chief Joseph had "fought for that which man calls patriotism when it has been crowned with success," signaled, from the outset, a decidedly sympathetic stance and revealed the first of many statements that grew into Wood's increasingly critical view of federal policy. In addition to providing an account of the war from Joseph's point of view, Wood explored the Nez Perce history of friendship with explorers Lewis and Clark, Bonneville, and Frémont, and their commitment to promises. The United States, on the other hand, failed to act in good faith by insisting that those Nez Perce who had refused to sign the 1863 treaty, with its land cessions, were still bound by it. The Nez Perce did not share the American view that a majority's view bound the minority. In fact, Indians maintained individual autonomy, and a leader's power was not absolute but depended upon his personal strength of character. Anarchist Wood found such a conception of individual autonomy attractive and espoused it as his own creed.[33]

This was not Wood's last word on the Nez Perce War. In 1895, he composed a letter about the famous conflict that eventually found its way into print. By the time of the surrender, Wood claimed, the number of able-bodied Indian fighting men was few, compared with "the number of sick, aged and decrepit men and women; blind people, children, babies and wounded, that poured out of their burrows in the earth as soon as it was known that they could do so with safety." The memory of the force that a powerful, industrial nation brought to bear against this ragged, weak band of fleeing Indians sickened him. He concluded that full responsibility for the tragedy rested with the U.S. government, and that the Nez Perce War was an outrageous tale of the strong prevailing over the weak.[34] That remained Wood's interpretation of this Indian war for the remainder of his life.

Yet for all his outrage about the injustices they suffered, Wood did little to redress past wrongs in any practical way. He did not plunge into the politics of Indian affairs. For some reason, the nuts and bolts of everyday Indian matters failed to attract his attention, interest, or passion. C.E.S. Wood preferred to write about Indians rather than act on their behalf. And as he continued to write about them, he depicted them as emblems of freedom, beauty, poetry, and simplicity, as well as victims of the white man's greed, hatred, and inhumanity. Typical is his essay, "What is Knowledge, What is Truth," a classic primitivist interpretation of a Thlinkit named Nah Sakh, who was "as harmonious with his setting in Nature as a star in the clear midnight sky." This man was one of the happiest people Wood ever knew because he found joy in simple pleasures: bright sunshine, a warm cabin, the delights of roast halibut dipped in seal-oil. In short, "All that went to make up the art of living he knew." True, Nah Sakh believed that stars were composed of pieces of ice which Yethl had kicked about the heavens and that thunder was the flapping of Yethl's wings. Furthermore, Nah Sakh had never contemplated matters such as evolution or revolution. Quite simply, Wood maintained, this "savage" had but one "firm conviction . . . which we savants have lost, and that is that each man was as free as he himself, to seek his living from the Mother breast and live his own life in his own way." Years later, Wood could still picture this man as he rested after a hard day of fishing, at peace with the world.[35]

In this highly romanticized vision of Indian life, Wood maintained that Indian ways, in all their presumed simplicity, proved far superior to the sterility of modern life. Happiness came not from vast knowledge or from accumulation of useless material objects. It came from simple pleasures; from emancipation from dogma, convention, and authority; from free expression of Self; and from living "in harmony with Nature for harmony with Nature is truth and happiness."[36] Today's readers will see at this essay's core, condescension, sentimentality, and perhaps even racism, but Wood did not mean it to be read that way.

He believed this "primitive," "simple" man exemplified all the rich possibilities of life that modern man had lost.

Wood conveyed a similar message, although he considerably muted his propensity toward sermonizing, in *A Book of Tales* first published by his fourteen-year-old son, William Maxwell Wood, and a friend on their children's handpress. The book, begun in 1898 and completed in 1901, was "Englished by Charles Erskine Scott Wood, One Time Lieutenant U.S. Army." It commenced with the following: "Here begin these tales heard in canoe, on horseback & by the camp-fire and told in all faith and simple belief by children of nature." Apparently, Wood collected Indian stories during his army days, and this little leather-bound volume represented the best of them. Before each tale Wood identified his informant and explained the circumstances under which he came to hear the story. John McBean, an interpreter and "half-breed," related "How a Beautiful Maiden Changed Into a Frog and Leaped Upon the Face of the Moon," during their days together in the 1878 Bannock War. The Thlinkit Tah-ah-nah-klekh told him tales about Yehl while Wood warmed himself by an Alaskan driftwood fire and watched the halibut toasting. Sarah Winnemucca, known as Pretty Shell among her own people, told him the story of "The Love of Red Bear and Feather Cloud." And of course, Debe shared stories while they loafed in the hot sun watching the women work or when they rested in the evening while roasting antelope ribs on coals.[37]

These stories were similar to other collections published by whites and reflect the antimodernist's fascination with folk tales.[38] Wood's voice most assuredly informs the narratives, in a word here or a turn of phrase there. Although the genesis of the book derived from actual experiences with Indian people, *A Book of Tales* is more romance than ethnology; more an extension of Wood's view of Indianness than an accurate rendition or replication of Indian story-telling; more a cooptation of Indian voices than actual ones. Nowhere is this more obvious than in the last and lengthiest story, "The Tale of Shshauni and Susshupkin." Wood admits this is not an Indian story at all, but rather one that came out of his own experiences in "the solemn desert wherein I have lain when I was three and twenty, looking into the infinite sky of flawless nights; and it is born of the longing in the heart."[39]

Although Max Wood and his friend initially printed only 105 copies of *A Book of Tales*, in 1929 Vanguard Press began reprinting it for a wider audience. Readers understood the book was not ethnological but believed that it spoke for and about Native American cultures. A *New York Times* reviewer, in fact, claimed the stories provided important views into Indian life and that Wood deserved praise for retelling them with a literary skill that retained "the simplicity of thought and language of the original, but sometimes, evidently, giving them touches of beauty that Indian originals do not possess." The *Saturday Review* believed the tales "quite definitely Indian and humanly revealing from the point of view of Indian culture."[40] Whether or not Wood sought out the job, simply by virtue of compiling the stories and offering brief explanations regarding their origins and supposed "authenticity," he became a spokesman for Indians.

Throughout his life Wood revisited this role as interpreter and spokesman despite the fact that after the 1870s, he had little contact with Indians. True, he sent his son to live with Chief Joseph, but the elder Erskine's interactions with the famous Nez Perce were limited to an occasional visit, such as when Joseph stopped in Portland to sit for Olin Warner's portrait. An episode in 1918 underscored the fact that Wood's relationships with Indian people were ephemeral. That year Wood wrote to his son, Erskine, that some Nez Perce visitors stopped by his Portland home but, after waiting an hour, were very disappointed when the father walked in. One of the Indians said, "'No, you are the wrong man; I want to see a young man, Erskine Wood.'" Eventually, the Nez Perce did acknowledge C.E.S. Wood was known among the Indians too: "he did me the honor to say . . . that he had heard Joseph speak of me very often, what a great man I was, with a really good heart." He simply had not expected Wood to still be alive since Joseph, White Bird, and all the others of that generation were now dead.[41]

Wood, of course, was still alive but his marriage was dying. He once wrote "the end of life is marriage and marriage is the end of life."[42] Marriage became the arena where Wood most clearly, and painfully, applied his philosophical beliefs to personal behavior, where he advanced a modernist approach to a traditional relationship. For Wood advocated free love and freely engaged in extramarital affairs which his wife apparently overlooked. But, in time, Wood could no longer live a life of deceit, and the marriage ended spiritually and practically, though not legally, in 1918. Wood maintained affection for his wife throughout her lifetime and certainly their children provided an important bond. In fact, it was Wood's concern for his family's material well-being that kept him practicing law as long as he did. He did not leave his wife until he had earned sufficient money to set up trust funds for the entire family. At the same time, he no longer felt he could deny himself the chance to live the life he wanted, as a poet, and with the woman he desired, Sara Bard Field.

Wood met Field, the wife of a Baptist minister and mother of two, at a 1910 Portland dinner party given by Clarence Darrow. Although thirty years separated Field and Wood, they saw in one another kindred spirits. By 1911, they had become lovers. Sara's sympathetic soul led Wood to show her his poetry. Field was not only a poet, but something of a critic and editor as well. In time, she worked with Wood to fashion his most significant work, *The Poet in the Desert,* into publishable shape. Moreover, Sara shared his radical views, his hopes and aspirations not only for literature but also for social revolution. In 1918, Wood left Portland to live with Field in California. His wife refused to grant him a divorce and so they remained technically married until her death in 1933. Wood and Field married in 1938.[43]

The marriage's ending was drawn-out, protracted, and painful for all parties. Because the issue proved so long-lived and frustrating, Wood often reflected on the philosophical and practical problems of marriage in letters to his children. Clearly, self-justification explained much of his writing on the subject, for this was the point where his deeply felt personal philosophy and everyday life most acutely intersected and conflicted. Sometimes Wood turned to philosophical naturalism to explain his point of view about marriage and sexuality. Sometimes he turned to Indians—and sometimes to a blend of the two. When son, Erskine, went off to Harvard in 1897, Wood wrote a lengthy, fatherly letter of advice, including a discussion of sex. In Nature, he wrote, the sexes mated simply to procreate, with no ties, obligations, or promises. "Savages," for instance, who are "close to nature" act on the basis of bodily attraction rather than affection. They mated when ready; separated when either chose. Such conditions precluded temptation, seduction, or adultery. However, Wood warned Erskine, the natural life was appropriate for "the animal man" but not for the social man of late-nineteenth-century Portland or Cambridge.[44]

In 1907, on the eve of his daughter Nan's wedding, Wood again took up pen on this subject, telling her that Nature was indifferent to the number of mates people took. "In fact," he claimed, "Nature is a persistent free lover and not at all moral according to present social ideas, but I believe her to be moral, myself, for I do not believe it is possible for any great law of Nature to be wrong."[45] In this rather unusual, perhaps bizarre, prenuptial letter from father to daughter, Wood went on to say he was not urging couples to take separation lightly. Rather, he simply meant to praise freedom against bondage and truth against hypocrisy and concluded the letter by announcing, "This is my opinion, but I am ahead of my time."[46]

By the time Sara Bard Field's daughter married, in 1927, Wood's ideas about free love had completely developed and he used "Indian ways" as a model for marriage. In a piece that begins, "It was a beautiful wedding . . . ," Wood goes on to say that every wedding is beautiful, at least every wedding that is made by love. He then elaborated on a "primitive wedding" he supposedly witnessed where the earth and sky served as the temple and the bride, dressed in beaded tunic and moccasins, wed her bridegroom simply by offering him a small, tightly woven basket filled with seeds. The man took the woman by the wrist and led her to his teepee. With that, the ceremony ended and the couple was married. "They would have stared very dumbly," Wood claimed, "if they had been told they must have a license or a priest. Primitive peoples are as stupid as children about some of our most valued institutions—such as poverty and marriage."[47] Once again, Wood called on "Indians" to provide an alternative to "civilized" forms of marriage, one which celebrated purity of love without bonds, restrictions, or limitations on freedom.

In the midst of this personal, marital turmoil, Wood and Sara Bard Field found time for creative work. Indeed, out of the tumult came Wood's best poetry, *The Poet in the Desert*, a lengthy work which included a denunciation of war, a paean to Nature, and a cry for revolution. Wood once explained the work's genesis to Max Hayek, who translated it into German. He wrote an early version in 1912, on the bank of the Blitzen River where he and his sons had camped. From the days of his earliest army assignment on the "edge of this desert" (a phrase Mabel Dodge Luhan would also use) he had loved the place. "It means youth to me and the smell of the sagebrush is the most delicious fragrance on earth; especially after a rain." While contemplating the beauty of the Harney Desert, he also thought about his years chasing and killing Indians, who had been "driven to revolt by the oppressions of that vague thing called 'government'" that powerful capitalists and industrialists controlled. After leaving the army, he learned the law was neither protector of the poor nor servant of justice but rather just the opposite. Drinking in the intoxicating loveliness of the Harney Desert, then, he became that poet in the desert "full of my lifelong meditations that this is a world distorted by man and founded on injustice, and with little thought of art I expressed my soul." Several years later, working in concert with Sara Bard Field, Wood pared the poem of some of its "propaganda sermons" and shared it with others.[48]

The first version, which Wood distributed only to personal friends in 1914, carried the uninspired title, "Civilization." Neither "savages" nor Indians appeared in this early edition. Here "civilization" represented ruin, corruption, and abuse. Wood admitted he did not particularly like the title, finding it both meaningless and unpoetic. So he alighted on "The Poet in the Desert" as an alternative.

The second edition incorporated Wood's major themes but succeeded in making it more "poetical." It again featured the desert as a gentle, loving, and feminized landscape.

> I know the Desert is beautiful, for I have lain
> in her arms and she has kissed me.
> I have come to her, that I may know Freedom.

In contrast, Civilization offered the roar of furnaces, the clang of hammers, "the bellowing of monsters which feed on men." It was "an iron world without a soul." Eschewing authority, privilege, and poverty the poet would instead go to Nature which fed him "with the honeycomb of Freedom." This time Indians had a role too, as part of the social criticism and as part of the solution. The poet encountered them, of course, in the context of warfare, where they represented victims of Civilization's most pernicious drives. The latter not only destroyed Indians but also encouraged Civilization's minions to forget, in the process of conquest, that "we are an universal whole." But the poet maintains,

> It is good to believe that the men, the women
> And children we kill are our brothers,
> Our sisters, our children.

Beyond their inherent value as fellow human beings, Indians offered another way to embrace life and death: "the wild men of this wilderness Take Death by the hand as they take Life by the hand." Forced by circumstance to put aside normal funerary practices, the poet and his fellow soldiers hurriedly wrapped their battlefield casualties in blankets and placed them in the ground. Far from being repulsed by this practice, the poet preferred it. Approximating Indian ways of death led to a simpler, more natural way to honor the end of life:

> These return unto the mother simply as the fall of a
> tree, but the burials of civilization are ugly.[49]

Proper treatment of the dead was just one of the lessons Wood learned from Indians. In the 1918 edition of *Poet in the Desert,* Wood elaborated on this theme:

> I have lain out with the brown men
> And know they are favored.
> Nature whispered to them her secrets,
> But passed me by.
> They instructed my civilization.
> Stately and full of wisdom.

Wood acknowledged a number of Indian teachers by name, including Joseph who "made bloody protest against Perfidy and Power" and Too-hul-hul-soot who taught him the Earth is Mother and who asked

> Who gave to the White Man
> Ownership of the Earth
> Or what is his authority
> From the Great Spirit
> To tear babes from the nursing breast?
> It is contemptible to have much where others want.

The poet went on.

> I sprawled flat in the bunch-grass, a target
> For the just bullets of my brown brothers betrayed.
> I was a soldier, and, at command,
> Had gone out to kill and be killed . . .
> Shrill yells of savages;
> Curses of Christians.
> The rifles chuckled continually.
> A poor people who asked nothing but freedom,
> Butchered in the dark.[50]

By 1918, the reluctant Indian Wars soldier had completely renounced his role as tool of the government and the capitalists who controlled it. In each new rendition of his masterpiece, Wood embellished the role of Indians, making increasingly clear that their defeat represented the triumph of greed and depravity, made even worse by the fact that the conquered people, who knew Nature's secrets, had lived lives of wisdom, grace, and, of course, freedom.

*The Poet in the Desert* received mixed reviews. One critic announced it was not great poetry. In response Wood wrote, "I did not want to write a *poem*. I wanted to say the say of my soul, and whatever poetry is there is to show the beauty of the world against which slowly writhes corruption." Still, he thought the piece had "patches of poetry" and he hoped those patches would help make its revolutionary doctrines more palatable to the laboring class, for whom he intended the work.[51]

When Wood wrote the introduction to the final version, which Vanguard Press published in 1929, he commented further on the issue of politics and poetry. Wood noted that Max Eastman, writing for *The Masses*, thought the first edition contained too much propaganda and too little poetry; while Emma Goldman claimed in *Mother Earth* it had too much poetry and too little propaganda. The second edition, a cheaper pocket-sized book, sold thousands of copies but mostly to people living in jail cells and boxcars and among workers, according to Wood. It remained unknown among the cultured classes, he claimed in a lament that strikes a chord with many authors, because it was never advertised. For the 1929 edition, Vanguard Press intended to reach a more educated audience by offering a revised and greatly augmented edition.[52]

Among the sections that Wood augmented were those dealing with Indians. He elaborated on the attractions of Indian societies:

> I have known people without "State" or "Statesmen";
> And without gallows, jails, palaces, police or slums;
> No poverty nor crime—none dreamed a man,
> Above the cunning, grey coyote-thief,
> Could have a wish to steal the common heritage . . .

These people were "nursed at Freedom's breast" and everyone lived in proud equality. Leaders governed not by force but by custom. Each owned what he or she made:

> What need of jails—police or penitentiaries?
> A simple people, whose smoked tepee tops scarce thrust
> Above the willows, where the rippling little river ran.
> No sky-assailing towers—no railroads, banks, no radios,
> Except the blackbird's whistle and the crane's high call;
> In every thought and act all free; from basket cradle
> Swinging on a willow bough or branch of juniper
> To the unmarked grave where the wind played with
> The grass and Nature stooped a moment but
> Refused to mourn. . . .
>
> Freely they gave and freely took without humility,
> And, unafraid, they wrapped their souls about them
> And lay down upon the mother breast, so close,
> They heard the beating of the cosmic heart:

Knowing that they were kin to all—and all
Were kin to them—and life—not property.
The destiny of Man.
Their houses, flitting as dry leaves in Autumn wind
Were frail to let the stars come in; and to them came
Freedom, Equality and Justice; to lie upon the black bear-robes
Spread soft before the central fire, whose thin
Blue smoke went straight up to the gods,
A happy people. I have heard their songs and flutes—
Their chants and drums—their stories, laughter and
Their weeping—a happy people—accepting the great mystery
Without rebellion . . .[53]

This, then, was Wood's culminating statement on Indians, dripping in romanticism and primitivism. Rooted in experiences fifty years old, these images represent the distillation of decades of memory, longing, and regret. Wood's initial role was destroyer of such "A happy people." But in his soldier's heart rested the sensibilities of a poet and, even as he took up a gun "to kill and be killed," the seeds of true understanding were sown. The germination period proved lengthy, but ultimately, the infantryman threw aside his weapons, returned periodically to the desert, and eventually articulated the wisdom that "Indians" knew all along.

Of course, Wood did not suggest his readers attempt to literally live like Indians. He believed the only solution to society's problems was revolution. The last stanza of his 1929 version sets the charge:

Through all the centuries of the toiling Poor.
The endless martyrdom of the patient Poor under the feet
Of their masters; their blood, welling up forever,
About the knees of the oppressors.
I heard them chanting:
"O Revolution—dark and Brooding Angel . . .
"Come and set the captive free . . .
"You are our only Hope—You are our only Redeemer . . ."[54]

Indians might serve as useful symbols of an integrated, just, and equitable society, but they were gone. They were vanquished and so had vanished. One could no longer join an Indian community (as his son had), but one could still foment a revolution.

By the time Wood penned these verses, he and Sara were living in a home they built together in the hills of northern California near Los Gatos. "I am tired now of being the reformer and agitator and only want a quiet nook where to dream poetry," he recorded in his diary. From the 1920s until his death in 1944, he at last realized his life's true ambition. Not only did he work and rework *The Poet in the Desert*, but he also published *Poems from the Ranges* and several other volumes of poetry, as well as his best-known work, *Heavenly Dis-*

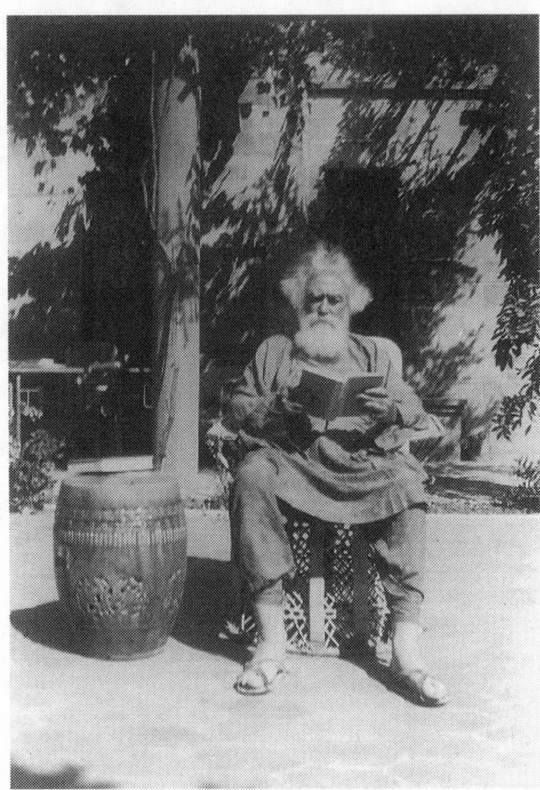

*C.E.S. Wood spent his final decades with fellow poet Sara Bard Field at their California home, "The Cats." There Wood perfected his most important work,* A Poet In the Desert. *Reproduced by permission of the Huntington Library, San Marino, California.*

*course*, which Vanguard published in 1927. The latter consists of fictional dialogues between various characters, including Jesus and Mark Twain, Satan and a pacifist, Carrie Nation and Margaret Sanger, on themes such as imperialism, war, marriage, and religious fundamentalism. Some of these satirical pieces first appeared in *The Masses* during World War I, and their twenty-plus printings over the years demonstrated a popularity that eluded all of Wood's other works. A few years after his death, Field collected his poems which Vanguard published along with a foreword by William Rose Benét. In none of these other works, however, did Wood feature Indians as prominently as in *The Poet in the Desert*.[55]

As Wood dreamed poetry in his quiet California nook, he also revisited his past, prodded in part by a woman who wrote her University of Texas English Master's thesis on his work, and in part by the inclination of a reflective old man to leave an autobiographical record for his great-grandchildren. Wood reiterated in letters to the graduate student the deep connection he believed existed between Indians and himself. Participation in the Indian Wars not only added a colorful aspect to his life, but also his "life with the Indians" deeply affected his social philosophy. And, of course, it was while campaigning against Indians that the desert captivated him. Simultaneously, he learned about the evils of a system which allowed men to own property and to control the water and the great forests. In other words, Wood concluded, his army years had been the crucial ones in shaping his philosophical, political, and poetic points of view.[56]

In the final years of his life, the nearly blind Wood dictated autobiograpical fragments that he never pieced together into a whole. He returned one last time to his experiences in the West, in Alaska, and in pursuit of the Nez Perce. He renounced one last time the futility and stupidity of war and repeated his belief in the power of Nature and human love to restore mankind to a healthy, happy existence—the kind he associated with Indians. Ironically, when he died in 1944, newspapers featured his military past rather than his poetic one, at least with respect to Indians. The *San Francisco Chronicle* noted his passing with this opening sentence: "A part of the era which wove Indian fighters, millionaries, artists and writers into the character of early California days passed into history yesterday with the death of Colonel Charles Erskine Scott Wood." And the headline over his *New York Times* obituary identified him as "Indian Fighter" rather than "Indian Lover," as he might have preferred.[57]

At times, Charles Erskine Scott Wood sounded more like a romantic transcendentalist of the nineteenth century than a cultural relativist of the twentieth. One finds in his writings not ethnographic information about actual Indians, but the aspirations and dreams of a discontented soul projected onto them. Debe, the Tklingit woman, and Chief Joseph were flesh and blood human beings, but in Wood's works they become the vehicles for his poetic and social vision. Yet, in developing intimate relationships with actual Indians (however fleeting those relationships proved to be), in sending his son to live with Chief Joseph, in sharpening his critique of government Indian policy, and in offering Indian ways as alternatives to aspects of modern life that he found abhorrent, Wood represented—at the very least—a transitional figure who bridged the centuries and anticipated others' efforts to reimagine and redefine the meaning of Indian for Americans in the decades to follow. For a man whose life began before the Civil War and ended only as World War II drew to a close, perhaps that is appropriate.

For his part, Wood believed he was ahead of his time, writing his daughter in 1937, "I wish I had been born fifty years later." Yet he was not forgotten by the generation that followed him, and his views of Indians struck a responsive chord with at least one influential member of that generation. Mabel Dodge Luhan, who also took up residence in the West on "the edge of a desert," wrote to Wood in 1933. Scribbling on the back of an article which indicated that New Mexico's Pueblos supported John Collier's candidacy as Commissioner of Indian Affairs, she asked, "Can you use yr influence to get Collier in?" Luhan and Wood had met in Carmel, California and shared mutual friends, Una and Robinson Jeffers. Perhaps Mabel also encountered Wood, or at least his work, through his contributions to *The Masses*. Moreover, Mabel probably remembered that in 1922 Wood added his name to a petition of artists and writers opposed to the Bursum Bill, which threatened Pueblo land and water rights.[58]

It is noteworthy that Wood rarely mobilized his pen to influence Indian policy in practical, everyday matters. For a man who operated at least part of the time in the world of law and politics, and to whom Indians seemed to be so meaningful, his reticence in such matters is puzzling. In 1919, however, he wrote a letter to Secretary of the Interior Franklin Lane regarding some Nez Perce grievances, about which his son Erskine had alerted him. Much of the lengthy letter recounts Wood's views of U.S.–Nez Perce relations with special emphasis on the conflict of 1877. Wood explained that he presented "this prolix history . . . because so far as I know I am the last person left who personally knows all the history of the campaign all of which I saw and part of which I was." In particular, Wood pleaded with Lane to provide the Nez Perce with an agent who would "see that these simple people of the forest get such indulgent and sympathetic treatment as they deserve and not be harassed with moralities against playing the stick-game and forced into fashion and customs, such as paying taxes and citizenship, which are absolutely foreign to them." Believing that the Nez Perce, like other Indians, will "not be long among us," Wood asked Lane to assign them an agent who would "not try to turn them into Billy Sundays."[59] It appears that Wood felt the battle to save Indians was already lost.

Fifteen years later, a new generation, with different, more optimistic expectations of Indians' cultural longevity, asked Wood to write another letter on behalf of Indians. Although Wood described himself as an "obscure western person," he wrote the letter Luhan asked for, addressing it to Mrs. Franklin Roosevelt. Wood did not appear to know a great deal about Collier, other than that he had battled against the Catholic and Methodist churches in their efforts to ban tribal religious practices. He also understood that Collier was "sympathetic with these aborigines—honest and courageous." Wood closed the letter by repeating his own now familiar credentials: he knew Indians from Alaska to Mexico, and he quit the army because he would not be a pawn of corrupt politicians.[60]

Charles Erskine Scott Wood had certainly come a long way from the days of the Nez Perce War. With his views of Indians evolving from enemy to inspiration, he was neither a typical Indian fighter nor a typical westerner. One can fault him for his romanticism, self-indulgence, and even vanity.[61] To be sure, his literary efforts, while significant, never reached huge audiences. His influence on Indian policy was not consequential. Yet among those people reexamining Indians and federal policy in the 1920s and 1930s, Wood was not only remembered—but valued. He *was* a man ahead of his time. No one better demonstrates that than George Bird Grinnell, Wood's contemporary, who spent much more time with Indians and who wrote much more about them. If Grinnell did more to alter Americans' ethnographic understanding of Indians, by emphasizing their humanity and the richness of their cultures and histories, he failed to share Wood's more radical conception of Indians as worthy not only of attention, but also emulation.

# 3

# GEORGE BIRD GRINNELL AND THE "VANISHING" PLAINS INDIAN CULTURES

GEORGE BIRD GRINNELL AND CHARLES ERSKINE SCOTT WOOD were contemporaries whose lives spanned the same decades. Both ventured west of the Mississippi River in the 1870s, when many Anglo-Americans still considered the West to be "wild," and there encountered Indians as friends *and* enemies. In encouraging their countrymen to understand and sympathize with Indians, they both championed the distinctions of Indians' cultures while simultaneously insisting on their shared humanity.

But where Wood was an insistently introspective and romantic poet, Grinnell was a thoroughly practical man of science who seemed, for the most part, unburdened by a complicated interior life. Where Wood was sensual and passionate, Grinnell was clinical, rational, and detached. Where Wood displayed a vivid, colorful personality, Grinnell's was restrained and quiet. Wood consistently used his conception of Indians as a springboard to reflect upon himself and the confines of his culture. Grinnell worried less about such things, preferring to understand Indians on *their* terms. Wood's discontent with modernity prompted calls for revolution. Grinnell pushed for, at best, limited reform well within the Progressive mainstream. Wood envisioned a different world. Grinnell lamented a lost one. Wood turned criticism of Indian policy into an indictment of his entire social and cultural milieu, whereas Grinnell's observations contained no sweeping recriminations. Rather, he kept his criticisms conscribed, limiting his complaints to individual agents or calls for increases in a particular reservation's annuities. Grinnell knew that the management of Indian affairs was fraught with deceit and corruption, but he never challenged basic policy goals or doubted the need for Indians to embrace acculturation and assimilation. A thoroughly nineteenth-century man in his sensibilities and inclinations, Grinnell seemed incapable of imagining a different kind of world than the one he inhabited. As an eastern patrician, with a Yale education, a fine home in New York City, and ready access to the politically powerful in New York and Washington, why would he want a different world? Grinnell, not sharing Wood's rebellious nature, was relatively content with the status quo.

Still, like Wood, he saw in Indian cultures something worth saving, if only on paper. Grinnell, as much as any man of his generation, worked diligently to commit Indian memories to the page and thus preserve them. He attempted to accomplish this with minimal interference and embellishment from "outsiders," including himself. At the same time, he believed that such a record could only be created by people like himself, who knew the "real" Indian life before conquest, spent time among them on reservations, and published their prose. Trained as a scientist, not a moralist, Grinnell wanted to log Blackfeet's, Pawnees', and Cheyennes' words, actions, practices, history, and religious beliefs as objectively, accurately, and faithfully as possible. He devoted many years and a great deal of effort to this project, expecting neither riches nor fame as a reward. Grinnell simply hoped to contribute to knowledge and to alter, however slightly, his fellow Americans' vision of Indians. By devoting so much effort to this decades-long ambition, Grinnell signaled the worth he ascribed to these people. Like the more professionally trained anthropologists, he underscored the value of their cultures merely by paying close attention to them.

If he did not share the antimodernists' deep foreboding about the future, Grinnell shared some of their concerns about the deleterious effects of modernity and sensed that the elimination of Indian ways, especially Plains Indian ways, would diminish the world. He understood that change inevitably meant loss, particularly of the supposedly free, unrestrained Plains Indians' life which could not survive in the modern world. So, Grinnell spent nearly half his lifetime recording histories, traditions, and cultural practices which, he concluded, slowly and relentlessly evaporated with the death of each "old-time Indian." The least he could do, as a man who had a taste of that life, was chronicle it for those who would never know the wonders, the dangers, and, most important, the human qualities of Plains Indians' existence.

Nearly every summer between 1870 and the mid-1920s, Grinnell traveled west to hunt, explore, climb mountains and glaciers, and eventually, interview Indians. He embraced what his friend Theodore Roosevelt called the "strenuous life," as an antidote to the intellectual life that dominated the bulk of his year. These western trips allowed him to revisit a preindustrial past and shake off the grey dust that had settled on his too-urban shoulders. In his unpublished "Memoirs" these trips eclipsed all other aspects of his narrative. It is as if his western adventures represented *real* life and the rest of the year, the mere recording of that life.

Grinnell's intense interest in Indians developed gradually. Only when he reached middle age, and perhaps found himself less physically able and less psychologically compelled to scramble about Montana's mountains in search of game, did Grinnell turn his sights from animals to Indians. Accompanying his growing sense of physical limits was the common tendency for an aging person to have a heightened appreciation for the past. Surely in his mind, he inextricably linked his youth with the last prereservation days of the Plains Indians. Yet he did not romanticize nor sentimentalize them. Nor did he urge people to emulate them, as others in this study would. He just wanted to explain them and honor their memory.

It was this compulsion, then, that led Grinnell to write a host of articles and a shelf-full of books about Indians. He believed that Indians deserved a historian, a cultural broker, a defender, and took on himself those roles. He could not imagine an Indian policy like Collier's, based on the assumption that Indian cultures could be preserved into the twentieth century or that acculturation and assimilation were not only preventable, but also deplorable. Yet his works on Indians asserted the value of their cultures, even as he believed such ways could not prevail in the modern world. His efforts, consciously addressed to nonscholarly audiences, paralleled the emergence of academic ethnography and anthropology. He belonged to that group of "horse and buggy ethnographers" who, according to anthropologist Margot Liberty, came onto the scene just as the U.S. Cavalry galloped off. Such people functioned in the "intellectual aftermath of war" and preserved a remarkable record whose value increases geometrically as the years go by.[1]

In this way, Grinnell's writings helped lay the foundation for a fundamental reassessment of Indians and thus contributed to an evolving perception of them as people worthy of interest and respect. Perhaps his motives sprung from nostalgia for an imagined past. Perhaps he underestimated the resiliency of Plains Indians' cultures. Whatever his motivation or the limits of his predictive powers, the output of Grinnell's ethnographic impulse was truly impressive and shaped many Americans' understandings of Indians in the twentieth century. Grinnell's essential message was this: Plains Indians were human beings with histories of their own, full lives, and complete cultures. If no one could stem the inevitable tide of evolutionary change ushered in by conquest, at least readers should consider and appreciate what had been destroyed. It remained for others, a later generation, to take the next step to push for policies that would honor and help revitalize the cultures, land bases, and sovereignty of Indian peoples.

Grinnell made one rare exception to his tendency to eschew self-reflection. In 1915, he sat down to compose a memoir which, he explained in the opening sentence, was meant for his nieces' and nephews' "amusement." Grinnell was sixty-six-years-old. He had taken almost annual trips to the American West for forty-five years. But if he learned something of himself during those ventures, if those experiences altered him internally in some way, Grinnell did not articulate it. The memoir is precise, factual, almost clinical, in ticking off the years between 1849, the year of his birth, and 1883, the date he had reached when the memoir stopped—in midsentence—as if someone interrupted him with more urgent business. He apparently never picked up the autobiography again. In the end, in marked contrast to Wood, contemplation or explanation of self carried little weight with Grinnell.

The memoir does, however, offer us a few clues about Grinnell's motives, compulsions, and interests as they relate to the West and Indians. Born in Brooklyn in 1849, he was connected to wealthy New York and New England families. Grinnell was a product of urban America. Yet his richest remembrances derived from the sylvan landscape of Manhattan's Audubon Park, where in 1856 his father purchased a home, on the former estate of naturalist John James Audubon. Not the least of Audubon Park's charms was the presence of Audubon's widow and his sons, especially John Woodhouse Audubon, who remained actively involved in natural history. Grinnell found the Audubon homes endlessly fascinating, and their contents sparked the interest of the impressionable boy for a lifetime. Beyond the deer and elk antlers, rifles, shotguns, and powder horns which festooned the walls, Grinnell remembered, "were many trophies from the Missouri River, a region which in those days seemed infinitely remote and romantic with its tales of trappers, trading posts and Indians."[2] Exotic birds and animals, the weapons to control them, and of course tales of Indians: What more could a nineteenth-century boy, living in Manhattan, ask for in terms of entertainment and inspiration?

Hunting and playing Indian thus began in the urban wilderness of Audubon Park, rather than the far reaches of the West. Grinnell watched his younger brother, Frank, transform their still younger brother, Mort, into an Indian by stripping him "stark naked in the chilly breeze." George too stripped down to short pants and tied feathers from a duster in a handkerchief around his head.[3] Yet, unlike his younger siblings, who eventually outgrew such games, George continued them, venturing west nearly every summer, hunting, and in a sense, playing Indian well into old age.[4]

Hunting, camping, and playing Indian, of course, did not constitute Grinnell's father's plans for his first-born son. In 1861, his parents sent him to day school at the French Institute and, two years later, to Churchill Military School at Sing Sing. He proved an indifferent student, with an academic record that would not help him get into Yale, where several maternal ancestors had received educations. Grinnell, like Wood, did not share his father's ambitions for himself "and tried to escape [them], but my parents had made up their minds, and I was not in the habit of questioning my father's decisions."[5]

Grinnell had harbored hopes of studying medicine, but again his father had other plans. George Blake Grinnell was principal agent on Wall Street for Cornelius Vanderbilt, controller of the New York Central Railroad, and he wanted to train his son in this lucrative business. Fortunately, just at the moment he was expected to forsake adolescence and enter the world of Wall Street, fate intervened. George learned that Yale Professor Otheniel C. Marsh planned a scientific expedition to the West during the summer of 1870 to collect fossils. Marsh wanted some young volunteers, fresh graduates of Yale, to accompany him. This was Grinnell's dream come true. Inspired by his connections with the Audubons and the writings of Captain Mayne Reid, whose travels in the West had thrilled him as a boy, Grinnell longed to visit such places which he "had supposed . . . were far beyond my reach." Happily, his parents consented, perhaps assuming this would be a last adventurous fling, and Grinnell joined the group of men and boys "bound for a West that was then really wild and woolly."[6]

When the party crossed the Missouri River on a stern-wheel steamer, Grinnell believed he "was now on the frontier," signaled by the presence of another passenger, who sported a long rifle and moccasins on his feet. Not long after, as the party moved west to Fort McPherson, impressions turned to hard reality. The day Grinnell arrived, several antelope hunters from the post fought off a small party of Indians, probably Cheyenne. The Indians shot one of the hunters in the arm with an arrow; in retaliation the hunters killed the young Cheyenne. The next day Major Frank North and Pawnee scouts arrived at the post to assume guiding and provisioning chores for the expedition. They took Grinnell and the other young men to the corral to select their horses from among those captured the previous fall during the Battle of Summit Springs. In 1915, Grinnell knew this was the battle where Tall Bull's village of Cheyennes had been destroyed and many of his people killed.[7] It is less certain that in 1870 Grinnell thought much about the fact that his expedition horse was actually a spoil of war.

In fact, Grinnell's 1870 expedition diary reveals little awareness of either politics or history. Rather, he comes across as an exuberantly youthful man, intrigued mostly with fossilizing and hunting. Indians attracted his attention only in passing and his country's expansion into Indians' territories, not at all. When the Marsh expedition came upon a Lakota gravesite, Grinnell helped himself to some beads, a medicine bag, bracelets, and moccasins. He did not muse about the person whose grave he was plundering, nor ponder the people who had laid their dead to rest there. He did not share Wood's inclinations toward Indians as "men and brothers." At this stage in his life, Grinnell saw them as just another feature of the endlessly fascinating Great Plains fauna, although unlike most other lifeforms, they could shoot back.[8]

He learned, however, that not all Indians were dangerous. Indeed, some were quite friendly. The Pawnees not only supplied directions and provisions for the Marsh expedition, but they also provided entertainment. Grinnell asked two scouts, "Tuck-he-ge-louks" and "La-oodle-sock," many questions about their peoples' history while Frank North interpreted their answers. Grinnell also engaged in boyish games with them. "We had lots of fun," he wrote in his diary, about their horse races.[9]

When the expedition shifted further west to Fort Bridger, Grinnell found an even more appealing way of life. Although the old trading post "had at that time lost some of the primitive attractions that had once clustered about it," Shoshones and Utes still brought furs there. It was at Bridger that Grinnell first encountered what he identified as Indian domestic life. There Ike Edwards and several other trappers, who had lived in that country for several decades with their Indian wives and mixed-blood children, continued to make their living by trapping beaver. Every morning during his Fort Bridger sojourn, Grinnell joined the trappers as they checked their traps. And he explored the river and surrounding hillsides, which offered abundant fish and game. To the urban-bred Grinnell, this was paradise. In fact, he found the existence "absolutely ideal. I desired enormously to spend the rest of my life with these people." In the end, the grief this would cause his parents meant returning east.[10]

But if familial duties dictated Grinnell's return to New York, they could not dictate his heart. By day, he worked for his father but during spare moments, he combed menageries and taxidermist shops, hunting for fossils and osteological material for Professor Marsh. He spent his evenings in the family's cellar, mounting unusual birds. He also dreamed of returning west. Finally, in 1872, Grinnell took a two-week vacation, a buffalo hunt with Frank North's brother, Luther, and some Pawnees. To his disappointment, Grinnell had seen no buffalo during the 1870 trip. Now he would participate in a hunt, in the company of Indians, no less. Thanks to his father's business contacts, who provided free-of-charge railroad passes, Grinnell traveled to western Nebraska in the luxury of a sleeping car. Moreover, settlers in the Republican River Valley signaled this was not quite the raw frontier Grinnell might have preferred. Yet the Pawnees who had left their reservation for their annual summer hunt (the last of its kind for the entire tribe, as it turned out) made an impressive sight. Only one or two of them carried a gun, the rest used "the ancestral bow and arrow" and the large body of hunters killed "enough buffalo to give us a very good idea of the methods employed in earlier days."[11]

After Grinnell left the Pawnees, his small party attracted the attention of about fifteen Indians who Grinnell believed were Cheyennes and who had, a few days before, attempted to drive off some of the Pawnees' horses. These Indians menaced Grinnell's group, firing a few shots and shooting a few arrows, none of which did any damage. Still, Grinnell felt threatened. His party had better weapons, however, and the Indians backed off.[12] Buffalo proved scarce and settlers inhabited the Republican valley, yet the Cheyennes still remained beyond the pale of civilization and offered the young adventurers a brush with a quickly vanishing way of life.

In September 1873, Grinnell's father retired and turned the business over to George and Joseph C. Williams, the firm's cashier. Three weeks later, the panic of 1873 "came on out of a clear sky" and the business failed. His father emerged from retirement to assure the firm paid all its debts, and in March 1874, George Bird fled Wall Street forever. Emancipated, at last, from family expectations and responsibilities, he could now pursue his own interests. He had begun writing hunting stories for *Forest and Stream*. He also volunteered as Marsh's assistant at the Peabody Museum at Yale, where he eventually earned a Ph.D. in paleontology.[13]

Hunting and exploring, of course, continued to head his interests. In late spring of 1874, General Philip Sheridan notified Marsh that he could assign a fossil collector to accompany Lieutenant Colonel George Armstrong Custer's expedition to the Black Hills. Grinnell leaped at the opportunity. "The Black Hills

*Grinnell and Walter McClintock both relied on Indian informants. Mad Wolf, or Siyeh, "adopted" McClintock, thus allowing him greater access to information about the Blackfeet culture, social structures, and religion. Reproduced by permission of the Yale Collection of Western Americana, Beinecke Rare Book and Manuscript Library.*

were then unknown . . . a region of mystery," he explained, ignoring Indian knowledge of the place.[14] However, by the expedition's end, Grinnell concluded that scientifically it was a failure.[15] The country seemed barren of fossils and the expedition's hurried pace allowed little opportunity for excavation.

The Black Hills were not, however, barren of Indians. Here and there they made an appearance in Grinnell's account. Custer's outfit included about fifty schoolboys from the Santee Sioux Indian school, uniformed and armed, "who were supposed to act as scouts." Twenty-five or thirty Arikara or "Ree" Indians from Fort Berthold also signed on and Grinnell expressed greater confidence in the latter's tracking abilities. The Arikara befriended Grinnell, he assumed, because of his relationship with Luther North, whom Grinnell brought along as his assistant during the expedition. North's ability to speak the Pawnees' language proved "a passport to the good graces of all the Rees," although Grinnell's rudimentary skills with that language helped as well.[16] As the expedition inched closer to the Black Hills, signs of less friendly Indians appeared. Thick smoke across the Missouri River, Grinnell assumed, meant Lakota and Cheyennes knew of the army's presence. But the only "hostiles" he encountered during the entire summer was a Lakota hunting party of five lodges which the Arikara scouts stumbled upon.[17]

If Grinnell was never seriously in harm's way during these 1870s trips, he certainly understood Indians and whites remained at war over the ultimate fate of the Plains.[18] He never doubted that whites would ultimately prevail, nor did the presumed Anglo-American triumph strike him as anything less than fitting. At the same time he demonstrated an interest in the Indian "allies" that suggested a more complicated, if not articulated, understanding of these events and their long-term significance. Although ethnography did not yet interest Grinnell in any sustained fashion, his interest in the Indian participants in these early expeditions indicated his potential for such work. In a way, he saw these people as living fossils, doomed to extinction but who could, for a time yet, speak, tell stories, and explain themselves. What he did not anticipate, however, was how quickly conquest would come and how quickly that conquest would alter the West. In only a few years, he witnessed a shocking decline in the numbers of game animals. In only a few years, Indians went from being perceived as genuine threats by Anglo-Americans to becoming their prisoners on reservations.

When Custer extended an invitation to Grinnell to join his 1876 expedition to the Little Bighorn, Grinnell was too committed to leave New Haven. Besides, a military expedition left little opportunity for collecting fossils. Had he gone, Grinnell later wrote, "I should have been either with Custer's command, or with that of Reno, and would have been right on the ground when the Seventh Cavalry was wiped out."[19] Like C.E.S. Wood, circumstances precluded Grinnell's participation in this battle and he fatefully escaped an early death.

That fall Charles Hallock invited Grinnell to become Natural History editor of *Forest and Stream*, a job which paid $10.00 per week, allowed Grinnell to remain in New Haven, and provided more experience in writing for nonacademic audiences. Over the next several years, Grinnell and his father gradually purchased enough *Forest and Stream* stock so that by 1880, the year he completed a Ph.D. in osteology and vertebrate paleontology at Yale, father and son controlled the magazine. Two career paths thus presented themselves: becoming a scientist or an editor. He chose the latter, returning to New York. The publishing career allowed him to pursue his true loves: hunting, conservation, and, eventually, Indians. This opportunity came just in time, for Grinnell was suffering from sleeplessness and headaches and a New York "brain" specialist advised him to change his work or "be prepared to move into a lunatic asylum or the grave."[20] *Forest and Stream* provided just the right niche for the ailing gentleman-sportsman.

The diagnosis raises interesting questions about Grinnell's psychological state, for this particular illness, ambiguous as it was, was increasingly common among people of Grinnell's class, race, and gender. Doctors discovered this new disease, neurasthenia, spreading particularly among middle- and upper-class men "due to excessive brain work and nervous strain." It threatened the body, rendering it less vital and virile. Historian Gail Bederman argues that concerns over this new disease, combined with challenges to upper- and middle-class white men's privileged position of power from immigrants, workers, and women's rights advocates, led many to endorse revitalizing manhood through athletics, the Boy Scouts, men's clubs, and by embracing "physical prowess, pugnacity and sexuality." The link between men and this disease is especially noteworthy. Many late-nineteenth-century Americans associated manliness with physical strength, hardiness, endurance, and the ideal of the "Masculine Primitive." The latter concept implied that all men shared certain savage impulses which could not, and should not, be suppressed. Rather, one should encourage or cultivate the ideal by hunting and developing one's "'natural' masculine strength and aggressiveness." Everyday opportunities to do so, however, decreased as the nation's frontier closed, and its men increasingly devoted their energies to business.[21]

Many aspects of Grinnell's illness fit this mold. So too did his remedies: the annual hunting trips, the celebration of physical prowess in his writings, and his numerous memberships and social contacts in men's clubs. Most revealing was his role in founding with Theodore Roosevelt the Boone and Crockett Club in order "to promote manly sport with the rifle." But Grinnell did not embrace all the cures. His love for the fair chase, for example, did not spill over to the "fairer sex." As a young man he disdained marriage and celebrated bachelorhood, showing little interest in women and apparently spending even less time with them. When he did eventually marry, at age fifty-two, to a twenty-five-year-old woman, the marriage elicited virtually no comment in his correspondence. Compared with the lusty likes of C.E.S. Wood and Charles Fletcher Lummis, Grinnell seems remarkably passionless, even asexual.[22]

In one other way Grinnell's actions and attitudes diverged from contemporary notions of manliness which also linked manhood with white supremacy and the "discourse of civilization." The latter notion maintained that only whites had evolved to the highest state of human development. "By harnessing male supremacy to white supremacy," Bederman explains, this Victorian gender ideology presented "male power as natural and inevitable."[23] To a large degree, Grinnell accepted this understanding of civilization which, of course, reinforced his claims to authority and power. Yet, in the long run, he could not follow this line of thinking to the same conclusions as his friend Roosevelt who, in *The Winning of the West*, demonized Indians, depicting them as rapists, baby-killers, unmanly men, and savages.[24] When Grinnell turned his considerable attentions to Indians, he forcefully, consistently, and purposely rejected such dehumanizing stereotypes.

All that remained for the future, however. For now, his bout with neurasthenia altered his life's work. His new publishing position allowed him to continue his annual treks west and remedied his illness, whatever its genesis. In 1881, he hunted in British Columbia. In 1882, Yellowstone National Park, newly accessible via the Northern Pacific Railroad, beckoned. The following year, Grinnell purchased a ranch in Wyoming's Shirley Basin.[25] The diaries he kept during these trips occasionally mentioned an Indian here and there. But clearly, Indians remained on the periphery. Hunting and preserving game most interested this sportsman.

The pattern changed in the mid-1880s when Grinnell commenced a systematic collection of Indian tales, history, and ethnography. It took fifteen years of western treks before he pushed beyond the relatively superficial relationships which he formed with Indian men on hunting expeditions and began to engage them in lengthy, deep conversations about their pasts. Paralleling his transformation from an avid hunter to a conservationist who preferred tracking game with a camera came a new dedication to collecting data about Indians and their cultures. By decade's end, Grinnell was on his way to becoming one of the most prominent, popular chroniclers of Indian life in the nation.[26]

What prompted this change? What sparked his interest in Indians? Grinnell was never explicit about this. Perhaps the turn toward Indian subjects was so gradual, so imperceptible, and so natural that he never felt the need to explain or justify. But certainly part of his motivation was his growing conviction that the Plains Indians cultures he glimpsed during the 1870s were disappearing forever.[27] He turned to them less because he wanted to "save" Indians and more because he wanted to retain a remnant of their past. He also wanted to learn from them, believing they had knowledge to impart. At the time, this was a fairly remarkable stance. In the 1880s, most non-Indians assumed it was Indians who needed to study the white man's ways. While Grinnell did not dispute this assumption, intellectually he pushed beyond it.

Not surprisingly, such impulses initially derived from hunting experiences. From his earliest days in the West, he looked upon Indians as instructors. Eventually, Grinnell published an article in *Forest and Stream* entitled "What We May Learn From the Indian" that addressed not only the hunt, but also broader social values. The article's subtitle summarized his basic point: "[The Indian] Protected the Game on Which he Depended and Practiced Methods of Economy in Hunting that American Sportsmen may well take to Heart." Using language commonly associated with the Progressive conservation movement, Grinnell attributed to Indians the values he hoped his countrymen would adopt. For instance, he argued that the Indian was intensely patriotic and that tribal welfare was of supreme importance. "[I]t was for the greatest good of the greatest number of his people that this game should not be wasted." Indians also took precautions for the welfare of future generations, assuring perpetuation of species. "But the white man with his acquisitiveness and selfishness wishes to secure everything for himself and is not willing that his fellows shall have the same chance that he has."[28] In what proved a relatively rare instance, Grinnell used Indians for purposes of social criticism, provoked by hunters' profligacy. The essay also represents an early example of later twentieth-century inclinations to envision Indians as models of environmental or ecological stewardship.

Grinnell's studies of Indians, however, moved well beyond concerns about the hunt. Evidence of his widening interests began among the Blackfeet in 1885. In late August, he visited the Southern Piegan agency school where he mingled with a small cluster of boys and girls, neatly clad and apparently interested in their lessons. Grinnell assumed they represented the future for the Blackfeet: indoors education, reading, writing, and eventually, farming. A little over one week later he came upon a Kootenai camp near St. Mary's Lakes where several boys especially impressed him. In fact, he was much more enthusiastic about them than the children in the agency school. "It was a wonderful thing to see that sturdy bowlegged boy march steadily up the steep face of that talus slope," he wrote in his diary, "never pausing for breath but going ahead as calmly and regularly as if he were walking up a pair of stairs."[29] Even as he understood the Blackfeet must change to survive, even as he embraced acculturation for all Plains Indians, Grinnell found their old ways extremely appealing. They embodied the vigorous out-of-doors existence to which he retreated every summer, evading the pressures of overcivilization and reasserting his connection with the "Primitive Male." As he explained to one correspondent, these trips gave him the chance to "change my life entirely for a little while and [I] become little better than a savage."[30] Grinnell, a paragon of civilization, could afford an annual reversion to temporary "savagery" or Indianness. The Blackfeet must renounce it forever, regrettable as that might seem.

Seeing the Piegan agency school, and other clues, signaled the impending transformation of Blackfeet ways. Sensing the cultural shifts, Grinnell sought to purchase war bonnets and shields, stone implements and weapons, tobacco and knife sheaths. He knew, by the 1880s, such "authentic" items were much less common than they had been only a few years earlier. With the deaths of Blackfeet men such as Red Eagle, Four Bears, and Almost A Dog, he lamented the lost opportunities to interview Indian old-timers. Grinnell complained, "one always feels that those old chaps, who had such glorious opportunities for getting at the bottom of matters connected with the Indians ought to have been crucified for not finding out and recording more facts." Grinnell decided there would be no cause to crucify him. He had already written the Bureau of Ethnology asking for any publications regarding North American Indians. He was especially interested in information on sign language.[31]

For the next forty years, Grinnell took upon himself this task—getting at the bottom of Indians—a chore located somewhere between work and play. He sought out old Indians, interviewed them through sign language and the help of interpreters, and recorded the conversations in his notebooks. He also relied on research assistants, including George Hyde, James W. Schultz, and mixed-blood George Bent, paying them for information they collected.[32] From the outset Grinnell intended to write for a general readership, preferring popular writing as a way to reach much larger audiences. He worried about professional anthropologists' criticism, but for the most part, his works received favorable reviews from layman and professional reader alike.[33] Grinnell did not aim to break new theoretical ground. Instead he focused on gathering data through systematic fieldwork among those he presumed represented the fading remnants of Pawnee, Blackfeet, and Cheyenne cultures. He attempted to record Indians' accounts without apparent embellishment or judgment and adopted a scientist's pose of objectivity. He also displayed unmistakable respect for his Indian informants.

By 1889, Grinnell began publishing his work in nationally prominent journals and magazines such as *Scribner's*, *Century*, the *Journal of American Folk-Lore*, and, of course, *Forest and Stream*. Like C.E.S. Wood, he first recorded Indian tales but, unlike Wood, Grinnell did not add his own romantic flourishes. He initially printed Pawnee stories in the pages of his own magazine and then collected them in book form. He followed this effort with several more collections of Indian tales, including *Blackfoot Lodge Tales: The Story of a Prairie People* (1892), *Blackfeet Indian Stories* (1913), and *By Cheyenne Campfires* (1926). "In each of these collections," according to historian Thomas R. Wessel, "Grinnell follows a familiar pattern. He acts as reporter, not interpreter, of the Indian's cosmic view."[34]

Grinnell's purpose transcended mere reportage. As he explained in the introduction to *Blackfoot Lodge Tales*, he hoped to humanize Indians and shatter stereotypes that perpetuated a one-dimensional view of them. American Indians had been shamefully treated throughout history and remained victims of threats, bribery, and fraud. Yet sensitive Americans, who cared about the well-being of starving Russians or Irish, seemed indifferent to Indians, Grinnell believed, because they "do not realize that Indians are human beings like themselves." In this volume, as well as the Pawnee one, Grinnell intended to fill that gap, allowing Indians to express their thoughts and feelings through their own stories. This story-telling would allow them to explain their perspectives, motives, and ways of reasoning unvarnished by the outsider's touch. The reader would thus get "the real Indian as he is in his daily life . . . [where he] is himself—the true, natural man." Like Wood, Grinnell was limited by certain nineteenth-century conventions such as the presumption that Indians were "a part of nature." In addition, he thought that the Blackfeet had the stature of men, but had undeveloped feelings and minds, like children. With education and civilization, with fair and judicious treatment, however, they had every capacity for improvement and citizenship. Grinnell clearly accepted the assimilationists' basic policy objectives.[35]

Yet he believed the so-called civilization program was a mixed blessing. In the closing decade of the nineteenth century, Grinnell witnessed first-hand the pathos of forced acculturation. "The Blackfeet will become civilized, but at a terrible cost," he wrote. They huddled together on a reservation which represented only a small portion of the great territory they had once dominated. They strove bravely to accommodate themselves to the new order, tried to reverse their whole manner of living, and though "scantily fed, often utterly discouraged by failure, they [were] still making a noble fight for existence." The change had been quick, dramatic, and tragic. "Only nine years have passed since these people gave up that wild, free life which was natural to them, and ah! how dear!"[36] Grinnell concluded with a chapter on contemporary Blackfeet existence, stressing recent starvation conditions, complaining about corrupt agents, and insisting that these Indians *could* prevail if they were treated fairly and encouraged to pursue stockraising. "With a little help," Grinnell explained, "with instruction, and with encouragement to persevere, he will become in the next few years, self-supporting, and a good citizen."[37]

By the time he published *Blackfoot Lodge Tales,* Grinnell was shifting his interest to other tribes, including the Cheyennes. He first visited the Northern Cheyenne in 1890 and by August 1895 had made sufficient contacts to begin interviews. Grinnell traveled to Tongue River and to camps on the Rosebud, where he interviewed Brave Wolf, Two Moon, Little Chief, White Bull, and others. He also talked with a missionary who told Grinnell he would share stories but, Grinnell noted in his diary, "he belittles their stories as a whole," something Grinnell would never do.[38]

He was not always successful in getting the Cheyennes to talk. Initially, Oldman Bear Coal refused to cooperate. So, Grinnell began to chat about how the Pawnees had captured the Medicine arrows. The old man agreed that Grinnell's version matched his own. "At first he said he did not know anything, but at last he said that he had always regarded these things as sacred and not to be talked about and he would prefer not to speak of it. I told him I could respect this feeling but not a lie."[39] With techniques such as this, which conveyed respect for Cheyennes' feelings—and truth—Grinnell usually found willing informants. The myriad stories he and his assistants collected among Southern and Northern Cheyennes filled notebook after notebook and, in time, became the foundation of his most important Cheyenne books: *The Fighting Cheyennes* (1915), *The Cheyenne Indians, Their History and Way of Life* (two volumes published in 1923), and *By Cheyenne Campfires* (1926), as well as a children's book *When Buffalo Ran* (1920).[40]

*The Fighting Cheyennes* chronicled their wars not only with Anglo-Americans but also with other Indians. At a time when the vast majority of Anglo-Americans showed interest only in the army's stories, Grinnell collected those from the other side of the battleline. At a time when many assumed "savages" had no history, Grinnell proved otherwise. The result was not a compilation of Indian views but a narrative, drawing on Indian and white accounts. What is truly remarkable is how much Grinnell depended on Indian testimony and the respect he accorded it.[41] As Grinnell explained in the introduction to *The Fighting Cheyennes*, "Since the Indians could not write, the history of their wars has been set down by their enemies." He wanted to balance the record. Moreover, now was the appropriate moment since "the wars are now distant in time, the Indians' own description of these battles may be read without much prejudice."[42]

It is not surprising that Grinnell focused first on Cheyenne warfare. That represented the context in which he first interacted with them.[43] It was also a topic that engaged and interested his Indian informants since warfare had dominated their lives in the nineteenth century. Moreover, Grinnell shared the antimodernists' fascination with the martial life. According to historian Jackson Lears, "those who coveted authentic selfhood" found "the warriors life personified wholeness of purpose and intensity of experience."[44] Surely, examples drawn from Indian warriors could suffice, as well as those from European knights. Finally, Grinnell's interest in Indian warfare intersected with late-nineteenth-century concerns about manliness. For one who believed the Old West was dying, the fading warrior ideal symbolized loss to all manhood.[45]

Grinnell's interests in the Cheyennes transcended the martial, however, and in 1923 he published perhaps his most important achievement, *The Cheyenne Indians*, a two-volume layman's ethnography. Although Grinnell relied occasionally on the work of historians, anthropologists, and other observers, most of the books' contents derived from information he had collected firsthand. Between his own frequent visits and the aid of interpreters, he gradually gained some Cheyennes' confidence and "to some extent . . . penetrate[d] into the secrets of their life." But Grinnell was humble, adding, "I am constantly impressed by the number of things about Indians that I do not know." This was not simply a public pose of feigned modesty. Privately, when Montana writer Frank Linderman once asked Grinnell if a white person could ever "get to the bottom of things with these people?", he responded, "I doubt it. I have reached the shell with two or three tribes, and perhaps have gotten a little way into the white, but way down deep there is the yolk of the egg—the heart of the matter—which I do not penetrate and perhaps no one ever will."[46]

Although he identified the Cheyennes as "primitive people" in the introduction to *The Cheyenne Indians*, the rest of the book belied that assessment as he chronicled the complexities of their lives and culture. In addition, Grinnell noted:

> *I have never been able to regard the Indian as a mere object for study—a museum specimen. A half-century spent in rubbing shoulders with them, during which I have had a share in almost every phase of their old-time life, forbids me to think of them except as acquaintances, comrades, and friends.*[47]

And then he added a most important point and constant theme in his Indian work: "While their culture differs from ours in some respects, fundamentally they are like ourselves." Here is Grinnell issuing an invitation to Indians to join the family of man or, more to the point, urging his readers to see that invitation as appropriate. Although he never articulated the theoretical leap to cultural relativism that such a comment could portend, he stopped just short of it.

*The Cheyenne Indians* offers a comprehensive study of nineteenth-century Cheyenne lives, focusing on such topics as smoking practices, marriage and divorce customs, horse equipage, children's games, musical instruments, tribal divisions and governance, hunting techniques, war customs and ceremonies, and religious beliefs. In page after page, the volumes present the Cheyennes, not as primitives, but rather as a people with a rich history and complicated patterns of living, thinking, believing, and being. They have communities, families, deeply held spiritual beliefs; in short, "a complex life . . . full of varied and diverse interests."[48] Grinnell also attempted to flesh out Cheyenne women by eschewing old stereotypes of them as slaves. He insisted they were their husband's partners, sharing equally in the work and affection of family.[49] Only occasionally did Grinnell drop his reportorial stance to make an editorial comment such as: "It often costs civilized man a struggle to carry out the precept to love his neighbor, but the Cheyenne did kindly, friendly or charitable acts of his own free will, and took no credit for them."[50] *The Cheyenne Indians* was a pioneering work that established the standard by which others of its kind would be measured. Throughout the remainder of the twentieth century, no historian or anthropologist who wrote about the Cheyennes failed to cite Grinnell's impressive work and build upon his foundation.[51]

By the mid-1880s, Grinnell began to utilize the power of his pen, as well as his connections in New York and Washington, to attempt some relief for Indian people. Political activism came naturally. As editor of *Forest and Stream*, Grinnell promoted game conservation and wise use of public lands. He helped establish the Audubon Society (precursor to the present-day National Audubon Society) and the Boone and Crockett Club, both dedicated to political action on behalf of game preservation. He successfully campaigned for game protection in Yellowstone National Park.[52] Unlike Wood, Grinnell did not separate what he most valued in the West from the knockabout, everyday political realities of the East.

True, regarding Indian affairs, he never challenged the fundamental acculturative policies of his day and never wandered beyond the basic boundaries of Progressive-era expectations for Native Americans. Yet he did not hesitate to criticize many particulars of policy. Grinnell deemed allotment and leasing of allotments as premature and detrimental to Indians' interests. He chided particular agents and worked to alleviate starvation on particular reservations. What began as a response to some Indians' pleas for help evolved into an unofficial advisory role during Theodore Roosevelt's presidency. Operating well within the constraints of his time, Grinnell nevertheless became one of the more dedicated and effective Indian rights' advocates of the early twentieth century.[53]

His political activism, which began when several Blackfeet and writer James W. Schultz appealed to Grinnell for help, paralleled his growing intellectual interest in Indians. Starving times visited the Piegan band of Blackfeet in the mid-1880s and they desperately needed relief. Grinnell shared their letters with Washington officials who saw to it that rations reached the reservation. The next year he visited the Blackfeet Reservation in Montana where various people, including Little Dog and Little Plume, greeted him enthusiastically and gave him an Indian name, "Fisher Hat" or "Pinutoyi Istsimokan." Grinnell began making reservation visits part of his annual western treks. Some Blackfeet welcomed his interest and viewed him as a potentially useful ally against their dishonest agent, M. D. Baldwin. The agent, however, had powerful friends of his own, and Grinnell's efforts to remedy the situation in 1887 went nowhere. When Grinnell returned to Montana for a hunt in the autumn of 1888, he learned more about their grievances against Baldwin, who allowed white cattlemen to invade the reservation, lied to the Piegans, sold agency goods to non-Indians, refused to acquaint the Blackfeet with their rights under treaty and severalty laws, and used his position for private gain. Grinnell was astounded and told the Blackfeet assembled before him: "I come from the east a private man. My business is to write. Many thousands hear my words, more people perhaps than live in all Montana." Grinnell then promised to report their complaints to the American people, "the Great Father," and the Commissioner of Indian Affairs, certain that things would improve once the public, the president, and the commissioner learned of the agent's abuses of power.[54]

True to his word, Grinnell wrote a lengthy letter to Commissioner T. J. Morgan indicating that Baldwin was "wholly unfit for his position." Grinnell reminded the commissioner that the Blackfeet had only a few more years' worth of annuities to rely upon before they would have to become self-supporting . . . or starve. This was not enough time to affect a revolution in habits, and to have their chances further undermined by neglect and broken promises filled them with despair. "I sympathise [*sic*] deeply with these Indians," Grinnell wrote, "I have known the tribe for some years. . . . They ought to be helped instead of hindered." As if to underscore his reliability, he went on:

> *I am no eastern sentimentalist on this question, for I have been familiar with Indians in their homes in the West for nearly 20 years, have lived with them on terms of intimacy and have met them in war; but I believe that the government might* [sic] *to, at least partly, fulfill its treaty obligations, and to give these people a chance to survive.*[55]

He ended by repeating his basic request: remove Baldwin and replace him with an "honest, conscientious man."

In a handwritten draft of the letter Grinnell wrote another, alternative appeal, arguing that the Blackfeet were people who loved their children and who had hopes and fears as well as joys and sorrows. "Though far away . . . they are human beings whose sufferings are as real as ours are to us." Perhaps he chose not to forward this version for he feared it sounded too sentimental. Grinnell's less passionate plea, however, went unheeded for Commissioner Morgan replied that his own investigator found things were going well at the Blackfeet agency. Grinnell answered that the inspector lied and then wrote a letter to the *New York Times,* cataloging misdeeds at the agency which the paper published on March 4, 1889. That fall's election ushered in a new president. That meant, in turn, a new secretary of the interior and other political appointees at lower levels. When Grinnell returned to Montana, the Blackfeet had a new agent.[56]

Pleased with his success, Grinnell engaged in some uncharacteristic boasting about his role in the Baldwin affair. He told the Piegans, whom he addressed as "brothers," that the new secretary of the interior removed the agent "wholly on account of [my] letter of charges."[57] Perhaps caught up in the emotion of the moment, Grinnell rather melodramatically told the assembled Blackfeet that he did not know if he would ever return their way, but added, "If I do not come back, I hope you will remember me for a little while. Think of Fishercap as one who will never lie to you and remember that when he says a thing it is so."[58]

The Piegans, apparently, shared Grinnell's belief that the New Yorker was responsible for Baldwin's removal. Several thanked him for his help and Whitecalf said, "Don't quit helping us . . . I guess the Great Father still listens to you for he knows you. He knows you have a good heart."[59] The Blackfeet, of course, had precious few white allies and in Grinnell they found someone who not only was willing to help but who also had the capacity to affect some change. Several of his Piegan correspondents most likely never knew that their notes of appreciation found their way into print. In summer 1889, Grinnell passed along several Piegan letters to the *New York Post* which published them. "Ah-ki-yah" wrote, "Fisher Cap. I send you my dream. When I was a young man it came to me. I have carried it in battles and it has kept me from harm . . . I thank you that you made such a bad agent leave us." Heavy Runner sent him a fur tobacco bag, apologizing that it was a poor present from a poor man. He thanked the New Yorker for ridding them of an agent who had referred to Grinnell as "a dog who runs about barking for nothing." Then Heavy Runner closed with, "The mountains looks inviting. I hope you will come and hunt with us again."[60] It is interesting that Grinnell released these letters to the press. Perhaps a bit of public recognition was the only compensation Grinnell exacted in exchange for helping the Blackfeet. Personally, he gained little from these efforts, other than a sense of satisfaction . . . and apparently a measure of self-satisfaction.

Grinnell proved less supportive of Blackfeet interests when they collided with conservation issues, however. In fact, in 1895, he played a more ambivalent role in reservation politics. That summer he traveled to Montana with several items on his agenda: hunting, interviewing Northern Cheyennes, and serving on a government commission to secure land cessions from both the Blackfeet and the Assiniboine/Gros Ventre reservations. The latter not only shaded his reputation among some Blackfeet and Gros Ventres in the early twentieth century, but also cast doubt on the depth of his sympathies in the minds of some late-twentieth-century observers.

In the early 1890s, whites began prospecting in the mountains on the reservation's western edge. By 1894, the Blackfeet's agent, Captain Lorenzo Cooke, pressured his "wards" to sell these lands as a solution to white trespass and as a means to buy themselves more resources and time for acculturation. Meanwhile, Grinnell had his own plans for the mountains. In 1891, he mused in his diary about starting a movement to buy the St. Mary's Country from the Piegan for a fair price and turning it into a national reservation or park. He thought the Great Northern Railroad would support such an idea and that Indians would like it too.[61]

Disturbed by rumors of gold in the mountains, in 1894, Grinnell urged Secretary of the Interior Hoke Smith to appoint an expert to evaluate their mineral potential. Instead, in March 1895, Congress provided funds for a commission to negotiate land cessions from the Blackfeet, as well as from the Gros Ventres and Assiniboines of the Fort Belknap Reservation. Secretary Smith requested Grinnell to serve on the commission and, although the Blackfeet wanted him to represent their interests (reflecting the trust they had in him), he declined both invitations. When Smith asked him again, Grinnell agreed but informed the official that he intended to offer the Indians a fair price, adding "I assume that you wish to have justice done in the matter." Grinnell found himself, then, in an anomalous position. He represented the U.S. government while the Blackfeet perceived him as their friend. Furthermore, he had his own interest in turning the St. Mary's Country into a national park. When the commissioners reached the Blackfeet agency, Grinnell noted in his diary, "The whole thing is amusing but sickening. See both sides of the game."[62]

Transcripts of the meetings between the Blackfeet and the commissioners indicate the Piegans viewed the sale as inevitable. The only matter of debate was how much would they receive for this cession. Some Indians asked for two million dollars, others three million. The commissioners publicly dismissed both bids as too high, and Grinnell noted in his diary their asking price was absurd. Understanding that many of these Blackfeet trusted him, he appealed to them on this basis. He assured them that Congress would never pay three million dollars, but they would pay one million. In the end, the Piegans capitulated to his arguments, compromised on a selling price of one and a half million dollars, and ceded the land.

Nowhere did Grinnell reveal any sense that he had betrayed Blackfeet interests. In fact, he noted in his diary that after negotiations concluded, many Indians thanked him. Possibly, he honestly believed the sale would cause no harm since the mountains had no agricultural value and the Indians did not have the ability to develop any mineral potential. Moreover, proceeds from the sale would help them acquire stock and implements to hasten acculturation. It would be easier to believe Grinnell acted solely in the best interest of the Indians, however, had he not harbored hopes that the land would become a national park. Still, in 1895, he had no assurances about park status and, in fact, what bothered him was not his role in the Blackfeet and Gros Ventres cessions, but rather the prospect of miners invading his beloved St. Mary Country. Once he returned to New York, Grinnell wrote, "It grieved me to think of that beautiful country being defaced by civilization and improvements so called, but there seemed no way to avoid facing conditions which existed." As Grinnell saw it, both Blackfeet and wild country must succumb to "progress."[63] Fortunately, the mountains lacked mineral riches. In time, Grinnell got his national park. But due, in part, to Grinnell's persuasive powers and the Blackfeet's trust, the Indians lost that land forever.

Most of Grinnell's activities with regard to Indian affairs proved less troubling. Usually, he intervened only to acquire more cattle and larger beef issues or to ensure Indian agents' honesty. Grinnell, for example, lobbied on behalf of the Northern Cheyennes when the government reduced their beef issue in 1902. He used the occasion to urge Secretary of the Interior Ethan A. Hitchcock to promote cattle raising among the Cheyennes who, he believed, were not ready for independence. In the long term, ranching would bring prosperity but in the meantime it was foolish to starve them. Two months later, a government agent at Tongue River Agency reported an increase of beef.[64] By this time, Charles Fletcher Lummis had enlisted Grinnell in his West Coast-based Indian rights organization called the "Sequoyah League." Grinnell shared his frustrations with Lummis in dealing with the Indian Bureau over the Cheyennes' beef issue, explaining that he engaged in protracted, wearisome arguments with the commissioner about it and that after six months of labor and five hundred dollars worth of time, the bureau finally granted the increase. He found it discouraging to work with the government agency because "they are so densely ignorant of conditions in the west."[65]

Finally, Grinnell occasionally addressed the federal government's efforts to suppress Indian religious and ceremonial practices. He did not support suppression, and when Secretary of the Interior E. A. Hitchcock asked Grinnell to comment on an inspector's complaint about the Blackfeet's Medicine Lodge Dance, Grinnell assured him it was "entirely innocent and harmless." Sometimes Indians used these dances as opportunities to criticize white people, but Grinnell claimed that "largely through my advice, [such] practices . . . have been eliminated from the ceremonies." Moreover, no nudity characterized these dances. They were "not 'orgies,' nor are they 'disgusting,' 'demoralizing' or 'degrading.'" When President Theodore Roosevelt asked Grinnell to investigate conditions on the Standing Rock (Sioux) Reservation in 1902, Grinnell's reports not only lambasted the government's unscrupulous leasing practices there but also criticized the commissioner's recent order that all Indians cut off their long hair. "Such an order was never before heard of in a free country, and the enforcement of it tends to make the Indians feel themselves slaves."[66]

By the spring of 1921 when the Pittsburgh *Dispatch* asked seven men to respond to the question: "Has the American Indian Been Fairly Treated?", Grinnell had no trouble deciding on an answer. His many years experience in Indian affairs led him to conclude no. Grinnell provided several explanations for the baneful state of affairs. Racial prejudice proved an insurmountable obstacle to fair treatment of Indians. Settlers and their congressmen regarded Indians as barriers to their own progress and never considered Indians' needs. The government made treaties and then broke them. Consequently, Indians believed they could never trust the white man. In fact, nearly all the Indian Wars derived from broken treaties or white encroachment onto Indian lands. Finally, their decline was inevitable. "The disappearance of the Indians is melancholy enough," he wrote, "yet in fact it is only the operation of law, which provides that the fittest shall survive and the weakest must be thrust to the wall."[67] This is a most telling statement and one that surely ties him more to nineteenth- than twentieth-century sensibilities. Grinnell, the Social Darwinist, was not insensitive to Indians' problems, but he believed their demise unavoidable, predestined, fated.

His response to the *Dispatch* seemed thoroughly enlightened, however, compared with that of Pittsburgh resident George Wright. This man concluded that the Indian *had* been well treated considering he is at best "a highly trained animal." Were he a human capable of education and assimilation, then he would have deserved better treatment. "As it is," Wright wrote, "nothing can be done with him except to offer him the same kindness that one would give a horse or an ox."[68]

Comments such as Wright's no doubt discouraged Grinnell. How could mere books change such attitudes? But such virulent racism did not immobilize him. Two years later Grinnell published his two volume work on the Cheyennes and wrote Lummis that he knew the public to which it would appeal was "very limited, but I am glad I lived long enough to see it come out."[69] Actually, he had also lived long enough to witness a new generation that read and appreciated his work on Indians. Among that group was writer Mary Austin who published a favorable review of his Cheyenne book in the *Saturday Review*. Pleased with her reaction, Grinnell wrote Austin:

> *I am taking the liberty of writing to you . . . to express my gratification that you comprehend my point of view about Indians. I have been writing about these people for a good many years, and always trying to tell of them so that the white people would realize that they were real "folks," just about like ourselves. It is only once in a while that I find someone who seems to understand that this is true, and those who do understand it are always those who have known Indians intimately, and, of course, sympathetically. You are one of those.*[70]

Just as Mabel Dodge Luhan reached out to Wood, so did Austin reach out to Grinnell. Austin was one of those people who viewed Indians in decidedly different ways than most of Grinnell's generation, representing a new spirit, one informed more by twentieth- than nineteenth-century sensibilities and experiences, one expressed through artistry, and one destined to grow more significant and influential in the decades to come.

It is noteworthy that Grinnell once attempted to convey his message about Indian humanity through "art" rather than science. The effort, a novel intended for adult readers, was a failure and never found its way into print. Titled "The Savage Lover," it is an elaboration of one of the earliest stories he published, "Comanche Chief, the Peacemaker," which appeared in *Pawnee Hero Stories and Folk-Tales*.[71] The manuscript blends his usual themes: educating readers about everyday Indian life while humanizing Indians. Alas, the stilted language and "romantic" story did not work as literature.

Grinnell was at his best when he was most straightforward. "The Indian is a man, just like one of us," Grinnell once wrote. "Like us he loves his wife and children; like us, he hates his enemies."[72] On another occasion he explained that the reason so many Americans felt contempt for Indians stemmed from the fact that they only conceived of them as enemies. "One who lives for a long time with Indians soon loses such notions for he sees another side of their character, the human side," Grinnell explained.[73] In the late twentieth century such sentiments strike one as obvious, hardly deserving of note. Clearly, in his day, Grinnell believed that acknowledging Indian humanity was necessary. Attitudes such as those expressed by Theodore Roosevelt in *The Winning of the West* or George Wright in the Pittsburgh *Dispatch* were all too common. Today Grinnell would find great satisfaction in knowing that many people, even if they have not known Indians intimately, understand his message about their humanity and appreciate his indefatigable efforts to preserve Pawnee, Blackfeet, and Cheyenne voices of one hundred years ago. Sadly, he died believing his message and his contribution went largely unappreciated.

Certainly, Grinnell was a product of the nineteenth century as his use of words like "primitive" and "savage," his Social Darwinism, his heavy-handed paternalism toward the Blackfeet and Cheyenne, his nostalgia for a romantic past, all attest. Moreover, he recognized the terrible costs of forced acculturation policy but could not imagine an alternative. Grinnell's significance here, however, rests less on his political actions than on his writings. In the depth of his research, in his books and articles on Native Americans, and his articulation of Indian humanity, rests Grinnell's contribution to the twentieth century. True, he forged these works out of a mistaken belief the Indian cultures he chronicled were vanishing. True, he shaped these works in an intellectual framework, an evolutionary model of human development, that scholars long ago rejected in favor of a relativistic one. But if he did not pursue the logical direction of his ethnographic work to arrive at a more pluralistic understanding of Indian cultures, many who read his books—the majority of which remain in print today—did. Finally, in his dedication to years of conversation with Indian people and to making their history, testimony, memory, and knowledge central to his works, Grinnell pointed the way to the use of Indian oral history, a method that some contemporary Indian critics insist modern historians still must learn to embrace.[74]

No white person can ever completely convey what it means to be Indian, and Grinnell never pretended he could. Yet through his efforts to faithfully record the words, feelings, perceptions, and experiences of the Pawnees, Blackfeet, and Cheyennes, he was one of the most dedicated and significant members of his generation to attempt it. Like C.E.S. Wood's, Grinnell's efforts did not go unnoticed by the generation that followed. Walter McClintock and Frank Linderman counted themselves among his faithful followers.

# 4

# AMONG THE BLACKFEET

*Walter McClintock and Mary Roberts Rinehart*

GEORGE BIRD GRINNELL WAS NOT THE ONLY YALE OFFSPRING to find his way to the Blackfeet of Montana at the close of the nineteenth century. Ten years after Grinnell's interest in these Indians was ignited, Walter McClintock entered their world. The son of a wealthy Pittsburgh carpetmaker, McClintock graduated from Yale in 1891. Like Grinnell, McClintock returned home to take a place in the family business, but a severe bout of typhoid fever allowed him to escape the humdrum commercial world of his father and go west. In 1895, McClintock visited Eaton's Cattle Ranch in North Dakota, the first dude ranch in the American West. It is a sign of the quickly changing times that a dude ranch even existed for such a comparatively tame option was unavailable to Grinnell in the 1870s. The trip apparently did the trick. McClintock recuperated but he traded one malady for another. He became addicted to the West.

The following year a chance to reprise his western adventure arose, as a member of a government commission assigned the task of recommending policy for management of the nation's forests. McClintock's Yale connections and friendship with Henry Graves, who would later became chief forester of the United States and dean of Yale's School of Forestry, brought him the opportunity to join Gifford Pinchot's 1896 expedition, surveying the forests on both sides of Montana's continental divide. McClintock served as official photographer. When the group reached Montana, William Jackson, a mixed blood also known as Siksikaikoan, and Jack Munroe, a white man married to a Blackfeet woman, signed on as guides. After their work was complete, Graves headed for Kalispell, Pinchot and Munroe left for Missoula, and Walter McClintock stayed behind with "Indian scout" Jackson, who took the young man over the divide and into a Blackfeet camp. McClintock's life was never the same.

It might be more accurate to say that this moment marked the beginning of Walter McClintock's life for his experiences with the Blackfeet defined, even obsessed, him for the rest of his days. Until his death in the late 1940s, he worked and reworked his impressions of that experience into one book (although he published two versions of it), an opera, and some articles. McClintock also presented illustrated lectures about the Blackfeet at venues across the country and in Europe between 1906 and the 1940s, although the lecture material, too, derived from that one story he had to tell about a young man from the East who lived, for a time, with the Indians.

For all their parallels, their privileged backgrounds, Yale educations, desire to escape the conventions of eastern life, an inclination toward timely illness with concomitant remedy through exposure to the West, and interest in the Blackfeet, Grinnell and McClintock did not, apparently, share a friendship or even correspond, although they did know of one another. True, a generation separated them. So too did intellectual breadth. Grinnell's interests were more wide-ranging, his curiosities broader, and his energies more robust. Compared with Grinnell's achievements, accomplishments, and skills, Walter McClintock's paled. And he knew it. McClintock was, at best, a mediocre intellect and a man of limited ambitions. Still, he believed he had an unusual opportunity to record, through photography and words, a glimpse of Blackfeet life at the dawn of the modern age. He told the story over and over again to anyone who would listen. To McClintock's credit, his listeners included Theodore Roosevelt, Andrew Carnegie, and the Crown Prince of Prussia. They also included readers and audiences from much less prominent walks of life who believed Walter McClintock had something to teach them about an attractive, friendly, generous, and spiritually rich people living, they all agreed, on the edge of extinction.

McClintock was too young to experience the West Grinnell knew. As a result, his work did not carry the same weight of nostalgia that informed the older man's writing. Nor did he share the same interest in manly pursuits of hunting and warfare. McClintock conveyed a softer, more spiritual, more romanticized image of Indians while simultaneously underscoring their individuality. Grinnell humanized Indians; but McClintock gave those humans a name, a face, a personality, a more precise identity. He also more explicitly contrasted their way of life to the "turmoil of the city, the dreary grind and slavery of business . . . [and] the shackles of social convention."[1] On this score he shared Wood's more pronounced antimodernist inclination to represent Indians as just the right antidote to contemporary urban life's routine, monotony, and materialism. One of McClintock's favorite images, one that he repeatedly offered in both photograph and word, was a Blackfeet lodge glowing from within, emanating a warm, radiant incandescence. Such an inviting image drew listeners and readers into a world seemingly far removed from the modern one. He tried his best to enter that lodge and explain its interior life to other Americans, in the process joining this growing chorus who celebrated Indian cultures and found in their distinctiveness something deeply compelling.

McClintock's life, before he met the Blackfeet, warranted no comment from the man himself. Other than hinting here and there that he had always loved the outdoors, he provided little explanation of what drew him to Indians. The best he could offer was "a love of nature and of the wilds" along with a pioneer spirit he must have inherited from an ancestor and "a yearning for a life of freedom beyond the frontier."[2] Initially, McClintock did not go west in search of anything, other than improved health and the possibility for some adventure. He simply stumbled onto Indians and then, having done so, grasped onto them for a lifetime.

That first encounter came in 1895, while hunting in Idaho. The guiding outfit's cook was a Paiute named Mrs. Smith, the daughter of Chief Winnemucca and sister of Sarah Winnemuca. McClintock described her as "unusual" since Mrs. Smith was outgoing, talkative, and friendly. He expected all Indians to be stoic. On the other hand, he also described her as "a typical Indian woman, waddling along not minding the deep dust and heat" as she searched for her pet antelope who had been chased off by dogs. McClintock facetiously called her an Indian princess.[3] At this point, he exhibited little interest in Indians and a ready willingness to resort to stereotype.

All that changed the following year when William Jackson took McClintock into a Blackfeet camp on the Cutbank River. Entranced with the people he met there, the young man from Pittsburgh decided to stay awhile. He purchased his own lodge and began to insinuate himself among these people who, evidently, expressed little objection to his presence. McClintock found it relatively easy to acquaint himself first with Blackfeet and, in time, their day-to-day life. Perhaps the fact that William Jackson (or Siksikaikoan as McClintock insistently identified him in his published work) introduced McClintock as someone who had come from the Great Father for the purpose of preserving the country's forests for future generations, helped. By presenting McClintock in this light, Walter believed Jackson created an image of him as "a friend and a man of influence and power."[4] McClintock did nothing to dissuade the Blackfeet of this impression and, in fact, exploited it for his own purposes. Throughout his life he tended to let misinformation slide, especially that which presented him in a more favorable, influential, or professional light than he deserved.

Walter wrote enthusiastic letters home, telling his brother about an autumn camping trip with a Blackfeet family. "You could not have finer people to camp out with," he told Norman McClintock. "They were the very nicest people on the reservation, the aristocracy," thus assuring his family that in embracing this primitive life he had not forsaken the imperatives of social and class distinctions. To his mother, Walter wrote about a Montana party that began at 8 P.M. and did not end until the following morning at 8 A.M. Indians, mixed bloods (or "breeds" as Walter identified them), and a smattering of whites intermingled. McClintock thought his mother would have been amused at the sight of him dancing with "the fair Indian maidens."[5]

To his father, McClintock wrote of more serious matters, especially his reluctance to leave Montana and return home to business, something he apparently was encouraging. Walter offered a variety of reasons why he should remain with the Indians. First, he could help out at a new school designed for the reservation children. Furthermore, his health was much improved in the West. Finally, he was observing the agent's chicanery and hinted he intended to keep track of his ill-doings for the purpose of helping his Indian friends. "People complain to me wherever I go," McClintock wrote, "but I discreetly keep my mouth shut. I would not have to try very hard to get into trouble here in short order. But I am going to continue to be a good listener."[6] In the end, listening—and eventually hinting in his books of their complaints—is the most McClintock ventured to do with regard to the Blackfeet's problems. He did not compose letters to the Indian Bureau about agency abuses nor did he publicly champion Indian rights. Walter McClintock was no George Bird Grinnell. McClintock claimed he lacked Grinnell's connections. More accurately, he lacked Grinnell's character, confidence, and maturity.

It is impossible to say which of Walter's reasons convinced his father to stop pressuring him to come home, but he stayed on for a few more years while his indulgent father bankrolled the adventure. Gradually, McClintock's purposes became focused. He wanted to record Blackfeet culture and his interaction with it. In the summer of 1898, he asked his father to send wax cylinders so he could record songs and stories. McClintock was most anxious to get them before the opportunities at hand vanished. Old men, young men, and even women seemed willing to talk with him, and he was astonished at how music proved all pervasive in their lives, explaining that "the Indians sing for everything they do, they are filled with music, which I think is not commonly believed." He took special pride in his ability to record Blackfeet women, telling his father, "yesterday I got three songs from a woman, this is rare as they are usually bashful. Mr. Grinnell said he could not get any and it was a very hard thing to do." Comparisons with Grinnell were inevitable and McClintock could not escape them. Someone told the Blackfeet that both men attended the same school, McClintock told his father, and that both would help Indians.

> *They think the world of* him, *and he certainly has done them much good, for he has influence in the East & rights their wrongs. I heard one of them liken Mr. Grinnell to a second Christ who has come amongst them, which shows the way some of them feel toward him. He certainly is a good man.*[7]

To be sure, such an assessment of a predecessor would be daunting. McClintock did not fashion himself the Blackfeet Savior, nor did he expect to compete with Grinnell's talents as ethnographer. He merely hoped to make his own modest contribution, in his own way.

Initially, McClintock's entrée into this world came through mixed bloods, such as Jackson, or whites who had married Indian women. The real breakthrough for McClintock came after he had spent several years on the reservation. At that point, an elderly man named Siyeh or Mad Wolf announced his intention to adopt McClintock. Siyeh was blunt about his motives. He believed McClintock would someday become a leader among his own people but would also help and advise the Blackfeet.[8] The implication was clear. McClintock would receive much from this adoption including information and a family relationship. He would accept responsibility in exchange. Siyeh viewed the relationship as reciprocal, expecting his "son" to provide help and guidance in dealing with other whites and the government. Siyeh also expressed affection for McClintock, and the latter believed he was accepted on the reservation, where people called him White Weasel, because of this relationship to Siyeh.[9]

The adoption was clearly a turning point for McClintock and, although it did not come until several years after his first forays into Blackfeet communities, he placed the event near the beginning of his books. McClintock did acknowledge that Siyeh chose him for this honor because he wanted to forge an alliance with a white man who would work sympathetically and faithfully for the welfare of the tribe. But he interpreted the elder Blackfeet's expectations in a self-serving way. "He wanted a white representative," McClintock wrote, "who had lived sufficiently long among his people, to become familiar with their customs, religion, and manner of life, and [who] would tell the truth about them to the white race."[10] Of course, this interpretation neatly coincided with McClintock's intentions. Yet the Blackfeet man's letters to McClintock reveal a different orientation, having more to do with immediate and practical problems than with the broader goal of teaching non-Indians about Blackfeet culture.

In letter after letter, Siyeh informed McClintock, when the latter returned periodically to Pittsburgh, of specific reservation problems and urged him to reply with news of affairs in the East. In one letter, Siyeh indicated that he had sold two horses and some other goods to acquire some old fashioned tobacco. "The reason I got it," Siyeh explained, "is because as I have taken you for my boy. I was willing to do this for you and to pay what I did for it." The elderly Blackfeet expected McClintock to reciprocate, by helping with the predicaments Siyeh chronicled in his missives. Sometimes he wrote about disruptive young Indian men on the reservation; other times he complained about white cattlemen on tribal lands or dishonest agents. Siyeh also fretted about cut-backs on rations and about property the federal government took but for which it never paid compensation. For many years the Blackfeet were uninformed about U.S. government actions, he explained, but now that some of their children were being schooled they had better access to information. Meanwhile, Siyeh's frustration with silence or secrecy about government policy was palpable. He urged McClintock to share his letters with Grinnell and pleaded with the Pittsburgh man to let him know "what is going on there." On another occasion Siyeh wrote, "If you can help me any about the matters I have written about, answer quick."[11]

The last letter McClintock received from Siyeh, in 1902, contained his final plea for assistance. He reported that cattlemen wanted to lease their land for grazing purposes, but that the Blackfeet objected to such a proposition. Although Siyeh knew their agent would try to force them to accept the lease, they hoped to prevail. Meanwhile, the Blackfeet wanted payment for land the government had purchased. Their agent had gone to Washington with their demand for compensation, but they had heard nothing from him. Siyeh was confident Grinnell would help them "kick against our present agent," and concluded, "Any advice may be received from you will be gladly acted upon."[12]

Five months later, McClintock responded. He said he had heard nothing from Washington or from Grinnell who lived far away. Moreover, in spite of Siyeh's heartfelt appeals for help, there is no evidence Walter corresponded with either the Indian Bureau or Grinnell about Blackfeet matters. He told Siyeh that he had been very busy working, that he did not expect to get out to Montana that summer, but that he hoped to hear news of reservation affairs. Such a lukewarm, ineffectual response would have disappointed Siyeh had he read the letter, but it was returned to McClintock with a message scrawled on the envelope: "Siyeh died 10 days ago."[13] In truth, McClintock's lack of action indicates that he left to others the chore of addressing practical and political concerns. About ten years later, Jack Big Moon informed McClintock that Blackfeet leaders decided not to adopt any more white people into the tribe.[14] To the extent such adoptions were political tools, McClintock's example demonstrated the limits of the device.

By 1900, McClintock was back in Pittsburgh working for the Opalite Tile Company, yet he returned regularly to Montana in years to follow in order to expand his written and photographic records of Blackfeet people and rituals. He lugged his camera equipment (which included a 3¹/₄ by 4¹/₄ Kodak with a Goerz lens and a 4 by 5 camera with tripod) and notebooks from camp to camp. The photographs survive, but most of the notebooks do not. An exception to this are notes from a 1903 visit that provide a glimpse into McClintock's methods and frame of mind. Siyeh had died the previous summer, but McClintock felt comfortable enough to pitch his own lodge among other Blackfeet. On a beautiful July evening he jotted down what he saw before him in the prairie camp: young men off for a ride, boys singing as they drove in the horses, a woman and her children dragging in a hide full of "chips," blue smoke rising from a fire in front of the sweat lodge—the cares and woes of hard reservation life nowhere in evidence.

Although a few men protested McClintock's photographing them and the sweat lodge, most did not seem to mind and several even joked about his compulsion to take photos. Spotted Eagle invited McClintock into his home and talked of various things, including the poor treatment they received from agency traders, the absence of credit, and the prices they paid for horses. Spotted Eagle, according to McClintock, was "continually making faces & often looking over nodding & winking as he talked, squinting & looking out of one eye. a great joker and frequently making smutty jokes."[15]

A few weeks later, McClintock found himself in the midst of another lighthearted group of men who had gathered in Last Gun's lodge. They shared the results of Last Gun's hunt and munched on service berries while debating the particulars of an important story. They disagreed about whether the North

Star was Scarface or whether he had become the Morning Star. As McClintock recorded the scene,

> *They all entered the discussion. Middle Calf held both were wrong that Scar Face was a small star near the Morning Star. Shorty broke in & laughed at them all saying they were all liars for none of them knew anything about the old stories. That the only people who ever knew are now all dead. The people tell the stories as they imagine them & they are all off. All laughed & enjoyed this tirade.*[16]

Laughter aside, McClintock found a certain pathos in Shorty's charge. Who *could* remember the story? Who *would* preserve these memories? Concerns about losing such stories certainly steeled McClintock's determination to make some kind of lasting record. And, of course, he was not alone. Among non-Indians, Grinnell had taken up this calling, as had a young anthropologist named Clark Wissler. Some Blackfeet too determined to keep alive the stories. McClintock's 1903 notebook conveyed a decidedly positive view of the Blackfeet who, while confined to a reservation and anxious to talk with him about their problems, still found opportunities to enjoy summer camps, religious ceremonies, and one another's company. In McClintock's eyes, their lives seemed filled with love, laughter, spirituality, and family connections—in marked contrast to those of whites living in towns on the edge of Indian country. There, according to McClintock, and in anticipation of Frank Linderman's similar views, gloom, violence, alienation, and loneliness prevailed. After spending a night in the Glendive railway station, McClintock walked into town for breakfast and found in the hotel office a cluster of "typical bronzed westerners" discussing the fight that had taken place the previous night.[17] McClintock scurried away from the violent cowboys and took refuge among the peaceful Indians camped in a cluster of lodges pitched out on the prairie. When he told the Indians that he was Mad Wolf's son, they welcomed him. In his experience, cowboys represented the bad guys, Indians the good ones; cowboys created violence; Indians offered refuge from it.

That night he returned to the railway station. While waiting for his eastbound train, McClintock met an immigrant who had been hopping freight trains but had stopped because the incessant rain and cinders had made such travel unbearable. "He felt bitter," McClintock noted in his journal, "against the new country into which he had come." Alone, with no horse and little money, the man despaired for his vision of American promise had soured. McClintock did what he could to cheer the man's spirits, encouraging him about the West Coast's prospects. When his train pulled into the Glendive Station, McClintock was happy to leave this dour fellow behind and felt "thankfulness for the comforts & pleasures which served to throng my life in comparison to his."[18] Although he did not explicitly state it, it is possible McClintock included among those "pleasures" *both* of his families, Indian and white. This experience, coming as it did in the wake of a summer spent with the Blackfeet, underscored his impression of Indians' lives as comparatively happy, healthy, and connected in community. Whites, by contrast, operated in a world of alienation, isolation, and loneliness.

Of course, McClintock seemed determined to ignore the desperate problems that plagued reservation life. He preferred the romance, not the reality, of it. In fact, Walter's first effort to share his knowledge of Blackfeet people came in the most unlikely form of all: an opera. McClintock would later explain that his own musical inclinations drew him to Blackfeet songs and moved him to "record and rescue them from the oblivion with which they were threatened." He found the younger tribal members unconcerned with posterity, future generations, or his project. But older men, who normally held themselves aloof from white men and were religious by nature, seemed "happy living in the dream world of myths and dances and ceremonies" and proved willing to share and work with McClintock.[19]

McClintock then asked Victor Herbert, conductor of the Pittsburgh Orchestra, to translate Blackfeet song and story for non-Indian audiences. Herbert demurred but suggested Arthur Nevin, a young musician, as a possible alternate. So, in the summer of 1903, Nevin and McClintock traveled west. At first, the camp fascinated Nevin, who was friendly with the Indians and enthusiastic about their artistry and music. The Blackfeet, in turn, liked him and called him "Don't Lace His Moccasins." But soon, McClintock claimed, Nevin grew tired of camp life with its hardships and lack of privacy. He spent most of his days smoking by the fire inside their lodge or stretched out on his bed. They did attend a Sun Dance ceremony and recorded songs. While sitting together at their lodge fire, McClintock claimed, he hatched the idea of writing a serious Indian opera based on the Scarface story. It would incorporate Blackfeet melodies in a setting of Indian camps on the prairie or in the Rocky Mountains. It was to be, as McClintock put it, an interesting and important conflation of cultures, "a thoroughly Indian and American grand opera in every way."[20]

Throughout the autumn and winter Nevin toiled away on the project, confident in his ability to compose original and unusual music for it. Meanwhile, McClintock created the Nevin Fund to provide money for the production. He appointed himself sole trustee and his father, Oliver, as first subscriber. Six others became financial backers. In June 1904, Walter and Nevin returned to Montana, living in a circle-camp and observing another sun dance. Walter stayed on to pursue his ethnological work while Nevin left in July to labor on the musical score back home. Eventually, they arranged for New Yorker Randolph Hartley to write the libretto.

Signs of dissension became evident, however, when Hartley complained to McClintock about an article he had read concerning "Pöia," as they titled the opera, "in which you practically claim authorship of the libretto."[21] The most McClintock could take credit for, of course, was providing Nevin and Hartley with access to the story and financial backing. Yet McClintock wanted a more public role and so began presenting lectures on the Blackfeet in 1906. His first venue was his hometown's Conservatory of Music, where McClintock offered a hand-colored lantern slide-illustrated talk with a sampling of Indian songs. In the meantime, Oliver McClintock did his best to promote his son's interests by acquiring a list of the nation's opera directors and urging them to produce "Pöia." While the Metropolitan Opera House responded it never presented anything that had not been thoroughly tested elsewhere first, the Pittsburgh Orchestra was more encouraging. It played two movements from the opera on consecutive evenings in January 1905. Two years later, Nevin conducted "Pöia" in concert form at Carnegie Hall, its New York debut. The Pittsburgh newspapers' music critics loved it. One paper declared it a "Splendid Triumph," noting that Nevin "has preserved the native melody and used it to convey to the world in song the passions and devotion of the red man." Another newspaper quoted well-known lecturer Captain Jack Crawford, who was in the audience that night: "'It's got plenty of Indian and lots of ingenuity, too.'" Both accounts mentioned that Commissioner of Indian Affairs, Francis E. Leupp, attended the performance, having made a special trip from Washington "to listen to the melodies of his redskin wards set to operatic score."[22]

Within the next several months, McClintock and the opera attracted greater attention. The chairman of the Pittsburgh Orchestra appealed to Andrew Carnegie to help open the way for "Pöia" to be performed abroad, declaring the opera both "authentic" and "American." Gifford Pinchot's mother hosted a Walter McClintock lecture in her Washington, D.C. home in March 1907, and the next month Walter, the now-recognized Blackfeet specialist, presented a lecture-recital about the opera at Theodore Roosevelt's White House. Such prominent audiences represented quite a contrast for a man who claimed, when Indians appealed to him for help that, unlike George Bird Grinnell, he lacked connections. At the White House, McClintock shared some stereoptican pictures of Blackfeet camps, sang Indian songs, and briefly explained the opera's genesis. Arthur Nevin then followed with a piano recital of some of the opera's music. Roosevelt, who of course sat in the front row, was an appreciative listener. After the performance he asked questions about the Blackfeet and told reminiscences about his own life on the western plains. Several weeks later, Roosevelt wrote McClintock, "I feel that you [have] done a real service in thus working for the preservation of the old Indian songs and music."[23]

Meanwhile, the partners decided to launch their full-scale opera in Europe when American producers refused to put it on. So, when Walter McClintock learned Andrew Carnegie would sail to Europe on *The Baltic* in May 1907, he decided to book passage on the same vessel in hopes of meeting him. McClintock did not want his money but rather his "influence," which he hoped Carnegie would use on "behalf of an American Work that came out of Pittsburgh." While crossing the Atlantic, the two men did meet. McClintock presented an abbreviated lecture with lantern slides in Carnegie's cabin and succeeded in getting the industrialist to write a letter introducing McClintock to Charlamagne Tower, American ambassador to Germany. Carnegie also mentioned in this letter that he believed the emperor and his family would be interested in McClintock's presentation.[24]

Once settled in Berlin, McClintock took his letter of introduction to Ambassador Tower whose interest was not pronounced. But his wife took an interest. Once she learned that money did not motivate McClintock, but rather that he had come to Germany (in his words) "to save for posterity the culture of a fine tribe of the American Indians who had no historian and were being destroyed by impact with white civilization," she became an important backer. So too did the American-born wife of the Danish ambassador to Germany, Lillie de Hegermann-Lindencrone.[25] Meanwhile, McClintock took up residence in a boardinghouse and began learning German. He wrote his mother that he felt confident about his ultimate success in Germany and was certain that his entrée into Berlin's highest social circles would ensure the opera's success.[26] Letters to his father emphasized the academic contacts he was making, particularly among German anthropologists. Such contacts eventually brought lecturing opportunities. In a May 1908 letter, he described his presentation at Berlin's Royal Museum as "the greatest success I have ever had," adding that Professor V. D. Steiman deemed McClintock "'a born Ethnologist.'" McClintock was beside himself with enthusiasm. Such a reception by the leading scientists and professors in Germany thrilled him, but fearing that perhaps he sounded a bit too boastful, McClintock added, "My head is not swelled; I am only encouraged."[27]

It is interesting that McClintock sought out academic approval, and that he did so in Europe. Possibly, he found such favor more easily obtainable across the Atlantic than in his own country. He lacked academic training in anthropology or ethnology and, while such credentials were not essential to carry on work with Indians in the early twentieth century, that was changing. McClintock must have been aware of his deficiency. It would be easier to peddle his lectures farther away from the subject, as well as the eyes and ears of academics such as Clark Wissler who might challenge his authority. McClintock was, at best, a layman or a "buff" along the lines of Charles Fletcher Lummis and Frank Linderman. Yet he wanted to be seen as much more than that. He wanted academic respectability, without going through the rigors of its training. European audiences and academics seemed willing to grant him this and he revelled in the prospect. As he told his mother in 1909, one year before he had been an unknown "but now my name will always be identified with Indian throughout Germany, 'me and [James Fenimore] Cooper.'" But McClintock's photographs and lectures offered "the real article." As a result, "I continue to get letters addressed Dr. McC. I will have to get Yale to give me that title now in self defense."[28]

Europe provided one more thing McClintock could not get at home: a brush with royalty. Through his diplomatic contacts Walter managed an invitation for dinner from the Crown Prince of Germany in 1909. The boardinghouse where McClintock resided was in an uproar over the invitation, and he imagined that American newspapers would take note of his royal visit as well. Sounding not unlike a Henry James character enraptured with Europe's aristocratic trappings, this American in Berlin shared all the details of his royal evening, in a letter to his doting mother.[29] Besides brightening his social life, Arthur Nevin would later claim, McClintock was dropping hints that his relationship with the Crown Prince helped bring "Pöia" to the stage. Whatever the truth of that, on April 24, 1910, Berlin's Royal Opera House finally presented the debut of what McClintock had called an "Indian and American opera."

"Pöia" royally failed. The evening of the debut, when the final curtain dropped, polite applause dissolved into whistles and hoots of disdain. Others expressed their dissatisfaction by jangling streetdoor keys or yodeling. After watching the performance, Willy Pastor, music critic for *Tagliche Rundschau*, reported that no one in America would produce the opera and he now believed, "Respect for McClintock may have caused this refusal." Pastor appreciated McClintock's enthusiasm for Indians and desire to share his knowledge with a wider audience, but called this an "operatic catastrophe." Nevin was, at best, a "mediocre musician," who hurriedly studied a little Indian music. Pastor warned readers, "do not confuse McClintock and his work with this caricature."[30]

American news reports emphasized not the quality of the opera, but rather the nationalism in the audience's response. According to the *New York Times*, the opera pitted "Red blooded American enthusiasm . . . against stubborn German stolidity." While Americans roundly applauded, Germans offered demonstrations of disapproval. Patriotic plaudits met a storm of German hisses.[31]· A Rochester, New York, newspaper offered the following lesson from "Pöia" 's reception in Germany:

> *The abuse of Nevin's opera, Pöia, by the Berlin press should be an object lesson to Americans who kowtow a shade too obsequiously to foreign opinion. It is not by imitating Germany that this country will ever become musically great. It is by being Americans.*[32]

The paper went on to muse about the possibility that German racism toward Indians played a role in alienating critics' sympathies and concluded that by damning the opera, Europeans would make Americans want to see it all the more. These American newspapermen embraced Indians as an integral part of American identity and nationhood. For his part, McClintock later claimed the German press's hostility to "Pöia" stemmed from resentment about its being produced by the Berlin Royal Opera House when so many German operas waited for a hearing.[33] Nationalism cut both ways and possibly pervaded the reaction to the effort on all sides.

For all the nationalistic fervor the opera's reception unleashed, however, there was no denying, in the end, it failed on its own artistic merits—or rather, lack of them. McClintock's friend John C. Symmes, who attended the first performance (McClintock was lecturing in Britain and so never saw the production), told him quite honestly the music was mediocre and the plot difficult to follow. It lacked the poetry of McClintock's lectures and photographs. Americans who tried to turn the matter into a nationalist affair were mistaken.[34]

Nevin, meanwhile, blamed McClintock and lashed out at him, accusing him of taking more credit than he deserved for the work, lying about his Indian linguistic abilities, and manipulating the legend for artistic purposes while claiming ethnological integrity. In short, he believed McClintock was a charlatan. Surely, this correspondence reflected deep hurt and anger at the opera's reception, and it leaves the impression Nevin was looking for a scapegoat. Still, his letters contain a measure of truth and insight into McClintock's Indian work. They certainly reinforce the impression that McClintock *was* claiming more credit for himself, particularly as an ethnologist, than he deserved. They also suggest that he was willing to stretch or manipulate the truth and that he engaged in some duplicitous behavior. In sum, his partner believed he was a "pretender." Some of McClintock's actions suggest this assessment was not completely off the mark.[35] The story of the opera and McClintock's role, then, reveals something about his methods, which sometimes proved questionable, and something about his motives, which included a measure of self-aggrandizement as well as goodwill. The opera is also noteworthy because it received attention at the highest levels of American political power and because it represented an effort to reimagine Indians for Europeans as well as American audiences. McClintock was the only one to consciously carry this effort across the Atlantic among the writers examined here.

Not only did the McClintock-Nevin friendship end in 1910, but so also did "Pöia's" prospects. After the Berlin Opera staged only four performances, "Pöia" died and remained forgotten until 1930 when Robert Nevin, Arthur's brother, asked McClintock's permission to pursue the possibility of having the opera adapted for the movies. Arthur and Hartley had already given their permission, and Hartley, who had just returned from Hollywood, was willing to write the dialogue. McClintock granted permission but apparently the film was never made.[36]

McClintock did not link his ambitions for his Indian material solely to the opera, however. He continued lecturing and he wrote a book titled *The Old North Trail: Life, Legends & Religion of the Blackfeet Indians* which Macmillan and Company published in London in 1910. This book, along with a 1923 Houghton Mifflin revised version, *Old Indian Trails*, represented McClintock's most widely read works.[37] *The Old North Trail* is McClintock's treatise on the Blackfeet. It is his effort to translate his experiences in Montana and Canada into something useful, tangible, and enduring. He made clear that his primary motive was to preserve the "rich treasures" of Blackfeet folklore and religious life by repeating the all-too-common assumption that these Indians "must soon lose their identity and disappear for ever." He reiterated his belief that their youth cared little for their history or culture and that his role was to record, through print and photograph, these things for posterity. McClintock also clearly identified the villains of the story: "the white race was like the invasion of a hostile army in its effect upon this Indian paradise." They brought smallpox, measles, and alcohol which resulted in the Blackfeet exhibiting a deep-seated distrust of whites and in a declining Blackfeet population. By McClintock's day, all that was left was "the pathetic spectacle of a dying race."[38]

From the first page of his book, it was clear that McClintock would play a major role in this story. While he was a white man—he was a different kind of white man. In an interesting reversal of history, McClintock approached the Blackfeet not from the east but from the west. As his guide took him toward the Plains, they crossed the Old North Trail which the Indians no longer used, "its course having been broken in many places by the fences and towns of the white man's advancing civilisation." McClintock would never forget his first glimpse of the Indian camp. It was inviting, tranquil, lovely. Moreover, being there was akin to a spiritual experience. As he camped out under the stars that night, he wrote in Woodlike revery, "Lying on my back and gazing up into the wonderful beauty of the heavens gave me an overwhelming sense of the infinity of God's universe and my own littleness by comparison."[39]

Littleness notwithstanding, McClintock loomed large in his Blackfeet book. Organization of the book's material signaled his intention not only to relay ethnographic information but also to create a compelling story revolving around himself. He had no sooner arrived in the camp, for instance, than Siyeh adopted McClintock and conveyed upon him an Indian name. In accelerating this adoption by years, McClintock reinforced his own centrality to the book as an adoptee and became the focal point of the adoption ceremony. Of course, he was also the interpreter that put him in the dual role of participant and observer. Interestingly, while McClintock occasionally referred to "superstitions" when writing about Indian religion, he also hinted that he was a *believer* and thus went a step further than Grinnell in legitimizing them. By connecting the stories and ceremonies to his own experiences, he gave them a veracity they might have lacked if he had simply recorded them as an "objective observer." Furthermore, by straddling the role of objective observer and believer-participant, McClintock made Indian religion more accessible to non-Indians.

Once, after listening to the legend of the Medicine Grizzly, he wrote: "I felt convinced that the huge grizzly, who had frightened me the night before, must be the dreaded 'Medicine Grizzly.'" Another time he entered into the spirit of the Crow Beaver Ceremonial. Onesta, who conducted the ceremony, asked McClintock to sleep in the sacred Thunder Tipi (where the ceremony took place) and told him he might experience a dream or vision in the process. McClintock agreed and later reported, "As I went to sleep I remembered having seen a large eagle. . . . He stood beside me in the night, advising what message I should bring to the North Piegan." That message, as it turned out, just happened to correspond to McClintock's interests for, as McClintock reported to his Indian friends, the eagle told him "'It is a good thing for you to visit the North Piegans, to learn about them, and to take their pictures.'" The Blackfeet looked him over carefully to see if he joked, but McClintock "maintained a solemn countenance . . . and I knew my vision was taken seriously."[40] In his 1923 version of this story, McClintock claimed that he was joking and that none

*McClintock's authority regarding the Blackfeet rested on firsthand experience garnered from living among them at the turn of the century. Reproduced by permission of the Yale Collection of Western Americana, Beinecke Rare Book and Manuscript Library.*

of the Blackfeet took him seriously. They understood such an opportunistic vision was a fiction.

For the most part, McClintock treated their religion with respect and care, even attempting to legitimize Indian religion by drawing comparisons to Christianity. He presented the Sun Dance, for instance, not as an opportunity for self-torture (as he assumed most of his readers perceived it) but rather as a "holy sacrament, the supreme expression of their religion." McClintock equated the feasting which accompanied raising the Sun Dance center pole to the Jewish Passover and Christianity's Last Supper. Throughout the book he repeated such comparisons. Tipi representations of the Buffalo, Otter, and Antelope, which signified the power these sacred animals had to protect the owners' family from harm, resembled Christians' use of the crucifix as an "outward sign to the world of the inward faith of many Christians." And the Indian practice of naming children in honor of a medicine bird or animal in order to invoke its protection, had its parallel in the Pilgrims' habit of choosing biblical names or the more recent custom of naming children after Christian saints.[41]

Not only did McClintock intend to interpret and legitimize Indian religion for his readers, but he also wanted to humanize Indian people. Grinnell shared this goal, yet McClintock proved more successful in achieving it. By placing himself at the center of the story, he magnified his personal experiences with individuals. Mad Wolf did adopt him and in the process not only became an informant, but also a father with a family. In his books, Grinnell maintained the position of detached scholar or scientist-observer who did not intrude in the narrative. McClintock, by contrast, jumped right into the thick of things. His relationships with individual Indians allowed him to observe and record facets of Blackfeet life that were revealed more readily to a family member than an outside observer. That he was allowed into these families and permitted to photograph so many aspects of their lives "attests to the wide acceptance of his presence by the Blackfeet," according to one recent interpreter.[42] It also explains why McClintock's photographs and prose transcended the more static images of other amateur and professional ethnographers. McClintock filled his volume with examples of Blackfeet humor. He interacted easily with the women in his adopted family and smoothly integrated them into his stories. Children played a key role as well.

McClintock lavishly illustrated both books, using photographs to underscore the reality and vitality of Indian people. His extensive photography collection represents his most important contribution to Blackfeet history and ethnology.[43] Containing over two thousand images, the collection includes rare views such as a series of time-lapse images of the construction of a Sun Dance lodge, many different ceremonies, and scores of portraits. Capturing such photographs required persistence and also the cooperation of his subjects. Sometimes the latter were forthcoming, sometimes they were not. Some women refused to cooperate, he claimed, because they had been told McClintock's camera could penetrate their clothes and he could see them nude.[44]

Most of his Blackfeet subjects agreed to McClintock's photographs, however, and the photographs had the effect of verifying his vision, of bringing his story to life. When he wrote about a person, say Siyeh or Brings Down the Sun or his "sister" Strikes-On-Both Sides, and then strategically placed a portrait of that individual in the midst of the prose, the person suddenly became more "authentic." More important, the images seemed to validate and corroborate McClintock's interpretations. Surely, Siyeh was noble, for didn't he appear so in the portraits? The same held true for his juxtaposition of photographs and written descriptions of ceremonies or pastoral scenes of tipis on the Plains. In a typical passage, McClintock presented an Indian encampment this way:

> *The picturesque lodges, with their painted decorations and blue smoke rising from their tops, were perfectly reflected on the surface of the quiet lake . . . In the surrounding meadows, large herds of horses were quietly feeding, while upon the summit of a ridge was a solitary horseman, who had left the noisy camp for quiet and meditation . . . When the tipis were lighted by bright inside fires, the circular encampment looked like an enormous group of coloured Japanese lanterns, and the flickering light of the many outside fires resembled fireflies in the summer's dusk.*[45]

McClintock then matched the words with appropriate images, including a solitary horseman gazing off at the village below, proving that this place was not a figment of his romantic imagination. After all, the Blackfeet still lived this idyllic life. If one doubted McClintock's word, one only had to examine the photos.

Equally important in interpreting and understanding McClintock's vision in *The Old North Trail*, however, is what he omitted. He masked the mixed bloods' presence by using their Indian names. He never photographed Indians next to frame, brick, or other European-American structures. Although McClintock took many of his photographs only yards away from Browning, Montana, one would never know it by looking at them. He never included whites in his photographs of Indians, except for himself. He rarely discussed and never photographed present reservation conditions or circumstances, and he consistently refused to engage in or acknowledge practical and political matters.

By omitting reference to mixed bloods, whites, and the presence of "civilization," McClintock wanted to convey an image of a people untouched by change, living their traditions (albeit doomed) in tranquility. In sum, McClintock's books offer a good deal of artifice as well as ethnology. Given McClintock's apparent interest in scholarly approbation, he might be disappointed by such an assessment. Clearly, all of the works studied here involve "constructions," representations, and manipulation of "facts." In the case of McClintock, however, evidence suggests a more decided manipulation than one would find, say, in Grinnell's books.

Like C.E.S. Wood with the Nez Perces, McClintock needed an image of the Blackfeet that would strike a dramatic contrast to the lives of most Anglo-Americans, for it was in the contrast of these two worlds that McClintock found his most important message. It was the North Piegan camp which inspired this key passage:

> *Seated in this ancestral place of meditation, and under the spell of my peaceful and beautiful surroundings, a strong doubt entered my mind as to whether the white races, in the pride of their civilisation, fit their natural environments much better than this patriarchal settlement of Blackfeet.*
>
> *While we have mastered and harnessed the forces of nature to do our bidding, and have achieved wonderful things in science and industrial combination, have we, with all our striving and complex life, attained a much higher average of character, contentment and loyalty to the community interests, than was attained under the simple life and few wants of the average Blackfoot family, before the invasion of the white race? We could look in vain in such camps as that of the North Piegans, nestled among the cottonwoods, to find the depravity, misery and consuming vice, which involve multitudes in the industrial centres of all the large cities of Christendom.*[46]

To McClintock, these Indians inspired an alternative to what he found most distasteful about life in Pittsburgh, New Haven, and other loci of Christendom. In classic antimodernist fashion, he acknowledged the achievements of science and industry, but quickly raised questions about their costs. In the mad rush to conquer nature, "white races" had forsaken compassion, happiness, and concern for their fellow man. Urbanization and industrialization brought "depravity, misery and consuming vice," things one could not find in the "simple" life led by the Northern Piegans. Of course, McClintock himself never truly abandoned Pittsburgh or New Haven for Montana. For one thing, he claimed the alternative offered by the Blackfeet was fleeting.

The final chapter of *The Old North Trail*, entitled "The Present and Future of the Blackfeet," made clear their present was grim and their future uncertain. The chapter began with an elegiac tone: most of the leading chiefs and medicine men he once knew were dead or ignored by young men, who preferred horse racing and baseball to Sun Dance ceremonials. The agent arbitrarily interfered with religious ceremonies, further demoralizing the devout. Conditions precluded the development of future leaders the likes of Siyeh or Brings-down-the-Sun whose "unselfish and patriotic lives, devoted to the welfare of their tribe, rise before me in strange and painful contrast with the selfish and sordid lives of many of the rich and powerful of my race."[47]

Yet, like Grinnell, McClintock could not imagine any other destiny for the Blackfeet. A prisoner of nineteenth-century conventions, he expressed deep regret for the ravages of Indian policy while simultaneously endorsing current policymakers' visions. He attacked reservations that herded Indians upon tracts of land, provided them with rations, and forced them into a life of paupery, degradation, and dependency. Instead, McClintock supported the "humane and progressive" policy of Theodore Roosevelt and Indian Commissioner Francis E. Leupp "to individualise the Indian," give him an allotment, and make him a citizen. In a position which made no sense whatsoever considering all that preceded it in this book, McClintock concluded that by embracing "civilised conditions," the younger generation of Blackfeet made "a striking contrast" to the older generation of Indians, who, "because of their fixed habits of hereditary savagery, are incapable of work, or a settled occupation." Finally, in the most amazing reversal of all, McClintock decried the "mental and spiritual slavery of the Blackfeet, under their 'Medicine' superstitions" and encouraged Christian missions to work among them. "The Blackfeet stock," he concluded in the last line of the book, "is endowed with as favourable qualities for grafting upon it the fruits of our Christian Civilisation, as was the Anglo-Saxon before its conversion to Christianity." The final chapter reads like a tacked-on, uninspired afterthought.[48] Of course, McClintock never pretended much interest in or enthusiasm for matters of policy. Perhaps it is unfair to judge him too harshly for a tendency to simply fall back on current practices of contemporary "wisdom." If Grinnell could not reimagine the contours of policy, why should we expect it of McClintock? His intended goal was not to challenge policy but to enrich readers' understanding of the Blackfeet and their religious life.[49]

Walter McClintock saw to it that various acquaintances in high places received copies. Theodore Roosevelt and Gifford Pinchot thanked him for their books, and the latter congratulated McClintock on providing a "real service to the country" in making such a record. Anthropologist Clark Wissler proved a bit more evasive in his praise, noting that McClintock had managed to give a "mass of details a rather artistic setting." Grinnell wrote a gracious and generous review. He described *The Old North Trail* as "a delightful story" of life among the Blackfeet as they lived ten years ago. Grinnell pointed out that McClintock's versions of traditional stories would be new to students of Blackfeet literature, but added that variations were normal and that all should be recorded. Finally, he credited McClintock with presenting the Indians "from the human point of view, seeing them as they really are as fathers, mothers, sons, daughters and friends, with all the simple kindliness and affection of a people still primitive and more or less unspoiled."[50]

Undoubtedly, McClintock cared what people such as Grinnell and Pinchot thought of his work. Presumably, he was also interested in the reactions of the less well known. At least one such reader corresponded with McClintock and indicated that the book touched her deeply. Alice Jacobs wrote that "there is a great deal we can yet learn from those we have been taught to look on as heathen." She was most impressed with the Blackfeet devotion and reverence in carrying out rituals and ceremonies, their love for one another and for the white man, who had caused them so much suffering, and their moral development which was far beyond the white man's. Jacobs ended her letter by stating that McClintock's book "has been a real blessing to me and therefore its mission has not been in vain."[51]

McClintock published *The Old North Trail* in Great Britain but waited a dozen years before moving toward an American imprint. Finally, in 1922 he approached Houghton Mifflin about publishing a new book, titled *Old Indian Trails*. He explained the manuscript dealt with the same general subject as his first volume but in a different way. He promised there was no repetition of text. Actually, *Old Indian Trails* was a condensed version of the original, offering less ethnographic detail, greater consolidation of the narrative, reorganization of material, and more nostalgia for by-gone days. Passage of time had deepened his sentimental feelings about these people and those emotions seeped into his prose. This time McClintock claimed his motive in visiting the Indians was to escape the turmoil and daily grind of city life, "the shackles of social convention," and the "slavery of business," where making money was the focal point of life. In rejecting the city, he simultaneously embraced "the lure of the wild" and the "new sense of freedom" he found in Montana.[52] Certainly, he still wanted to present a record of Blackfeet life, but the antimodern impulse took a more prominent place in this second book.

On the other hand, *Old Indian Trails* is more forthright about McClintock's methods and contacts. He offers more information, for instance, about William Jackson or Siksikaikoan, "the scout." This time McClintock admitted Jackson was a mixed blood and a rancher. Throughout the volume McClintock acknowledged the presence of other mixed bloods, as well as white men married to Indian women, and conceded they most often served as his primary contacts and conduits to full bloods. Furthermore, he presented these "types" in completely positive ways—in marked contrast to many racist nineteenth- and early twentieth-century observers, who depicted "squaw men" and mixed bloods as debased and depraved. He credited a mixed-blood friend, named Yellow Bird, with proving especially helpful in introducing him to the Blackfeet.[53]

One other contrast between *Old Indian Trails* and its predecessor is the new work's greater emphasis on McClintock's immersion into Nature as a central theme. Although his chronology was always fuzzy, in the second book McClintock organized the material around the device of a year's changing seasons. The story begins in late summer, moves through a cold and brutal winter, briefly touches on spring, and ends with a summer's Sun Dance. The effect is a more organic, artfully constructed narrative. He also more pointedly connected the peacefulness he felt in the West with the "close communion with nature" he experienced there. Stories of McClintock's camping, hunting, birding, fishing, and botanizing, then, take greater prominence, although he made it clear that he engaged in such activities in the company of Indians who taught him much. In fact, it was the close connection the Blackfeet maintained with Nature, their brotherhood with birds and animals, that McClintock found especially appealing.[54]

Finally, McClintock concentrated less on religion and more on humanizing the Blackfeet. Their humor, their love for one another, and their supposed domestic bliss received more emphasis in the second version. Once again he takes the reader into those Japanese lanternlike lodges on the Plains, sits us down at their hearths, and includes us in the ceremonies, the joking, and the storytelling. Time and again women reach out to McClintock, helping him assemble his botanical collection, altering the appearance of his moccasins so they would more closely resemble theirs, and assisting him as he erects his own lodge.[55]

*Old Indian Trails* ends with a description of the Sun Dance, this time given by Mad Wolf. In a conclusion obviously contrived by McClintock, Mad Wolf addresses the congregated Blackfeet before they disperse at the ceremony's close. Mad Wolf urges them to send their children to school, learn English, obey the law, and accept the fact that the white man's way was now predominant. Then the "tribal camp melted quickly away; and I was left alone on the prairie." That was, McClintock claimed, the last time he saw his Indian father and "now all that old generation of Indians have followed him."[56] In this version McClintock offered no bromides on policy. He simply let the Blackfeet fade away.

Once again McClintock placed copies of his book in the hands of the wellborn, famous, and prominent. Crown Prince Frederick William, now living in exile in the Netherlands, for example, thanked Walter for sending a copy of *Old Indian Trails*. McClintock apparently made no effort to share his work with old friends from Montana—Indian, white, or mixed blood. Not until seven years after publication, did McClintock hear from some Montana folk who discovered the book on their own and wrote friendly letters. A mixed-blood woman named Pearl Wetzel Hagerty, presented in the book as "Katoyisa," discovered the book in 1930 and wrote a glowing reaction. She found that McClintock pictured people "just as they were" and surmised that he must have kept clear notes. Pearl found his description of her, which emphasized her "slender graceful form," "shapely head and good features," and "courage and character," especially pleasing. In fact, she admonished McClintock for neglecting to tell "that Indian girl . . . what you thought of [her] those days or you might have played a different part in life." Now that she was fifty-three and "fat," she wondered how he would describe her.[57]

Apparently, McClintock responded because Pearl wrote again. "Received your letter and really felt thrilled," she wrote. "Say! the word Indian kind of makes me happy. I hated it when you knew me. I looked at the dark side and I was miserable for a long time, but now I [illegible] it is real blue blood. So many fine people like you . . . and Mr. Grinnell have changed my ideas."[58] McClintock must have enjoyed this. First, he found himself in the company of Grinnell. More important, he had evidence that he had altered someone's perception of Indianness. Here was a middle-aged, mixed-blood, Montana woman who had lived much of her life embarrassed and ashamed of her Indian heritage. McClintock's work helped to erode that shame and replace it with pride. It changed at least one ordinary person's view of herself and of Indians.

In the end, ordinary, educated people constituted McClintock's primary audience. His work, with its "artistic" elements and liberties, limited its usefulness to scholars. McClintock probably knew that. So, he contented himself with lecturing to nonacademic audiences across the country, presenting his lantern slide-illustrated lectures at places such as Chicago's Field Museum and Pittsburgh's Carnegie Museum and Academy of Science and Art. McClintock did not make much money on the lecture circuit, nor did he need to; he just wanted to share his message about the Blackfeet with as many people as would listen. The lectures, carrying titles such as "My Introduction to the Blackfeet and Adoption by Chief Mad Wolf" and "Sun Festival of the Blackfeet," offered the same material found in his published works. In fact, any audience member who had already read McClintock's books might have been disappointed by the absence of fresh material.[59]

What the lectures offered that *was* new, however, were color images. Between 1905 and 1933, McClintock created a large collection of colored slides which he believed improved in quality and artistry over time. Especially important to him was that central image: the tipis glowing with light from within. Around 1905, McClintock hired Charlotte Pinkerton, a Chicago-based slide colorist, to work on his black-and-white photographs. He sent her written directions, relying on notes taken from a field journal that he kept handy while snapping the original photos. He consulted a book of spectrum colors so he could be as accurate as possible in delineating hues of painted tipis, costumes, and mountains. Pinkerton also consulted Chicago's Field Museum Blackfeet

*Walter McClintock devoted his life to writing and lecturing about the Blackfeet. Reproduced by permission of the Yale Collection of Western Americana, Beinecke Rare Book and Manuscript Library.*

collection for accuracy. By the early 1920s, McClintock's collection contained over 377 colored enlargements made from negatives and in 1923 he exhibited the master set at the Carnegie Museum. Later, partial sets were on exhibit at Los Angeles's Southwest Museum and Yale's Sterling Library.[60]

To a late-twentieth-century eye, accustomed to the truer colors afforded by improvements in film technology, the glass slides seem artificial and romanticized. Whereas the black-and-white photographs impart an authenticity to his interpretation of these people, the colored slides seem to undermine it. They render the Blackfeet less real, more dreamlike, and distant. McClintock's early twentieth-century audiences probably reacted differently. Perhaps, in the absence of any comparison, they thrilled at the sight of color images.

While McClintock realized his main audience was the layman, he never relinquished his hope for academic endorsement. He sought recognition from scholars and received a measure of satisfaction. In 1911, Yale granted him an honorary M.A. degree, and in 1929 Clark Wissler, by then an anthropology professor at Yale, offered him an opportunity to work on a project concerning the present condition of the Blackfeet. McClintock, as volunteer investigator, would find his name formally listed in the New Haven Anthropology Department. Yet Wissler warned McClintock that scientists would insist his work be grounded in "specific statements of fact." Noting that a brief paper McClintock had sent him was both interesting and appealing, Wissler suspected "the serious reader will look upon it with suspicion because it does not give a number of the plain homely facts upon which it was based." McClintock could be as literary as he liked, as long as he supplied simple, "homely" facts.[61] It is unclear if McClintock took on this task. It is also unclear what motivated Wissler. Possibly, Yale hoped to inherit McClintock's photography collection.

If that ambition partly motivated the university, the plan worked. By 1934, McClintock had donated at least some of his photographs to Yale's library which, in turn, named McClintock curator of the McClintock Indian Collection. As part of his duty, he traveled to New Haven every fall to deliver a lantern slide-illustrated lecture. "This became his sole hobby," according to one Yale alumnus. "He had little interest in life except the preservation of the story of the finest tribes of American Indians who held themselves aloof from white men and their civilization." The Anthropology Department, according to historian Howard Lamar, found McClintock so amateurish they "froze him out." But the "wiser, shrewder" library staff took him in, rounded up students and staff to attend McClintock's annual lecture, and in the end became the recipients of McClintock's collection and endowment. Sadly, every year McClintock gave the same lecture about the Beaver Bundle. As a result, students dubbed him "Old Beaver Bundle" and eventually stopped coming to hear him. If McClintock noticed, he did not penalize Yale or its students. To this day, his bequest includes an annual McClintock prize of cash to a graduating student who writes a senior essay about Indians.[62]

In 1927, the Southwest Museum announced McClintock's appointment as a Research Fellow in Ethnology.[63] He gave lectures at the museum, published some short pieces in their periodical *Masterkey*, and produced a number of small booklets on Blackfeet topics. In one booklet, "The Tragedy of the Blackfoot," for instance, McClintock recounted his return to Montana after lecturing in Europe and commented on the disruptions the younger generation wreaked upon the reservation, particularly after returning home from distant schools and colleges:

> *Now they had short hair, modern clothes, and manners strange. At first they made a fight and failed, as anyone would fail, without employment and exposed to the ridicule of families and friends. Quickly disillusioned, their education became a bitterness. They deteriorated morally and physically. White men took away their old culture and gave nothing to take its place.*[64]

McClintock blamed agents for further undermining Blackfeet culture by failing to understand or sympathize with Indians ways. Consequently, they made no effort to incorporate the sound and ethical aspects of Indian religion into their teachings. Finally, he claimed, a Carlisle-educated mixed blood, who spoke English fluently and learned lessons of corruption from white men, demanded McClintock pay him $300 before taking any more photographs or notes on Blackfeet ways. When McClintock refused to pay the bribe, the "half-breed grafter" spread malicious rumors among the Indians that McClintock made a lot of money from his work. "Here a new and modern element entered into my relations with the tribe," McClintock lamented.[65] But the "tragedy" McClintock referred to in the brochure title was not the emergence of Indian grafters but the federal government's determination to interfere with the Sun Dance. "My sympathy was with the Indians," McClintock asserted, rather than with "their narrow and bigoted agent." Finally, in this 1930 essay, McClintock lambasted a policy which, he believed, had destroyed a once vibrant, generous, and healthy culture.[66]

Of course, by the 1930s, such policies of forced acculturation were already under wide attack. To be sure, no one could charge Walter McClintock with initiating challenges to either the means or ends of Indian policy. Instead, he chose the quieter corner offered by the literary arena. McClintock's contribution was to chronicle what he believed to be a fast disappearing way of life in books written for ordinary people and slide-illustrated lectures for middle brow audiences at local natural history museums.

If McClintock ever met Mary Roberts Rinehart, there is no evidence of it. That is somewhat surprising given the fact that both hailed from Pittsburgh's wealthy set (although McClintock was born to it and Rinehart worked her way into it), wrote books, and shared an interest in Montana's Blackfeet. On the other hand, Rinehart's involvement with the tribe proved comparatively fleeting and her writings on Indians represented only a small part of her literary output. She deserves some attention, however, because she was one of the few women who wrote about Indians of the Northern Rockies and one of the few figures in this book who wrote primarily for female audiences. A brief comparison between Rinehart and McClintock also suggests that gender played a role in limiting women's access to tribes such as the Blackfeet. A young man, like McClintock, had the freedom to impose himself upon a group of Indians in the early twentieth century. A similar prospect was not available to women. Actually Rinehart did not initiate a relationship with the Blackfeet. They initiated it with her. She encountered them in the context of a national park, under the care of a "tour guide." Finally, Rinehart sought adventure, but it was not the same kind as McClintock's, for her adventure would be comparatively tame, controlled, and protected. But when it came to doing battle on behalf of the Blackfeet, Rinehart demonstrated more pluck, confidence, and aggression than her male Pittsburgian counterpart.

Rinehart exemplifies how fleeting fame can be. Well known in the first half of the twentieth century, she is now remembered only among a few avid readers of mystery books. Between 1904 and 1957, she published scores of articles in such periodicals as *Scribner's, The Saturday Evening Post, Harper's*, and *Ladies' Home Journal*; achieved fame as a European war correspondent during World War I; and authored plays which were produced on Broadway and turned into Hollywood films. Rinehart was best known, though, for her mystery books, including *The Circular Staircase, K, The Bat*, and *The Breaking Point*. She was born into modest circumstances and had only a public school education where she learned that "the British were a bad lot, and so were the Indians. . . . It appeared to be my patriotic duty to hate them both, and hate them I did." Rinehart worked as a nurse and eventually married a doctor. But it was her books, plays, and articles which brought the Rineharts significant wealth.[67]

None of her major works had anything to do with Indians. Yet Rinehart's growing fame as a popular writer led to growing celebrity which, in turn, led to opportunities for travel adventures and the chance to write about them. In 1915, Howard Eaton, born in Pittsburgh but operating a dude ranch in Wyoming's Big Horn Mountains, invited Rinehart to join his party on a trip through the newly created Glacier National Park. This was the same dude ranch operator McClintock had visited in 1895, though in a different location. The publicity would be good for the tourist trade and Rinehart, always anxious for new adventure, agreed. *Collier's* willingly published her account and Houghton Mifflin subsequently printed it in a book called *Through Glacier Park*.[68]

During this 1915 excursion, Rinehart met some Blackfeet when, as she tells it in her autobiography, several came into her camp, brought by the National Park Service "from their adjacent reservation to give [the park] color." When the Indians learned that she had been to war, they decided to initiate her into the tribe. "This was before such things had been commercialized," she claimed, "so that now almost any tourist who may be of value to the Park becomes a Blackfoot Indian."[69] She did not apparently consider the possibility that they "adopted" her because she, as a writer, could be of value to them if they enlisted her sympathy, aid, and influence in addressing their problems—the same tactic they used with Grinnell and McClintock, with mixed results. They named her in honor of their own traditional woman warrior, Pitamakin, and eventually gave her a painting which depicted this heroine's story. Rinehart hung it on her Pittsburgh billiard room wall.

This time the "adoption tactic" worked. Rinehart took an interest in their well-being and after listening to stories of the tribe's condition outside the park boundaries, she decided to leave the riding party for one day and visit the reservation. Conditions there shocked her. "The previous winter had been one of starvation," Rinehart wrote, "and old chiefs with tears in their eyes told me of the deaths of their children from famine." The Blackfeet, a tribe of hunters, could not be remade into farmers and the government was indifferent to their need for food. Indignant with what she saw and heard, Rinehart promised to use her influence on their behalf. In return for this pledge of aid, the Indians showered her with gifts, including moccasins, belts, a parfleche, necklaces, and "their last war-pipe; a relic which they had carefully preserved."[70]

True to her word, on her next trip to Washington, Rinehart arranged a meeting with Secretary of the Interior Franklin Lane. Armed with her notes and memories of "those tragic old full-bloods," she appealed to Lane that all around her "was a country enriching itself by the war, [while] these helpless wards of ours were dying." According to Rinehart, Lane promised immediate food for the reservation's inhabitants and a thorough investigation of conditions there. "From that time on," Rinehart wrote, "I became a sort of mother-confessor, adviser, and friend to the tribe.[71]

In identifying herself as "mother-confessor," Rinehart took up the timeworn convention of parent to Indians and situated herself as all-knowing and all-powerful. This pose stands in marked contrast to McClintock's, who depicted himself as student and *son* of the Blackfeet. Rinehart, as woman warrior and mother, charged back to Washington in full fury. In her brief encounter with the Blackfeet, she may have missed the mysteries of their religion that McClintock captured, but she tried to address more pressing, immediate problems and, if she is to be believed, got things done.

Nevertheless, the condescension was profound. In 1916, the Rinehart family returned to Glacier National Park and attended a rodeo at Kalispell, Montana, where Mary found, to her dismay, some Blackfeet sitting across from her in the grandstand. Several weeks earlier she had met with these same men and, as she related in her 1918 book *Tenting Tonight*, they had promised that they would return immediately to the reservation. "They were going to be good Indians." Now she found them miles from the reservation, without the agent's permission. There, Rinehart wrote, "in all the glory of their forefathers—paint, feathers, beads, strings of thimbles and little mirrors—handsome, bland, and enjoying every instant to their full in their childish hearts, were my chiefs."[72] In good parental fashion Rinehart "scolded them all roundly." Yet she also sympathized with their desire to attend the rodeo, where a few captive buffalo grazed nearby.

> *These, my Blackfeet, had been the great buffalo-hunters. . . . They who had lived by the buffalo were now dying with them. A few full-bloods shut away on a reservation, a few buffalo penned in a corral—children of the open spaces and of freedom, both of them, are now dying and imprisoned. For the Blackfeet are a dying people. They had come to see the buffalo.*[73]

"Mother" Rinehart took pity and asked their agent not to punish these "children" for their transgressions.

Rinehart's depiction of the Blackfeet is deeply patronizing. It is also steeped in stereotypes of a doomed people. She hardly knew them and certainly, compared with McClintock, spent virtually no time with them. As interpreter to general audiences, particularly women readers, Rinehart's view of these Indians offered little that was new or challenging. In her day she would have been classified as one of the so-called Friends of the Indian, a well-meaning do-gooder who hoped to ease the "plight" of native people as they gradually moved toward extinction.

Such an assessment of Rinehart's attitudes toward all Indians, however, is incomplete. Her experiences in the American Southwest, among the Hopi and Navajo, led Rinehart, as it did other women writers, to different assessments of those peoples' cultures and their possibilities for survival.

*The Out Trail,* published in 1923, contains several travel pieces about adventures in Arizona and Montana, again with Howard Eaton. Although she wanted to convey an image of "roughing it," her party traveled with eight automobiles and three trucks which carried food, bedding, and the cook. Rinehart was especially attracted to the Hopi with their almost inaccessible villages and their "tribal integrity." Especially impressive was the way they mastered their environment. "Not long ago," she explained, "came experts from an agricultural college to these Indians, to teach them dry farming. The experts came, and stayed to learn, for the desert Indians are the original dry farmers of the world. They can raise corn where a white man could not raise a rattlesnake." She attributed their success to knowledge of water resources, patient work, and "indomitable courage." The power Hopi women wielded within the family also impressed Rinehart, and she wrote at length about witnessing the Snake Dance, where she found herself "carried away . . . [by] a sense of the essential dignity of religious ritual however primitive, of custom sanctified by antiquity, of faith and its undying quality."[74] Clearly, the Hopi inspired respect rather than maternalism.

Rinehart's brief sojourn in the desert introduced her to a different kind of Indian than she had encountered in the Northern Rockies. She was undeniably impressed with the character and integrity of the Southwestern cultures. Not once did she refer to them as children. Not once did any of them appeal to her for motherly aid. Unlike the Blackfeet, who were still in the throes of a difficult transition to a farming, sedentary reservation life, these Indians had endured centuries of conquest. In spite of all these pressures, Rinehart noted, the "Indian of the Southwest has not changed."[75]

Rinehart did not ponder the implications of her positive reaction to the Hopi any more than she had reflected on her inclination to "mother" the Blackfeet. She was, after all, simply a tourist, passing through and jotting down impressions. Others, however, would share her positive reaction to Southwestern tribes—and return again and again or, in the case of Mabel Dodge Luhan, come to live among them. Rinehart had no deep interest in Indians. But in her reconsideration of Indians in Arizona, if not Montana, this very popular writer of fiction and travel essays signaled a sea-change in the representation of Indians.

McClintock certainly gave more thought to the Blackfeet and dedicated his life to writing and lecturing about them. Rinehart's interest was sincere but less devoted. Both wrote about Indians in ways that stressed their humanity and cultural value. "Foreign" yet indigenous cultures still existed within American boundaries. The Blackfeet, they agreed, would have to change. The tribes of the Southwest, however, suggested a different scenario. Perhaps such Indian cultures could survive; perhaps such a prospect was a welcome one.

# Part II

# Western Enthusiasts

# 5

# NATIVE SON

## *Frank Bird Linderman*

THE LURE OF THE WEST struck Frank Bird Linderman early and inexorably, just as it had Wood, Grinnell, and McClintock. In 1885, at age sixteen, he left his family in Illinois and lit out for Montana Territory, hoping he was not too late to experience the authentic frontier. Naive, romantic, and determined, Linderman convinced another boy and the latter's black servant to accompany him. In contrast to Huckleberry Finn, these American boys had parental approval and even some money. For transportation, they chose neither a raft nor a flatboat up the Missouri River; rather, they boarded a westbound train. Once they reached their destination, Linderman's companions quickly became disillusioned with the adventure and returned home, sharing neither his dreams nor his compulsions. Frank stayed. He found, in Montana's Flathead Lake area, a corner of the West where he could realize his fantasy of becoming a trapper, if only for a few years. Five years later, the Census Bureau announced the "frontier" closed, and eight years later, Frederick Jackson Turner gave that pronouncement an academic stamp of approval, but Linderman managed to squeak through the portals of an officially defined "frontier experience."

Besides the frontier, Linderman found something else: Indians. In fact, without Indians it is doubtful the young Midwesterner would have considered his section of Montana authentically wild. He anticipated meeting Indians with a mixture of fear and fascination. Would they be friendly or hostile? Would they see him as intruder or kindred spirit? As it turned out, Linderman claimed some Indians as friends and others as antagonists. The Flathead or Salish, Cree, Chippewa, and Crow befriended him; the Kootenais did not. All of them entered into his imagination as "real" Indians, that is, Indians who lived in the days before confinement to reservations. If Linderman is remembered at all, it is because of his efforts, through his writings, to preserve a record of these "endangered authenticities," people supposedly unblemished by contact with Europeans and untarnished by reservation life.[1]

Starting in 1915, thirty years after he first ventured west, Linderman began writing about Indians who represented, for him, the most powerful symbol of a West that was no more. Like many of the writers examined here, his earliest work was a collection of Indian folk tales. His later, and most enduring, books centered on the life stories of two Crows, Plenty Coups and Pretty-shield. Throughout, Linderman's voice is clear and his point of view unmistakable. Indians, regardless of tribe, symbolized a pure, clean way of life unsullied by the corruption of Anglo-American or European cultures. Their religions, indelibly stamped with a spirituality both foreign and compelling, represented a sensibility and reverence for nature unappreciated by Christians. He acknowledged that Indians demonstrated human faults and frailties. Yet, he believed, their virtues went unrecognized. "Ever since our advent in North America," Linderman wrote in his autobiography, "the red man's misdeeds have had willing heralds." Linderman's intention, by contrast, was to herald Indians' "finer qualities" for "it is only the discovered good in man that builds humanity." He explained that Napoleon, upon reading *The Iliad*, commented on how the heroes' rude manners struck him more forcefully than their loftier characteristics. "The Indian has startled us by the same contrast," Linderman went on, "and so confounds us in our final estimate of the race we have conquered—from whom we might have learned needed lessons, if we had tried."[2]

Without a doubt, strong currents of nostalgia, romanticism, and antimodernism inform Linderman's works on Indians. On one level Linderman's Indians, like those of Wood, reveal more about his longings for an imagined past, his disillusionments with the world he inherited, and his doubts about the future than they do about Indians themselves. Linderman, of course, would have disputed this assessment. He would have pointed to the years he spent with Indian people as trapper, defender, and interpreter as evidence that his books represented the truth about Indian ways. He would have emphasized the weeks he devoted to carefully listening to, watching, and interpreting Plenty Coups' and Pretty-shield's life stories as proof that "their" books closely approximated their own versions of themselves. And he would not be entirely wrong. If he could not expunge himself entirely from those records (and there is no evidence that he ever felt the need to do so), still those accounts *do* contain useful information about Crow people. Linderman intended to approximate Grinnell's scientific achievements. Simultaneously, in his Crow books, he shared McClintock's intention to humanize his subjects. Plenty Coups and Pretty-shield emerge as fully formed individuals with compelling lives. Yet at the core of Linderman's compulsion to tell their stories was a deep disdain and disillusionment with the modern world. Indians offered a refuge. But he did not flinch from engaging the world he inherited. Linderman operated for many years in the place where Montana's Gilded Age politics intersected with Indian affairs, hardly a spot for romantics. He fought to carve out a small Montana reservation, called Rocky Boy, for the Cree and Chippewa who had fled Canada during the Riel Rebellion of 1885, and he succeeded. In certain respects, Linderman was a hard-nosed realist who accomplished things. Indians who lived on the Rocky Boy Reservation saw him as a genuine friend.

Yet, whether he recognized it or not, Linderman was a full participant in the Anglo-American cultural process of reimagining Indians in the early twentieth century. From his earliest days as a child, pouring over maps of the Great West, the contours of this reinterpretation were already set. If his timing was a bit off to experience the "real frontier," (George Bird Grinnell and C.E.S. Wood would attest that he was too late) his timing to participate in reimagining Indians could not have been better. He rode the rails into a Montana that was already conquered. What remained for those of Linderman's generation was to interpret the consequences of that conquest and to acknowledge its costs. He did so with greater assurance than Grinnell or McClintock. Consequently, he not only lamented the damage done to Indians but also worked to redress those wrongs in new ways; to question not only the damage done by forced acculturation, but also to imagine alternatives to that approach. In fact, Linderman was among the first of the Northern Rockies writers to see in John Collier's policies another way.

Linderman was born in the middle of the country, in midcentury, into a middle-class family. For all this middling, however, his equilibrium was off and as a youngster he demonstrated a drive, an "ache" as he put it, to move off-center, into the West. Later, he attributed this westering impulse to family blood. Lindermans had immigrated to the United States in the early eighteenth century and kept moving westward from New York, to Pennyslvania, to Ohio (where he was born in 1869), and finally to Illinois.

Frank received a common school education in Lorain and Elyria, Ohio, and enrolled for one year in Oberlin's School of Commerce (a business college that operated outside Oberlin College) before dropping out to go west. His mother, who attended Oberlin College's preparatory school, introduced him to Shakespeare and instilled in her son a lifelong love of literature. Quite likely, she encouraged Linderman to read James Fenimore Cooper's novels. If so, Frank never acknowledged the acquaintance, perhaps fearing that to do so would be to convince others his Indians were not "real" but rather romantic, informed not by actual experience but by sentimental literature. Whatever the source of his westering impulse, by age sixteen his greatest fear was that he had missed the frontier altogether: "How I feared that the West of my dreams would fade before I could reach it!"[3]

Linderman examined maps of the Pacific Northwest and concluded that the Flathead Lake region of Montana posed the greatest possibilities for a would-be trapper. It seemed the farthest from railroads. "I had to have unspoiled wilderness," Linderman explained, and the Flathead Lake country "seemed yet to be the farthest removed from contaminating civilization." Moreover, it was a country where Indians still lived, presumably uncorrupted by Europeans. So, there he went. While homesickness and howling wolves quickly convinced his companions to return to Chicago, Linderman set about exploring the area around the little cabin they had hurriedly constructed, engaged in some hunting for subsistence, and enjoyed the timber wolves' calls. He worried about Indians, however, not knowing their disposition toward whites. Finally, one day he heard the whinny of horses. Armed with a Bowie knife and an antiquated Kentucky rifle for self-defense, he sought out their owner, but to no avail. Upon returning to his cabin, he found the man seated at Linderman's own hearth. He stopped, fascinated. Apprehension dissolved for the middle-aged Indian, ensconced by the fire, smoked a pipe "with such an air of peace and contentment that I fairly ached to shake hands with him, if he'd let me." Hearing Linderman's approach, the man allowed Linderman to shake his hand and also extended his own in friendship while making certain the youngster understood he was Flathead rather than Kootenai. His name was Red Horn, a well-known warrior who had counted many coups and taken many scalps. "What a fine face he had, that red man!", Linderman later remembered. Red-Horn, "my first Indian," was all he could have hoped for: a "real" Indian warrior, yet one who was friendly to whites.[4]

For the next half dozen years, Linderman pursued the life of a trapper, which he assumed was the closest a white boy could get to being Indian. "Instead of going to town or mining camp I went to the wilderness where I learned Indian ways, and lived as they lived." Moreover, he later testified, Indians befriended, hunted, and trapped with him "when they were real, and unspoiled by civilization."[5]

But not all Indians proved friendly. The Kootenais took on the role of "bad Indian" in Linderman's works, although he hesitated to demonize them for fear such depictions would undermine his ultimate purpose. To soften his accounts of belligerent Kootenais, Linderman acknowledged they resented white men settling in the Flathead country and murdered not out of mindless savagery but because intruders built fences across their old trails. Yet Linderman, himself a white man after all, neither left the country to the Kootenais nor saw himself as part of their problem. In fact, he resented Kootenais who crowded *him* off the trail, jeering at him as they passed. He believed a Flathead friend who told him it was Kootenai who entered his cabin and stole food, traps, and a rifle.[6] And it was Kootenai who delivered the greatest humiliation he experienced at the hands of Indian people. It happened when Linderman squatted on a site where he intended to construct a cabin. Forty Kootenais began destroying his property. When he confronted them, one slapped Linderman. "He counted a fine coup on me," he wrote, "and now when I look back, I respect him for his bravery." But at the time, Linderman ached to kill him.[7] What prevented Linderman from doing so was the realization that the other Kootenais would kill him.

While Linderman couched all his darker images of Kootenai with explanations for their hostility and with guarded respect, the same was not true of his depictions of mixed bloods and whites. Linderman consistently assigned full-blood Indians the heroic roles, mixed bloods and whites the depraved and sometimes villainous ones. Without a doubt he believed that the white man's blood, his alcohol, and his propensity toward violence corrupted. For instance, Linderman wrote about two mixed-blood Flatheads, Dominick and his brother Baptiste, who "had different portions of white blood." The brothers became thoroughly drunk at a Fourth of July celebration, rode their horses into Frank's cabin, and began shooting their guns, bullets piercing Linderman's roof. An occasion meant to celebrate a momentous episode in Anglo-American history only served to debauch Indians—at least, mixed bloods who seemed to embrace the worst elements of American culture. An even more loathsome Fourth of July celebration in the little town of Egan resulted in not only drunken half-bloods but a murdered one as well. In a scene reminiscent of McClintock's experiences with his countrymen in Cutbank, Linderman observed as the whites launched a "free-for-all fight." Outfitted in moccasins, he climbed up on a billiard table to escape the row. Those moccasins could not transform him into that more virtuous and purer race, but at least he could literally rise above the vicious, violent white men, even if he had to use another symbol of depravity, a billiard table, to do so.[8]

In Linderman's world, then, the most wicked men were neither Indians nor mixed bloods but rather whites. He offered as evidence the notorious "Fight in the Cypress Hills." Some Indians had stolen horses from thirteen Americans, including "wolfers, buffalo hunters, and whiskey peddlers." Determined to avenge themselves and regain some horses, these men attacked an unsuspecting, innocent camp of Crees across the Canadian border, killing eighty Indians, including women and children. The Canadian police arrested the Americans but a court acquitted them. The men also came before a legal proceeding in Helena but were not punished there either.[9] That two supposedly civilized systems of justice viewed the murder of eighty innocent Indians unworthy of punishment only underscored the horror of such an explosion of white violence.

Linderman, then, found confirmation once he reached Montana that it *was* better to be Indian than Anglo. His expectations of Indian virtue were only reinforced by the comparatively savage behavior of whites and the debauchery of mixed bloods. Although he knew he could not exchange his own blood for that of the Flatheads, he could don their mocassins, take on the outer trappings of Indian identity, and approximate their way of life as a hunter. Moreover, he took great pride in the names that various Indians gave him, including Iron-Tooth among the Blackfeet, Sign-Talker among the Crow, Bird-Singer among the Kootenai, and Glasses or Sings-like-a-bird among the Cree and Chippewa. He shared "the oldtime Indian" belief that "the white man is the natural enemy of all natural things" and concluded "the wilderness, my wilderness, did not last long. The railroad came to it, and then the country began to settle rapidly. The old days were forever ended for both the Indian and me." Further sealing his identity with that of the oldtime, prereservation Indians, Linderman wrote another correspondent that "newcomers are stealing the west and it isn't fair." Finally, Linderman claimed to understand and share Indian enmity for whites which he described as "natural, and thoroughly deserved."[10]

Linderman's notions about the purity of wildness and the corruption of civilization, found reinforcement not only in the rural parts of Montana, but the urban ones as well. There, not only regret, but also disgust overwhelmed Linderman as he witnessed Montana's economic and political transformation at the turn of the century. Ironically, when he decided that "his wilderness" was indeed gone and his days as a trapper numbered, Linderman did not eschew the future. He did not fade deeper into the past (by moving to Canada or Alaska, for example, where he could have pursued trapping and evaded civilization), but rather he embraced modernity. Linderman left his trapper's cabin and walked straight into the heart of industrial Montana. He explained it was a woman who determined his fate, for Frank met Minnie Jane Johns and knew that to marry her he must find more suitable work. No longer a boy, he chose to leave the world of wilderness and Indians behind, "for a girl who weighed less than ninety pounds."[11] Between the railroad ruining his wilderness and a woman kindling his domestic urges, Linderman gave up trapping for mining. Unlike Grinnell and McClintock, Linderman in his twenties put aside youthful impulses for more manly, mature ones.

In 1892, Frank found employment as a watchman and eventually an assayer at the Curlew Mine in Ravalli County. When that mine closed down, he moved on to chief assayer and chemist for the Butte & Boston Smelter in Butte. In contrast to the lush wilderness of his earlier haunts, Butte offered no trees, not even a blade of grass for Linderman and his growing family. They hated their neighborhood. Moreover, life in the mines was, at best, distasteful. Linderman expressed little sympathy for miners' complaints about work conditions or wages and disdained the immigrants who worked the mines. In fact, the most revolting aspect of Butte for Linderman was the imprint immigrants made on the community. Hardly anyone spoke English, he claimed. Across the street from the Lindermans' house sat a saloon where "beer-guzzling Austrians" drank, sang beneath the Lindermans' window, and inevitably quarreled with one another. The Italians, Welshmen, Cornishmen, and Irish who flooded into Butte, he wrote, brutalized their wives and each other. Burglaries were commonplace. Sometimes the thieves demanded no more than a man's lunch box, demonstrating hunger and desperation. Such conditions, he concluded, "fostered political filth, and politically Butte was filthy."[12]

Linderman contrasted his early days in Montana to this immigrant-induced squalor. Occasionally, Indians appeared for fleeting moments, to underscore how times had changed and to heighten Linderman's sense of loss. Once, he set off to investigate a new smelter under construction when a sight out of his past thrilled him: four Indian lodges stood across the valley. Transfixed by the sight of these symbols of a purer, preindustrial past, Linderman noted that the way the mountain shadows rested upon the lodges suggested that they belonged "to another world altogether." Upon approaching the tipis, he discovered they belonged to a group of Cree, whose acquaintance Linderman had made years before in the Flathead region. One of the men, Muskegon, had shared Cree stories with Linderman. Now, he looked discouraged and haggard in his "ragged portions of white men's apparel, [which] seemed to have lowered both his morale and personal appearance." Linderman found their presence so near a big mining camp puzzling, although they explained that they had come to sell polished buffalo horns in town. Hard times had befallen the Cree and, although he did not realize it then, Linderman's first political action regarding Indians would eventually revolve around finding them a home.[13]

In 1898, the Lindermans left Butte for Sheridan, Montana, where Frank pursued the assaying business and invested in a small mine of his own. By the next year, he abandoned mining altogether and purchased the Sheridan newspaper as well as a furniture store, managed by his parents who joined him in Montana. He also entered that realm which he supposedly detested, politics, winning election to the state legislature. From the start, Republican Linderman found Montana politics corrupt, and his autobiography contains various tales of skullduggery. He writes of being offered and refusing very attractive bribes. Under tremendous pressure to capitulate to powerful but fraudulent forces in the state, Linderman held firm to his principles and his integrity. When the legislature took up its responsibility to name Montana's senator, for example, a group of Republicans from Linderman's county agreed to rebuff party politics and oppose Republican Tom Carter's election to that office. In Linderman's assessment, the pro-Carter people represented corruption; his own group, virtue. Linderman dubbed his confederates in this fight, "Indians." "A good deal of pressure was brought to bear upon the 'Indians,'" he wrote, "The tribe lost four of its members before it had fairly taken the warpath." Political patronage further weakened the Indians' resolve until "like a bubble, my tribe went to pieces." In the end Linderman was the only "Indian" who remained true to his principles, proving impervious to bribery and voting against Carter.[14]

Although this stand earned him a great deal of scorn and open hostility in the legislature, it also led to another political opportunity. Montana's secretary of state, A. N. Yoder, who knew Linderman from their Butte days, offered him a job as assistant secretary of state. Linderman accepted the Helena position and held it between 1905–1907.[15] During his Helena days, Linderman's life, again, intersected with Indians. As early as 1906, members of the Cree and Chippewa bands, whom he first met in the Flathead and Swan valleys, informed Linderman of their destitute condition. They had no reservation and no consistent means of feeding themselves. For a time they camped on Helena's outskirts, living on slaughterhouse offal and the town's garbage. As Linderman tells it, he begged food and clothing for them, often reaching deep into his own pockets. He tried to find employment for one man, named Young-Boy, but the Indian could not secure the position because he did not belong to the union, and, in classic irony, the union refused him admittance because he was Indian.[16]

Linderman's commitment to the Little Bear and Rocky Boy bands of Cree and Chippewa stemmed from his earliest impressions of these people as vital, genuine Indians. When he first encountered them, they were refugees from Canada's Riel Rebellion, rebels who had fought Canadian troops. "They were pictures in the extreme," he remembered, "and full of fight." But rather than fighting with Linderman, they shared their stories of "long ago" and looked upon him as a family member. "In fact," Linderman explained, "I am a Chippewa by adoption and as the Cree and Chippewas claim kinship and have always been allies, I feel myself to be as much a Cree as a Chippewa." Moreover, these people reminded Linderman of his own and Montana's unreclaimable youth. He had known them "when whitemen were not wanted" along the shores of Flathead Lake, when "Manitou was king," and when "both that country and I were young." Now that these Indians were in desperate straits, Linderman intended to help as he would any family member. It was a gesture for friends in need and a gesture in honor of his own past.[17]

He realized the only long-term solution for the Cree and Chippewa bands lay in a permanent reservation. By 1908, Linderman and William Boles, editor and owner of the *Great Falls Tribune*, began a campaign to convince Congress to create such a place. They understood many Montanans would oppose creation of another reservation within the state's boundaries and so they commenced a letter-writing campaign to politicians. Artist Charlie Russell, Linderman's friend, started a fund to raise money for the Indians and wrote to Senator Henry Myers in support of a new reservation. Russell's arguments hinted at the same propensity toward nativism one can find in Linderman's work. In Linderman's and Russell's view, it was unconscionable for the government to provide support and succor to immigrants while it ignored the "real Americans."[18]

In 1908, Congress appropriated $30,000 to establish a home for the Montana Cree and Chippewa, but the reservation failed to materialize. The Indians, in the meantime, continued to wander back and forth across the state, some camping on the Blackfeet Reservation, some staying near Helena, and others heading for the Havre area. Meanwhile, Congress's appropriations wasted away on rations, many of which never reached their intended recipients. When word came in 1911 that the U.S. army intended to abandon Fort Assiniboine, about twenty miles south of Havre, a Chippewa named Full-of-Dew, a Cree named Little Bear, Linderman, and his allies believed they had found the perfect solution: let the Cree and Chippewa take up the abandoned military reservation. Havre citizens fought the plan and the *Havre Plain Dealer* ridiculed Linderman, who they charged "has gained his knowledge of the noble redman from a too faithful reading of Leatherstocking Tales."[19] In truth, according to the newspaper, Chippewas were "trifling, lazy, renegade" Indians.[20]

Linderman worked hard to counter such racist arguments. He enlisted prominent Montanans such as Charlie Russell to support his cause as well as national figures, most notably, George Bird Grinnell. Linderman evidently knew of Grinnell's work with Montana Indians and believed he could be counted on for support. Grinnell agreed to do what he could, namely, write letters and talk to people in Washington. In the meantime, Linderman and Boles went to Washington in December 1913 to lobby for the reservation and offset the efforts of a Havre group that had traveled east to fight its establishment. Boles negotiated with the Montana opponents, reaching an agreement that the southern portion of the former fort, the farthest away from town, would become part of an Indian reservation. Linderman was not satisfied with this, however, for that property contained mostly untillable land. Resolution of final reservation boundaries stalled for another three years. Finally, on September 7, 1916, with congressional approval, President Woodrow Wilson created the Rocky Boy Reservation, the last to be carved out of Montana. It included some agricultural land.[21]

Linderman best expressed his point of view about this drawn-out affair in his letters to Cato Sells, Commissioner of Indian Affairs. He insisted that citizens of Havre aside, most people of Montana wanted a permanent home for these Indians. He testified that the Cree and Chippewa were good workers who would "help themselves, if they get anything with which to work." Linderman assured Sells that his interest in these Indians was neither personal, selfish nor based upon ignorance of Indian character. He *knew* them and offered as evidence the fact that Charles Scribner's Sons of New York recently published his book, *Indian Why Stories*. Finally, if the federal government failed to act on behalf of the Cree and Chippewa, he threatened to take up pen again and write a thoroughly illustrated article to provoke sufficient public sentiment on behalf of the Indians. Linderman evidently believed this threat carried some weight, for one month after writing this letter, Grinnell informed Linderman that Mary Roberts Rinehart had scared the Interior Department into providing sufficient winter rations to the Blackfeet by threatening to publish an article about their destitution in the *Saturday Evening Post*. Linderman, who privately criticized Rinehart as an instant authority on Indians who had minimal experience with them, shot back this response to Grinnell: "You say that Miss Rinehart threatened the officials in Washington, in promising to publish articles dealing with the Blackfeet. Well, I did the same thing, and I must say it did more good than two or three years of begging."[22]

To be sure, Frank Linderman deserves credit for his efforts to assure the Montana Cree and Chippewa gained a home. A desire for justice and humanitarian impulses motivated him, as did paternalistic instincts, evidenced by his consistent identification of the Cree and Chippewas as "my Indians." Throughout the Rocky Boy Reservation creation-episode, Indian voices are sparsely recorded and when they are, always through white intermediaries. Yet evidence exists these Indians did appreciate Linderman's efforts. They comprehended, probably better than anyone, their precarious and relatively powerless position when dealing with state and federal governments. They understood their dependency on the friendship and support of whites such as Linderman. As Big Rock wrote Linderman in 1916, "Times are hard just now . . . I will do as you say. You must try very hard and find the means of a good living for us poor Indians, as I might say that we are helpless." They turned to Linderman because he was sympathetic, sensitive, and in a position to help. In early twentieth-century Montana, Indians welcomed political allies no matter how paternalistic, patronizing, or sentimental.[23]

This propensity for "sentiment" led Linderman to fight to preserve some semblance of an Indian present. It also led him to record, through literature, a semblance of an Indian past. It was not mere coincidence that the timing, creation, and publication of Linderman's first Indian book paralleled the creation and realization of the Rocky Boy Reservation. For Linderman, political and literary proclivities went hand-in-hand. He sought out publication to promote his political agenda. At the same time, his political views shaped his literary efforts.

Linderman's first book, then, joined a few Cree and Blackfeet tales to those of Chippewa friend, Full-of-Dew. He compiled the collection, entitled it *Indian Why Stories: Sparks from War Eagle's Lodgefire,* and submitted it to Charles Scribner's Sons in 1914. Reminiscent of Wood's and Grinnell's early works, Linderman's book offered tales with evocative titles such as "Why the Kingfisher Always Wear a War-Bonnet" and "Why the Curlew's Bill is Long and Crooked." Linderman introduced the stories, as did Wood, by explaining the circumstances in which he heard them, as a way of authenticating them. Unlike Wood, Linderman added none of his own fanciful tales but rather made clear he included only stories told him by *older* men. He also indicated he wanted to tell the legends in a way that kept as near as possible to the Indian style of story-telling.[24]

Scribner's rejected the manuscript. Convinced Linderman's project had merit, however, a friend encouraged him to try again. The following year O. M. Lanstrum, a fellow Mason and head of Montana's Republican Party, dropped the manuscript off at Scribner's offices. This time Linderman received a different response. Apparently, Charlie Russell's willingness to produce illustrations and George Bird Grinnell's endorsement of him as an Indian authority made the difference. After the publisher was assured that Linderman's book did not duplicate Grinnell's works and that Russell would indeed provide illustrations, Scribner's agreed to publish it. They marketed this book, and all the Linderman work they printed thereafter, for a juvenile audience. Between the subject matter and the simple literary style, that seemed to them the logical strategy. They also advertised it as an Indian version of Joel Chandler Harris's work, hoping the stories would prove as popular as Uncle Remus's tales.[25]

Linderman would have preferred comparison to Grinnell. Clearly, the latter's work provided a model and in an effort to secure the association, as well as express what he evidently felt to be an honest debt to the New Yorker, Linderman dedicated *Indian Why Stories* to Grinnell as well as to Russell. Grinnell, possibly taken aback by the honor, neglected to remark about Linderman's choice until the Montanan prompted a reaction by asking if he had any objections. Grinnell responded that he was greatly flattered. He also took pains to warn Linderman that he should not expect to make much money from the book. "I repeat," Grinnell wrote on another occasion, "your reward for the work on the book will come not in the shape of money" but rather in the satisfaction of trying to help Indians by awakening interest in them. Linderman should rest assured that *Indian Why Stories* was a good piece of work and that it would make an impression on a good number of people.[26]

Linderman took Grinnell's encouragement to heart, but he ignored his warnings about the limits to financial remuneration. For the rest of his life Linderman continued to produce books on Indian themes, but he became increasingly embittered about his inability to make a living from them. Still, in 1917, he felt sufficient financial security to quit his insurance sales job in Helena, move his family to a large log home on Flathead Lake, and pursue a longtime dream of returning to his boyhood haunts to write books. Apparently, he hoped the royalties would prove sufficient to support his family. The dream turned nightmarish in August 1919, when a forest fire swept through the Flathead Lake area. As the family prepared to evacuate their home, Mrs. Linderman asked her husband what she should salvage. His answer: Rain-in-the-face's pipe, a shirt, and a pair of shoes. Linderman stayed behind to saturate the roof with water and, in the end, succeeded in saving the home from the blaze. Among the prized possessions he lost in the conflagration was his highly valued Indian lodge (decorated by Indian friends with thirty-six drawings or paintings) and all its contents.[27]

In some respects the fire was a portent of other disappointments, if not disasters. Scribner's liked the Linderman-Russell collaboration, reprinted *Indian Why Stories* as a school edition under the title *Indian Lodge-Fire Stories* in 1918, and encouraged more work. Linderman, anxious to comply, hoped to publish another book of Indian tales in 1919, but this time Russell could not produce the illustrations in time for Christmas sales. While Linderman wanted to go ahead without them, Scribner's refused to move without the cowboy artist's illustrations. This created a crisis and, in fact, a serious rupture in the Linderman-Russell friendship. Although Linderman never published his version of these events, his daughter claimed that Russell's wife, Nancy, obtained a commission for Russell to paint something for the Prince of Wales' Canadian lodge and decided that job took precedence over any commitments to Linderman. Russell could not finish the illustrations until he completed the commission, worth approximately $10,000. The Lindermans were not sympathetic, blaming Nancy more than Charlie. Frank dashed off an angry letter to the artist, believing this turn of events financially disastrous for himself. Russell responded, "I got your note an [*sic*] am sorry you got snuffy. . . . If you haent been up against a string of hard luck I might get sore at you." Several months later, Russell sent the tardy drawings and told Linderman, "am sorry they wer to late . . . you can pay for those pictures when your book is published I've been playing lucky and you ain't win a hand, latly . . ." The book, *Indian Old-Man Stories: More Sparks from War Eagle's Lodge-Fire*, came out in 1920, but the Russell-Linderman friendship was seriously damaged, and they never collaborated again.[28]

*Taking pride in his friendships with many of Montana's tribes, Frank Bird Linderman hoped to gain financial remuneration, as well as literary accolades, from his books about them. Reproduced by permission of the heirs of Frank Bird Linderman and the Mansfield Library, University of Montana, Missoula, Montana.*

Although Linderman saw postponement of *Indian Old-Man Stories* as a financial blow, he remained hopeful that writing could make him a living. He continued to mine both Indian and Western themes to that end. The same year *Indian Old-Man Stories* came out (1920), Scribner's also published Linderman's *On a Passing Frontier: Sketches from the Northwest*. Most of these stories focused on whites in mining towns, trading posts, and other frontier settings. Whiskey, guns, and card-playing played major roles in the tales. White characters were portrayed as sometimes comical, sometimes sympathetic, sometimes colorful, and sometimes dreadful, but overall, neither particularly attractive nor dignified. The few tales that involved Indians, on the other hand, presented Native Americans reverentially in an elegiac tone. In contrast to whites' ragtag towns, Indians lived in unsullied places. Linderman described a Blackfeet village as situated on the banks of the Marias River, where "that sweetest of perfumes, the breath of wild roses" wafted up to the lodges. In another vignette, an old prospector acknowledged a spiritual debt to his wise Indian partner, who was "right in a heap of things," particularly in his devotion to the natural world. Of course, this man was now gone, no longer part of the Montana scene.[29]

In the years to follow, Linderman pursued the literary path he blazed in these early works. In 1921, Scribner's published another collection, *How It Came*

*About Stories*, and a book of Linderman's verse called *Bunch-Grass and Blue-Joint*.[30] Scribner's hoped to snare Russell illustrations for the first volume and, although Linderman gave the publisher permission to approach Russell, the artist refused. When an editor asked Linderman about the possibility of renewing agreeable relations with Russell for the purpose of supplying drawings for the poetry book, Linderman wrote, "I would rather not ask Mr. Russell to draw anything for me—not even a cork."[31]

Linderman continued to struggle with the conflict between his dedication to telling "the truth" about the West and his need to make money by writing commercially viable books. He juxtaposed his quality work, based on authentic sources, against others' financially successful books which were often tawdry, clichéd, and hopelessly flawed. He insisted on writing the former and became bitter when they flopped financially. Linderman fretted about sales and urged Scribner's to get his works into national parks in order to take advantage of tourists' dollars. He complained that people all across the country were trying to purchase his books but could not find them. He was especially frustrated that Montanans had trouble locating copies. In the end, Linderman believed that Scribner's failed to market his book energetically and that the eastern publisher's failure to promote a Westerner's books reflected deeper regional divisions. "I suppose the East will never understand the West," he wrote in 1921, a sentiment shared by Mary Austin, "I know that the Eastern idea of the West has been derived from miserable sources which are cheap, shallow, and unreal."[32]

With the exception of a 1933 novel, *Beyond Law*, and a collection of animal stories, most of Linderman's remaining publications focused on Indians. His most notable achievements came with publication of two Crow autobiographies, or more accurately "as told to" stories, that of Plenty Coups and Pretty-shield. Linderman first encountered Plenty Coups, who he called "a perfect specimen of manhood," just at the moment he was forsaking his trappers' life. Plenty Coups fit Linderman's definition of a real Indian, for he remembered a Montana that preceded white man's domination plus he had fought several battles with Flatheads. Plenty Coups provided the perfect blend for Linderman's purposes: he was an authentic warrior who was friendly to Linderman. In fact, he gave Linderman the name "Sign-Talker."[33]

The genesis of the idea to record Plenty Coups' life is a bit cloudy. In autumn 1926, Linderman admitted to his publisher that, although he had never been close with the Crow tribe, he spent most of the spring and summer with them gathering material for another book of tales. The following summer (1927) he shipped off this Crow manuscript, which Scribner's declined to publish, having already warned him such books were not selling well. Though undoubtedly disappointed, Linderman was not discouraged. He set his sights on a new genre, Indian "autobiography."[34] In his own autobiography, Linderman claimed that he had wanted to interview Plenty Coups for a long time, but not until the Crow man "sent for him" did the opportunity arise. Other evidence suggests Plenty Coups had less to do with Linderman's timing and involvement than did potential competition from other writers with the same idea of preserving the old man's story for posterity. In spring 1927, James Sladen, who lived at the Crow Agency, informed him that Frank Shively, who Linderman identified as a "Carlisle [Indian boarding school] man," was also thinking about writing Plenty Coups' story. Sladen believed Linderman the better person for the job, however, and convinced Shively to help the published author. Linderman hurried out to complete the project before it slipped through his fingers. Alas, Linderman left little record of the process of interviewing Plenty Coups or of transforming this raw material into the finished book. He only indicated it was difficult and that he wrote it twice before submitting it to Scribner's. The publisher refused it. The John Day Company, however, published it in 1930 under the title *American: The Life Story of a Great Indian, Plenty Coups, Chief of the Crows*.[35]

The book reads like an on-going conversation between Linderman and Plenty Coups. Adopting what one scholar called the technique of "Self-Conscious Editor," Linderman placed himself squarely in the center, asking the questions and recording the Crow leader's responses. Among the subjects Linderman inquired about were childhood, play, and its implicit training for a male adulthood devoted to hunting, warfare, and horse stealing. Plenty Coups talked much about religion, including his vision quest and how the Chickadee-person came to be his medicine. The lion's share of the book, though, focused on warfare, small raids and counterraids, tales of valor and loss. Coup counting, horse stealing, and friend avenging dominated Linderman's interests and possibly Plenty Coups's, as well. Only when Linderman asked the Crow man to discuss reservation life did he reputedly refuse to talk. Given Plenty Coups' active involvement in reservation politics, it is quite possible that Linderman was the one who preferred to ignore contemporary life. It did not fit his romantic image.

In taking on this project, Linderman moved beyond collecting tales and attempted to enter an Indian world via one man's life. Of course, the final product reflected Linderman's interests, questions, and values. He cut, pasted, and rearranged the material. His inquiries literally structured the book. Well meaning as he might have been, Linderman undoubtedly altered Plenty Coups' story in the telling of it. On the other hand, the work offered a variation on more academic models of ethnographic authority for the book *was* identified as a collaboration and thus offered a shared vision of reality. Linderman and Plenty Coups created this together, through the process of dialogue. The resulting representation of that dialogue was Linderman's. But, as historian James Clifford noted, in ethnographic encounters of this kind, the interviewee maintains considerable control over the knowledge.[36]

Moreover, the concept of autobiography was not unknown to Indians. Many Native American cultures produced narratives including coup tales, less formal stories about hunting and warfare, self-examinations to account for misfortunes, self-vindications to explain behavior, education narratives, and stories of acquisition of powers. By injecting himself into the book, explaining the social situation in which Plenty Coups related his stories, and by presenting the tales as discrete narratives, Linderman maintained their integrity. He avoided the fiction that Plenty Coups' work was like other "seamless, western autobiographies." Linderman, then, in this way, attempted to present Plenty Coups' point of view and way of telling his story.[37]

Although Linderman assigned himself the role of arbiter of authenticity, he did not claim to truly understand Indians and, like Grinnell, doubted any white man ever could. "I have studied the Indian for more than forty years," he wrote in the preface, "yet even now I do not feel that I know much about him."[38] Yet he saw himself as sensitive and believed Indians shared their old customs or religious beliefs with him because he empathized. To underscore his own veracity and reliability, Linderman placed Plenty Coups' thumbprint and these words on the book's frontispiece:

> *I am glad I have told you these things, Sign-Talker. You have felt my heart, and I have felt yours. I know you will tell only what I have said, that your writing will be straight like your tongue, and I sign your paper with my thumb so that your people and mine will know I told you the things you have written down.*[39]

Linderman wanted readers to understand that Plenty Coups trusted him. Time and again, in his correspondence, Linderman harped on this theme: he was not a "fakir." He was dedicated to preserving the truth about the Old West and if that "queers it with publishers" then so be it. Finally, Linderman was absolutely certain that he could never learn valid information about Indians from younger generations, "certainly not from the offspring of these warriors, who know next to nothing about their people's ancient ways. Now it is too late to learn. The real Indians are gone."[40]

This last remark was, in part, a poke at anthropologists who relied on younger Indian informants. Linderman occasionally revealed a sensitivity about his lack of academic credentials. Once, he complained that professors knew only what they had learned from books, while his own knowledge and credibility rested on his experiences and relationships with Indian people. He took pride in being a "Doer before [he] became a Teller." While Linderman cared more about commercial success than academic respectability, still he welcomed the latter. No doubt the mixed review of his Plenty Coups book that appeared in *American Anthropologist,* written by Crow expert and eminent ethnologist R. H. Lowie, disappointed Linderman. Lowie claimed the book contained "some absurdities." At the same time, Lowie also acknowledged "a great deal of value [was] sprinkled through the book" and that it "supplies some worthwhile facts for the ethnographer." Other professionals agreed Linderman had a contribution to make. The University of Chicago Anthropology Department invited him to work on an Indian project, assembling biographical vignettes of Northwestern Indians. The project excited Linderman not only for its promised income but also because it implied academic approval of his past work. Unfortunately, the timing of this project proved fatal. The Depression intervened, making it impossible for the University of Chicago to raise an endowment to fund it and, in the end, the plan never materialized.[41]

By this time Linderman must have become accustomed to disappointment. Still, he did not let such frustrations paralyze his efforts to record the Indian past. In 1932, John Day Company published *Red Mother*, an account of Crow woman Pretty-shield's life. Linderman had never displayed concern about gender equality, so it is difficult to pinpoint his motive for writing a woman's story. But in 1930, Linderman received a letter from a reader who praised *American*, yet remarked that it presented "almost wholly a man's world—a world of battle, hunting, adventure, friendship. Women seem like trailing shadows behind the men. . . . The part that women played in Indian life is not apparent. Why is this?"[42] Perhaps promptings like this, as well as the commercial potential of a book marketed to women readers, motivated Linderman to capture an Indian woman's story for print.

In the course of his many years in Montana, Linderman always found Indian women to be "diffident, and so self-effacing that acquaintance with them is next to impossible."[43] So his first challenge was finding a suitable woman, someone "equally able and old." Linderman hoped to write the story of Deep-nose, a Crow, but she died before he could accomplish it. By the spring of 1931, however, Linderman learned that Pretty-shield was willing to talk with him. She met his requirements in several ways. She was mentally sharp, willing to talk freely, and old enough "to have known the natural life of her people on the plains." According to Linderman, she agreed to the collaboration because her own children and grandchildren lacked interest. Moreover, he knew more about Crow culture than many Crow men his age. Self-serving as this explanation was, it gave Linderman added credibility—notably because an Indian granted it to him. Finally, Pretty-shield knew of Linderman's work with Plenty Coups and perhaps shared his desire to get the "woman's side" out.[44]

During the interviews, conducted in the Crow language through an interpreter, Linderman found the "old girl is keen" and she "is a pippin . . . Bright & keen as a fox." On the other hand, he feared that in the course of relating her life's hardships, Pretty-shield was not giving Linderman "enough of the gentle side of it."[45] Clearly, he had certain expectations of what the book should convey about Crow women, and he intended to shape it in light of those expectations. But in this ethnographic encounter, Pretty-shield controlled the knowledge and played a considerable role in determining the contents of her story.

Once again Linderman, as self-conscious editor, offered readers an extended conversation. From the outset he told Pretty-shield he wanted "only a woman's story." Of course, he never told Plenty Coups to tell only a man's story. Nevertheless, she took this admonition to heart, repeating on several occasions she was telling only stories about women in an effort to give Linderman what he wanted. Most of her material related to domestic life, childhood adventures, marriage, and child-rearing. Linderman asked little about women's work and so Pretty-shield talked little of it. She discussed briefly her spiritual helpers, the "ant people." And she told stories about warfare, although not about the fighting itself for "that is a man's business." Rather, Pretty-shield discussed the costs of warfare to women and children, who lost their husbands and fathers and found themselves subsequently dependent on others. "We women did not like war," she explained, "and yet we could not help it, because our men loved war." Women tried to dissuade men from fighting, but such efforts proved futile: "this was like talking to winter-winds."[46]

Yet Pretty-shield took pride in women warriors, a subject she correctly assumed Plenty Coups had not broached. She talked about a sixty-year-old woman who fended off a Lakota war party, armed only with her root digger, while singing her medicine song. Bullets flew all around her. Frightened by her powers, the Lakota retreated but, Pretty-shield said, the Crow men "never tell about it. They do not like to hear about it." Nor did they discuss the two Crow women who fought with General George Crook at the Battle of the Rosebud.[47] To his credit, Linderman included these stories in the book, although he offered no commentary on them or on the fact that Plenty Coups had not acknowledged them. This was not "the gentle side" Linderman was looking for, but he did record and print it.

Of course, Linderman rearranged Pretty-shield's material in creating the book. He balked, however, when an editor suggested further rearrangement. For instance, the editor wanted Linderman to place Pretty-shield's comments about the Battle of the Little Bighorn at the end of the book, thus making that tale the climax. The editor believed that readers would find Pretty-shield's commentary about the battle of greatest interest and importance, and he apparently cared little about what it meant to her. Linderman resisted, not because it might warp the meaning of the story to Pretty-shield, but because he preferred to make the decisions about arranging and rearranging material, about the creative aspects of the book. Linderman believed he knew best how to make the story "sound" authentic. "I can make my stuff sound more Injin than you can," he wrote the editor, "so that if there is any writing—and there must be—I wish to do it myself with your suggestions." In the end the publisher insisted and Linderman capitulated, placing the Battle of the Little Bighorn at the book's conclusion. Linderman refused to budge, though, on the title. He wanted *Red Mother*. When Richard Walsh of the John Day Company expressed fear people would think it a book about Russia, Linderman refused to surrender. His original title remained on the cover, accompanied by a subtitle which signaled this was a story about an Indian woman.[48]

Linderman received many accolades for *Red Mother*. Hugh L. Scott, a former army officer and authority on Indian sign language, indicated that Linderman's portrayal of Crow girls matched Scott's remembrances of them. His only complaint was that Linderman should not have included Pretty-shield's claim that Custer was drunk during the Battle of the Little Bighorn. Ethnologist Robert

Lowie wrote a positive review for an academic journal and pronounced it the most valuable of Linderman's works on the Crow. Even Lowie learned something from "this layman's production." At the same time, Lowie expressed regret that Linderman had not taken advantage of published and accessible data on the Crow (presumably his own) and pointed out errors. He noted, for instance, that Pretty-shield's claim that Plenty Coups shot another Crow woman, Sitting-heifer, while she was dancing a Sun Dance, could not be true. Linderman, describing himself as "very much upset" by this mistake and, ever the perfectionist, took pains to discover whether or not his informant was, in fact, wrong. Once he learned Pretty-shield had made an error, Linderman told University of Montana Professor Harry Turney-High that he would have the correction made in all unsold books as well as in future editions. He asked the professor to pass this information along to Lowie.[49]

Others lauded Linderman's Crow books without reservation, particularly white writers who shared his interest in Indians. Marie Brace Kimball, who published a book about her army officer-husband's experiences in the West called *A Soldier-Doctor of Our Army*, thought *American* "an invaluable contribution to our knowledge of Indian history and folk-lore." Frank Van de Water, who eventually wrote a well-known book about Custer and who had lauded *American*, told Linderman, it is "too good for the present," but would eventually be "'discovered' by someone long after you and I are dead." Van de Water, who also applauded *Red Mother*, complimented Linderman's beautiful style with its "grand delicacy of touch." Walter Campbell, better known by his pen name Stanley Vestal, also liked *Red Mother* very much and told Linderman he was lucky to find an Indian woman willing to talk so freely of intimate matters.[50]

The one note of dissent from his fellow popular writers came from Oliver LaFarge, who was also academically trained. LaFarge believed *American* contained "too much Linderman . . . these are not the old Chief's words." Linderman reported LaFarge's complaints to his editor, complaining that LaFarge believed "that I 'fall down badly' in telling about the Indian. I reckon he *knows*." Professional jealousy may have piqued Linderman a tad here. LaFarge and Linderman directly competed for audiences, LaFarge more successfully after he received the Pulitzer Prize for *Laughing Boy*, a Navajo story, in 1930. In time LaFarge altered his estimation of Linderman, however. In 1935, he told a magazine editor that Linderman was "the man to ask about Indians," which clearly pleased the Montanan. Upon hearing this, one of Linderman's friends expressed pleasure that LaFarge "is seeing the light" and added he always believed LaFarge to be "honest and well-intentioned and . . . [would] gladly give you due recognition."[51]

Crow reactions to the "autobiographies" are difficult to discern, although it stands to reason their publication made something of a stir. The Crow Indian Woman's Club read and discussed *Red Mother* and also commented on the Sitting-heifer controversy. The book became a vehicle for increased Indian-white interaction in the vicinity of the Crow Reservation. Pretty-shield and six other Indian women from the Crow Agency agreed to attend the Woman's Club meeting in Forsyth, as well as the biennial meeting of the state federation. The president of the Montana General Federation of Women's Clubs later reported that the Crow women enjoyed the Forsyth meeting and that club members thought it one of the best programs ever. Pretty-shield also talked at the Forsyth High School assembly.[52]

Linderman's works, then, reached sympathetic ears both inside and outside Montana, Indian and white, scholar and layman. Within his adopted state, he was hailed as one of its premier men of letters. Still, Linderman doubted his achievements because he never achieved financial success. George Bird Grinnell warned him from the outset about elusive royalties, but Linderman never stopped hoping for them and he continued to link financial accomplishment with intellectual achievement. If his work was truly good, he believed, it would sell. Rejection and weak sales "are gut-shots to me," he said, "and make me double up." Many editors and writers understood he was discouraged, yet urged him to continue writing. His friend Hermann Hagedorn reassured Linderman that his work had a lasting value beyond that of most books which made money. Hagedorn concluded that *American* and *Red Mother* would live on for one hundred years and so had greater value than anything of Hagedorn's that "brought in coin of the realm."[53] Such words of reassurance may have provided temporary balm for Linderman's wounds but they never cured his craving for financial success.

Not only did Linderman fail to sell his books, but he also failed to sell himself as a political candidate. Simultaneous with his writing efforts, he pursued national political office, running for the House of Representatives in 1916 and 1918 and for the Senate in 1924. All three times, Linderman lost. Not the least of the reasons, in Linderman's estimation, stemmed from two of Montana's, and the modern world's, most disagreeable elements: feminists and immigrants.

Linderman claimed he decided to run for U.S. House of Representatives while trying to explain what Congress was to "my tribesmen," the Chippewa and Cree. He thus linked personal political ambitions with the welfare of Montana's Indians. Alas, Linderman ran against Jeanette Rankin in the Republican primary and she beat him. She went on to win the election and serve as the first woman to sit in the House of Representatives. This was a blow not only to Linderman's political aspirations; it was a blow to his manhood and his sense of the world's well-being. Ridiculous as his reaction may seem today, one must admit it probably was difficult to be the man to lose to the first woman elected to Congress. Certainly, Linderman feit compelled to explain his defeat, telling his father that woman suffrage was the "fad" that did him in. He went on to say, he would have been embarrassed to take a seat in Congress with a woman as a member. "I am old fashioned in this belief I suppose, and out of date, but my ideas concerning the ladies are of a good deal higher grade than those possessed by the ones who boom their candidacies for congress." He told another friend that he did not object to women "controlling a rightful portion of things" such as the office of Superintendent of Public Instruction. But he did object "when on a sudden jump they wish to sit where wars and the nations' troubles are passed upon." Perhaps his attitude linked him to an earlier age, but Linderman believed that feminism and women's ambitions for public office represented the end of "the beauties and niceties of the old times." He concluded that he was being "perfectly honest in that expression and have no sore spots because of my defeat, but I fret and worry over the condition of things today, just the same."[54]

Linderman naturally looked to Indians for comfort. Such a turn of events, such a topsy-turvy realignment of men's and women's roles, he believed, never occurred among the Blackfeet or Crow, Chippewa or Cree. Yet in modern Montana among its white residents, this election proved that the "war bonnet has passed from the buck to the squaw and soon the medicine pipe will follow," he lamented. When George Bird Grinnell wrote, indicating that he heard a Montana woman received the Republican Party nomination for Congress, which he hoped was not true, Linderman responded:

> *Regarding the election, I was defeated by a woman. This fact I have failed to explain to my Indian friends. . . . I am glad that I have counted a good many snows and that I lived when I did, because in many things I believe I see the crumbling process that has afflicted every nation since the beginning.*[55]

Linderman lost to a woman and the whole world was going to hell! He was certain that his Indian friends would never understand.[56]

Defeated but not completely discouraged, Linderman ran for the Republican nomination for Congress again in 1918. He won the nomination, only to lose in the general election. This time Linderman blamed his defeat not on faddish feminists, but on fraud in Butte and, consequently, on immigrants. In the years to follow, leading up to his 1924 bid for the Senate, Linderman's nativism became more pronounced. The twenties was a period of intense xenophobia and Linderman found fellow compatriots. He wrote to author Gertrude Atherton that immigration had injured the nation, "American ideals are being dimmed or lost in the rabble from other lands." Moreover, immigrants robbed America's children of their "birthright of opportunity." He urged one of Montana's senators to introduce another bill restricting immigration. And when friends began urging Linderman to run for the Senate, he thought he could win but also believed "the Sinn Fein element would fight me to a stand still." In composing an autobiographical sketch for the Senate race, Linderman described himself as an ardent patriot whose love for country dated back to his childhood, when he used to argue with his mother about immigration. Clearly, Linderman hoped to perpetuate an image of himself as anti-immigrant and pro-American. He succeeded in convincing at least one Butte resident that he was "a true-blue American and a real He-man," but he still lost the election.[57]

Linderman never took rejection well and these losses fed his despondency.

Friends, once again, tried to buck him up, including one who told Linderman he was actually fortunate to have lost the congressional elections because congressmen only serve for a few years and then are lost to the public eye. Linderman's books, on the other hand, "make land markes [*sic*] that stand out through life's journey, to which we can always point with pride and when time and adversity has depressed the soul, we find a hiding place between the pages." It is possible that had Linderman won political office he might never have written Plenty Coups' and Pretty-shield's stories. Whatever the case, there is no doubt that his experiences in the political arena and his political point of view colored his approach to those projects. It is no coincidence that he chose *American* and *Red Mother* as his titles. They underscore Linderman's theme of a vanishing world—not only an Indian world, but also one where red-blooded, Anglo-Saxon Americans held supreme against immigrants and one where women knew their place as mothers rather than as congresswomen.[58]

If Linderman could not win an election, the prospect of appointment still held out possibilities. He was particularly interested in an office tied to Indian affairs. For a brief moment in 1929, some political friends dangled the possibility of becoming Commissioner of Indian Affairs before Linderman. A former Nebraska governor nominated Linderman for the job, without asking his permission. The governor informed the Hoover administration that Linderman's qualifications included his expertise on Indians which derived from living in the West for forty-five years, his careful studies, and his sympathies for them. Additionally, he argued, Linderman wanted to see Indians become independent of governmental assistance and would work to end federal involvement in their lives. Linderman wanted the job but quickly learned that President Herbert Hoover preferred to appoint a wealthy man. Linderman lacked those credentials and did not get the job.[59]

Up until that time, Linderman's most direct involvement in Indian political matters had come with his efforts to create the Rocky Boy Reservation. Beyond that episode, however, he did not regularly comment on or present well-thought-out viewpoints regarding the proper ends of Indian policy. He offered only occasional tidbits. In 1928, for instance, he suggested the Bureau of Indian Affairs be abolished altogether, after Indians had time to prepare for self-sufficiency. On another occasion, Linderman urged the Rocky Boy Reservation inhabitants to reject allotment, although the reason for this counsel is unclear. Most clearly, throughout his life, Linderman advocated Indian religious freedom. Certainly, his books present Indian religion sympathetically. Sounding not unlike Walter McClintock, Linderman admitted he found Indian ideas believable.[60] Linderman had no particular religious bent of his own. In fact, the closest he came to a religious affiliation was involvement with the Masons, which he believed, in its ritual and pageantry, had connections to Indian religion.[61] He found Indians free of bigotry and evangelical impulses and so he urged, "Let us be as broad as is our helpless ward."[62] He resented missionaries who tried to force their religion on others, particularly onto Indians. "'Isn't it a great pity that we are unable to give the Indian a better God?'," a missionary once asked him. Linderman thought such a thing was impossible.[63]

Linderman, then, urged the federal government not to interfere with Indian religious observances. In 1916, Linderman asked Cato Sells, Commissioner of Indian Affairs, to rescind any orders to cut Indian men's hair and to prohibit the annual Sun Dance on the Rocky Boy Reservation. Sells replied that he appreciated Linderman's efforts on behalf of Indians and explained that no order to forcibly cut men's hair was in effect, although the Office of Indian Affairs hoped to convince the younger men to cut their hair and "give up the old non-progressive Indian customs." On the other hand, Sells unequivocally refused to rescind the order to stop the Sun Dance, claiming that to allow the Sun Dance at Rocky Boy would set a dangerous precedent and reverse a long-standing policy to discourage harmful Indian practices. While Indians might view forced abolition of the Sun Dance as a hardship in the short term, Sells believed, they would benefit in the long term as they moved toward civilized life. Meanwhile, while Linderman and Sells corresponded, the Rocky Boy Reservation Indians went ahead with their Sun Dance. Official permission mattered little to them and apparently nobody on the reservation tried to stop it.[64]

Still, Linderman hoped to achieve an official change of heart. The following year he tried again, and again failed. The Indians held the dance anyway. In 1925, Linderman still hoped the official ban on sun-dancing would be dropped, if only to relieve concerns that in the future someone might try to prevent the ceremony. That year he urged the Rocky Boy Reservation superintendent to allow it and the superintendent responded that he had not forbidden the dance. Over the last decade the Indian Office had softened, now allowing dances and ceremonies as long as they involved neither immoral or injurious behavior nor the giving away of property. Several Indians on the reservation believed Linderman was primarily responsible for this change and asked Evan Jones, a Havre harness-maker, to express their appreciation to him. As Day Child told Jones,

> *I want you to know how I like Frank Linderman. My father is dead. I loved him, but if my father came back and stood on one hill and I saw Frank Linderman on another hill I would not go to my father, I would go to Frank Linderman. You know I do not lie. This is the Truth.*[65]

Jones also informed Linderman that the local missionary disapproved of traditional religious practices, but that he would never win the old men away from them. On the other hand, the missionary had greater success with the young men which, Jones wrote facetiously, "goes to show that God is helping him in his work."[66]

Linderman, then, had formulated and acted upon some ideas about Indian issues, but he did not have a well-thought-out, comprehensive plan for Indian policy reform. Meanwhile, if his chances for the commissionership were remote under a Republican administration, they were nonexistent under a Democratic one. He would not be considered by Franklin Roosevelt's regime.

Linderman, however, never seemed especially devoted to partisanship. During the Rocky Boy Reservation controversy, he worked with Democrats as well as Republicans to achieve their shared goal. And although he probably did not vote for Roosevelt in 1932, Linderman was supporting him by the fall of 1933. The hardships brought about by the Great Depression clearly influenced him. "I'm making Injin medicine for the nation's good luck during this winter," Linderman explained to a friend. "I'm worried, have been worried for a long time. Anyhow our new President has enough guts to bait a deadfall for grizzlies, and I'm for him strong as mustard." Linderman told Van de Water, "I never had any time for the man Roosevelt until he became President and made his first ante in the big game. Then I saw that he was guts on legs and threw in with him." It is quite possible that among those actions Linderman found appealing was Roosevelt's Indian New Deal.[67]

Linderman and John Collier apparently never met, yet during the twenties it is very likely they knew of one another's work. When Collier became commissioner, Linderman commenced a correspondence with him. He told Collier that he had read several of his speeches and liked them, particularly his condemnation of using tribal funds for administrative purposes and his denunciation of off-reservation boarding schools. He went on to request an expansion of the Rocky Boy Reservation boundaries, by ceding more acreage from the former Fort Assiniboine military reservation. Linderman lauded the memorandum Collier sent to all reservation superintendents ordering no further interference with Indian religious life or ceremonial expression. Collier also declared it was desirable for Indians to know not only English but also their own "vital, beautiful and efficient native languages" and that Indian arts and crafts were "to be prized, nourished and honored." Although pleased with this memo, Linderman cautioned that the true art was gone, irretrievable, "emasculated."[68]

Clearly, Linderman was heartened by the Indian New Deal and Collier's positive response to Linderman's pleas for an extended Rocky Boy Reservation. Linderman, in kind, did his part to explain Collier's policies to the Cree and Chippewa. In the spring of 1934, he traveled to Rocky Boy to help the reservation Business Council decipher the Indian New Deal. In the spirit of self-determination, Linderman made it clear he would not tell these Indians what to do. Rather, he counseled them to think carefully and deliberately about the New Deal adding, with only a hint of paternalism, to "not quarrel among yourselves. The time has come to forget about tribes, or families, or old quarrels. You must now be *one* family."[69] Linderman found great solace in Collier's approach to Indian affairs. Though Indians had changed irrevocably and many of the old-time ways were lost, Indian people *finally* stood a chance of surviving.

A few months before Linderman died in 1938, a sculptor named George Blodgett asked him to support his dream, a National Gallery of the American Indian. Having read *American* and *Red Mother*, Blodgett thought Linderman a likely ally who would lend his name to the project. Blodgett particularly hoped Linderman would help enlist Indian involvement in order "to make the gallery *their* gallery as much as it is *our* gallery, for we are not white anthropologists and ethnologists who look upon Indians as 'specimens' but primarily artists, poets, writers, etc. who know and love them as human beings very much alive with something dynamic to contribute." Linderman agreed to help but died before he was able to do so. His works never cracked best-seller lists, but, among those Americans interested in Indians, his work carried weight. Through his collections of Indian stories and his autobiographies of Plenty Coups and Pretty-shield, most of which are still in print, he undoubtedly helped form many twentieth-century readers' understanding of "Indians." Collier may or may not have read them, but Linderman's works represent a Northern Rockies version of that cultural groundwork which authors, toiling in various corners of the West, laid for the reforms Collier had in mind.[70]

It is ironic that Linderman, as a young man, could hardly wait to forsake the East and embrace the West, and then as an old man considered reversing the process. Disappointed with his various failures in life, particularly the languid sales of his books, Linderman once toyed with the idea of moving to Mystic, Connecticut. "I'm ready to quit Montan [*sic*]," he wrote Frederick Van de Water, "it's no longer Montana to me. And there's nothing here for me." Of course, he did not go. All his life Linderman struggled with his own internal pessimism regarding his writing career, his Montana, his nation. Only a few months before threatening to "quit Montan" he groused, yet again, about what a mess the world was in and claimed that if he was a single man, even at his age, he would pick up a few blankets and a rifle and head for the hills. He concluded with a telling admission: "I've often wished I'd been an Indian a hundred years ago."[71] During his early years in Montana, Linderman had attempted to approximate such a life. He dedicated the rest of his years to commemorating it in words and to assuring its perpetuation, in however truncated a form, through political activity. In this he found fellow enthusiasts in other sections of the West.

# 6

# CHARLES FLETCHER LUMMIS AND THE FIGHT FOR THE MULTICULTURAL SOUTHWEST

HAD CHARLES FLETCHER LUMMIS BEEN BORN WITH LESS AMBITION, he might have become a pugilist rather than a publisher. As it was, he found a way to combine his literary talents with his combative temperament. Through much of his career Lummis took up not fists but pen to defend Indians and to battle for recognition of the Southwest and California's diverse archaeological, historical, and cultural heritage. A New Englander by birth and education, Lummis literally walked through the heart of New Mexico, Arizona, and California in 1884. From that point on, his allegiance and his soul belonged to the Southwest. The region's impact struck Lummis as potently as a religious conversion and as a result, according to historian Edwin Bingham, "he became a self-appointed and zealous missionary in its name."[1]

Lummis's errand into the "wilderness," however, took a different turn from that of his New England forebears. What he discovered in the West was neither a howling wasteland in need of taming nor a savage people in need of a Puritan-inspired metamorphosis. Rather, in Spanish and Indian cultures Lummis found attractive cultural alternatives to his New England heritage. In addition, Indians jolted him out of his complacent assumption that America's history began with the English colonists' efforts on Atlantic shores. Long before the latter even considered the possibility of sailing to Virginia or Massachusetts, New Mexico's Pueblos were tilling the soil and "living in temperance, dignity, peace and prosperity." The Southwest's Spanish and Mexican people convinced the Harvard-educated Lummis that while his conscience was Puritan, "my whole imagination and sympathy and feeling were Latin." Once free of his own repressive region, Lummis, in a quick, efficient act of appropriation, "began to see that the generous and bubbling boyish impulses which had been considerably frosted in New England were, after all, my birthright."[2]

These boyish impulses developed into "manly" attributes once Lummis settled in the Southwest. To the extent that manliness meant, for some members of Lummis's generation, engagement in rigorous sports or physical activity, a willingness to fight, and a display of robust sexuality, Charles Fletcher Lummis filled the bill on all three. He demonstrated physical prowess by walking 3500 miles from Cincinnati to Los Angeles, a fighting spirit by defending the honor of Indian and Spanish peoples, and a healthy virility by taking several wives and many lovers during his Southwestern sojourn. Such rigorous manliness spilled over, of course, to his work and his writing but with, perhaps, unexpected results. While some of his contemporaries saw the nation's triumph in the West as evidence of Anglo-Saxon superiority, Lummis's view, like Grinnell's, was more complicated and sometimes contradictory. First, he learned Indians still lived in communities hundreds of years old. The Pueblos were neither brittle nor brutal savages but enduring and attractive people. Then he discovered remnants of Spanish culture that cultivated beauty, poetry and romance, all attributes sorely missing from Anglo-American culture. Neither Indians nor Hispanics were innately inferior to the "Saxon" tribe. What threatened to despoil all this, in fact, was the growing presence of Anglos. True, the numbers of the former were dwindling. But Lummis wanted to stem that tide and revive the best elements of Indian and Spanish cultures, not hasten their disappearance. If he shared a belief in the ultimate dominance of the Anglo-Saxon, he did not applaud that outcome. Antimodernist-inspired doubts, misgivings, even pointed critiques of his own culture accompanied Lummis's albeit hopelessly romantic, and sometimes racist, assessments of Southwestern people.[3]

Lummis, as self-appointed missionary, determined to present his newfound wisdom to the rest of the country. For forty years he produced a stream of newspaper articles, magazine columns, and books dedicated to educating Americans, especially Easterners, about this "strange corner of the country." Acknowledging the Indian and Hispanic ingredients of Americanism would reintroduce romance, adventure, fantasy—the very things Lummis, like C.E.S. Wood, believed the modern world lacked. This heritage offered a dose of grace and gentility to counter Yankee aggression, coarseness, and materialism. At the same time, acknowledging the value of Indian and Spanish-Mexican cultures and their place in the family of man would strike a blow against racism, bigotry, and anti-Catholicism.

Lummis, aptly characterized as a "bantom cock of paradox" by historian Kevin Starr, did not always maintain an intellectual or ideological consistency on these matters. He sometimes wrote himself into corners, particularly when he addressed historical conflicts between Indians and the Spanish. What happens when two heroic groups collide? In Lummis's contentious world, one must take on the role of villain. And that is what happened to Indians, say, in his renderings of the Pueblo Revolt of 1680. One can certainly find evidence of nativism and racism in Lummis's voluminous writings which spanned four decades. Sometimes he demonized Indians; sometimes he infantilized them. Yet an examination of his complete works reveals Lummis also attempted to challenge the racial and religious bigotry so common in his day, to give faces and voices to Native Americans and Hispanics, and to incorporate them into a more dynamic and inclusive vision of America.[4]

Lummis did not write the brand of popular ethnography that characterized the work of George Bird Grinnell or even Walter McClintock. Nor did he produce the chronicles of individual Indians' lives such as Frank Linderman's *Plenty Coups* or *Pretty-shield*, although he did collect and publish Indian stories, following the pattern of Wood, Grinnell, and Linderman. Neither Lummis, nor any of the other Southwestern-based writers examined here, demonstrated the compulsions regarding "salvage ethnography" or revealed the same deep-seated anxiety about vanishing cultures that characterized writers on the Northern Plains or Rockies. Rather, it was the continued presence of Indians in the Southwest, as the nation pushed out of the nineteenth and into the twentieth century, that inspired them. The Pueblos, in particular, stood out for several reasons. A sedentary, agricultural, Spanish-speaking people, who practiced both Catholicism and their own religious traditions, were living proof of the Indian capacity to adjust and survive. They had endured physically, culturally, and spiritually not only centuries of contact with Europeans and their descendants, but Anglo-Americans as well. It was the Pueblos, more than any other Indian group on the continent, who convinced antimodern writers and reformers that Indians not only had a long history of coexistence with whites, but a future too; that a policy which perpetuated these "endangered authenticities" was possible; and that Anglo-Americans could learn something of value from Pueblos and save themselves in the process. Lummis did not travel as far along such lines of thinking as did Mary Austin, Mabel Dodge Luhan, or John Collier, but he certainly began that journey and encouraged others to travel the same road.

In the end, Lummis was more promoter than social critic, more popularizer than scholar. As editor of the California-based periodical, *Land of Sunshine*, later renamed *Out West*, his purposes included the practical goal of encouraging immigration to southern California. Celebrating the Southwest's cultural heritage and insisting elements of it remained alive contributed to that cause. In addition, Lummis's attitudes toward Indians took root in nineteenth-century experiences and assumptions. He never completely shed the consequences. Yet when examined over time, starting with his first impressions of Pueblos in 1884 to his 1920s writings in support of John Collier, Lummis' outlook demonstrated an elastic, evolving character. Certainly, Lummis' work regarding Indians made its mark on Collier's generation. Mary Austin and Anna Ickes knew this, but no one expressed it more clearly than Collier himself who, upon Lummis's death, acknowledged his debt to this "westerner." Lummis, Collier wrote in the American Indian Defense Association's journal, "was a founder of the Indian Defense movements. Indeed, he was its forerunner by half a generation."[5]

Born in Lynn, Massachusetts, his father sent two year old Lummis to New Hampshire to live with his maternal grandparents after his mother's death. At age eight he returned to his father and began an academic education. Methodist Reverend Henry Lummis served as principal of the New Hampshire

Seminary and Female College, but his son's refusal to cooperate with his teacher led him to conclude Charlie was best suited for home study. Under Henry's tutelage, Lummis learned Latin, Greek, and Hebrew and ten years later enrolled in Harvard College.[6]

Intellectually prepared for college, Lummis was not emotionally ready. He preferred athletics to academics; women to work—not unusual, perhaps, but in Lummis's case such propensities had dramatic consequences. In 1880, Lummis and Dorothea Roads, a Boston medical student, secretly married, and the following year he withdrew from Harvard just days short of graduation. The details of these rather crucial events remain cloudy and, for the rest of his life, Lummis retained a decided hostility toward Harvard. He once wrote to David Starr Jordan, then president of Stanford University, that Stanford was the only university to which he would ever consider sending his son. "I wouldn't send this Western Boy to Harvard for anything—not even for salary." In his autobiography Lummis also noted that if Jordan had headed Harvard instead of Stanford, he would never have become "the Greatest Educator in America. . . . Harvard would have smothered him in its conventions."[7]

Such sentiments reflected resentment over his personal problems, as well as the school's class divisions which delegated him to a subordinate position. They also revealed Lummis's later western regional chauvinism. Nevertheless, the Harvard years allowed him acquaintance with a future president of the United States. Although Lummis and Theodore Roosevelt did not prove intimate friends during their years on the Charles River, the Harvard connection undoubtedly made it easier to renew the acquaintance later in life. The school also brought him under the tutelage of mentor Charles Eliot Norton, who encouraged Lummis to examine culture through art, artifacts, and antiquities—lessons he would apply with vigor once ensconced in California. Lummis later proudly stated that Norton pronounced him "the best thing Harvard has sent West." Clearly, Ivy League approval still mattered. Yet more typical was Lummis' assertion that "my chief thankfulness about the whole matter is that four years of Harvard didn't make a fool of me."[8] Leaving Harvard a few days shy of graduation might lead some to question that assessment.

Fool or not, Lummis and Dorothea landed in Ohio where he supervised his father-in-law's Scioto Valley farm. Soon tired of the agrarian life, Lummis turned to journalism and edited the Scioto *Gazette* for several years. In his spare time he pursued a budding interest in archaeology, hunted, and fished. Finally, in 1884 at the age of twenty-five, a robust Lummis pushed off for the Far West, his destination: California and a job with the *Los Angeles Times*.

Eschewing a conventional westward journey, Lummis decided to walk, writing dispatches back to Ohio and forward to Los Angeles along the way. While some aspects of Lummis's westward journey undoubtedly approximated that of earlier nineteenth-century overlanders, his trip differed in one fairly dramatic way: Lummis followed the railroad tracks—perhaps the most potent symbol of industrial America. Like McClintock and Linderman, he could not pretend to be a pathfinder or an explorer of unknown geographical regions. Instead he would "discover" cultural regions and in the process attempt to redefine not the nation's physical borders but rather its cultural ones. Nothing in the record, however, suggests that Lummis set out to accomplish such a purpose. In 1884, he simply wanted an adventure and walking across the continent satisfied that impulse. Yet the experience proved transforming. Following the railroad tracks led Lummis into new worlds and, in time, convinced him that he ought to introduce into American life an antidote to its increasingly sterile, pallid dreariness. New Mexico's Spanish, Mexican, and Indian worlds, he believed, provided that remedy. Moreover, the further these people lived from the railroad, the greater their value to Lummis and the greater their potency as partial cure to what ailed modern America. Like Linderman in Montana, Lummis had to range far from the beaten path to find American authenticities. "The railroad ruins an Indian with marvelous rapidity," he once wrote, noting that the Zuni, for instance, "'Grow no better fast' under its baleful influence. Therefore if you would visit the aborigine, find him as far as possible from all the adjuncts of that dubious thing which calls into civilization."[9]

Lummis's first encounter with Indians during this trip occurred in a once-defined border region. By 1884, Kansas qualified as a well-developed state and the Indians he met there were not "wild." Rather they enrolled in the Lawrence, Kansas, Indian School and fully engaged in the nation's civilization program. At this point, Lummis supported such a policy. It surprised him that while some appeared "stolid and dull looking," others displayed "really bright faces." Breezing through Lawrence, Lummis pronounced in letters back to Ohio, that stereotypes of Indians as lazy and stupid were wrong and noted, these children were anxious to learn.[10]

When Lummis reached southern Colorado and northern New Mexico, surprises continued. Initially suspicious of the Mexicans he encountered, Lummis's racism ran rampant. "The Mexicans," he wrote in mid-November, "are a snide-looking set, twice as dark as an Indian, with heavy lips and noses, long, straight, black hair, sleepy eyes, and a general expression of ineffable laziness. . . . Not even a coyote will touch a dead Greaser, the flesh is so seasoned with the red pepper they ram into their food in howling profusion." By the end of the month, however, Lummis was already reconsidering, noting in his next dispatch that while the whites were "all on the make," the Mexicans were "not half bad people," who shared whatever they had with a stranger. Generosity, hospitality, kindness, Lummis now claimed, typified the Mexicans.[11]

New Mexico's Pueblo Indians underwent a similarly speedy transformation in Lummis's letters. His first glimpse of these people came at Española where he saw "Bucks" drinking whiskey, "squaws" carrying papooses, and Indian youngsters "keeping up an incessant jabber." Later that day, however, he stopped at San Ildefonso Pueblo where he encountered "the best looking Indians I ever saw" and remarked on the courteous reception he received in one of the homes. Moving on to Santa Fe, Lummis lingered and learned a little about Southwestern history, including the Pueblo Revolt of 1680. In his first rendering of this event, Lummis took the Indian side. With the carefree, even flippant style that typified these bulletins, Republican Lummis explained, "These old Spaniards appear to have been Southern Democrats, every mother's son of them, for they stuffed the ballot boxes, bull-dozed the majority, and kept the poor Pueblos down in regular slave fashion. Then the Pueblos arose on their ear—in 1680—and ran their oppressors out at the end of a pointed stick."[12] As time went on, Lummis reformulated his interpretation of these events.

Lummis's initial impression of federal Indian policy regarding off-reservation education was also positive. He reported that the Pueblos' agent was an honorable man who had made great strides in enrolling children in the Carlisle or Albuquerque boarding schools. The older generation opposed such innovations, he claimed, but younger people favored compulsory education. Lummis declared that Indian children performed better at schools removed from parental and tribal influence. He also asserted that the Catholic Pueblos "are all as good Christians as you are—perhaps a good deal better," that no "Christian American community in the world . . . can approach in morality one of these little towns of adobe," and that "I wish they [Pueblos] would send out missionaries to their American brothers."[13]

Lummis's fleeting, though positive, first impressions of the Pueblos did not transfer to other Indians. He recounted conversations with New Mexicans about their bloody feuds with Apaches, Navajos, and Utes. Whereas Lummis pronounced the Pueblos clean, honest, charitable, and moral, he found the Navajos "dirty, thievish, treacherous and revoltingly licentious." To underscore the difference, Lummis reminded his Ohio readers that the Pueblos were farmers, the Navajos stock-raisers and hunters. In short, Pueblos were civilized, Navajos "still mere savages." He reserved his harshest commentary, however, for the Mojave Desert's Hualapais: "These Indians are as worthless as a pair of last year's linen pants. They don't make blankets, pottery, or anything else, and their only industry seems to be prostitution."[14]

By the time Lummis sauntered into Los Angeles in early February 1885, his introduction to things Southwestern was complete and his conversion to westerner status well underway. His cross-country tramp proved a formative experience, much as Wood's Indian Wars campaigns and McClintock's sojourns with the Piegans had proven to them. Like them, for the rest of his life, Lummis drew upon that experience—sometimes reinterpreting the place, its people, and its history from his original renditions but never swaying from his fundamental purpose: to promote and celebrate the region. Periodically, he returned to the heart of the Southwest, each time gathering material for his cultural campaign.

His next opportunity to stockpile weapons for this crusade came, suitably enough, in the context of a military campaign. In 1886, Lummis's boss, Harrison Gray Otis of the *Los Angeles Times*, capitulated to Lummis's urging and assigned him to cover the Apache war. Lummis pushed for this assignment because he found the office stifling and longed to feel his blood flow freely and his muscles expand. Now as he sat in his urban office, scratching out a living as a newspaperman, "my thoughts go drifting out of the windows and across the mountains to—well, I call it *life*." In a sentiment reminiscent of Grinnell, he went on, "The best that civilization can give is not much more than existence. However, by the time this Indian complexion fades out . . . I shall have gotten over the edge of my hunger for the wilderness probably."[15] Neither the hunger for adventure nor the "Indian" complexion had faded completely, however, and by March 1886, Lummis was on his way to Arizona to cover General George Crook's campaign, bringing Chiricahua Apaches back to their reservation.

His stories about the war, some composed in Arizona and others back in California, reflected a reporter's necessarily superficial, sometimes sensational, off-the-cuff rather than well-considered, assessment of events. In an early dispatch, Lummis described Geronimo as "the gory Chiricahua" and one month later characterized the Apaches as "BORN BUTCHERS—hereditary slayers." Long before Caucasians entered Arizona, Apaches attacked the "agricultural Aztec, peaceful Pueblo or plodding *paisano*" and "what he has done to keep his gory hand in since blond scalps first amused his knife, I need not remind you now." Still, Lummis could not refrain from describing the Chiricahua as attractive and, especially important to Lummis, manly, tough, strong, resolute. In fact, by the end of his Arizona experience, Lummis' sympathies had begun to shift toward the Apaches. He noted that Crook would not allow him to telegraph the surrendering Apache's destination in Florida until the night before their departure for the Indians required soldiers' protection. Danger came from "'civilized' whites along the way . . . who would jump at the chance to signalize their bravery by shooting a captive squaw through a car window, if they had received sufficient notice to brace themselves with 'brag and whisky.'"[16]

Such statements hint at the genesis of Lummis' gradually altered attitudes toward Apaches, a reconsideration that emerged full-blown near the end of his life in "The Man Who Yawns," a poem about Geronimo. In this posthumously published work, Lummis presented Geronimo as victim of a corrupt Indian agent, an intrepid and ephemeral foe whom army troops never conquered militarily, and a man who in the context of war would kill, though never on the scale of his white adversaries:

> He spared nor child nor womankind;
> but Pagans never knew
> How Christians *wholesale*—Like Cheyennes, or St. Bartholomew!
> In years he killed of them about
> a half the toll that we
> Shot down of Indian squaws and babes
> one day at Wounded Knee.[17]

Shades of C.E.S. Wood, this view of Geronimo and the Apaches as heroic figures, it must be emphasized, reflected Lummis's later view, just as Chief

Joseph and the Nez Perces took on deeper significance as symbols of a purer, less corrupt people for Wood as time went on. In the 1880s, Lummis's vision was less precise and consistent, for in 1886, he was still a neophyte in the study of Southwestern history and culture.

That neophyte status changed dramatically when Lummis, who today would be labeled a workaholic, found himself literally unable to get out of his chair, the victim of a paralytic stroke. As with Grinnell and McClintock, sickness allowed Lummis to submerge himself into Indian life and excuse himself from civilization. A physical breakdown, for this most physical of men, brought Lummis an opportunity to reacquaint himself with people of the Southwest. In February 1888, he decided to convalesce in New Mexico, living for a time on Amado Chaves's hacienda near San Mateo and then moving on to the Isleta Pueblo. Altogether Lummis stayed in New Mexico for nearly four years, cementing his emotional and intellectual ties with the region and living in closer proximity to, and longer duration with, Indians than most others in this book. In the course of that New Mexico sojourn, Lummis's marriage to Dorothea ended, and he wed Eva Douglas, a Connecticut-born schoolteacher working at the Isleta Pueblo and sister-in-law of the Isleta trader. He met Adolph Bandelier and assisted the Swiss archaeologist on several projects in the Southwest and Peru. He broke horses, hunted rabbits, and mastered rolling cigarettes with one hand. He listened to Pueblo stories and photographed the New Mexican penitentes, archeological ruins and, when possible, Indians. He occasionally wrote articles for newspapers and magazines and, perhaps most significantly, gathered material for the cascade of articles and books he began publishing about the Southwest and its inhabitants in the early 1890s.[18]

Lummis derived his insight into Pueblo people by living within the Isleta Pueblo, south of Albuquerque, where he rented a house at the Abeita family compound. Apparently, Lummis's paralysis provided the unusual opportunity for an Anglo to take up residence there. One year before Lummis's arrival, the pueblo cacique had died after enduring a similar paralysis for four years. Thus, Lummis's appearance was viewed as a coincidence of spiritual significance. Still, not all Tiguas welcomed him and the *alguacil* or constable repeatedly sent him messages to that effect. Determined to remain, in order to "learn all that the elders would teach him," Lummis persisted and prevailed earning the nickname "Por Todos" for always sharing his tobacco.[19]

Lummis's relationship with the prominent Abieta family and a Carlisle-educated Tigua boy, whom Lummis hired to teach him the pueblo's language and history, helped the journalist ingratiate himself with the rest of the community. Lummis's stay at the pueblo also taught him that federal policy, particularly regarding education, was not as beneficial as he had originally supposed. He observed Indian young people who returned to their communities with skills irrelevant to reservation life. He witnessed healthy young Pueblos "turned into consumptives by being transported to unfriendly climates and forced into alien ways." He realized that teachers violated the children's dignity

*Lummis lived in New Mexico's Isleta Pueblo while recovering from a stroke. He championed the Pueblos from that point onward. Reproduced by permission of The Huntington Library, San Marino, California.*

and self-respect by stripping them of their Indian names and cutting their hair with sheep shears.[20] Lummis became acutely aware of the cruelty of this educational system when Abieta's three children were shipped off to boarding school. Lummis helped his landlord acquire a lawyer and a writ of habeas corpus to regain custody of his own flesh and blood. According to Lummis's own children, Keith and Turbese, "He had many things in his life to regret, but against them he set the day he took those three boys back to Isleta and the mother whose arms hungered for them." Several days later, Lummis and a group of Indians from the Pueblo brought home thirty-seven other children.[21] To launch a fight and win undoubtedly satisfied Lummis. It may have also reinforced his tendency to see Indians as powerless unless assisted by sympathetic whites. Some of this was paternalism; some reflected political realities of the time. Lummis did not stop with local activism. He wrote critical newspaper articles about boarding schools and consequently incurred the wrath of eastern philanthropists and government bureaucrats. No less than Commissioner of Indian Affairs Thomas J. Morgan found Lummis's publications "a slanderous attack upon the entire government system of schools."[22] He was getting someone's attention.

This experience sensitized Lummis to the darkest aspects of forced acculturation and represented an important turning point in his view of Indian policy. Just at the moment he positioned himself as a student of Indian life, just as his education into the beneficial aspects of Pueblo culture began, Lummis suddenly understood his own culture's determination to destroy it. Once awakened to this prospect, the fighter in him rallied to the cause—first, by actively seeking legal redress; eventually, by stirring up publicity about the odious aspects of assimilation, and by educating his fellow countrymen about what he perceived to be the beauty and the value of Pueblo ways.

Still, the sensitivities of this bantom cock of paradox had their limits, particularly when they interfered with his ambitions regarding promotion of things "Indian." Pueblo elders allowed him to hear Tigua traditions, stories he eventually published, to their dismay. He also understood that many Indians did not want to be photographed and admitted as much in several of the articles he published in 1889 and 1890. Yet he found such reluctance aggravating, noting that Pueblos and Navajos alike shared a "superstition about photographs, and my appearance around a corner with a camera in hand was the signal for an instant and incontinent stampede of the whole visible population." To overcome this impediment, Lummis resorted to various ruses (also practiced by George Wharton James), including luring children into the camera's lens view with candy, "bush-whacking" older women before they could escape, and replacing his 5 x 8 camera with a smaller Kodak "to the knowledge of whose subterfuges my aboriginal friend had not yet graduated."[23] Such practices, along with his publication of Pueblo stories, hastened Lummis's alienation from residents of Isleta.

Even after his estrangement from the Tiguas, Lummis never forgot the importance of his Pueblo experiences in helping to frame the intellectual foundation of his work and life. He credited God with having "been kind enough to knock me down with paralysis in the midst of the newspaper game." That paralysis drove him to New Mexico, "doubled my own fighting quality against helplessness and misfortune," and brought him into closer acquaintance with Spanish-speaking people, Pueblos, and other Indians. It introduced him to the history and prehistory, languages, folklore, and customs of "the First Americans." Finally, it brought greater self-realization: "For I had at last Found Myself," he wrote in a phrase echoed by every author examined here. "And while there wasn't very much left of me when I first made this finding," Lummis went on "it was worth while, because it was Mine and with no Collar. I never have worn a Collar since."[24]

Significantly, then, both a collision and collusion with the West and its people helped Lummis not only regain his health, but also define his American self. It is noteworthy that he chose to mold his new identity, however, not on an Indian model but rather on a Spanish one. In time, he called himself "Don Carlos," served Spanish cuisine at his California home which he named "El Alisal" (the Alder Grove), strummed a Spanish guitar, collected old Spanish songs, and rolled his own cigarettes in the style of old Spanish vaqueros. Actually, Lummis took great offense when his first wife told people that his second wife was an Indian. Referring to this "gossip," Lummis wrote Dorothea, "it is unpleasant to us and bitter to her—for while she likes Indians, she doesn't care to figure as one." Significantly, while eschewing an Indian identity for himself or his wife, Lummis embraced it for his children. He referred to daughter Turbese, who was born at Isleta Pueblo and received her Tewa name meaning "Rainbow of the Sun," as "my splendid little Indian." When his son, Amado, died, Lummis dressed him "like a little Indian and in a white Moqui blanket." For paternalistic Lummis, an Indian identity suited children; it would not do for adults.[25]

By 1892, Lummis had traded in his businessman's collar for the corduroy suit that became his trademark garb and returned to Los Angeles with new wife and child. He began to write. His paralysis now gone and his conversion complete, Lummis launched his crusade to give the Southwest and Indians their due. There is no doubt that he saw his publications in moral terms, declaring that his work had "a moral right to be."[26] The opening salvo came with Scribner's 1891 publication of *A New Mexico David and Other Stories of the Southwest*. It was especially important for Lummis to establish his credentials, noting in the book's preface that this depiction of the region came from years of residence and study. No "random tourist," Lummis situated himself as a Southwestern expert who had much "intimacy with [that region's] quaint peoples, its weird customs, and its dangers."[27] At the same time, Lummis claimed no scholarly or academic expertise. Quite the opposite, Lummis saw his role as popularizer, messenger to the general reading public, "'advance agent' . . . who tried to drum up an audience for his better," as he wrote to ethnologist Washington Matthews. Such a label allowed Lummis to play fast and loose, at times, with facts (although he was always quick to criticize other writers for their lack of precision or factual errors).[28] It also meant that Lummis felt no compulsion to display either scholarly detachment or consistency in his work. Prone to allocate moral qualities to the cultures of the Southwest, this New Englander-turned-Westerner assigned the roles of "good guy" and "bad guy" to Indian groups capriciously.

For the most part, Lummis depicted Pueblos as quiet, quaint, friendly, intelligent, and industrious farmers. Such qualities, he maintained, reflected their historical traditions. In the story, "The Enchanted Mesa," for example, Lummis presented the fifteenth-century Queres in pleasant domestic scenes and as peaceful people who took up weapons only to defend their homes. In fact, they lived on the top of a mesa, a nearly impregnable city, because they hated war. On the other hand, Lummis apparently worried that the Pueblos, his ideal Indians, might appear unmanly. So, he presented them as both capable fighters and hunters, using conventions more typically found in descriptions of Plains Indians. Lummis's description of a rabbit hunt, for instance, bore more resemblance to a buffalo than a bunny hunt. "Ambrosio, a young Apollo in bronze," Lummis wrote, "wheeled his big gray like a flash, and dashed in pursuit . . . thundering down the plain, devouring distance with mighty leaps, [the mount] plainly glorying in the mad race as much as did his rider." The end result of a day's work of rabbit-hunting which included "thirty-five miles of hard riding and fourteen 'surrounds' [was] on the cantle of every saddle bump a big mass of gray fur."[29]

Lummis's strained effort to provide Pueblos with masculine attributes, which he defined primarily in terms of hunting and fighting, could have been fairly easily resolved had he chosen to see the Pueblo Revolt as an act of courage and even patriotism, his original interpretation. By the early 1890s, however, Lummis could no longer see it that way. The moral waters had become muddied by his enthusiasm for Spanish and Mexican peoples. At this point, the Pueblos exchanged white hats for black ones. Although he believed the Pueblos were "the most wonderful aboriginal race on earth," he also saw

New Mexicans as "the descendants of the Spanish heroes who were the first real pioneers of this new world." But when "the most wonderful aborigines" fought and expelled the "most wonderful pioneers," something had to give. Although the Indians initially exhibited hospitality and patience, they eventually rose in revolt. For this rather dramatic alteration in attitude and action, Lummis provided no explanation. Rather, he simply declared "the long and wonderful war" was over when Don Diego de Vargas Zapata "reconquered the awful wilderness of New Mexico" and "heroic priests . . . settled themselves alone in the Pueblo towns to convert the suspicious natives to Christianity." In later renditions, the Pueblos fared even worse. It is difficult to say if Lummis recognized the inconsistencies in his tale. Why would such wonderful aborigines rise in revolt for no apparent reason? How could such gentle, industrious, house-dwellers become, virtually overnight, inhabitants of an "awful wilderness" and "suspicious natives"? Lummis could hardly call the Pueblos "savage," for he had already assigned that term to the Apaches, Comanches, and Navajos.[30] The "bantam cock of paradox" betrayed no awareness of these inconsistencies.

The explanation for such contradictions, however, is fairly straightforward. Lummis's purpose was not to provide a balanced, scholarly rendition of the Pueblo Revolt. His aim was to jolt the East into a recognition of western significance. First, he wanted to make the point that the Pueblos had lived in this country for hundreds of years before Europeans ever dreamed the place existed. He wanted to awaken people in the East, who, Lummis believed, knew more about Australia's aborigines than they knew about the Pueblos, that aborigines existed within the United States, as well.[31] But Lummis had an even more important goal:

> *I hope some day to see a real history of the United States; a history not written in a closet, from other one-sided affairs, but based on a knowledge of the breadth of our history, and a disposition to do it justice; a book which will realize that the early history of this wonderful country is not limited to a narrow strip on the Atlantic seaboard, but that it began in the great Southwest.*[32]

Some scholars have emphasized Lummis's fairness and accuracy in his depictions of Southwestern Indians, but such assessments oversimplify his view of Indians and miss Lummis's main purpose.[33] While Lummis worked hard, at times, to humanize Indians, at least the Pueblos, he quickly jettisoned that approach when it threatened his larger goal of redefining American history and culture. He intended to develop a new cultural myth for America, one which provided the Spanish with what he saw as long overdue credit for their heroism. Such an endeavor required little faithfulness to facts or recognition of historical complexity, both of which could make that effort more difficult. When his quest demanded presenting Navajos, Apaches, and even Pueblos as treacherous, Lummis did not hesitate.

Lummis elaborated on these themes in a series of books that quickly followed *New Mexico David. A Tramp Across the Continent*, which sanitized his 1884 letters to the *LA Times*, resurrected that journey. In the book version, his edited original letters, now tempered by the four-year sojourn in New Mexico, underscored a variety of themes which would dominate his writing. First, he wanted to strike a blow against race prejudice, acknowledging that he too had carried "silly inborn race prejudice" with him to the West. "We all start with it," Lummis wrote, a "few of us graduate from it. And yet the clearest thing in the world to him who has eyes and a chance to use them, is that men everywhere—white men, brown men, yellow men, black men—are all just about the same thing. The difference is little deeper than the skin." Not only did Lummis promote the generosity and kindness of Mexicans and Pueblos, but also Italian immigrant laborers, hinting at the senselessness of class as well as race prejudice.[34]

Naturally, the Pueblos made this case most effectively. Far from fitting the "lo the poor Indian" stereotype, Lummis wrote, "the Pueblo, the most striking ethnologic figure in our America today, is emphatically an Indian who is not poor from any point of view." Lummis particularly admired Pueblo biculturalism (to use a contemporary term for it), wherein they enjoyed two religions (Pueblo and Catholic), two sets of tools (Stone Age and Industrial Age), two sets of laws (their own and the Supreme Court's), and two languages. Pueblos had a rich folklore, poetic imaginations, and a sense of humor. They were athletic and healthy "for [they had] not yet degenerated into the fullness of civilization." Their multistoried architecture and the fact that Pueblos, who learned neither architecture nor agriculture from Europeans, gave the latter their first lessons in irrigation, also impressed him. At the same time, Lummis stressed the gifts the Spanish brought to the Pueblos, including domesticated animals, iron products, and Christianity. "It is fortunate, that the Spanish was his brother's keepers," he wrote, "Had the Pueblo enjoyed sixteenth-century acquaintance with the Saxon, we should be limited now to unearthing and articulating his bones."[35]

Of course, Lummis returned on several occasions to the story of the Pueblo Revolt, remarking how "the swarthy insurgents" butchered twenty-one priests in one day but adding such bloodshed was now in the past. The Pueblos he met peacefully cultivated their corn, squash, and watermelon and attended church. They were also citizens of the United States by virtue of the 1848 Treaty of Guadalupe Hidalgo, although the powers in Washington, D.C. seemed to ignore that fact. Lummis also railed that Easterners were oblivious to all aspects of Spanish and Mexican involvement in the United States, past or present. Making this point, of course, allowed Lummis the chance to reiterate several of his favorite themes: the partisan nature of American history that ignored the primacy of Spain in the New World and overlooked its record of heroism and the narrow-minded sectarianism that encouraged anti-Catholicism.[36] Hispanic peoples and their religious traditions, he argued, deserved respect.

Lummis occasionally hinted that Indian religions too deserved the same consideration, although on this score he was much less emphatic. At times, his proclivity for jaunty journalism or the easy joke superseded consideration. For example, he noted in his description of Isleta Pueblo's Day of the Dead festival, where family members placed food on graves, that those buried in front of the Pueblo church would "have the first square meal they have enjoyed in a twelvemonth." He never subjected Spanish traditions to such irreverent humor. While Lummis often treated Pueblo religion with dignity, he did not do so consistently.[37] In *Some Strange Corners of Our Country* (1891) Lummis, emphasizing "oddities" in keeping with the theme trumpeted in his title, characterized Indian religion as both superstitious and pagan. He devoted an entire chapter to the sensational aspects of the Hopi Snake Dance and referred to religious leaders as "conjurors" and "magicians." He used terms such as "civilized" (for Europeans or Anglo-Americans) and "savage" (for Indians). In this work, Lummis wished to arouse curiosity about and encourage Anglo tourism to the Southwest. If that meant depicting Indians as savages and their religion as pagan, so be it.[38]

In the final analysis, Lummis most wanted to encourage a broader appreciation of the Spanish and the Catholic Fathers whose heroism and devotion, he believed, qualified them as early martyrs. As he pronounced in the preface to *The Spanish Pioneers*, published in 1893, textbooks had not given them due recognition. But, "now, thanks to the New School of American History, we are coming to the truth,—a truth which every manly American will be glad to know. In this country of free and brave men, race-prejudice, the most ignorant of all human ignorances, must die out." Manhood was more worthy of respect than race or nationality, he went on. Championing masculinity and nationality in highly gendered language that nearly suffocates the reader, Lummis claimed, "We love manhood; and the Spanish pioneering of the Americas was the largest and longest and most marvelous feat of manhood in all history." The Spanish experience, as Lummis construed it, had one more quality he wanted to celebrate: ROMANCE. Although *The Spanish Pioneers* was meant as a "guideboard" rather than an exhaustive history of Spanish presence in the New World, Lummis hoped it would provide at least "a general understanding of the most romantic and gallant chapter in the history of America."[39]

Lummis, as antimodernist, described romance as "the chief riches of any People." In fact, he went on,

> *the most enduring and the most valuable things in the world are those you can not buy, nor sell, nor weigh, nor see—Sentiment—Beauty—Romance. The more universal the Sentiment, the older the Romance, the better.*[40]

For Lummis, the Spanish of New Mexico and California were the most sentimental, most romantic people in the country's history. Father Junipero Serra, for instance, belonged to days of "Chivalry and Romance and Adventure," although Lummis's description makes him sound as if he would be perfectly at home in the industrial age. More than a missionary, he was a leader of men, an adventurer, a "captain of industry, a fighter as well as a founder. Yet he has left

*Charles Fletcher Lummis promoted the Indian and Hispanic heritages of California and the Southwest throughout his career as journalist, publicist, and writer. Reproduced by permission of The Huntington Library, San Marino, California.*

so gentle a memory that his name is almost one of sainthood. I have never heard even a Ku Kluxer, rabid against his church," Lummis concluded, "fling a verbal rock at Fray Junipero."[41]

He also celebrated the secular Spanish settlers, publishing a book of photographs of Camulos, the ranch that served as inspiration for Helen Hunt Jackson's novel, *Ramona*. In this volume Lummis commemorated the ranch, and the Spanish way, through poetry:

> Untaint by greed of riches,
> That is our modern shame;
> Unchanged as in those far old days
> When Padre Serra came;
> Its white adobes face the sun,
> Its myriad wood-doves call—
> Its heart the heart of mother Spain—
> Of Spain before the fall![42]

The magazine, *In The Land of Sunshine,* which Lummis began editing in 1895, became the vehicle for his ideas and the outlet for his energies. Under Lummis's editorial control, this periodical, originally a business-supported journal for promotion of southern California, printed articles boosting California's climate, fruit, and appeal to both industry and tourism. But Lummis worked hard to increase the literary dimension of the magazine, publishing works by Mary Austin, Eugene Manlove Rhodes, Sharlot Hall, William E. Smythe, Joaquin Miller, Elizabeth and Joseph Grinnell, Ina Coolbrith, Charlotte Perkins Gilman, Theodore Hittell, L. Maynard Dixon, Grace Ellery Channing, and of course, Lummis himself. Significantly, the first article Lummis contributed was entitled "The Spanish-American Face," followed in succeeding issues by "The Old Mestizo" and "At the Old Hacienda." His enthusiasm for things Spanish became most evident in his announcement of a monthly column called a "A New Crusade" to save decaying California missions on the verge of total ruin. The preservation group named itself "The Landmarks Club," and Lummis dutifully printed the association's news in a monthly column. For Lummis, saving the missions was important, in part, because he believed tourists came to see romance. His motives, then, blended cultural and artistic impulses with crass commercialism. Still, Lummis and the Landmarks Club undoubtedly contributed to salvaging the physical remains of a number of southern California's premier historic structures, including the missions at San Juan Capistrano, San Fernando, and San Diego.[43]

Early issues of *Land of Sunshine* contained only an occasional article relating to Indians until 1899, when Horatio N. Rust's article, "A Fiesta at Warner's Ranch," signaled a new direction for the magazine. Rust described the festival in order to make a political point. "The white man's government generally breaks any pledge to an Indian if a white man asks it to," Rust wrote. "Unless some of the white men whose color strikes in as deep as their heart shall aid these simple children of nature, these first Californians, to keep their rights, they will be elbowed out from their little patrimony."[44]

Always ready for a fight, Lummis leaped in several months later with his own Indian concerns. Before long, his interest turned from writing about them to acting on their behalf. His initial effort focused on Indian education. After a meeting of Indian educators in Los Angeles, Lummis began an editorial series entitled "My Brother's Keeper," in which he renewed his campaign not against the goals of Indian education, but against the eastern philanthropists' philosophical, impractical approach to it. Unaware of the scientific studies of Indians carried on by Henry Lewis Morgan, Adolph Bandelier, and Washington Matthews, most eastern philanthropists were ignorant of Indian history, social organization, and, most important, humanity. He did not intend to slur the majority of Indian educators, mostly women who were "humane and womanly. There were some manly men, too." Rather, he aimed his literary arrows primarily at Carlisle Indian School founder and premiere Indian educator of the day, Richard Henry Pratt, "one of the most undilute materialists ever born in civilization." Pratt too was a "manly man," but "he has not yet learned that the Indian has a soul; that he loves his parents and his children, and even the birthplace that we have stolen from him." Particularly reprehensible to Lummis was Pratt's cruel practice of separating Indian children from their families. Philanthropists of Pratt's ilk, he concluded, "are no less heartless than the Apaches whose roasted victims I have seen 'pegged out'—only that they fool themselves (as well as us) into believing that their torture is a means of grace."[45]

In the issues that followed, Lummis expanded on these themes, adding that forced separation of families was unconstitutional and reminiscent of slave traders' tactics. When Pratt replied to Lummis's charges by dismissing him as "'a fantastic litterateur'" and *Land of Sunshine* as "'a thin little magazine,'" Lummis, the bantam cock, became further aroused. His attacks turned increasingly personal, devoting one entire article to haranguing Pratt for having neither the heart nor soul nor mind for Indian education, "a field out of which he has procured a very handsome living."[46]

Lummis's own talent rested more with pointed reproach than constructive suggestions for alternative approaches to Indian education. He did urge, however, cessation of separating children from their families, recommending instead they be educated in their own communities, where parents could simultaneously be brought into the educational process. Lummis also suggested the curriculum be adopted to Indians' capabilities, although what he meant by this is not entirely clear. Nowhere did Lummis describe Indians as innately inferior and so unable to benefit from education. In fact, he worried that the present system was designed to turn Indians into "a class of constitutional peons" or servants. What Lummis objected to was a curriculum which taught skills that proved irrelevant back on reservations. What, he believed, Indians needed most was to learn to read and write English, mostly to protect themselves from voracious whites who continued to covet Indian lands. Scientific farming and the rudiments of sanitation also made logical subjects for Indian study. "It would be best of all," Lummis wrote, "if he might learn that the New People who are so much smarter than he were also as decent; that only the vilest would impose on him and that they should be punished inevitably. That no man of us would turn father against son or son against mother; and that we really respect a home."[47]

Home was especially important to Lummis. His complaint about boarding schools focused not so much on their destruction of valuable cultures, but rather on valuable human ties, on families. Writing at the edge of the twentieth century, Lummis was not yet prepared to take on the whole concept of acculturation. Lummis was neither a radical reformer of Indian affairs nor an intellectual of great depth. Most often his commentary on Indians seemed more visceral than calmly considered. Still Lummis's demand for respect of Indian families and even Indian constitutional rights signaled an important step in the direction of overhauling Indian policy and the dominant culture's view of Indian people. His attacks on forced acculturation represent the beginnings of a more thorough-going reproach to "civilization's" Indian program that would emerge twenty years later.

In the meantime, Lummis expanded his Indian concerns beyond education issues, throwing himself into the case of the Warner's Ranch Indians. He disclosed, in the summer of 1901, that a group of prominent people was organizing on behalf of these Indians "whose only crime is that they were here first and that they have lands that stronger people hanker for." The February 1902 issue of *Land of Sunshine* announced the birth of the Sequoyah League whose vaguely stated goal was "To Make Better Indians." Among the concerns of these western reformers, the fate of California's so-called Mission Indians ranked highest. This organization of well-meaning white people bore all the characteristics of a paternalistic reform movement. Lummis's declaration of intent added his characteristically pugilistic comment:

> *If there are people who think they are strong enough to fight this organization to secure simple fair play, let them try; if there are people who think they are foxy enough to fool this organization, let them try . . . People who really knew better have maltreated the Indians just because it was no one's organized business to stop them; now it is some one's business.*[48]

Joining Lummis, who served as chair, on the Sequoyah League's Executive Committee were George Bird Grinnell, David Starr Jordan, and C. Hart Merriam. Beyond addressing the needs of California's Indians, the League intended to cooperate with the Indian Bureau while maintaining "a friendly watchfulness over" reservations. It expected to lobby for legislation that would assure Indians' security of home, family, and individuality; encourage education; and provide a market for Indian arts and crafts. Certainly, with its emphasis on education, individuality, and industry the Sequoyah League offered no wholesale rejection of the existing acculturation policy, although it rejected allotment as a panacea. Its essential thrust remained assimilationist. What the League particularly critiqued was eastern control over Indian affairs. Lummis seemed especially driven to inject insights from the West into national Indian policy.

For this reason, it was of utmost importance to Lummis to detach the Sequoyah League from eastern reform groups. He spent much time thinking about a name for this California-based organization and ultimately pushed for "Sequoyah," representing California's giant redwood trees, over "Tecumseh," "Tipi," and "Calumet" League, alternatives which carried eastern associations. Not the least of the League's advantages, in his estimation, was its physical proximity to actual Indians. In fact, he argued that his western organization represented "the nearest large highly civilized community to the largest number of Indians and Indian tribes."[49]

Furthermore, among Lummis's goals was the insinuation of more "Westerners" like himself and George Bird Grinnell, people who knew Indians because they had lived among them, into the national planning process for Indian affairs. Unlike the eastern-based Indian Rights Association which battled the Indian Bureau, Lummis thought the Sequoyah League should cooperate with the bureau by providing "authentic and disinterested information . . . actual knowledge, common sense, Patience and Steady Pressure." He wanted his organization to be as far away as possible from eastern philanthropists and to keep the latter from gaining control of the League. Lummis believed that President Theodore Roosevelt and the Indian Bureau sincerely wanted a better policy, that a sentiment of fair-play had grown in the American public, and that "we are it." As he wrote to Grinnell, "You and I have ached for [fair-play] for years—and now, I believe with all my heart, our hour has struck. Let's pile in; soberly, patiently, tactfully, but like good Out-Door men who know about what we want."[50]

For all of Lummis's talk about representing a western approach, many members of the Sequoyah League's Advisory Board were Easterners, including Grover Cleveland, ethnologist Alice Fletcher, and reformer Wendell P. Garrison. Grinnell and Merriam also lived in the East. Lummis's western emphasis was more rhetorical than substantive. In addition, nothing in the Sequoyah League's fundamental philosophy or approach to Indian reform signaled a significant departure from that of eastern groups. Finally, it is noteworthy that Lummis included the Omaha Francis LaFlesche, who lived in Washington, D.C., on the board in order "to have one real Indian."[51] But no other Indians, including those who wrote books and articles on Indian topics, engaged in political activity to institute reform, or hailed from California, New Mexico, and other western places, were invited to participate. In assuming Anglos were best qualified to direct Indian affairs, the Sequoyah League marched in step with other Indian reform groups of its time.

The first order of business for the Sequoyah League was to help the Cupeños who faced eviction from Warner's Ranch in southern California. They forfeited title to this property, according to a U.S. Supreme Court decision, by failing to present their claim to the Board of Land Commissioners which Congress had created in 1851. Consequently, the federal government concluded that they must move. The League put pressure on the government to either prevent the eviction or provide an alternative home and in 1902, partly through the influence of Lummis's acquaintance with Theodore Roosevelt, the League won some concessions. Lummis was appointed to the Warner's Ranch Indian Advisory Commission. After explaining to the Cupeños that Congress could not buy the Warner's Ranch land for them because its owner would not sell, the advisory commission traveled thousands of miles looking for a suitable alternative home. Eventually, they settled on some property at Pala, California. Congress appropriated the funds to purchase the land, and although the actual move from Warner's Ranch to Pala was characterized by confusion, sadness, resentment, and delay, the last of the group relocated by March 1903. The Sequoyah League leaders claimed victory and Lummis pronounced the case was the only one where the Indian was "moved to a better home than he was deprived of."[52]

After this long, drawn-out episode, the Sequoyah League and Lummis turned their attention to other Southwestern Indian issues. As a result of their efforts, in 1906, Congress appropriated $100,000 to purchase lands for San Diego County Indians. Less sanguine results, however, came from Lummis's campaign against Charles E. Burton, Superintendent and Disbursing Agent among the Hopi and Navajo. In 1902, Commissioner Jones encouraged agents to monitor, and discourage, Indians' long hair, dancing, dress, feasting, and body piercing. He especially wanted to discourage returning boarding school students from taking up such practices and suggested withholding rations and jobs and even jailing those who disobeyed these orders. Public outcry across the country convinced Jones to retreat, but some agents did not refrain from pushing the policy anyway. Burton was among them. He further incurred Lummis's wrath by sanctioning raids on Hopi homes to search for school truants and by allowing the use of corporal punishment in the schools. Lummis did not claim Burton was a scoundrel or a cheat but rather that he was an unfit agent. Dubbing him "Mr. Pinhead Burton," Lummis drew up a list of charges against the superintendent, sent a copy to Roosevelt, and demanded an investigation. But when a subsequent inquiry exonerated Burton, Roosevelt sent Lummis a sharp rebuke and Secretary of the Interior Ethan Allen Hitchcock demanded a public apology. Hitchcock also told Lummis that his "serious charges couched in excited and unwarranted language, correspondingly diminishes the value of your representations to the Department."[53]

While the Sequoyah League achieved some minor local victories, it never attained national prominence and by 1907, the organization disintegrated. Its inability to take off was noted as early as 1903, when Lummis wrote Grinnell that the League failed to arouse greater support. He still held out hope that his personal relationship with Theodore Roosevelt would help push Indian reform along, although he was vague about the nature of that reform, other than ending the more brutal aspects of forced acculturation and replacing incompetent Indian Department personnel with men who knew something about Indians. Lummis also harbored hopes of taking Roosevelt to Isleta and Acoma Pueblos where he could "see Indians, unboiled," for the President "doesn't yet know that the Indians are human." Alas, Roosevelt's trip west in 1903 did not allow time for such a visit and Lummis had to be content with meeting him at the Grand Canyon. Lummis continued to believe that if he could only get Roosevelt to Isleta Pueblo he "could teach him more in two hours . . . than he is likely to learn in his whole life about the real insides of Indians."[54]

In some respects Lummis's cantankerous personality proved the greatest impediment to his, or the League's, ability to influence policy. Eastern philanthropists had been wary of him since his early newspaper attacks on boarding schools. A Californian warned Roosevelt that Lummis was a "consummate crank" and by 1904, Roosevelt himself dismissed Lummis as "a wild coot." Even his ally, Grinnell, who allowed he was "picturesque" and "possessed of great activity and energy," admitted that Lummis, "like the rest of us," had his peculiarities.[55]

Lummis, of course, was not easily discouraged and though his influence with the president had weakened, he still hoped to install a knowledgeable and compassionate Commissioner of Indian Affairs. Lummis thought C. Hart Merriam or Grinnell, both true western men, could turn the agency around. To Lummis's overtures, however, Grinnell responded that he had never coveted the commissionership, partly because he had to earn a living but also "because I do not care to walk into the infernal regions of my own volition. The job is one of extreme difficulty, and if a man is going to put his heart into it I can fancy that it would come near driving him to drink, or to a lunatic asylum." Lummis explained that Merriam had suggested Grinnell's candidacy, assuming Grinnell would be willing to make the sacrifice for the chance to do some good. Although privately he had some reservations about Grinnell's suitability for the job, Lummis went on: "All the efforts of all the friends of the Indians for twenty years scattered around and doing little odd jobs here and there, no matter how well done, cannot effect one-hundredth part as much as if we can get the right Commissioner." All discussion came to an end when Roosevelt nominated Francis Leupp, former Washington agent of the Indian Rights Association, to the position.[56]

In the end, Lummis's hope for significant Indian reform on a national scale did not materialize for another twenty years until, a few years after Lummis's death, President Franklin Roosevelt appointed John Collier to the commissioner post. Yet when this new reform movement first appeared on the scene, Lummis was ready to endorse it. True, he did not lead the new movement—intellectually or politically—but he saw in it possibilities, values, and attitudes that he could support.

The fact that John Collier's interest in Indians began with New Mexico's Pueblos provided an important initial link between the two men. In the years following the Sequoyah League's demise, Lummis turned his attention to his job as Los Angeles City Librarian and to his dream of creating the Indian-oriented Southwest Museum. In the early 1920s, however, interest in Southwestern Indian affairs reignited with the Bursum Bill's threat to Pueblo land holdings and water rights. As the General Federation of Women's Clubs, under the leadership of John Collier, geared up to help the Pueblos fend off this latest assault on their property, Lummis enlisted in the fight. He wrote a "Sequoyah League Form Letter" on behalf of Collier and sent it to various contacts in New Mexico with personal messages attached. "For the first time since any of us can remember," Lummis wrote, "there looks to be a reasonable chance to hope for a betterment of Indian conditions in the Southwest." Both Indian Department bureaucrats and "Tenderfoot Philanthropists" had proved unequal to the task of providing justice to Indians, but now an intelligent, influential, committed movement had emerged under the leadership of John Collier. Among Collier's attributes: he lived for a year among the New Mexico Pueblos and he was "no tenderfoot nor wild theorist nor dreamer, but a fine fellow, earnest and sane and sympathetic, and a man of much weight." In handwritten notes on several letters, Lummis added this comment about Collier: "Now here is what we have been looking for a long time."[57] Lummis had found his man!

It is not clear how or when Collier and Lummis met, but by 1922, they were corresponding with one another. Collier assured Lummis his approach to "the Indian question is not romantic, but it is fundamental, and it is a good feeling to be thus working wholly *with* the Indians, from within, in a manner they thoroughly comprehend." By the next year, Lummis prepared to turn over the now dormant Sequoyah League's mailing list to the newly created American Indian Defense Association. He saw the new organization as a logical extension of his League and also regarded it as the "most vital and promising movement now afoot for justice to our Brown Brothers."[58]

That Collier's position was more "radical" than Lummis's of earlier decades apparently posed no problem. As a matter of fact, Collier assumed Lummis shared his views, for he sent Lummis a copy of a letter he wrote in response to the president of the General Federation of Women's Clubs' charge that Collier favored paganism over Christianity. Collier insisted that Indians had every civil right to religious freedom and expressed disappointment that this effort now numbered among its opponents the president of the General Federation of Women's Clubs.[59] Apparently, the letter quieted criticism from that corner. That Collier sent Lummis the letter suggests he expected Lummis to share his sentiments. By the 1920s, they saw one another as kindred spirits.

Lummis's failing health limited his full participation in this new movement for Indian reform but, in the last years of his life, Lummis managed to return to New Mexico and threw his support behind Collier and the new reformers. In 1926, he spent a day with Collier at the All Pueblo Council where Sotero Ortiz, president of the council, thanked God for sparing Lummis's life and then thanked Lummis for helping the Pueblos. Touched by their gratitude, Lummis spoke in Spanish and English to the assembly and when the meeting broke up, each Pueblo delegate shook Lummis's hand. A few of the oldest even embraced and prayed over him.[60]

Lummis continued to offer Collier advice about Indian affairs and in 1927 Collier, who looked upon Lummis as an ally, asked him to write letters to the Pueblos urging them to reject the Indian Bureau's call for a Pueblo council to replace their own All Pueblo Council. Lummis responded to this request with great energy, encouraging them to retain their All Pueblo Council and to insist the bureau meet with that body. Lummis concluded by reminding the Pueblos they had dignity and honor "as the First Americans" and should stand fast for their own representative council. A few weeks later Lummis wrote to Antonio Abeita of Isleta Pueblo about the council issue, adding that he wished he could attend the All Pueblo Council at Santo Domingo. "I would love to be there with My Pueblos, and to give them whatever advice I could." Critical of the Indian Bureau's tendency to infantilize Indians, Lummis ironically failed to see that tendency in his own interactions with them.[61]

Lummis made his last trip to New Mexico in the summer of 1927. The place, he wrote, "gets dearer to me all the time as I daily hate more and more the in rush of God-fearing chumps and tenderfeet from Ioway [*sic*] and waystations who have stolen the California that Was."[62] If California was spoiled, New Mexico still provided respite. That his own books and articles in *Land of Sunshine*, which promoted the region, might have contributed to California's supposed ruin did not occur to him.

By December 1927, Lummis realized he was dying, having been diagnosed with brain cancer. He informed friends he was not depressed but rather happy, serene even.[63] Still he wanted to get a few more things done and set to work writing. He turned to his favorite theme: the Romance of California and the Southwest. He had been disappointed, he once wrote to ethnologist Edgar Hewett, that the Southwest had failed to inspire a School of Writers. The fault lay not with the region but with "the times in general—we are not producing apostles or Crusaders or Conquistadores to whom the Southwest is a Gospel."[64] Lummis, then, poured himself into a final effort to create a Southwest literary tradition, publishing a book of verse entitled *A Bronco Pegasus* in 1928 and a collection of stories, *Flowers of Our Lost Romance*, posthumously in 1929.

In the introduction to *Bronco*, Lummis indicated he had devoted little time to verse in recent years as he was engaged in building a museum, saving missions, and fighting for Indian rights. Now, in the last years of his life, Lummis wanted to celebrate through poetry his heroes who included Theodore Roosevelt, Geronimo, and a Pueblo Indian man named Santiago Naranjo. In his poem about Geronimo, which Lummis described as the "last thing I ever wrote and the most powerful," it was clear that his perception of the Apaches had mellowed considerably over the years. Now they represented to him the essence of true heroism that the modern world could only mimic through the shallow, shadowy reflections of Hollywood movies.

> But here an Epoch petered out,
> An era ended flat;
> The Apache was the Last Frontier—
> The Tragedy is *that*!
>
> ENVOY
>
> It had to be—it *has* to be!
> The Primitive must go!
> We keep the Ten Commandments—yes—
> ten reels—a picture show!
> Our life alike the movie mob,
> all scurrying, bad and good—
> *Ah*! Give me back Geronimo—
> the Border—and Leonard Wood![65]

As if uncertain that his poetry would make the point emphatically enough, Lummis added a prose version which detailed the Apache side of the 1886 war.

ummis explained in 1928, were not savages or primitives (his on to that effect notwithstanding). Rather, their political, so- ous "culture-stage was well-advanced." And although "progress" . the Apaches be kept restrained on a reservation, it did not dictate hould be cheated by Indian agents. As a result of fraud and villainy on them, these people "had far deeper grievances than led our forefa- ring the bell at Lexington." Speaking from his forty-four year, intimate ledge of Indians from Canada to Chile, Lummis concluded, "If halfway norably treated, they are everywhere good citizens."[66]

It is a sign of Lummis's evolving attitudes that an Apache warranted such a view. It is a sign of Lummis's ability to sustain an idea, over the course of time, that his most positive image of Indians came in the poem about the Pueblo man, Santiago Naranjo:

By Rio Grande's Chama-reddened flood
That drains the Sandstone Giants of their blood—
What see you in the West? The urgent day
When this our upstart, Panic Hour shall pay
The price they pay who fall from Reverence
And worship Smartness and the Present Tense.

Or see you backward until the world was young,
When here your fathers autochthonic sprung—
No immigrants, but First Born of the Soil,
Who wrought here through millenniums of toil,
That aristocracy was ancient when
Our forefathers bruted in some British fen? . . .

Of Poet, nor what Greek Philosopher?

Yet we forget you in the nation's plan—
An Indian—THE FIRST AMERICAN.[67]

In his final contribution to Southwest myth-making, *Flowers of Our Lost Romance*, Lummis was less inclined than in earlier versions to undercut Indians. He acknowledged the cost of Spanish conquest to Indians and noted that Indian subjugation was "accomplished by equal subversions—religious, linguistic, educational, and commercial." Moreover, in contrast to earlier renditions, he now consistently argued that Indians offered their share of mystery, idealism, imagination, and romance. Indians, like the Spanish, "had the natural human heritage of those poetic qualities, which in the Puritans were warped and soured by peculiar circumstances and by an ingrowing pietism, with an abhorrence of joy as a danger to the soul."[68] At the end of his life, Lummis found himself exalting both Indian and Spaniard and, to the very end, disparaging New England's Puritans.

That he maintained his personal identity with Spanish rather than Indian people, however, was revealed in the epitaph he wrote for himself:

> Chas. F. Lummis
> March 1, 1859 to———
> He founded the Southwest Museum
> He built this house and gave it to
> the Museum as an Auxiliary.
> He saved four Old Missions.
> He studied and recorded Spanish America.
> He tried to Do his share.[69]

Apparently, he did not feel his efforts with regard to Indians warranted mention.

Scholars who have examined Lummis's work agree he was not a great writer but conclude he was, as Kevin Starr put it, "a dynamic force for regional identity." According to another scholar, Lummis needed constant attention and to get it, he wrote quickly and impatiently. As a result his books, intended for popular audiences, were neither well documented nor scholarly. They lacked intellectual depth and were promotional, superficial, and romantic. Yet, for all his weaknesses, Lummis remains a significant source for popular Southwest cultural history. Historian Edwin Bingham agreed Lummis was not a skilled writer but went on to conclude that as a pioneer in the literary discovery of the Southwest, Lummis deserved recognition. Moreover, Bingham maintained, Lummis was an effective fighter for Indian rights, successful preserver of historic landmarks, and founder of the Southwest Museum. "He got things done."[70]

Among the other things he got done: publishing eighteen books over forty years, most printed by major East Coast publishing houses; editing *Land of Sunshine/Out West*, a journal that appealed primarily to educated people from the middle and upper-middle classes who were inquisitive about California and the Southwest; organizing, if only for a few years, a West Coast Indian rights group that saw tangible results for a handful of California Indians; serving briefly as a consultant to Theodore Roosevelt on Indian affairs; and near the end of his life, throwing his support behind John Collier and the next generation of Indian reformers. Collier certainly believed Lummis was influential, honoring him posthumously in a poem entitled "The Indians' Charles Fletcher Lummis."

> Dead! . . . And I see in thought, as long ago,
> Angels of earth—dark rains by mesas far;
> And Indian holy land, your dream now know
> Past age where no pueblo Camelots are.
> Tongue, deed, and bronze, and dye; none yet have shown
> Like your emprise, that desert's mystic span;
> From your dead deed, that Indian life is sown,
> A deathless harvest to eternal Man . . .

ıly—the sweet old men, who long have known
ıiend great in the changed and conquering time.
ıen welcome their own, their own;
gone, has gone into the prime.
Lummis has gone into the longed-for cloud.
Has gone into the grass which answers prayer,
Has gone where Indians round the great drum crowd.
The world soul takes its own. Lummis is there![71]

Lummis would have enjoyed this image of himself. He also would have appreciated Edgar Hewett's final assessment: "To him," Hewett claimed, "life was battle. His very dreams, beneficent as they were, brought him into ceaseless conflict and repeated failure; yet from failure came fruition, came mastery of life."[72]

Walking into the West in 1884, Lummis collided with other cultures, ways of life, and people he had never heard about in New England. He devoted the rest of his life to sharing these newfound insights with his countrymen and fighting those who insisted on defining American culture from an East Coast perspective. In the process, he contributed to his nation's reconsideration of Indians, helped prepare the American reading public to accept a view that venerated Indian cultures, chided an Anglo-American culture intent on destroying them, and in his last years, supported reforms instituted by John Collier. Finally, he fostered, and of course fought with, other Southwestern writers who shared his views. George Wharton James became one of Lummis's favorite punching bags.

# 7

# OUT OF ARIZONA

## *George Wharton James*

JANUARY 1900, THE DAWN OF THE NEW CENTURY, found Charles Fletcher Lummis particularly perturbed. He was infuriated that George Wharton James, a disgraced Methodist minister-turned-Indian-and-Southwest-enthusiast, was speaking on Indian subjects at such prestigious venues as New York's Columbia University. James, according to Lummis, was a "notorious scoundrel—not a mere libertine but a fellow degraded from the pulpit for unspeakable vileness—a notorious liar who even lies about science to puff himself." It was outrageous, Lummis wrote to ethnologist Washington Matthews, that such a man, one of those "pimps that prostitute science and live upon the earnings of her shame," should address "honest students."[1] His sin? George Wharton James had plagiarized a report by Matthews on the Navajo Fire Dance.

Up to this point, Lummis told Matthews, he considered James too contemptible to acknowledge. But now that he had published a book on the Grand Canyon and, one presumes, threatened to challenge Lummis's self-imposed role as sole interpreter of the Southwest, James "need[ed] exposure." Moreover, James's sins as writer found corollary in his sins as a man. Drawing on a large reservoir of righteousness, Lummis informed Matthews that James was once a Long Beach, California, minister who "was caught in unutterable vileness, tried by the church & expelled." He disappeared for a few years but eventually reemerged in southern California, where he found employment at tourist hotels. He worked at the Mount Lowe Hotel until he was "caught in flagrante with a Irishwasher." Eventually, he married the "ancient widow" of a Methodist elder and made a precarious living by lecturing and guiding tourist parties to the Grand Canyon. "He is a dead beat," Lummis concluded, "He isn't a rising scientist; but with his gall & oily speech he gets in with the ignorant tourists & they support him."[2] Lummis wanted to ensure James would not secure further recognition from eastern sources.

Actually, Matthews was less aroused about the plagiarism than with the distortions of Matthews's original meanings and the false additions he made. To his disgust, the Bureau of Ethnology had invited James to write a paper on the

Havasupai because he had lived among those people for several summers. Apparently, Bureau ethnologist Frederick W. Hodge extended the invitation believing that "'even a sponge would have absorbed information in that time.'" A flawed person's work was better than no work at all. Demonstrating his own capacity for venom, Matthews told Lummis that "compar[ing James] to a sponge is a libel on that stupid but honest little animal." Finally, Matthews closed with, "I pity the poor little dishwasher who could find no more worthy lover."[3]

Lummis next struck out by publishing an attack entitled "Untruthful James" in *Land of Sunshine*. Matthews did his part on the East Coast. When James attempted membership into the American Philosophical Society, Washington Matthews assured its doors would not open to "*that* man."[4] Lummis and Matthews, powerful enemies, managed to slam shut many a door when James tried to slip his foot into a room of scientific respectability. People have looked upon James's work with suspicion ever since.[5] Such detractors cast a long shadow, but they were not mighty enough to silence James. Nor did James return these attacks with counter-attacks. He simply ignored them, turned the other cheek, and kept writing and lecturing about the West and its Indians, reaching audiences not only in California but also all across the country.

To be sure James felt the sting of Lummis's charges and took great pains to assure his readers that he did have credentials, particularly personal experience among Indians. In his book on Navajo blankets, for example, James testified that the work resulted from long study and personal association. He had spent thirty years among the Navajos, visiting them, watching weavers work, eating their food, and listening to their stories. He also insisted upon his honorable intentions to give full and complete credit to his sources. He cared less about being perceived as an "*original* writer" than a thorough one reading widely among the more scientific or academic works on Southwestern Indians and always giving full credit to these authors when he incorporated their insights into his own publications.[6] In fact, so many of James's books contain lengthy quotations from scholars' writings that one is more inclined to charge him with laziness than theft.

Nor was he faint of heart. James believed southern California could support more than one writer about Indians. Although he could not have mistaken Lummis's deep disdain, even hatred, James corresponded with him anyway, asking in 1907 for information on the Sequoyah League to be used in a book on California Indians.[7] In 1912, he interviewed Lummis for a series of articles on literati. And for all of Lummis's efforts to set himself apart from James, the two had much in common. They shared a basic interest in and sympathy for Indian cultures, although neither had scientific or academic training in archeology or anthropology. They both imparted their vision of Indians through popular, rather than academic, works. They used Indians as vehicles for social criticism and denounced certain aspects of U.S. Indian policy. Finally, they encouraged perpetuation of Indian cultures. James, however, put greater emphasis on the supposed universal artistic and spiritual aspects of Southwestern Indians' lives, pushing for recognition of their place in the "family of man" on that basis. He also went further than Lummis in offering up Indians as models of "the simple life" and as counterpoints to the unattractive, unhealthy aspects of modernity. James, in fact, devoted an entire book to the subject of what the "white race," and the modern world, should learn from Indians—a work published over one decade earlier than Mabel Dodge Luhan and John Collier began their campaign to promote Indians as examples for emulation.

Like the other authors examined here, James's path to Indians was indirect. Unlike them, however, James was not American born. He hailed from Gainsborough, England, where he was born in 1858, the son of a cooper and basketmaker. After only a few years of formal schooling, James became a bookseller's apprentice. He began preaching in the local Methodist Church and writing articles about local history. From an early age he exhibited predilections that some of his fellow countrymen may have seen as peculiar. At age twelve, for instance, he became a vegetarian. A few years later he decided to stop shaving and grew a lifelong beard. By age twenty-three, he had married a grocer's daughter, immigrated to America, and found work as an itinerant Methodist minister among the miners of Nevada. Apparently, a search for good health explained the move to America. Eventually, the James family moved to California and, although British by birth he was, according to one historian, "rapidly becoming a 'Westerner' in his informal ways and addiction to nature study."[8]

In 1889, James held a pastorate in Long Beach when his wife charged him with adultery, brutality, incest, and several other less inflammatory crimes, and moved out of their home.[9] Scandal erupted. James countercharged his wife with adultery. The newspapers gobbled it up and James lost his job, reputation, and family. He was, according to his biographer, "an unwelcome and reviled man in California."[10] In the wake of such personal crisis, James wandered off into the wilderness, camping under the open skies of Arizona and New Mexico, becoming acquainted with some of the Southwest's Indians, and finding solace in Nature and Nature's people. Unlike Walter McClintock, James did not settle in with one group or tribe. Although he spent months with the Havasupai, he did not engage in deep, long-term observations of them. Rather, he kept on the move, visiting many tribes including Hopi, Zuni, Navajo, Wallapai, and Pueblos of the Rio Grande. God's natural creation, more than His scriptural works, became the foundation of the new life James built after the shambles of Long Beach. Although he never forsook Christianity, his sermons now took the form of more secular lectures, articles, and books about Nature, the Southwest, and Indians.[11]

James also lived in Chicago during his self-imposed banishment from California. It was those years, from 1890 to 1892, that he developed a new career, lecturing, a popular form of entertainment. He toured Midwestern cities, offering programs from a menu of over one hundred lectures he had prepared, many of them slide-illustrated. James touted himself as "Professor," although he had no academic training which entitled him to that appellation. Finally, in 1893, he returned to southern California where he found employment as social director of the Echo Mountain Hotel, a resort in Pasadena. In time he offered more professional tours for organizations such as the Southern California Hotel Association. His writing commenced in 1894 and James published *Nature Sermons*, a work in which he now "found God in His works, in Nature and its beauties."[12] Several guidebooks followed, as James developed a tour business. By the time of his death in 1923, he had churned out numerous books and myriad articles, edited several magazines, become something of an amateur anthropologist, collected Indian artifacts including baskets and blankets for trade, boosted California and its literature, and campaigned for Indian rights.

Most likely the vast majority of James's readers, as well as the tourists whom he guided, knew little if anything of the scandal that disrupted his earlier career. Yet those personal troubles led James to Indians and to the region which offered a different path. His books, "widely read and widely reviewed," according to one analysis, "promoted the region as . . . a place in which a man, reveling in the midst of God's pristine creation, can reshape his life to its full potential."[13] James could point to no better example than himself. Although he provided none of the lurid details, James did confess that when he was young and when "life seemed a horrible nightmare, when men and women shunned me for that which I was not, I fled them and sought refuge in the solitudes of the desert and canyon." There he encountered only Indians, birds, and animals. There he regained his bearings and found peace, serenity, and joy. And there "my real spiritual birth occurred."[14]

Like many a new convert, James felt compelled to share the story of his personal regeneration. Most of his books, however, revealed greater zeal than skill. In fact, most lacked enduring literary merit, while exhibiting many of James's worst excesses, boosterism, overenthusiasm, and bald-faced hucksterism. James was more entrepreneur than scholar. Moreover, his own Radiant Life Press published a good number of his books. But at his best he was a moving celebrant of the West, and some scholars today agree that *The Wonders of the Colorado Desert* is his finest work, containing passages that reach the sublime.[15]

James was also a celebrant of Indians. His approach to Indians, as Lummis certainly understood, proved less than systematic, scientific, or sensitive. In addition, his methods of collecting information could be downright offensive. It is something of a wonder that he was able to garner as many photographs, acquire as many baskets and blankets, and gather as much information as he did. James barged into many situations, took what he could get, and gave no thought to what the long-term consequences of his actions might be for others who followed him.[16] Of course, when he thought about the proper approach to Indians, as subject of camera or pen, he recommended sensitivity. The ethnologist, he explained, need not be a scientist but he did need to be humble. He should not display scorn for Indians' social and religious practices, for who would want to share the inner meanings of ceremonials with a person who saw them as foolish or superstitious? Instead, the ethnologist should be nonjudgmental, friendly, open, and honest. He should not ask questions and should demonstrate great patience. James waited over ten years before the Havasupai invited him into their sweatlodge. But once welcomed, he claimed, "there came . . . an open sesame to all the songs and ideas of the people . . . Patience paid." Finally, James cautioned against offering money for information. Such practices did more harm than good.[17]

In reality, James broke all these rules—time and again. He proved particularly obnoxious with his camera. Amazingly, he recorded detailed descriptions of his offenses, apparently assuming readers would sympathize with him rather than with his reluctant Indian subjects. When he first visited Acoma Pueblo, for instance, he understood the Indians there opposed his efforts to photograph them. James would not be denied. One morning he knew the pueblo's governor and his staff would be attending mass. So, James placed his camera before the church door and waited for the entourage. When the governor arrived, James interested him in a microscope he brought along as a diversion. Just when the Pueblo men relaxed and sat down to smoke on the church steps, James sauntered over to his camera, pressed the bulb, and captured the image. "The moment they heard the click of the shutter, however, they jumped to their feet in alarm & another photograph, made not more than 30 seconds later, shows them wrapped up in their blankets, half angry & half alarmed. It took me some time to conciliate."[18] When the Hopi allowed him into the Antelope kiva, they asked him to take no photos. James ignored the request, removed the cap from his lens, and let the dim kiva light do its work on the sensitive plate. The result, he boasted, was a fine photograph. He also pursued Indian children, insisting on capturing their images when they proved reluctant. Bribes of candy, a tactic Lummis also used, helped bring them around.[19]

James was especially proud of his nonposed portraits. He criticized the work of a more celebrated photographer, presumably Edward Curtis, whose posed pictures distorted the realities of Indians' lives. In contrast, James boasted, his subjects were rarely posed. "I catch him on the fly or wait until he begins to talk to some one naturally or unaffectedly."[20] In short, James stole his pictures and unapologetically acknowledged that his subjects often objected. He described one portrait of a Chemehuevi man he met along the Colorado River this way: "His face clearly shows questioning, antipathy, and the querulousness of an old man who asks an unwelcome visitor, 'What on earth have you come for? Why don't you leave us alone?' "[21] Distasteful as his methods may strike late-twentieth-century readers and as obvious as some Indians' contempt for him was, he was able to capture Indian people in moods that eluded other photographers, including annoyance and disdain.

Not only did James deliberately ignore Indians' requests concerning photography, but he also forced himself into sacred places, offered bribes for both information and artifacts, asked all kinds of questions, and violated taboos with abandon. While visiting Zuni Pueblo, James "laughingly" suggested to his escort, Dick Tsnahey, that they take several figures from the "Ma-a-si-lima" and "Ah-a-yu-ta shrine." Tsnahey was terrified at the thought of the consequences such depredation would bring down upon him. James stole nothing but admitted his "cupidity was aroused." When he wanted to go to another sacred site called "Unahikah," Tsnahey denied its existence. His son, who had attended one of the government-sponsored Indian schools, however, agreed to lead James there. The young man's education had caused him to question Zuni ceremonies and to conclude they were superstitious. He had learned something else "from his white association and teaching," according to James. "[H]is earnest query was: 'What you give me, I show you Unahikah?' "[22]

And so, Dick Tsnahey, his son, and James visited the site. After James had taken his photographs, the elder Tsnahey asked James to leave first, to assure himself that the white man stole nothing. James refused because he had every intention of taking not one but two of the "idols." Argument turned to negotiation and finally James spirited away two Zuni figures. He claimed that this was the "first and only attempt at plundering a sacred shrine I ever made." Yet he was unrepentant. After all, he might add, he had Zuni coconspirators working, although reluctantly, with him. Moreover, he retained the two figures in his possession and "as I have not dried up, been blown away, or had any other fearful thing happen to me, I am fain to believe that the conduct I have related has not brought upon me either the censure, disapprobation, or vengeance of the gods."[23]

That it might bring the censure or disapprobation of the Zuni or other Indians did not apparently concern him. To make his behavior appear even more pernicious to modern sensibilities, James presented this story in a book designed to attract tourists to New Mexico. He offered a model of how to be an offensive visitor and an antiquities thief, with no caution about why this kind of behavior might be inappropriate, illegal, or counterproductive to long-term friendly relations or mutual understanding and respect.

Sometimes James made friends and discovered willing informants among the Indians of the Southwest. Sometimes he irritated and infuriated them. Sometimes he amused them. Tawaquaptewa and Monroe Fredericis remembered that the Hopi thought James was a "chica-wimpke" or clown because of his long beard. When he asked them funny questions, they gave him funny answers. James himself was aware that he frequently became the butt of Indian jokes. His Havasupai guide's recital of an exploration into Beaver Canyon gone awry, because of James's failure to secure the rope that would help them climb out again, provided much mirth around the Havasupai cookfire. James didn't mind. "Knowing the joking propensities of his people and their utter indifference to the feelings of any person out of whom they can extract a little fun, I was prepared for the rude jokes and vulgar witticisms expended upon me, and sat eating and drinking with the stolidity of a Hottentot—or a Havasupai."[24]

On another occasion, James found himself the target of both Indian humor and hostility. While visiting Hosteen D-a-zhy, a Navajo, he mentioned that when he visited the Hopis, Acomas, and Zunis, the women shampooed his head. So, Da-a-zhy asked his daughter to give James a shampoo. At first she resisted, complaining that she already had enough to do, shampooing her husband. But when her father admonished her for being rude to the stranger, she relented. During the shampoo, however, she made "droll" remarks about James's beard and when she asked if he would like her to clean that as well, he agreed. "Laughingly I bade her put [the suds] everywhere she liked, and just as my mouth was at its widest she brought up a handful of suds and filled it full." James's choking only made them laugh harder and then the Navajo woman added, "'It is a good thing that you got a mouthful. White men need to have their mouths washed out pretty often!'"[25]

Whatever the nature of his relations with Indians, whether friendly or hostile, spiritual or commercial, substantive or superficial, for over thirty years James collected information, stories, anecdotes, art works, blankets, baskets, and religious objects. Some of these objects found their way into his own collection. Others found their way onto the market. In some respects, all that he gathered became grist for his entrepreneurship. For above all, James meant to make a living out of his relationships with Indians. It is not surprising, then, that some of his published works focus on Indian artistry, in part because of its commercial potential. Yet he saw it as much more. His book on Indian basketry, for instance, is a guidebook for the serious collector or dealer, offering detailed information on the uses of Indian baskets from one tribe to another and the various symbols and designs found on them. It is also a treatise on the supposed universal art impulse that Indians, particularly Indian women, demonstrated through their work: "mythology, religion, worship, poetry and history [are] all woven with busy brain and tireless fingers into baskets which the unversed regard as mere examples of crude and savage workmanship," James declared.[26]

Countering his readers' presumed assumptions about Indian inferiority, James insisted that while these artists were "primitive," they were also "thoughtful, sentient, poetic people."[27] Just as whites produced paintings, poetry, sculpture, and architecture which expressed their "art instinct," so too did Indian women create baskets as the repository of their own poetic impulses and aspirations. In short, while the novice observer would merely see a pleasant or harmonious design in an Indian basket, the expert would discern "a heart's thankfulness, a poet's song, a devotee's prayer, an artist's masterpiece."[28]

Beyond celebrating Indian artistry, James struggled to answer these questions: From where or what does the artistic instinct derive? What led Indian women to experiment with color, form, and symbolism? Did the designs originate in a distant shore or did they emerge from Indian minds? In the end, he admitted he did not know the answers, although he had a strong hunch that observation and imitation of Nature provided initial inspiration. Furthermore, he was certain that the complexity of designs was neither purposelessness nor merely imitative but rather signified a deep meaning to the weaver. James asserted, in a statement reminiscent of C.E.S. Wood, that understanding the weaver's artistic inclination would bring his countrymen "a long step nearer the goal of knowledge which will reveal the Indian to us, not the dumb, unintelligent, unimaginative, unreligious character we have too long regarded him, but as a mentally alert, intelligent, observant, imaginative, poetic and religious being."[29]

Navajo blankets performed the same purpose. They too functioned as specimens of the human race's "art development" and served as powerful deterrents to those inclined to dismiss Indians. The variety of designs Navajo women weavers incorporated into their blankets, for example, revealed "that the 'artistic temperament' is to be found among the aborigines as well as in the most 'advanced' civilization."[30] True, James relied on such terms as "aborigine" and "advanced civilization" but by inserting quotation marks around the latter, he began to undermine the validity of such categories. Finally, he revered those blankets which had small imperfections. They were especially valuable because they signaled "the *human touch*, that flash of life and reality that sets it distinct and apart from machine work. It makes it the work of a personal, living, sentient human being."[31] James, the antimodernist, cherished blankets and baskets with irregularities or imperfections. Tiny flaws meant the baskets and blankets were individualistic, artistic, and authentic rather than homogeneous, manufactured, and mechanical. By virtue of both their imperfections and their artistry these objects demonstrated that Indians were human beings who deserved their place in the brotherhood of man.[32]

Of course, James could not deny that commercial impulses had invaded Navajo blanket making, with unfortunate consequences. In earlier days, before commercialism had overtaken many of the Navajos, the weavers blended into their blankets reverent thoughts, religious ideas.[33] The baneful influence of a "money-mad civilization" had changed that. Yet James believed that the Navajo remained an essentially religious people and that their blanket designs retained some sacred and mysterious meanings. Moreover, their ceremonials could vie with those of any people for allegory, symbolism, and intricacy of ritual. The same was true of other Southwestern Indians' religions. While an intelligent Protestant could grasp the meaning of complex Catholic ritual in a very short time, it would take "half a lifetime" to grasp the full significance and complexity of Pueblo religious symbolism.[34]

Many Americans failed to understand this, however. Just as many dismissed Indians as savage and thus missed their artistry, so did they categorize Indians as heathen and miss their deeply religious natures. While most cultured Americans would assume nothing good could come from the prayers and songs of a barbaric Navajo, James confessed that he hoped songs, blessings, and benedictions had been sung over the blankets he purchased. "I like to think that the Navaho woman . . . before she began work upon [my blanket] prayed that only beautiful things should come in touch with it."[35]

Given James's background as a man of the cloth, it is not surprising that Indian religion interested him. What is perhaps more unusual is his advocacy of tolerance or religious relativism. White men, James believed, would never be able to understand Indian religions until they had banished their prejudices and approached the subject with an open mind. That entailed a willingness to see their religious ideas *"as the Indian himself sees them."* Unfortunately, this was particularly difficult when it came to religion. Few people could understand another's religion, and it was especially difficult for white men to understand an Indians's reverence for a rattlesnake.[36]

He meant to open his readers' eyes and hearts. The Navajo believed in shamans and the cowardly among them called upon these men to exact revenge on their enemies. But was this so different from white men, those "despicable wretches [who] attack their foes through the columns of newspapers or in the pages of magazines?", James asked, in a rare swipe at Lummis.[37] In the end, he tried to encourage the ethnologists' ethic of observation and description without judgment. If James did not always realize this goal in his work, in relaying this basic concept—or aspiration—to people who read his books, took his tours, or listened to his lectures, James spread the idea far wider than could its more scholarly and academic adherents.

Like George Bird Grinnell, James wanted to break down his countrymen's resistance to acknowledging fundamental Indian humanity. In the process, he did not intend to ignore their faults or turn a blind eye to their evils. But he did want to point out their capacity for good, which James believed had been ignored. Moreover, when their "goodness is combined with the simplicity and childlikeness of the uncorrupted Indian, then there is a combination that is as delightful as it is rare. This combination I have found far more often among the Indians than I have in my own race."[38] The reason whites refused to acknowledge the good in Indians, James maintained, was because of a strange psychological tendency among people to deny the honorable and noble in those they have injured. Whites willfully closed their eyes to positive Indian qualities and acknowledged only meanness and evil because whites have acted so unjustly to Indians. Indians, he acknowledged, had murdered and terrorized whites in the past, but such behavior usually derived from self-defense as they were driven to warfare by whites. James was now dedicated to altering images of Indians, not by ignoring their vices, crimes, or ignorance, but by being honest and just and promoting Indians' good qualities to the world.[39]

James went one step further to conclude that, in some respects, Indians were superior to whites. Nearly twenty years after his congregation spurned him and he ventured out into the desert, James published *What The White Race May Learn From the Indian*. The title was designed to startle its readers, to jolt them out of complacency about presumed Indian inferiority. James found much to criticize about American civilization. James, the former minister, found many sins in society. Finally, James, the scorned and reviled, found delicious pleasure in turning the tables on the sanctimonious, who had tossed him out of his Long Beach pulpit, by preaching that Indians, who many believed to be iniquitous, heathen, and unethical, were actually, in many ways, superior to their Christian brothers.

He did not deny Indians' shortcomings including smoking, wearing dirty clothes, mistreating animals, using coarse language and humor, and drinking dirty water. But, he argued, one could still learn from imperfect people. The book, which seems thrown together and sometimes downright silly, is hardly a systematic critique of American culture or a carefully crafted defense of Indian cultures. Yet there is no mistaking James's simple life philosophy at the book's core:

> *I call upon the white race to incorporate into its civilization the good things of the Indian civilization; to forsake the injurious things of its pseudo-civilized, artificial and over-refined life, and to return to the simple, healthful, and natural life which the Indians largely lived.*[40]

*What the White Race May Learn* is James's most self-conscious construction of Indianness, inspired partly by experiences with actual Indian people but mostly by James's obsessions, compulsions, interests, and imagination. It is a "how-to book on health, an anthropological study . . . a manual on morality . . . a catalog of James's fantasies," as one scholar put it.[41] The book summarizes his own ideas about how people should live, raise children, eat, and exercise. It did not evolve from any serious study of Indian cultures or careful observation of Indian ways. Quite simply it offers James's view of the world grafted onto American Indians, although it is interesting that he believed claiming this as Indian behavior would help his case.

One can certainly imagine Lummis gritting his teeth upon reading portions of it. How could anyone take James's authority on Indians seriously when he argued that among the beneficial lessons one could learn from Indians was the art of nasal breathing?[42] But James also encouraged readers to imitate Indians' outdoor life. Only when he began climbing up and down canyon walls, wandering the southwestern deserts, rowing and swimming the Colorado River, and coming into intimate contact with many Indians, did he realize the tangible benefits of a "simple, natural, and therefore healthy life." Vigorous exercise outdoors would not only restore health to the body, but also the mind and soul. James believed that the outdoor life was responsible for insanity being practically unknown among Indians. In addition, the outdoor life encouraged the Indian to be an early riser and early retirer in contrast to the "civilized habit of turning night into day, living in the glare of gas and electric light" which is "artificial, unnatural, and unhealthful."[43]

Interestingly, throughout this paean to the Indians' outdoor life, James never called upon actual Indians to support this message. Instead, he turned to European or American writers for reinforcement: John Muir, Robert Lewis Stevenson, and the editor of *Good Health*, Dr. J. H. Kellogg. James claimed that he knows "scores and hundreds of dusky-skinned Henry D. Thoreaus and John

Burroughses, John Muirs and Elizabeth Grinnells," but never does he name one.[44]

Other aspects of Indian life James prized included their belief in the dignity of physical labor. They were not ashamed to get their hands soiled. Rich and well-educated Americans, on the other hand, avoided it. One might wonder whence such an idea came, for James himself never engaged in manual labor as a bookseller, minister, or author/tour guide/lecturer. Whatever his own acquaintance with manual labor, James celebrated its advantages not only for Indian men, but women as well. As an example, James offered up, without a hint of irony, the "woman who honors us by coming to our house weekly to do the heavy work." But why did he deny his own wife the opportunity to achieve "the refinement of a gloriously healthy woman radiating physical, mental, spiritual life upon all those who come within the sphere of her influence"?[45]

James, in fact, found much to commend in Indian women. They taught their children about sex in an open and wholesome way. They did not joke about it, keep it a secret, or assume it was unholy or unclean. When they gave birth, he testified, they did so free from pain. Loosely fit clothing, an openness and freedom with their bodies, exercise, outdoor living, and, of course, nasal and deep breathing all explained their easy births. James lauded Indian mothers who breast-fed their babies and scolded civilized ones who refused to do so because they feared it would destroy the contours of their breasts, demand too close confinement, or keep them from attending club and other social functions. He also applauded the Indian practice of allowing children to run nude and decried those missionaries and teachers who taught them to be ashamed of their bodies. "[W]e are foisting on to them our hateful, impure, and blasphemous conceptions of nudity," he wrote. James, something of a nudist advocate himself, admitted that Indian adults did not go nude, but he believed in the "sanctity of nudity" and encouraged the end of shame when men saw nude men or women saw nude women. Although he did not advocate open nudity between men and women ("Let the sexes remain apart") and while he opposed what he called "promiscuous nudity," he was equally opposed to the attitude that nudity was wrong or "that the Creator did not know His business when he created us both nude and of different sexes."[46]

Other Indian attributes James promoted included a simple diet and slow, thorough chewing. He could not claim that Southwestern tribes were vegetarian, but they did not eat meat habitually and so, he maintained, they were more or less vegetarians. Mealtime provided an opportunity to observe another Indian characteristic which James urged his readers to imitate: genuine hospitality without ostentation or extravagance. When a person arrived unexpectedly at an Indian's door, the visitor was expected to join the family for a meal. It was not a matter of invitation but rather "the daily expression of their lives." As noted earlier, hospitality could sometimes go beyond sharing meals to shampoos. Indians, James informed his readers, shampoo and take steambaths regularly. He had never felt so clean as when he took a Havasupai sweat-

*George Wharton James found in "Indians" models for alternative practices ranging from nudity to vegetarianism. His rather unorthodox ideas, and a tendency to rely on others' work, brought him the scorn of Charles Fletcher Lummis. Reproduced by permission of The Huntington Library, San Marino, California.*

bath, jumped into cool waters, rubbed down with mud, and then jumped back into the river. For those who assumed that Indians' ragged and dirty clothes signaled a dirty body, James cautioned that appearances could be deceiving.[47]

One other aspect of Indians' life that James wanted white people to emulate was their aversion to accumulating things. This is somewhat surprising given that he made a living, in part, from collecting and selling Indian baskets and blankets. Yet Indians' supposed commitment to simplicity, to ridding themselves of luxuries, excesses, and the "superfluities of life," appealed to James. He did not encourage a complete lack of luxury,

> *but I do long with all my heart that we might . . . find the golden mean between their life and our too complex and superfluity-laden life* [with all that] *. . . a commercially-cursed, bargain-counter, curio-living, bric-a-brac adoring, showy, shoddy civilization can give.*[48]

Speaking of superfluities, James never let one adjective suffice when six could be attached. Still, James was apparently sincere in advocating simplicity, although he failed to live up to it in his prose or personal life.

Although much of the book chronicles outer aspects of Indian life, James did not neglect the inner life. He admired Indians' honesty and frankness. They did not lie in order to be polite. If they did not like you, they would tell you (as James no doubt experienced more than once). They engaged in no pretense or hypocrisy. They did not exhibit self-pity or weep and wail over lost joys or better days. They mourned their dead but did not dwell on such misfortunes. Instead, they minimized sorrows by constant labor and by concentrating on happiness. Of course, James went on, they attained such serenity of mind and soul because they were essentially childlike, accepting the will of the gods with youthful acquiescence and a faith and trust civilized people had lost.[49]

Finally, James returned to themes explored in earlier works exalting the Indian as ecologist, artist, and religious soul. Indian sincerity, earnestness, and reverence in worship offered a model to Protestants and Catholics alike who could be quite rude, whispering and displaying other discourteous behavior during ceremonies and services. Picking up on a theme explored by George Bird Grinnell, James pronounced that Indians never killed any animals to extinction. They demonstrated their capacity for self-restraint and providential foresight by husbanding resources for the future, unlike American fur traders such as John Jacob Astor and buffalo hunters such as Buffalo Bill who nearly destroyed the nation's supply of bison, elk, and other animals. Only when these species stood on the brink of extinction did Americans pass laws to protect game. Indians had required no such laws since they were governed, not by the white man's greed, but by good sense and moderation. Finally, it was close observance of Nature that provided a constant source of food, as well as artistic inspiration. Indian artists found their most compelling designs in the natural world which put to shame the absurd and foolish fancy-work of white women who spend hours on designs that "are a crazy, intricate something to be dreaded rather than admired." True art development, James asserted, came only "from familiarity with Nature in all her varying moods."[50]

Lodged throughout *What the White Race May Learn*, then, is a fairly consistent critique of Anglo-American life. The book takes its place in a long-standing and venerated European-American tradition of exploiting Indians as convenient instruments of social criticism. What differentiated James's effort from earlier ones, however, was the dogged, determined, extended length to which he went to make his point. That Indian cultures have genuine value was no passing thought or rhetorical tool. It was a deeply felt conviction. True, James's observations were sometimes superficial, patronizing, silly, and even ridiculous. Often they were thinly veiled attempts to foist his own enthusiasms onto readers in the guise of Indian ways. But he was seriously committed to the basic notion that "in the hurry and whirl of our money-mad age and our machine-driven civilization, we have scarce time to sit down calmly and contemplate anything, hence my earnest plea for a return to the simple things, to the outdoors, to the quiet contentment of the Indian." Many readers no doubt took him at his word.[51]

James's certainty about the benefits of Indian ways, however, did not translate into a consistent indictment of those who attempted to extinguish them. His longest commentary on Indian-white relations focused on the Spanish missionaries' activities in California and New Mexico. Perhaps on no other subject did James and Lummis have more in common than this thorny one of Spanish priests' impact on Indians. Here James faced the same intellectual dilemma that Lummis encountered: How can you applaud the pious faith and selflessness of the padres and simultaneously promote the sanctity of Indian religions and the principle of religious freedom? How can you celebrate the development of California by venerating her first European settlers, while simultaneously pointing out the disastrous consequences for Indians? James dodged these predicaments by separating the California experience from the New Mexican one. The California missions supposedly symbolized the best of Spanish colonization: loving, gentle efforts to usher Indians into the world of civilized and Christian men. New Mexico represented the worst of Spanish excesses: harsh and brutal conquest which sparked revolt among the Pueblos.

James, like Lummis, ever the promoter of southern California, judged Father Junipero Serra and the other Franciscans as "the best the Spaniards had to offer of earnestness, power, ability, and sympathetic brotherhood."[52] Likewise, James fashioned California's Indians into primitive hordes of "untamed" people or "savages." Not that they were "abject savages" for they did have the mental capacity to learn, construct magnificent mission structures, and cultivate crops. Also, it was not true that California Indians had no religion. They practiced "a rude kind of Nature worship with personified dieties." But James harbored no doubts that Indians were better off under the Spanish missionaries who taught them to wear clothes, raise and manufacture what they needed, and understand the basic elements of the Catholic faith. He could imagine the padres' joy when Indians became baptized and their despair when their disciples displayed moral lapses or, even worse, mounted a rebellion.[53]

Mention of rebellion, of course, raised complications. Why would Indians rebel if the Spanish mission system was essentially beneficent? What happened to those 30,000 Indians who inhabited California during the mission days? Why did only scattered groups remain? James refused to fault the missionaries. California Indian revolts sprang from their own savage tendencies or resulted from abuses they experienced at the hands of Spanish soldiers. As to the long-term decline of California's Indians, James blamed this squarely on those who secularized the missions. With secularization, "vulture politicians" obtained the missions, the vineyards, and the herds and thus "cram[med] their own maws with the fatness they so envied and lusted after." Once removed from the watchful eye of the missionary, the guileless and trustful Indians became victims of these scoundrels, neglecting their cattle and converting their property into money and whiskey. It was the secular politicians, not the missionaries, who deserved the blame.[54]

James's desire to protect the memory of missionaries issued from several different inclinations. In part, he supported the efforts of "the virile editor," Charles Fletcher Lummis, to preserve California's mission structures as tourist destinations. A positive, even romanticized, image of the missionaries would prove more helpful to that cause, for surely potential donors and visitors would prefer to commemorate heroes rather than villains. Also, James used his depictions of California's Catholic missions to attack sectarianism and fierce anti-Catholicism, common in his day. By presenting Catholics in a positive light, he could counter narrow-mindedness, ignorance, and prejudice.[55]

This was not James's final word on Catholic missionaries, however. When he turned his attention to New Mexico, the tone changed considerably. There the missionaries came as part of an invasion. They exhibited a zeal, an ambition to win God's approval, and a fervor that led them to force their religion upon the natives. In New Mexico the Spaniards were unkind and impolitic in their subjugation of the Pueblos. Moreover, Pueblos in revolt were not savages but patriots, and their leader, Popé, was "a true aboriginal Patrick Henry and George Washington rolled into one."[56] For these people

> *had arisen in defense of their hearts, their homes, the graveyards of their ancestors, their cornfields, their hunting-grounds, their religion, their ceremonies, their honor, their families, and the preservation of their national existence.*[57]

It was the Pueblos, not the Spanish, who deserved his readers' sympathies, James insisted. The Spanish provoked rebellion by their cruelty.

How do we explain James's shifting perspective? Of course, Lummis helped pave the way for this bifurcated view of the Spanish missions, and James was not inclined to challenge his nemesis on this issue. In addition, by the twentieth century, the relative status of Indians in California and New Mexico was quite different. Revolts against the Spanish in California had failed and the Indians had seemingly disappeared. Only weakened remnants of their cultures remained. The Pueblo Revolt, on the other hand, achieved a measure of success. The Pueblos rid themselves of the Spanish conquerors and missions for about one dozen years and even after Spanish reconquest, not to mention years of Mexican and Anglo-American jurisdiction, they retained their homes, communities, cultures, and religions. They persevered.[58]

Moreover, the world had changed by the time James's book on New Mexico was published in 1920. The recently terminated World War unquestionably influenced James as he contemplated troubling issues of conquest and the rights of the conquered to protect their homes, ways of life, and religious traditions. Woodrow Wilson became the first statesman in human history, in James's estimation, "with vision enough, purity of heart sufficient, and moral courage assertive enough to dare to defend the rights of all *people* to determine the course of their own lives." No nation should be allowed to subjugate a weaker or smaller one. All people have the right to political self-determination and religious freedom, including freedom from the "evil" effects of missionaries.[59]

By the 1920s, then, James had turned an intellectual corner. He censured not only the Spanish but the entire mission system as well. Cracks in confidence about Christianization and concomitant acculturation policies became more pronounced. He leveled his greatest indictments against U.S. Indian policy and seemed to delight in comparing Spanish with the more rapacious American policies. The "loving power the Franciscans held over the Indians," James maintained, contrasted vividly with American authority which lacked honor, character, and truth. "It was bad enough to rob them of their lands, their homes, their hunting grounds, but to rob them [the Indians] of their character and to let it go on record that they were without honor or any spiritual development was an injustice as cruel as it was criminal," he wrote. Of the three distinct phases of rule in the Southwest (Spanish, Mexican, and American), the third and last was by far the worst.[60] In book after book James launched attacks on Americans' treatment of Indians. Quite simply, Americans wanted Indians' land and took it. Let us be "manly" enough, James charged, to call ourselves by our proper names: bigots, debauchers, liars, and murderers.[61]

James did not concern himself about the particulars of policy.[62] Nowhere did he offer a sustained or intellectually consistent discussion of policy. At times he could be quite critical of particular reservations. The Navajos' experience on the Bosque Redondo Reservation, for example, offered one example of wretched, abominable treatment. But James did not quarrel with the reservation idea nor did he deny that the Bosque Redondo experience forever quieted the Navajos and made it possible for Americans to pass through their country unharmed. In fact, he concluded, the "Bosque lesson, though severe, was needed, and it proved salutary." As for education, on the one hand, he commended government schools for Indian children. On the other hand, he criticized them for separating children from their families and providing the children with an inappropriate education.[63]

The two exceptions to James's vacillations on policy came, perhaps not surprisingly, in the areas of religious freedom and artistic expression. His views are instructive because they parallel areas where Collier's Indian New Deal instituted reform—reforms James would have applauded. His support of Indian artistry derived from a belief that it held intrinsic value. James also believed it marketable, if it had integrity, and that it could ensure Indians' economic self-sufficiency. In a proposal which anticipated the New Deal's Indian Arts and Crafts Board, James recommended that Indian schools hire and provide adequate compensation for Indian women to teach basketmaking and weaving. Forget the useless practice of teaching Indian girls embroidery, James wrote. Instead, encourage perpetuation of native dyes and allow the Indians to devise their own shapes, designs, and symbols. In the end, both Indians and whites would profit—financially and otherwise—from such an artistic renaissance.[64]

If American agents', missionaries', and teachers' efforts to supplant Indian artistry with embroidery and other "twaddle" annoyed James, their efforts to stamp out Indian religions angered him. He was enraged to learn of Indian Office instructions designed to discourage ceremonies that took Indians away from agricultural work or included intoxicants and drugs. James had no problem with the prohibition of illegal drugs and intoxicants, but he fumed at efforts to suppress other religious activities. Bureaucrats had no conception of what these ceremonies meant to Indians nor did they comprehend their deep solemnity. Such politicians' powers paled in comparison to God, who "gives to all men the same freedom, the freedom to worship Him in any way and every way they deem wise and desirable." As far as James knew, God had not granted superintendents and agents the right to determine when, where, and how Indians worshiped Him. Moreover, the Constitution, "which as far as I have yet learned, even the Indian Department has not yet abrogated," assured that Congress would establish no state religion or prohibit people the freedom to practice their own. Americans should recall their own struggles to assure religious freedom and rise up in protest against public servants' efforts to deprive others of this same right. The more James read the Indian Office's "outrageous message" the more indignant he became "at the bold impudence, audacity and arrogance of it."[65]

Such a deposition on religious freedom strongly suggests that James would have found John Collier's commissionership compatible. And he did join other writers weighing in against the Bursum Bill, which James described as a congressional attempt to justify the theft of Pueblo lands and water. He felt certain the infamous legislation would not pass, in part, because of the "valiant and informing articles written by John Collier."[66] Alas, James died in 1924, nine years before Collier's appointment to the commissionership. Given James's commitment to Indian religious freedom and artistry, as well as his evolving thoughts on Indian autonomy and self-determination, it is reasonable to assume, however, he would have shared Lummis's view on Collier: this is the man we have been looking for.

Historian Patricia Nelson Limerick has noted James's maddening inconsistencies regarding deserts. Sometimes he painted deserts as havens from artificial civilization; sometimes he presented civilization as refuge from deserts. Sometimes he applauded the development of towns upon deserts; other times he commended the raging Colorado River which drowned them out. Yet for all his inconstancies, Limerick noted, James was a "crucial figure in the transformation of attitudes" toward the desert.[67] He played a similar role in the transformation of attitudes toward Indians.

James lectured, wrote, and preached about the West and Indians for over four decades. Every year he addressed thousands of Easterners at his lectures. Thousands more read his books and articles although, according to his biographer, the "total verbal output of his life cannot be measured; nor can we measure the influence of his words."[68] Perhaps a 1910 letter from a fan, however, represents the sentiments of many listeners and readers. May S. Wood heard James lecture in Pasadena and decided he was the perfect person to advise her on how to find work helping the Indians. She did not want employment with the government and its "clumsy and arbitrary service rules," nor did teaching "damnation" (as missionaries supposedly did) appeal. She hoped James had an alternative. Wood also indicated she wanted a copy of *What the White Race May Learn From Indians* because its message reinforced her own belief: "Indians can teach us as much—more than we can teach them."[69] Surely, May Wood was not James's only listener who shared this point of view.

Nor was she the only woman drawn to Indians, particularly those of the Southwest. By the end of World War I, several unconventional, outspoken women came to New Mexico and turned their attentions and energies to Indians. More radical in their cultural critiques than James or Lummis, they liked what they saw in Indians' cultures, became determined to "save" them, invited John Collier to the West, and transformed the preceding generation's doubts and misgivings about forced acculturation into convictions and determinations. They labored not only to alter the nation's hearts and minds about Indians but also to reform policies. It was Mary Austin, Anna Ickes, and Mabel Dodge Luhan, then, who brought the reimagining process to its early twentieth-century climax.

# Part III

# Mothers of Reinvention

# 8

# SISTERS OF THE SOUTHWEST

## *Mary Austin and Anna Ickes*

SOMETHING ABOUT THE SOUTHWEST attracted independent, unconventional women. In part, the desert climate and the landscapes appealed. So too did the open vistas, swept clean of obtrusive vegetation, allowing an unimpeded view of the distant horizon. Most compelling of all, however, were the Indian occupants of the region. In particular, the Pueblos of the Rio Grande fascinated these women who believed that in those small northern New Mexico communities, they had found nearly perfect societies. Agrarian, domestic, seemingly peaceful, rooted, artistically and spiritually vital, the Pueblos attracted the feminine eye. No other geographical region, not the Pacific Northwest, the Northern Rockies, or even California, packed quite the same punch. No other Indian group, not the Blackfeet, Nez Perces, Crow, or Yavapais, had quite the same appeal. Only in the Southwest and among the comparatively sedentary, agricultural Pueblos did women comfortably settle in and join men in reimagining Indians.

Like Lummis and James these women, including Mary Austin, Anna Ickes, and Mabel Dodge Luhan, were not inclined to keep the wonders of the region and its Indian occupants secret.[1] They wrote books, essays, and poetry. They invited others to experience the Southwest and meet its people. They helped publicize Pueblos' political problems. They sparked John Collier's interest in Indians, leading to his appointment as Commissioner of Indian Affairs by Anna Ickes's husband, Harold, in 1933.[2] They thus helped set in motion fundamental reform first by exercising whatever political power they had at their disposal, then by turning to men such as John Collier and Harold Ickes to complete the work.

Ironically, while Austin complained that being a woman proved an impediment to a writing career, her gender partially explains why she has received much recent scholarly attention. Over the last decade or so, scholars hunting for a woman's voice found Austin's and revived her long-neglected work. Mabel Dodge Luhan, too, has been the object of recent historical scrutiny inspired, at least in part, by efforts to recover women's experiences. Most of the men examined here, on the other hand, still await biographers.[3] What brings them all together in this work, of course, is their shared interest in Indians. Certainly Wood, Linderman, and Lummis anticipated much that these women would say and do but it was Austin, Ickes, and Luhan who brought this long-brewing cultural development to its early twentieth-century culmination. In their *words,* one finds the most explicit antimodernism, the most outspoken cultural critiques. In their *works*, one finds the most determined efforts to undo the policies of assimilation and acculturation and usher in a new day of significant reform.

It is not surprising, given the gender dictates of her time, that Mary Austin's move to the West from Illinois was not at her own instigation. Neither professional compulsion nor personal ambition, health, or desire for adventure (those motivations which pulled most of the men in this study west) explained her migration. Rather, familial duty dictated the move. In 1888, her brother James decided to try homesteading in California, and his widowed mother followed. Mary thought it a poor idea, believing her mother clung to James in a most unhealthy way after her husband's death. But the mother prevailed and Mary dutifully accompanied her.[4]

Born in Illinois in 1868, Mary Hunter had been content to stay in the Midwest where her "foremothers" pioneered several generations earlier. Although Mary's father immigrated from England to Illinois in 1851, her mother's family's presence in America was long-standing. Austin grounded her autobiography (throughout which she referred to herself in the third person) in tales of grandmothers and great-grandmothers who she believed deserved recognition for settling the wilderness. Polly McAdams, for instance, came to Illinois "while the Black Hawk Hunting-Ground was still infested by Indians incited by the French." Relying upon language she would have eschewed had her ancestors been Spaniards among the Pueblos in the 1680s, rather than Anglos among the Sac and Fox in the 1830s, Austin maintained such American women "were trained to win the land from savage hordes."[5] Nothing in the text suggested Austin meant this ironically.

By Mary's day, the Indians of Illinois were long gone, removed across the Mississippi River and relegated to supporting roles in family stories about pioneer days. Even her father, upon traveling up the Mississippi in the early 1850s, caught only a glimpse of Indian canoes trading to the south, moving out of sight. So the family might have remained out of sight of Indians had Mary's brother and mother decided to stay put. But the westering urge, shared by so many of his countrymen, infected James, and the rest of the family trailed behind. They crossed the continent by train and dropped down to southern California, where Mary pronounced the Los Angeles area unappealing, "all the uses of natural beauty slavered over with the impudicity of a purely material culture," she later wrote.[6] Happily, the Hunter family's final destination was the Tejon country which Mary found more inviting and to her taste. There she discovered Indians.

Austin came to California literally and emotionally malnourished. Mary believed her mother neither noticed her ill health nor, more significantly, cared. She believed the Tejon region, on the other hand, took her to its heart and restored her vitality. Every day she rode horseback, sometimes all day, watching spring come to the dry country; making acquaintance with sheepherders, Indians, and Spanish-speaking cowboys; and establishing a deep relationship with the region simply through knowledge of it. She met and befriended Edward Fitzgerald Beale, first Indian Commissioner of California, who related the region's history and introduced her to Indians such as Sebastiano, "one of the half-dozen authentic Mission Indians Mary was to know."[7] Rebuffed by a loveless, seemingly sterile, desertlike family life, Austin turned to the Tejon and its native people for solace, comfort, acceptance, and illumination:

> *She began to learn how Indians live off a land upon which more sophisticated races would starve, and how the land itself instructed them. As she saw these things, the whole basis of her social philosophy and economy altered beyond the capacity of books to keep pace with it. She was altered herself to an extent and in a direction that nothing she has yet written fully expresses.*[8]

What the Harney Desert did for Wood, New Mexico for Lummis, and Arizona for George Wharton James, the Tejon region did for Mary Austin. What Indians did for all examined here, also affected Mary. Her contact with them inspired an acute sense of personal regeneration and encouraged self-expression. The Indian as other, as outsider, legitimized Austin's difference and bolstered her resolve to articulate her view of the world. Among California's Indians, then, she discovered the themes that engaged her during a lifetime of writing and the voice through which she would express them. Those themes included the belief that Indian artistry and aesthetics deserved recognition in American art and letters, that men deprived women of power, and that the East ignored the West's aesthetic which was based upon startling natural beauty.[9]

From the beginning, western experiences prompted Mary's pen. Her initial journey into the Tejon, in fact, inspired her first publication. "One Hundred Miles on Horseback" appeared in her college's periodical, *The Blackburnian*, and offered the fairly simple and straightforward message that nature heals. She also hinted that Indians lived closer to nature's restorative power.[10] Austin's writing career did not take off immediately, however. First teaching to supplement her mother's household income and then marrying Stafford Wallace Austin occupied Mary's early years in California. The marriage proved no happier than life among the Hunters. Wallace, from all appearances a decent man, did not match Mary's intellect or satisfy her yearning for a mate with whom she could communicate truly and deeply. Mary also blamed her husband for their only daughter's mental retardation. Eventually, Austin institutionalized Ruth and divorced Wallace.

Throughout these personal travails, Austin never abandoned her ambition to become a writer. Actually, she became "completely committed to the idea that she was to write of the West . . . and [its] strange growths and unfamiliar creatures."[11] Tucked between pelicans and phylloxera, Austin listed Indians on her string of local inspirations. On one level, they were just another element of the flora and fauna. On another level, here and elsewhere in her work, they appeared more abstract than human, more conceptual than flesh and blood. For Austin, Indians represented a way of experiencing life, of seeing and expressing it artistically. Or, as she put it herself, "I lapped up Indians as a part of the novelist's tormented and unremitting search for adequate concepts of life and society and throve upon them."[12] She needed them, both emotionally and intellectually and, as Mary construed it, they obliged. Only rarely did an individual merit mention by name or receive recognition of personal attributes in her published work. In this, Austin shared much with fellow poet, C.E.S. Wood. Both used Indians for literary purposes, remained the most dedicated primitivists of all the writers examined here, and transformed experiences with actual people into ideas about art and politics.

Austin never approached Indians with a blank slate, completely free of expectation or purpose, but, from the start, she never pretended to be an objective outside observer. Austin not only openly acknowledged her need for Indians, but she also identified with them personally in a way matched by no one else in this study. Quite simply, Mary believed she *was* Indian. Somewhere in her distant ancestral past, Austin claimed, she had an Indian ancestor, "an uncorrupted strain of ancestral primitivism, a single isolated gene of that far-off and slightly mystical Indian ancestor of whose reality I am more convinced by what happened to me among Indians than by any objective evidence."[13] On another occasion, Austin declined the role of Indian authority but added, that, at times, she simply became an Indian.[14] Thus, in discovering Indians, Austin merely tapped into a heretofore buried but meaningful aspect of herself. Consequently, in articulating the meaning and significance of Indians to America, she felt completely comfortable projecting onto them the mysticism, spiritualism, and artistic impulses imprinted on her own soul. In this, too, she shared much with Wood. Austin was not a student of Indians in the ways of Grinnell, McClintock, or even Lummis. She was not a close observer or recorder of Indian cultures. Rather, she defined her role as articulator of Indianness which, in the end, was mostly an extension of her self.

The process of becoming an Indian articulator began in earnest around 1892 when the Austins traveled to San Francisco. While Wallace discussed an irrigation venture with his brother, Mary made contact with California's literary community. She met poet Ina Coolbirth, editor of the *Overland Monthly*, who became Mary's mentor and eventually published several of her stories. When Wallace moved on to the Owens Valley, Mary followed, arriving at the moment when the Owens Valley was on the brink between old and new. It was a time before "modern America ha[d] laid a greedy, vulgarizing hand" on it. It was a place where people still remembered the Paiutes "last stand" before being "driven into the bitter waters of the lake, and dying, sank there."[15] Survivors of this tragedy still inhabited the area, however, and told stories of their struggles with one another and of Commissioner Beale's efforts to remove them all to the Tejon country.

The Owens Valley, then, provided Mary Austin the opportunity to deepen her acquaintance with Indians. True, the stories provided fodder for her "folk interest." But she also became friends with individual Paiutes, who, alas, typically remained anonymous in her recollections of those days. When her daughter Ruth was born, Austin became ill and received little help from anyone except Indian women. A Paiute woman nursed Ruth, as well as her own child, after Mary consulted with a white doctor to make sure it was medically safe. Several years later, when her daughter was still not talking, that woman brought her dried meadowlarks' tongues to make Ruth's speech nimble and quick. The remedy, unfortunately, did not resolve Ruth's retardation. But, according to Austin, such experiences allowed her to begin genuinely knowing Indians. Not far from her home, was a small encampment of brown wickiups which, she thought, resembled wasps' nests. Sometimes Mary would join the women from the camp as they gathered seeds and dug wild hyacinth roots. She absorbed their knowledge of the natural world, learned which plants proved suitable for the dinner table or for the medicine cabinet, and picked up the rudiments of basket weaving and snare making.[16]

Contact with the Paiutes also brought spiritual lessons. A Paiute Medicine Man taught her how prayer could be expressed in dance, music, words, and rhythm. It was "an outgoing act of the inner self toward something not a god, toward a responsive activity in the world about you, designated as The-Friend-of-the-Soul-of-Man." Gradually, she converted to an "Indian" understanding of spirituality, finding it much more satisfying than the Methodism of her Midwestern upbringing. This slow transformation, she explained, "began as adventure and became illumination." In time, by immersing herself in the Indian life around Lone Pine; by studying Indian verse, artistry, and rhythm; and by entering into "the strange secret life of the tribe, the struggle of Whiteness with Darkness, the struggle of the individual soul with the Friend-of-the-Soul-of-Man," she learned how to live . . . and how to write.[17]

Owens Valley days not only inspired Austin's writing, but her political activism as well. The federal government's Indian school at Bishop introduced her to what she deemed the Indian Bureau's meanness and cruelty and transformed her into "a fierce and untiring opponent of [its] colossal stupidities." Associating Indian rights with the other great social and political causes of her day including women's suffrage, labor organizing, and religious and intellectual freedom, Austin claimed Indians as one of the underdogs her generation took to heart. She personally threw herself into the cause of Indian rights rather than that of labor because the former seemed the more offended and, besides, were close at hand. She would have done as much, Austin later wrote, even if she had not gained so much insight and knowledge from them. Finally, engagement in Indian rights issues provided her with further confirmation of her own culture's brutality, emotional savagery, greed, and hypocrisy.[18]

In 1898, Wallace decided, without consulting his wife, to move from Lone Pine to Independence. Mary promptly suffered a mental breakdown and, in the summer, she headed to Oakland for treatment. By this time, she knew she could not follow Wallace to Independence, but she was also unprepared for divorce. Over the winter months of 1899, Mary took Ruth to Los Angeles, supposedly to seek medical help for her daughter's disability. There Austin met Charles Fletcher Lummis and, for a while, enjoyed the stimulation of the "Arroyo Seco" literary group which gathered around him. Mary was initially quite impressed with Lummis, who encouraged her writing and served as something of an inspiration for her own career, particularly regarding Indian work.[19] Certainly, both Lummis and Austin shared interests and political inclinations regarding Indian affairs. They also shared a tendency toward monumental egotism and so the potential for friendship between such types was perhaps inevitably doomed. Lummis, as earlier noted, seemed incapable of sharing the role of interpreter of the Southwest or Southwestern Indians. Initially, however, he assumed the role of mentor to Austin, although his advice could sometimes be quite sharp. "If you are 'not in the least ashamed of Spanish derivations' then you ought to be," he wrote her in 1904, critical of her translations. "I don't try to write about the things I am ignorant of."[20] Many years later, Austin remembered Lummis this way:

> *Mr. Lummis did not take to her, nor she to him. She had no genius, he said; talent and industry and a certain kind of knowledge, but little gift . . . Mary shrank from him a little; thought him romantic; felt that he rested too much on the lesser achievement; on working too many hours a day; on sleeping too little; on drinking too much; on his wife's translations of Spanish manuscripts.*[21]

That thirty-year-old barb, regarding Mary's faulty Spanish translations, apparently still stung.[22]

For all their spats, however, in 1899, Lummis helped restore Mary's health and stimulate her writing. She resigned herself to Wallace and Independence but, most important, began writing in earnest. She sold stories to *Atlantic Monthly* and other periodicals and in 1903 published *The Land of Little Rain,* one of Austin's most famous and most admired works. As the title implies, it focused primarily on the desert. Here and there she mentioned Indians and celebrated their close connection to and deep understanding of the natural world. They were, quite simply, rooted in it. "The Shoshones," she wrote, "live like their trees." Moreover, young Shoshones are like quail, "knowing . . . to be still and keep on being still, at the first hint of danger or strangeness." She compared the Indian campoodie or village, in an image she used more than once in her writing, to "a collection of prodigious wasps' nests" and, once again, noted its "inhabitants have the faculty of quail for making themselves scarce."[23]

Austin intended these images, not as insults implying Indians were little more than animals, but as compliments conveying the natural, organic relationship between them and their physical surroundings.

In another vignette, Austin humanized her Indian neighbors a bit more through a sketch of Seyavi, a basket maker. This woman attracted Austin's attention because she offered a model to women of how to live without a man and how to live a life of artistry. According to Austin, Seyavi once told her men must have women, but women could do well with only a child. More compelling than her self-sufficiency and freedom from male domination, however, was Seyavi's work. She "made baskets for love and sold them for money, in a generation that preferred iron pots for utility."[24] She was an artist. But then, according to Austin, every Indian woman was an artist, even though she did not philosophize about her work, but simply saw, felt, and then created.[25] Beyond the technical skill and even cleverness displayed in their baskets was something else: "The weaver and the warp lived next to the earth and were saturated with the same elements."[26]

For all Seyavi's self-sufficiency and artistic ability, of course, Austin still deemed her, and other Indian women, primitive. In fact, her very simplicity constituted the core of her attraction. Austin, as primitivist, believed the deep connection between art and culture was most discernible among such so-called primitives. This was the connection Mary hoped the modern world would somehow reclaim. And though she was primitive, Seyavi was nevertheless a repository of wisdom, "nourishing her spirit against the time of the spirit's need."[27] Austin did not expect her readers to abandon their comfortable homes for the Paiutes' wickiups or to accept Indian beliefs, but rather to approximate the demeanor, discernment, and sensibility of such people, who found profound connection and contentment with the natural world. What Austin promoted was an aesthetic practice rooted in authentic experience of essential reality.[28] This was how she imagined all Indians lived.

Interestingly, Austin's primitivism was tied to an understanding of Indians which, like that of Grinnell and James, rested on an evolutionary view of culture. In this regard she represents a throwback to an earlier generation. She never reconsidered her fundamental assumptions about human cultures and the evolutionary framework throughout her writing career which spanned forty years; took her from Independence to Carmel to New York to Santa Fe; and included twelve books of nonfiction, nine novels, three plays, fifty short stories, and many articles and poems. In short, Austin believed that the Pueblos, for instance, proved useful in "showing us the mind in the making." One merely had to "slip inside the bubble of pueblo [*sic*] thinking" to discover "the life before we lived this life."[29] Civilized people existed on a plane further removed from "the Infinite Subjective Mind," a god-concept, force or power, and so their relationship to it was less vital and less readily linked. It was more cerebral and less elemental.

She shared these ideas with William James when they met in 1898, and believed he validated her notion about the continuum of religious experience. "What I got out of William James and the Medicine Man," Austin wrote, "was a continuing experience of wholeness, a power to expand the least premonitory shiver along the edge of primitive apprehension to the full diaspon of spiritual sophistication, which I have never lost."[30] Clearly, Mary believed a link existed between Indians' ideas about prayer and the most sophisticated metaphysical theories of her own culture. Only Europeans and Anglo-Americans such as William James and Mary Austin, however, could follow this experience to its most complex and sophisticated manifestation.

Austin's brand of primitivism and social evolutionary thought did not lead her to conclude, however, that Indians were destined for extinction. Nor did she share Grinnell's belief their cultures were vanishing. But she did assume them static. They could travel just so far toward an understanding of the world they live in, and no farther. And, she added, this was true of all Indians regardless of tribal and cultural distinctions.[31]

Such explanations of human differences demonstrate Austin's limitations and, further, have racial implications. She expressed distaste for, even fear of, African-Americans, although she tried to overcome this among the artistic element. Her disdain of Jews revealed her anti-semitism.[32] She saw Indians, however, as racially pure and, because they were rooted in the American environment, authentic. Jews and African-Americans were foreign and thus unauthentic. Finally, although she placed Indian cultures on the primitive end of her cultural spectrum, she did not mean to deny their moral, artistic, or spiritual value. In fact, she found their supposed closer proximity to the "Infinite Subjective Mind" and to the earth itself admirable and worthy of emulating.

When Austin turned from sociology to history, it became even more clear that if she rather thoughtlessly adopted the language of social evolution, she did not adopt its nineteenth-century moral assumptions. In her view, the brutes and barbarians were not Indians but rather the Spaniards and especially the Anglo-Americans who succeeded them in New Mexico. In her historical account of the Spanish presence in the Southwest, which departs in significant ways from Lummis's, Austin explained that Spanish policies forced the normally peaceful Pueblos to bloody revolution. It was the Spaniards' suppression of free spiritual expression and their brutal labor system that naturally led to resistance and ultimately insurrection. The Pueblos, who "opposed . . . the destruction of their own way of reconciling themselves to the universe," simply revolted and in doing so meant to "scour . . . themselves clean of the contamination of baptism."[33]

Pueblos were not a militant people, however, and harbored no long-standing hatred toward the conquistadors. Conversely, when the Spaniards returned, they came somewhat chastened. After reconquest, they no longer hung medicine-men, stopped employing forced labor at the mines, and accepted baptism and a reasonable attendance at mass as sufficient signs of conversion. For the next two hundred and fifty years, Pueblos and descendants of the Spanish lived peaceably. Some Indians welcomed intermarriage. Others opposed "the contamination of their blood" and, Austin claimed, one could still find Pueblo villages where Mexicans were not welcomed. In fact, Indians might have regained complete control had the Anglo-Americans not arrived.[34]

Entrance of Anglos spelled changes even more disastrous than those precipitated by the Spaniards, for between Protestant missionaries and Indian Office bureaucrats the Americans "made a dull, debasing smear over the lovely and aesthetic culture of the pueblos [*sic*]."[35] True, the Franciscans had forced their religion and destroyed much beauty in the process, but at least they left some beauty behind, including their architecture. In contrast, the "alien, inappropriate buildings of the Indian Bureau eat into the beauty of the landscape like a pox."[36]

Anglo-Americans forced their ugly, brutish culture onto the Pueblos. After Kit Carson, who represented an American type which was aggressive but gentle, chivalrous, honorable, and just, came a wholly different and inferior type. His successors were men bred of violence and destruction, who considered all Indians "varmints" and all Spanish-speaking people "Greasers." These lowly men, reminiscent of the type disparaged by Linderman and McClintock in Montana, were profoundly ignorant, laughed at the New Mexicans' courtliness, spat, swore, and murdered one another for little cause.[37]

Such coarse men plundered the peaceful Pueblos and genteel Hispanics of the Rio Grande. Moreover, their destructive tendencies spread beyond that river's watershed to the Navajos, who were rounded up and forcibly removed to the Bosque Redondo Reservation, a disgraceful chapter in American history.[38] But antimodernist Austin reserved her deepest lamentations for the Pueblos who, to her, represented

> *the vase, the cup in which had mellowed for a thousand years the medicine for want of which the civilized world is tearing out its own vitals. For in the cultural frame which we hold so obstinately . . . lies the only existing human society that ever found, and kept for an appreciable period, the secret of spiritual organization.*[39]

For all the efforts to supplant Pueblo culture with a Christian one, for all the centuries of contact and waves of conquest, those little communities in northern New Mexico still survived and offered Americans a model of how to live.

The Pueblos' secret of survival, and the essence of their attractiveness to Mary Austin, rested in their ability to meld the spiritual and social through community. By the time the Spaniards first stumbled upon them, the Pueblos had developed an essentially utopian society with no rich or poor, no criminals, no orphans, no prostitutes, no lonely people. Although by the twentieth century that idyllic life could no longer be found, "three centuries of Christian contact have not quite cured [the Pueblos] of their superior achievement."[40] True, by refusing to honor the Pueblos' rights to their lands the government allows poverty to undermine them. Diseases such as trachoma and tuberculosis saps them of their vitality. Most people remain tragically ignorant of the richness of their cultures. "Yet still, in that dust, blossom and smell sweet, concepts for the lack of which our age goes staggering into chaos."[41] The concepts Austin particularly felt her countrymen lacked was an inherent understanding of the spiritual rootedness of man and woman in community.

By contrast, European and American cultures consisted of societies with a million alienated souls. Such people are essentially incapable of discerning any meaning in their lives, blinded by a cloud which underscores their separation from one another. Only occasional artists, poets, and prophets, in whose company Austin would certainly have placed herself, "detach themselves and go sailing skyward in a lovely world of their own seeing." By contrast, for Pueblos community was the center of life and seldom did the personal transform into complete individualism. Alienation was unknown. Connection with one another provided the bedrock of meaning, purpose, and integration with the world.[42]

Making the Pueblos', and other Indians' ways, even more appealing to Austin was their easy, artful expression of the link between the body and the mind, the earthly and the spiritual. The meaning and value of Indian art rested in its understanding of the unity of all things. Austin came to understand that genius or artistry was rooted in awareness of such connection. She also realized that Indians understood this long before she did. "I have written about the earth performance, the multitude of bright and shining things that contribute to the sense of beauty and fitness, and find that the aboriginal has anticipated them."[43]

In fact, Austin argued that American Indian expression formed the foundation of a national culture, particularly poetry. She became convinced that Indian verse articulated the essence of American experience because the American environment shaped it. Believing that verse found form in the poet's geography and even in the rhythm of his food supply, Indians, long before Anglo-Americans arrived, were "singing in precisely the forms that were later to become native to the region of Spoon River, the Land of Little Rain, and the country of the Cornhuskers." Austin claimed that when she realized she could listen to Indian languages on a phonograph and place them geographically in the locales that produced them, she became convinced a relationship existed between Indian and the later American poetic expressions that emerged from those same places. They shared an environment which, in turn, shaped their art and, more broadly, American literature.[44]

Austin reiterated one of her major themes, the communal aspect of Indian expression. Even though these peoples' cultures were of the "neolithic" type, their poetry both expressed and evoked their social nature.[45] In fact, she maintained, these communities were "the only societ[ies] in the world in which culture exists as an expression of the whole." Differences of class or caste, property or power did nothing to disrupt this cultural wholeness. Euro-American society did not even have a word for such holism and integration, because it had never experienced it. At the same time, deep within, all people were collective. "At the core of *our* [my emphasis] Amerind life we are consummated in the dash and color of collectivity." She remained optimistic that Americans were capable of experiencing, naming, and bringing this hidden collectivity "to consciousness" and could learn this from the Pueblos. That prospect was in doubt, however, because through missionaries and boarding school teachers Indians remained vulnerable to destruction at the hands of those very elements in society who made up for their own spiritual impotency, by imposing themselves on rich Indian cultures. America robbed Indians of their lands, destroyed their self-confidence, and crushed their most colorful spiritual expressions. Unless this stops, the "great Left Hand of modernism [will close] over the Puebleno," Austin warned, and Anglo-American culture would go down with him.[46]

Mary Austin did more than muse about such prospects. Beyond warning about modernism's murderous compulsions, she enlisted in campaigns, both cultural and political, to alter Americans' understanding of and treatment toward Indians. In publications and lectures, for example, she repeatedly promoted the Indian aesthetic as an elemental part of American culture. This was the cause that mattered most to her. She met resistance everywhere. In 1922, students at the University of California rejected Austin's advice that they study Indian life and literature. She wrote to Mabel Dodge Luhan, "They have a snobbish notion that they ought to be above anything the Indian has to teach them." If students questioned Indians' value, the East Coast literati were even more resistant. She tried to convince New York editors and critics to admit the Indian among American influences. She met limited success. Few would publish her "re-expressions" of Indian poetry, for example. Mary presumed the problem rested not in her interpretation of Indians, but in New Yorkers' refusal to acknowledge valuable aspects of American culture that derived from west of the Hudson River. As she explained to Luhan, "For years now, I have been telling New York new things, things New York never heard of before, and things contradicting what New York believes at the moment, like the importance of the Indian in our culture. And it still strangely lingers in the New York mind that the telling ought all to come from New York," she complained in words that would warm Lummis's and Linderman's hearts, "and not from any other part of the country."[47]

Occasionally, Mary announced a minor victory. *The New Republic* published a review of several Indian books in 1926, which she prematurely interpreted as acceptance of Indians as key factors in national life and culture.[48] She took particular pleasure in this since writer Walter Lippmann had once ridiculed the idea. More often she experienced failure. Her play, *The Arrow-Maker,* flopped. The script offered a feminist message wrapped up in an Indian story. She tackled the theme of the waste of women's talents in an Indian setting, believing that in such a context no tradition prevented women from exercising their powers. Austin hoped that this contrast between primitive conditions and contemporary ones would convince the audience to support the "struggle of Femininity to recapture its right to serve . . . with whatever powers and possessions it finds itself endowed."[49] Reviewers and audiences were not impressed and the 1911 New York production closed after eight performances. It is noteworthy, however, that the *New York Times* reviewer thought the characters seemed more like "Anglo-American Indians" than American Indians.[50]

If Austin's cultural crusade often faltered, her political activities proved more successful. This was due, in part, to the fact that she had some powerful, dedicated allies in Mabel Dodge Luhan and John Collier. The three first met in pre-World War I New York City where Luhan, a wealthy woman, hosted a weekly salon attracting intellectuals, artists, writers, society people, and radicals. Austin encouraged Luhan to focus on the Indian "crisis." At this point neither Luhan nor Collier, a Georgia-born social worker who was intrigued with immigrant communities, seemed interested. Only after Luhan's 1917 move to Taos, New Mexico, did Indians take a more prominent place in her consciousness. She then encouraged Austin to visit New Mexico and introduced Collier to the Taos Pueblo. By 1922, Collier became consumed with Indian reform issues and when the Pueblos faced the threat of significant land and water loss through the Bursum Bill, Luhan and Austin joined forces with him to defeat it.[51]

This controversial bill became the first test of intellectuals and artists such as Mary Austin to transform their ideology into political action. Collier began a publicity campaign on behalf of the Pueblos and both Luhan and Austin helped. He published an article, entitled "The Red Atlantis," about the Pueblos that called for policy reform to preserve their way of life and end the destructive goals of allotment and assimilation. It was, according to one scholar, the "first article to . . . weave together the romantic, primitivist rhetoric of the ideology of regeneration with a practical program of action designed to save the Indians from economic and cultural demise."[52] This became the heart of the Indian New Deal reform ten years later.

Mabel Dodge Luhan leaped into the fray, gathering artists' and writers' signatures for an anti-Bursum Bill petition and encouraging friends to write pro-Pueblo pieces. By 1923, Albert Fall, secretary of the interior and advocate of the bill, was experiencing political problems of his own, linked, among other things, to the Teapot Dome scandal. Yet the Bursum Bill remained alive. Luhan and Collier decided that an East Coast publicity campaign and Pueblo testimony in Congress would help their cause. Luhan encouraged Collier to enlist Austin's aid, for the latter apparently felt overlooked in all the flurry surrounding the anti-Bursum Bill activity and was, consequently, angry. After all, she had been engaged in Indian affairs long before these Johnny-come-latelies. Collier wrote Austin a "mollifying letter," and by late January 1923 joined forces with her in the East. Austin reported to Luhan that during his publicity trip to New York, Collier "was wonderful." Furthermore, she patronizingly reported, one of the Pueblo men who participated in the tour, Antonio Romero, surprised her with his articulate speeches and quick mind.[53] Her enthusiasm was most pronounced in recounting their appearance at New York's Cooper Union, where the laborers and Pueblos established a rappport "that was of immense spiritual value to both." It was as if Indians and laborers "for once . . . had truly discovered the brotherhood of man."[54] Such efforts eventually paid off. The Bursum Bill was defeated.

But the euphoria Austin expressed during Collier's New York publicity swing did not last. Although Collier and Austin certainly shared a great deal, Mary always believed she knew much more than he did about Indians, particularly Indian arts and crafts. "Why is it," she wrote Luhan, "that people always feel certain that they know what is good for Indians in inverse proportion to the length of time they have been interested in Indians." Austin also doubted Collier's political skills. Unhappy with an alternative to the Bursum Bill which the Senate was considering, she wondered if Collier was part of this "stupid blunder" and doubted that Collier was a practical enough politician to be effective in Washington. Finally, Austin thought Collier's interest in Indians was "too philosophical and too largely economic" and not sufficiently romantic to catch on with the general public. "He doesn't know how to make them seem exciting and romantic figures, as the public likes to see them." Austin added that everyone thought the Indians sang and danced better when she managed them.[55]

Austin's longer association with Indians served, in part, as the foundation of her abundant self-confidence regarding knowledge of Indian cultures and art. Neither Luhan nor Collier challenged her on this. But Collier did contest Austin's judgments regarding practical politics and, consequently, they sometimes clashed. Frankly, issues of political rights, land tenure, and water did not engage Mary Austin. As Collier became more deeply engrossed in Pueblo land and other economic issues, Austin never wavered from her commitment to preserving Indian artistry and encouraging an American cultural revolution based on an Indian aesthetic. When it became clear that Collier's American Indian Defense Association, which he organized in 1923, would not put art before land issues, Austin and others in Santa Fe organized the Indian Arts Fund to protect the finest examples of pottery and weaving, rejuvenate Indian artistry (which they believed assimilationists had nearly crushed), and educate Anglo Americans about Indian art forms. She expected the latter would come to recognize the Americanism in Indian art and "make it a vital, redeeming part of modern American life."[56] By 1928, John D. Rockefeller, Jr. provided funds to finance the Indian Arts Fund's growing collection and to construct a building to house it. Austin promoted this fund as the leading national authority on Indian arts and crafts and, after Herbert Hoover's election in 1928, encouraged Charles J. Rhoads, new Indian Commissioner, to lift government restrictions on Indian artistic expression.[57]

In the meantime, Collier, who never intended to forsake Indian arts and crafts altogether, put together his own legislative plan and hired an advertising executive to pursue an Indian owned and operated corporation that would funnel profits into tribal funds. He also wanted the Bureau of Indian Affairs to assure authenticity through a trademark system. Austin did not approve. She worried more about the art's integrity than its marketability. Moreover, she did not believe the government's judgment on authenticity or integrity could be trusted. To make matters worse, Collier had proceeded without consulting her or the Indian Arts Fund. Once again, Austin was overlooked and angry.[58] In a series of testy letters, Austin expressed her displeasure with Collier's bill, assuring him that no need for legislation fostering Indian arts and crafts existed. They simply had to get the Indian Bureau to stop barring it from Indian schools. She went on: "When I advise you about Indian matters, I do not proceed by argument, but by intimate personal knowledge." And she imperiously added,

> *you must try to understand that for most of us the inciting motive is not philanthropic, but a thing much profounder, more intimate and more universal. . . . I fully realize that your particular temperament requires argument and formalization of your attitude. . . . But in reference to the arts one does not proceed in that manner.*[59]

Collier did not fold even when Austin chastised him for his "snootily" written responses. In the end, he suggested that further correspondence over the issue would be futile since "unconnected universes of discourses are involved." He did believe practical work required facts rather than "divinations."[60] In the short term, Austin prevailed simply because the deepening Depression doomed Collier's arts and crafts legislation. In the long term, though, he prevailed. After Roosevelt tapped him as commissioner in 1933, Collier ushered an Indian Arts and Crafts Bill through Congress.[61] Austin's contentiousness and sometimes downright eccentric behavior encouraged some to avoid her and others to ridicule her. Despite their differences, Collier did neither. In later years, he acknowledged that she was one of three or four Santa Fe friends upon whose support he could always count.[62]

In 1929, Austin told Mabel Dodge Luhan that what they shared at that point in their lives was the freedom of menopause, a fortunate turn of nature that "has provided a space of years in which we can put all our gathered wisdom into the game, stripped of its excess of personal emotion, a period in which we can be returned to society as purely social factors, no longer under the biological stress of being chiefly female." At age sixty, Austin was astonished at the influence and power she had exercised over the last ten years. "I hope just such a decade is before you, and that we may be able to work out some things together."[63] Clearly, among those "things" Austin hoped to work out, was Indians. By this time, they had found one other especially useful, middle-aged woman-ally, Anna Wilmarth Ickes, who joined them in writing about and politicking on behalf of Indians. She also, by 1933, brought into the equation a husband of some note: Harold Ickes, secretary of the interior.

On an August day in 1935, Anna Ickes left Mabel Dodge Luhan's Taos home, heading back to her own adobe ranch house near Coolidge, New Mexico. She never made it. Somewhere, on the road from Taos, her automobile crashed. Ickes died. "She was here at 3 all laughing and jolly," Luhan wrote to a friend, "and at 4 she was dead. Awful."[64]

Anna Ickes's demise on an isolated New Mexico road ended a productive but not completely happy, life. Her marriage to Harold Ickes, for one thing, was less than ideal. They weathered a separation in the mid-1920s, but when Franklin Roosevelt tapped Harold for his cabinet in 1933, the marriage appeared intact. This was far from a traditional marriage. Anna, a Republican member of the Illinois legislature, refused to surrender her seat to join her Democrat-husband in the nation's capitol. For a time, she prevailed. Anna assured a newspaper reporter that she was able to balance wifely and legislative duties while also managing "to wedge in several months every year for the Indian hobby she has brought to the importance of a vocation." She also told the reporter that no conflict existed between her Republicanism and her husband's role in the inner circle of a Democratic administration's cabinet.[65] By 1934, however, the political pressures to step down proved overwhelming, and Anna decided not to seek reelection. In a newspaper article titled, " 'Wife's Place Is With Husband,' " Anna indicated the situation had become too complicated.[66] An accompanying photo depicted Anna, Harold, and their sons Raymond and Robert all looking quite glum. Mrs. Ickes went to Washington.

Anna grew up in Chicago, the daughter of Henry and Mary Jane Wilmarth. According to one newspaper account, her parents were pioneer Chicagoans of wealth and prestige who gave their daughter the finest private school education that city, and Boston, could provide.[67] Her mother involved herself in Chicago civic affairs, serving as organizer and first president of the Chicago Woman's Club. She also supported the settlement house movement, sat on the Hull House Board of Trustees, and attended the 1912 Progressive National Convention as delegate-at-large with Jane Addams. Mrs. Wilmarth saw that her daughter, after travel in Europe and a debutante party, enrolled in the University of Chicago, one year after its opening. Anna attended the university for three years until her marriage in 1897 to James Westfall Thompson, an instructor who later became a well-known historian. The Thompsons, who had one son and adopted a daughter, divorced in 1909.[68]

Two years later Anna married Harold Ickes, a Chicago lawyer whom she first met during their University of Chicago days. The couple had one son and adopted another. They shared an interest in social reform and progressive politics and, by 1912, Anna and Harold helped form the Progressive Party in Illinois. Anna also supported the Women's Trade Union League, providing bail money for women strikers and even taking a place on the picket line when garment workers struck against Hart, Schaffner and Marx in 1910. As the Progressive Party's fortunes waned, the Ickes returned to the Republican fold. Anna's own public service career began in 1924, when the governor of Illinois appointed her to the University of Illinois Board of Trustees, normally an elected position. Later that year she won election and maintained her board position for five years.[69]

By the mid-1920s, the Ickes marriage was in trouble and in September 1925, they separated. Anna informed Harold she would allow him to return to the family only if he became "a responsible head of this household." She also wanted no more "shocks" or "humiliations," most likely over his extramarital affairs. Harold responded, "If you have been humiliated it has been of your own doing. Lately you have been gradually discarding the armor of good breeding."[70] Although the couple reconciled, Harold's proclivities toward extramarital affairs did not end. In the early 1930s, Ickes's mistress's *other* lover alerted the newspapers about Ickes's affair. In a gesture quite unlike modern tendencies to probe and publicize public figures' personal lives, the newspapers chose not to write about it. If Anna knew about it, she did not move toward divorce court.

Whatever the emotional state of their marriage, the Ickes remained political partners. In 1928, Anna ran for and won a seat in the state legislature with Harold as her campaign manager. She was reelected in 1930 and 1932, campaigning as a reform-minded legislator. By this time, however, her husband was head of the Western Independent Republican Committee for Franklin Roosevelt. This infuriated Anna who feared it would imperil her own political career. To mollify her, Harold promised to ask for the commmissionership of Indian Affairs, if Roosevelt won the presidency. Once in office Roosevelt offered not the B.I.A., but rather the entire Department of the Interior.[71]

Sacrificing her own political career and moving to Washington to support Harold's had at least one benefit. It allowed Anna more time, and opportunity, to devote herself to her long-standing avocation: Indians. She saw herself as an amateur archaeologist, as well as advocate of Indian cultures and Indian welfare. These interests, which her husband shared, stemmed from courses both took at the University of Chicago, where they were introduced to the new anthropology of Franz Boas and concepts of cultural relativism. Anna's introduction to actual Indians came in the early 1920s when, for health reasons, she began spending a part of every summer in New Mexico. Eventually, she established a vacation home near Coolidge, close to an archaeology dig, where she volunteered her services, and to the Navajos and Pueblos, who fascinated her.[72]

Anna Ickes's experiences in the Southwest eventually formed the foundation of her book about Indians. *Mesa Land*, published in 1933, was part travel book, part amateur anthropology, part popular history. It is somewhat reminiscent of George Wharton James's works, without the irritating assumptions of authority, the circus barker–promoter mentality, or the insensitivities. It paralleled Austin's appreciation of Southwestern Indian cultures, without the limiting and increasingly old-fashioned frameworks of primitivism and social evolutionary theory. Ickes's work, though simply written, was actually more sophisticated in its acknowledgment of non-Indians' fundamental ignorance about Indian cultures and up-to-date in its bedrock assumption of cultural relativism. Finally, the book shared Lummis's, James's, and Austin's belief in the intimate connection between the land and its Indian occupants. "The setting is so much a part of the life of the Indian today," Ickes wrote, "that any discussion of the Southwest must emphasize it." She took this idea a step further than her predecessors by not only encouraging the reader to shed normal standards of appreciation and beauty, but also to suspend traditional notions of ethics and morality. The desert demanded a new aesthetic, new standards of beauty. Indians required an openness to alternative ideals for they approached life from different premises than did Anglo-Americans. If the traveler can truly unlock his eyes, mind and heart "to this marvelous land and its mysterious dwellers he need never seek distant countries for interests historical, artistic or archeological."[73]

Ickes peppered the book with references to the works of archaeologists and ethnologists such as Washington Matthews, Jesse Walter Fewkes, and Edgar Hewett. She included a bibliography of scholars' works for further reference. But *Mesa Land*, intended for popular audiences, had a simple message: understand "the eternal brotherhood of mankind" and practice tolerance. She hoped the book would encourage people to look at Indians "not merely as a bit of local color, not as a romantic or grotesque figures . . . but as a man among men, a woman among women."[74] Anna did not idealize Southwestern Indians such as the Pueblos. She acknowledged their human propensity to bicker, fight, and engage in rivalries. But she also recognized their endurance, mystery, complexity, and distinctiveness. Whites had audaciously tried to transform Indians into white men, but so far, happily had not been successful. "They may disappear under uniformed compulsions. But become like us? Never!" She argued the "racial strain" was too deep, too distinctive to ever be eliminated. Then she added, "Mutual tolerance might effect a compromise and allow a civilization within a civilization to exist."[75]

Of special interest to Ickes, as it had been for Austin, Lummis, and James, was Indian religion and spirituality. The mysterious, secret aspects of Indian religion seemed especially compelling. But whereas Austin believed she not only understood Indian spirituality but also could interpret it for others, Ickes made no such claim. In fact, she maintained that white penetration had not unraveled the deep mysteries of Indian religion, except in the most superficial ways. Although the Pueblos sometimes allowed visitors to observe their ceremonies, they still carefully guarded their beliefs. Ickes' presentation of Native American religion is, in fact, unique among the writers' works examined here, because of her insistence that Indians maintained power over their practices and over outsiders' access to them. These religions were viable and vigorous and Indians remained in control. Ickes expected to be rebuffed rather than welcomed. She explained that she never forced her way into a ceremony (in sharp contrast to George Wharton James), and she urged her readers, who might someday visit a village and meet an emissary who asked them to turn back, to do so. In the past, insensitive tourists had closed Indian doors to future guests through laughter, thinly veiled sneers, or rude intrusions.[76]

If allowed into the Indians "land of myth and story and religious beliefs," however, one would "find the human approach to God similar in far-separated races. Brothers we are in the deep and significant things of life."[77] Nowhere, however, did she suggest Indians were primitive brothers. Austin's search for the universal forms of expression led her to collapse all Indians into "a generalized primitive" culture.[78] Ickes did not share this inclination. She did not differentiate the primitive from the sophisticated. Presumably, her anthropology courses at the University of Chicago taught her the folly of such constructions and sensitized her to the diversity and complexity of Indian cultures. Still, she believed at the heart of all cultures rested some core beliefs, values, and needs which brought people together, even equalized them.

It seems no one could write about the Southwest without engaging its Hispanic heritage and so, in keeping with Lummis, James, and Austin, Ickes offered her own history beginning in 1540. She criticized the Spanish conquistadors' treatment of Indians but admired their courage and stamina. Towing a middle line between Lummis's glorification and Austin's condemnation of the Spanish, Ickes defined the Pueblo Revolt as "the last desperate attempt to throw off the yoke of the invader" and described Popé as a hero. Spanish conquest cost the Pueblos dearly. Many lost their lives. Many communities disappeared. And yet one could still find Pueblos living today as they had before the Spanish came.[79]

In fact, neither Spanish conquistadors nor Anglo-American boarding schools had destroyed the Pueblos. More optimistic than Austin, Ickes maintained "the daily life goes on, and two thousand years have made little change in the habits of living or the habits of thought." Yet Ickes still feared that their unique civilization, complex ceremonial life, and art was jeopardized by contact with a dominant race whose outlook on the universe was so different. What threatened them went unsaid, but her growing concern about their future and belief that these villages contained something worth saving was undeniable.[80]

Although Ickes admired the Pueblos, her home was actually situated closer to the Hopis, Zunis, and Navajos. So she included these people in her amateur anthropological account, providing capsule views of their respective customs, character, and beliefs. In the process, of course, she hopelessly overgeneralized about them. The Hopis, Ickes claimed, were home-loving, peaceful farmers. The Zuni, perhaps more than any other tribe, lived in a world of symbolism where ritual and life closely intermingled. Moreover, they had managed to maintain the integrity of their social and religious lives in spite of white encroachment. Their ceremonies remained virtually untouched by outside influences. Finally, the Navajos were merry, given to joking, and likely to take on a sober demeanor only as a protective mechanism when near whites. Moreover, Navajo women exercised influence and power. Some even became medicine-women. All were very adaptable, acquiring art, religious observances, and economic practices from others. Yet in the most essential things, they remain untouched by white influence. The only trait Ickes found unattractive about "my Navajo" was their willingness to flock to Zuni Pueblo during their house blessing ceremonies, "uninvited and not over-welcome," to eat. The Navajos were taller, more dynamic, and less philosophical and contemplative than the Pueblos. But they were intensely religious and became "a bit puzzled when white folks [came] to them preaching a God of love and demonstrating only too often a God of hate." Finally, Ickes asserted that like all people of all races, the Navajos felt themselves above all others. Tribal outsiders were not only foreigners, but also inferiors.[81]

Ickes demonstrated greater humility than Austin and others when it came to claiming either the authority or the ability to define Indian religious values or explain rituals or ceremonies. But she shared their inclination to essentialize Indian cultures and revealed a hint of maternalism in references to "my Navajos." She urged tourists to approach Indians with sensitivity and to see the beauty of their cultures. At the same time, she perhaps unconsciously encouraged them to intrude into Indian homes and ceremonies, presenting them as curiosities or fodder for the tourist appetite. Finally, she brought to her study of Indians a familiarity with the concept of cultural relativism, yet littered her work with concepts of racial difference.

Ickes was not an intellectual, an artist, or a professional writer. She called her book "my very unpretentious effort" and was most grateful for Mary Austin's kind review in *The Nation*. *The Washington Star* review suggests that not all readers understood Anna Ickes's purpose in writing the book. Focusing on the more superficial aspects of *Mesa Land*, the newspaper urged visitors to the Southwest to take it on their next vacation if they wanted something beyond the guidebook providing hotels and other facts. "Different Indian dances are described with great vividness and many of the taboos are humorously compared with our own customs."[82] Alas, the review made no mention of Ickes's brotherhood of man theme.

Of course, Anna Ickes's true milieu was politics, not literature, and throughout the 1920s she involved herself in the New Mexico arena of Indian reform. She attended the All Pueblo Council meeting at Santa Domingo, which convened to discuss the city of Albuquerque's plans to build a dam that would flood out Santo Domingo. The Pueblo Legal Aid organization advised the Pueblos on strategy. Charles Fletcher Lummis and John Collier attended. Anna watched as Lummis translated from Spanish into English, and vice versa, for hours. Later she happily remembered him that day as energetic, precise, and in good humor.[83] He died soon after. But Collier, of course, was just in the dawn of his career, and he and Anna Ickes worked well together from that point on. In contrast to Austin and Luhan, neither of whom had experience with or an understanding of practical politics, Ickes was a potent political partner.

Collier called on Ickes, then, to help lobby the Senate regarding the Pueblo

Conservancy bill and other legislative maneuverings in the late 1920s. He relied on her reports including one on Navajo reservation schools.[84] Anna's disappointment when President Roosevelt chose her husband to head the Interior Department rather than the Bureau of Indian Affairs was soothed, in part, by Collier's appointment as commissioner. They worked beautifully together and shared basic beliefs about appropriate goals for Indian policy reform. As she told a reporter in 1933, she was delighted in the choice of Collier as commissioner and that she intended to keep advising him that Indians needed the opportunity "to run their tribal affairs in their own way."[85]

Once in power as commissioner, Collier did turn to Anna Ickes for advice in dealing with the Navajos as he tried to find allies who would support his reform efforts on their reservation. Ickes and Collier discussed B.I.A. personnel issues and they worked together to usher Collier's Indian Reorganization Act through Congress. It is interesting that while Anna Ickes criticized past policymakers for failing to distinguish between tribes, she did not express the same misgivings about Collier's all-encompassing reform. She believed that all Indians would, indeed, benefit from the legislation which Collier identified as the "Indian Land and Self Government Bill." And when he asked Ickes for her public support at meetings, press conferences, and national radio broadcasts, she obliged.[86]

In this capacity Ickes participated in a meeting at the Cosmos Club where attendees discussed changes in policy, including repeal of Indian allotment, restoration of traditional communities, and replacement of government paternalism with Indian self-government. Collier, Dr. Lewis Merriam of the Brookings Institute, and writer Oliver LaFarge joined Ickes in this discussion. In the meantime, Mary Austin attempted to recruit Ickes to her side of the conflict with Collier over Indian arts and crafts, but Ickes astutely sidestepped that complication, telling Austin that if she had any ideas relative to the topic, she should put them in writing and Harold Ickes would give them immediate, personal attention.[87]

By 1934, Anna Ickes was in the public eye, not because of *Mesa Land* but because of her position as wife of the secretary of the interior. She used the publicity attendant on that role to promote her interests in Indians among newspaper readers, especially women, who found most pieces on Anna Ickes in the society or women's pages. As one newspaper account put it, "Next to Mrs. Roosevelt, Mrs. Ickes takes the prize as the most active lady in the Cabinet. Her average is about three speeches per week plus as many dinners. Her favorite topic has been described as 'Indians—Just Indians.'" The article went on to say that Anna was even more interested in Indians than her husband. An *Indianapolis Star* account claimed that Anna's interest in Indians explained, at least in part, her husband's selection as secretary of the interior, although his interest "nearly equalled" hers.[88]

Her annual trips to New Mexico also attracted attention and she used those occasions to educate readers. She dismissed reports that she spoke "Indian fluently," had been adopted into a tribe, or given an Indian name explaining that such stories perpetuated wrong images of Indians who, she asserted, never adopted non-Indians or gave people Indian names. Her purpose in living among them was not to become Indian or pry into their lives, secrets, or customs. She lived near Coolidge, New Mexico, simply because of its proximity to the site of her archaeological studies. The Indians who lived nearby "I have incidentally learned . . . to love . . . as individuals, not as picturesque oddities, which seems to be some Americans' conception of them."[89]

Of course, most journalists made no distinction among tribal groups, and so when Collier and Ickes visited the Seminoles in Florida, Anna had to explain she had no expertise regarding these Indians. The article went on to claim, however, that in the "realm of the Indian, Mrs. Ickes is probably much more at home than her husband." In a move designed to calm the concerns of the likes of Frank Linderman and others upset with women in politics, Mrs. Ickes somewhat disingenuously added, "in the soft, feminine voice that makes her career as a public figure seem incongruous, 'It is the Indian lore, archeology, home life and psychology that have interested me more than the phase of the problem conveyed in the term Indian affairs.'"[90] Clearly, however, Indian affairs remained a vital interest.

A few months before her death, Anna Ickes attended a masquerade party at the White House. She dressed as a Zuni woman, complete with moccasins and authentic jewelry. The *New York Herald Tribune* printed some photographs from the party, including one of Mrs. Ickes.[91] The costume did not suit her, making her apppear stout and even portly. One wonders how the Zuni would have felt about her masquerading as one of them. Still, in some respects, it was a moment of triumph. The costume represented her commitment to Indians; the occasion represented her position at the apex of national political power. Finally, the opportunity to institute substantive change in the nation's treatment of Indians had arrived, and she was well positioned to help. Sadly, her untimely death in 1935 meant Anna Ickes would not live long enough to witness the results.

# 9

# MABEL DODGE LUHAN

## *Muse of Taos*

MABEL DODGE LUHAN has long been identified with northern New Mexico and the Taos Pueblo. Yet her first trip to the American Southwest brought her, not to Taos in 1917, but to El Paso in 1913. Accompanying her lover, journalist and radical John Reed, who was covering the Mexican Revolution, Mabel Dodge dashed off postcards from the border's edge to friends Gertrude Stein and Carl Van Vechten. On the back of a card featuring a scout from Pancho Villa's army dressed in sombrero, bandoleer, blanket, and sandals, Luhan wrote facetiously: "Here is part of the 'world spirit' on the loose—our constant companions." She found El Paso "the vulgarist town in the United States," and its people, whether Indian, Mexican, or Anglo, unappealing. Luhan concluded, "I'm afraid the West is a man's world & that woman's sphere is in New York."[1]

All that would change dramatically four years later when she returned to the Southwest, this time to join her new husband, artist Maurice Sterne. He sought inspiration and found it among the Indians of northern New Mexico. Within a short time, Luhan decided not only that the West, or at least Taos, could be a woman's place, but that it was also a place of mystical power. The Indians, in particular, moved her both figuratively and literally. Convinced that she had found a source of spiritual power, harmony, and inner peace, Luhan moved to Taos. She then assigned herself the task of finding a literary mediator who could interpret and publicize the world she had discovered. Assuming the mediator would be a man, and a European or Anglo one at that, Luhan still carved out a central role for herself. She would be the muse, the force that would help give voice to what she fashioned to be the inspirational but inarticulate West and its supposedly mute Indian inhabitants.

Although one historian has dismissed Luhan as insignificant in the context of eastern intellectual and cultural matters, a similar assessment cannot be made concerning her western life.[2] She did not dabble in the region, she helped define it. She did not merely visit it, she lived it, making the West her home for over forty years. She did not simply "play" Indian, she married one. Luhan not only lured a large number of writers and artists, including D. H. Lawrence,

Mary Austin, and Georgia O'Keeffe, to New Mexico to become important interpreters of the Southwest, but she also wrote about it herself. Finally, in the political realm she appointed herself the "savior" of Indians. If her own direct involvement in Indian reform proved limited, there is no denying her importance in bringing John Collier to New Mexico in the first place. She introduced Collier to Indians and helped launch his career as antiassimilationist reformer and eventual Commissioner of Indian Affairs.

For all these reasons, then, Mabel Dodge Luhan represents the culminating figure of this study. She reimagined Indians in a most dramatic, emphatic way. She worked hard to undermine assimilationist impulses and to save Indian, or at least Pueblo, culture from Anglo domination and ultimate destruction. Undeniably, primitivist impulses played a role in her thinking. It is also true she did not shed completely nineteenth century concepts of race. Yet she helped push peoples' understanding of Indian beyond old forms by insisting on the value, and even superiority, of their cultures. For, in the end, Luhan claimed the Indians saved her—and offered the modern world a chance for redemption. She fervently believed the Pueblos' example presented the possibility for personal and cultural regeneration. The "future of these continents," she wrote repeatedly, "lies with the Indian Americas."[3] Others in this study, certainly, moved in this direction. Luhan was there. She most clearly and consistently articulated this view of Indians in her own books and in her relationships with other nationally significant cultural movers and shakers of her generation.

Luhan's reintroduction to the Southwest was accidental. By 1917, her reputation as a Greenwich Village salon-keeper was well established. She mingled with American intellectuals such as Gertrude Stein, Max Eastman, Walter Lippmann, and Emma Goldman. She flirted with radical politics, participating in the Paterson, New Jersey Strike Pageant. She promoted the groundbreaking Armory Show of 1913, which brought Post-Impressionism to the American art scene. Luhan enjoyed her relationship with the avant-garde and saw herself as a proponent of modernism in America. Clearly her position was buoyed by family money (she hailed from a wealthy Buffalo banking family), for Luhan was neither an intellectual nor an artist. Her wealth, social standing, and fame garnered her many invitations to join and support radical causes. Yet Luhan saw her primary role as a "muse," a "mirror for men's imaginations." Lacking the focus and confidence to take on personally many of the political and literary tasks that came her way, according to one of Luhan's biographers, she preferred being "woman as earth mother," whose purpose was to "regenerate society by inspiring its great male talents."[4]

By the winter of 1915, however, Luhan had retreated from the world of New York's intellectuals and political radicals for a farm on the Hudson River. There she discovered psychotherapy and began a long association with analyst A. A. Brill. She also met Russian-born artist Maurice Sterne and became his patron, muse, lover, and eventual wife.[5] Nothing was further from her mind than the West and its Indians in 1917, the year she married Sterne. This was Luhan's third marriage and it was probably doomed from the start. Several years into their relationship, but before they married, she wrote Sterne that their mutual passion had subsided and their new phase of love was one of friendship. Sterne's amorous adventures with others also posed problems. But they married anyway. The *New York City Herald* reported that when queried about his romance Sterne replied, "'It was no romance at all . . . we just decided to get married. There was no need of telling everybody about it, because marriage after all, concerns only the contracting parties.'"[6] As if to underscore the absence of romance, Sterne headed west for a honeymoon—alone. Luhan provided him with the funds to go first to Wyoming, and eventually New Mexico, in search of subjects for his work.

Although Sterne found Wyoming physically stimulating, he did not find it intellectually, artistically, or spiritually invigorating. In November 1917, he headed south to Santa Fe and Taos, destinations known, even then, to attract artists. Sterne was skeptical, noting that famous places usually failed to interest him, whereas unknown and undiscovered places such as Bali had much greater appeal. He had stumbled upon Bali during a 1912 tour of Asia and, moved by the beauty of the landscape, the people, "their exquisite aesthetic sense," and their harmonious society, he stayed for two years. While Sterne admired their "well-defined group consciousness" and the "harmony that functions person to person, and also between man and his land," he ultimately left Bali precisely because of this group consciousness that evoked fears of "death and the loss of individuality."[7]

Once in New Mexico, however, Sterne forgot the darker aspect of Balinese group culture and found the Pueblos' communities similarly attractive. He decided to stay awhile, moving into a room at San Idelfonso Pueblo. Although he later claimed he never liked New Mexico or Indians, his 1917 letters indicate otherwise. He became acquainted with and grew fond of the people of San Ildefonso. Moreover, his experiences there caused him to wonder, in a letter to Luhan, "why . . . beauty vanishes with civilization." He went on to elaborate a theme his wife would eventually take up in her own work and writing regarding Indians: modern western civilization encouraged individualism which made people awkward and self-conscious. But Asians and American Indians were neither making their every pose, every movement beautiful. Still, for all its attractions, Sterne never seriously considered locating permanently in New Mexico. After the year he expected to sail for Italy, where he planned to settle down and work.[8]

In the meantime, Sterne remained ambivalent about the prospect of Luhan joining him in New Mexico. He did not want her to come until he was deep into his work. He did not want her to travel alone, nor did he believe she, a woman long accustomed to luxury, could possibly live in an Indian pueblo. At the same time, Sterne encouraged her. He was certain she would love Indians and have great rapport with them, especially the women.[9] But perhaps the greatest prod came with Sterne's clarion call to action:

> *Do you want an object in life? Save the Indians, their art, culture—reveal it to the world . . . That which Emily Hapgood and others are doing for the Negroes* you *could if you wanted to do for the Indians—for you have energy and are the most sensitive little girl in the world—and above all there is a strange relationship between yourself and the Indians.*[10]

Sterne envisioned Luhan organizing Indian dance performances in New York and Washington, D.C. to encourage an American realization that other forms of civilization besides theirs existed.[11]

Little did Sterne realize how quickly and seriously Luhan would take his advice. Unwittingly, he set into motion the passionate work she would pursue for the rest of her life, not to mention the end of their marriage. Without Sterne's flattery about her supposed rapport with Indians and his urgings to save them, it is quite possible Luhan never would have come to New Mexico. Certainly, she hesitated before making the fateful move. While still in New York, Luhan confided to a friend that Sterne was living in "an indian mud hut . . . and I must say it doesn't seem just my kind of thing." She urged Sterne to pick out an Indian family, hire them as models for six months, and house them in a cottage near her home at Croton-on-the-Hudson. There he could study their habits, rhythms, and poses. Seeing them as objects rather than people, Luhan thought moving some Indians to New York would resolve their dilemma: Sterne could pursue his art and they could be together. Apparently, he was not interested in this arrangement.[12]

Sterne's musings about her affinity with Indians, meanwhile, intrigued Luhan. She thought it possible that some part of her might parallel their lives—at least "the live part of me," she wrote, for "[my] inner life is a life that finds no counterpart in western civilization & culture."[13] At this moment, life in New York seemed spiritually sterile, and Luhan longed for something with which to connect, for her involvement in radical politics and modern art left her emotionally unsatisfied. She began to exhibit, in fact, that strain of antimodernism which sought mystical and spiritual experiences. Hungering for an intensity seemingly absent in the modern world, such antimodernists took great interest in medieval mystics.[14] Luhan, though, would find her source of otherworldly spirituality not in Europe's mystics but among the West's Indians. Significantly, this all began for her in a powerful dream.

She had been deliberating whether or not to join Sterne one night in November 1917, when she woke up, opened her eyes and saw Sterne's face, or more accurately Sterne's face in composite with an Indian's face, suspended in the air over her night table. Frightened and certain that this was a visitation from Sterne's soul, she worried that he was in harm's way at that moment. Later, Luhan claimed the Indian face she saw in her dream was that of Antonio Lujan, the Taos Pueblo man she eventually married. Once in New Mexico,

*In 1917, Mabel Dodge Luhan found her way to Taos, New Mexico. Reproduced by permission of the Yale Collection of Western Literature, Beinecke Rare Book and Manuscript Library.*

when Tony told Mabel that he had dreamed of her before she came to Taos, she replied, "'I saw you in a dream, too, before I left New York. It made me come here.'"[15]

Whatever the reason for the move, Luhan arrived in December 1917, with certain expectations about Indians and her relationship to them that Maurice Sterne had undeniably shaped. He would live to regret it. Although they had their reunion in Santa Fe, Luhan wanted to hurry to Taos, which she learned about at a Taos Society of Artists show just before leaving New York.[16] By the spring of 1918, Luhan was completely smitten with that little northern New Mexican village, writing to friend Neith Hapgood, "We are in the maddest, most amusing country in the world—in the freakiest—most insane village you ever dreamed of and *I* would like to stay forever!" Among the attractions of her new life "'on the edge of the desert'" were Mexican penitentes, "extraordinary" Americans who, like medieval mystics, starved and scourged themselves in order to see God. She was especially thrilled with the Indians. Of the latter Luhan wrote, "I am in love with the indians and they think I am one and talk to me in indian."[17]

What she failed to mention in her letters was her relationship with Tony Lujan. Only many years later, in her autobiography, did she present a public rendition of her early days in Taos. That version of the relationship emphasized the deep, spiritual connection she made with Tony, beginning with their very first meeting. Immediately, she recognized him as the Indian from her dream and claimed that merely by being in his presence she experienced an acute sense of life's rich possibilities. She did not deny Tony's physical attractions, with his face "like a noble bronze." In fact, Mabel acknowledged Tony reached her "on all levels of body, soul and spirit" and compared his awakening of her soul with her first orgasm at age eighteen. But she emphasized the psychic and emotional elements of their relationship and the way Tony provided a "deepening reality of life." She insisted they made this connection before they became lovers. Although psychically intimate, Luhan insisted, they did not become lovers until after Sterne left Taos.[18]

Sterne's version differed. He granted that when Luhan first arrived in New Mexico she was immediately entranced by the Pueblos, their drums, their music, even their silences. She hardly spoke during her first days in Taos, but Sterne could tell "she was deeply stirred." When Luhan announced that this was where she belonged and where she intended to stay, he was not surprised. From the beginning Sterne believed she did belong; he even thought she had probably inherited some Indian blood from her maternal ancestry.[19] He believed her general interest in Indians, however, was soon eclipsed by her infatuation with Tony Lujan. Rather than finding an affinity with Indian women, as he had anticipated, she found it with one particular man of great sexual and spiritual attraction. "That my appeal to her to save the Indians would be wholly focused upon one magnificent symbol of a vanishing race, had never occurred to me," Sterne dryly wrote, adding he did not like Lujan from the start. "[H]e had a well fed arrogant look." When Sterne inquired if Lujan was a chief, another Pueblo supposedly laughed at the thought and pronounced him "'a no-good show Indian.'" Lujan's fondness for Anglos and ease with their culture, according to Sterne, stemmed from his experience in a Wild West Show that once played Coney Island. Yet Luhan was attracted to him, Sterne claimed, because he had "form." "That it was petrified—that it had come to a stop and was not creative," he added sourly, "she did not in the least mind, because all she needed was a powerful tree with roots in the earth."[20]

As Sterne bitterly remembered it, Luhan declared their house too stuffy at night and so she acquired a tepee, which became Mabel and Tony's trysting place. Sterne would awaken with the sound of horse's hooves nearby, followed soon after by Luhan returning to bed. Those nocturnal meetings disgusted Maurice and the fact that this affair was common knowledge in the small town of Taos only deepened his humiliation. Finally, Sterne fled for New York, turning his "back upon Taos and its odious associations," leaving Luhan "to tackle a more powerful antagonist."[21]

The Sternes' marriage was emotionally finished but did not technically end until their divorce in 1922. In the meantime, Luhan provided Sterne with a monthly allowance and occasional letters. Luhan wrote about the house she was building adjacent to Pueblo property. She continued to enthuse about Indians noting, "We all need to dream . . . That is why the indian thing satisfies me. It is a dream." About Tony she remained silent, although Mabel impatiently dismissed Sterne's reports of New York gossip concerning her new life in the West. Moreover, Luhan indicated she was healthy, occupied, contented. Writer Mary Austin was visiting and others were coming. Plowing and planting was underway. Finally, she summed up her Taos life: "now as always my way of life is an honest endeavor to find out the essential *meaning* of life."[22]

For all of Tony's apparent allure, Mabel continued to insist much more was at stake in Taos than her individual happiness or personal regeneration. It became clear that Luhan believed Indians understood the "essential meaning of life" and she longed to share this insight with others. A hope for nothing less than social regeneration eventually enveloped Luhan. In 1919, she wrote friend Neith Hapgood that while everyone sought "acute spiritual realization" Luhan had, at last, found it in Taos. "The indians say that Taos is the beating heart of the earth," she explained. "The indians have made this place what it is—and consciously." She urged Hapgood to come to New Mexico and share in its spiritually cleansing properties.[23]

Luhan's ambitions for the Taos Pueblo as model moved beyond a handful of friends. Over the next several decades, Luhan summoned a remarkable collection of writers, painters, musicians, and intellectuals to her Taos home. Luhan wanted these visionaries to experience the place and people as she had and to spread the word about its potential healing power. This cluster of creative people, cultural radicals, and counterculture types of the interwar period who accepted her invitation included Andrew Dasburg, Marsden Hartley, Mary Austin, Carl Jung, Willa Cather, John Marin, Georgia O'Keeffe, Ansel Adams, Edmund Wilson, Aldous Huxley, Maynard Dixon, Leopold Stokowski, Martha Graham, Frank Waters, Laura Gilpin, and, of course, D. H. Lawrence and Robinson Jeffers.[24] In addition to inviting people into New Mexico, she also attempted to send a part of New Mexico out into the world. Mabel sent Maurice, for example, a series of paintings by Pueblo artist John Concha and asked him to show them in New York. She wanted a label, indicating that Mabel Dodge Sterne sent them, prominently displayed "because at the 1st big independent show I exhibited Gertrude Stein's 'portrait' *& launched her*." Maurice replied that this was the sort of thing he had in mind when he first wrote to her about saving Indians. "But I fear it is hopeless—everything with which the white race has come in touch with is bound to be destroyed. I mean everything beautiful, spiritual, powerfully sublime."[25]

That note of pessimism did not discourage Luhan. Schooled in the art of both politics and propaganda during her Greenwich Village years, she set about applying those lessons to the Pueblos' problems. In 1920, Luhan invited social worker John Collier out to New Mexico, just in time to observe the Christmas ceremonials at Taos Pueblo. They knew one another from New York days when Collier devoted himself to social justice causes, particularly regarding immigrants and workers. He believed the preservation of immigrants' communal traditions would help them survive in America's cities. For over a year, Luhan wrote letters to Collier, urging him to visit New Mexico and see the "magical Indians." Finally, he succumbed and became her "most important convert."[26] She took him not only to Christmas Eve ceremonies but also to the Red Deer Dance at Taos Pueblo where he found, at last, the genuine community of art, individual, and spirit that he had been seeking. It changed the direction of his life, just as it did Luhan's. By spring 1922, he began a new job with the General Federation of Women's Clubs Indian Welfare Committee.[27]

The first campaign to draw Collier back to New Mexico in summer 1922 was a New Mexico senator's bill to confirm all non-Indian claims to land and water where they could prove continuous possession. The Bursum Bill, as noted earlier, mobilized not only Collier but also Luhan and others of the Santa Fe and Taos artistic/literary set. Mabel sent Tony and Collier out in her car to read the Bursum Bill at every pueblo and to urge their collective action against it. She also advised the Pueblos to petition Anglos for their help. Meanwhile, playwright and poet Witter Bynner composed an anti-Bursum Bill petition for artists and writers, signed by, among others, C.E.S. Wood, Mary Austin, and George Wharton James. Such efforts brought so much publicity to the Pueblos' situation that, she claimed, every newspaper in the country, except for the *Taos Valley News*, opposed the bill.

Luhan also composed publicity material for Collier in 1922. Five years after her arrival in New Mexico, she was prepared to write her first manifesto on the meaning and significance of Indians to all Americans. Pueblos were mobilizing, she wrote, to awaken an interest in Indians which had been asleep in the American consciousness. This small group of "other-world men" was penetrating the American soul and demonstrating that Americans loved Indians and would not allow government policies to destroy them. Echoing Lummis's comments of twenty years earlier, she claimed that visitors to Indian schools became depressed when they saw the Indian children in awkward uniforms and with shaved heads, stripped of their own grace and dignity. Even more disheartening was the assault on their "mental modes—despoiling them of their ancient vision of the land and its culture for which they had a deep, poetic love, and substituting other symbols for their ancient life-giving ones." Artists and writers especially wanted to abolish this school system and preserve Indian cultures, for they understood that Indians could give Americans "knowledge of the beauty and wholeness of that almost secret nation within the nation."[28]

Publicity such as this helped defeat the odious Bursum Bill. Luhan, however, was not satisfied solely with political victory. As she explained to Leo Stein, Gertrude's brother:

> *My desire now is to keep this publicity of the indian question* alive *and have it become a part of our racial consciousness instead of our* unconscious-ness. *Only in this way can we stem the tendency to sweep out indian culture.*[29]

She elaborated on her grand plans for Indians as models, not just for Americans, but for the entire world. If Mary Austin anticipated a national aesthetic revolution inspired by Indians, Luhan hoped for a vaguely defined global revolution of consciousness. She even offered her Taos property as headquarters or "base of operations *really* for a new world plan," the center for this global transformation. To underscore her determination she told Collier, "I am really *in* the indian current . . . I mean Tony is a kind of symbol for my having gone over into an 'otherness'. . . . When I left the white people's world I *really* left it—it was not mental attitude or superficial sensational gesture." Collier replied that their fight was just beginning and the first step was to establish their right to dictate Indian policy "before we can demand for the Pueblos the kind of thing you write of."[30]

That Luhan's perception of things Indian began and ended with the Taos Pueblos was already apparent. Even neighboring Pueblos were inferior. She deemed the people of Santo Domingo Pueblo fierce and more barbaric and those of Cochiti as less pure than Tony's people. Mabel had little interaction with other Southwestern tribes and no conception whatsoever of those who lived in other corners of the country. Her fixation on the Pueblos, and Taos Pueblo in particular, would eventually cause a rift between Luhan and John Collier when he ascended to the commissionership in the 1930s. Even in 1922, she urged Stella Atwood, chairman of the General Federation of Women's Clubs Indian Welfare Committee, to release Collier from all responsibilities except those relating to the Pueblos, maintaining that "there is something big & fine & new" to come out of work with the Pueblos.[31]

Atwood was not completely unsympathetic to Luhan. Yet she was determined to see that economic and health conditions were addressed first. Once people were well-fed and healthy, then reformers could move on to revamping the Indian Office's education program and encouraging knowledge of Pueblo life. As to Luhan's plans for a new world order, the conservative Atwood remained silent. In the meantime, Atwood needed Collier for problems brewing beyond northern New Mexico. Other Indians also required attention and "although they are not quite so picturesque perhaps," Atwood gently chided Luhan, "yet they . . . all have their value, not alone in an economic way, but ethnologically." Atwood was certain that had Luhan landed among the Navajos she would have been taken with their ceremonies, prayers, and inner life.[32]

In truth, Luhan was not completely oblivious to political realities. She feared that living with Tony while unmarried would be used to discredit the pro-Pueblo movement. Apparently, that concern provided at least partial motivation for Mabel and Tony's marriage in the spring of 1923. Correspondence with Collier also demonstrated Luhan's awareness of everyday, practical issues among the Pueblos. She donated money for medical aid to Taos Pueblo, although Tony's brother-in-law suspected she would eventually demand land in exchange for the donation. She wrote letters about the Blue Lake controversy and the Middle Rio Grande Conservancy Act. In the work-a-day world, small issues grabbed people's interests and energies. Mabel could not stay out of them either.

Yet it was the larger issues—the philosophical, metaphysical ones, which most excited her. Even in the midst of the Bursum Bill crisis, Luhan admitted she was "preoccupied with that wretched Lawrence."[33] After reading several of D. H. Lawrence's books, including *Sons and Lovers*, *Psychoanalysis and the Unconscious*, and *Sea and Sardinia*, Mabel decided, in 1922, he was the person best suited to articulate the essential qualities of Taos and its Indians for a broad readership. She concluded he would be able to understand and convey to others the spiritual power that hovered over Taos Valley. So, she invited him to New Mexico, describing Taos as a quiet, pastoral land far from the railroad. Lawrence wrote back, asking if the Indians were dying out and if that wasn't terribly sad. He went on, "I believe what you say—one must somehow bring together the two ends of humanity, our own thin end, and the last dark strand from the previous, pre-white era. . . . Is Taos the place?" Clearly, Luhan believed it was and she enlisted others' assistance to convince him. Leo Stein encouraged Lawrence to accept Luhan's invitation, writing about the wonders of Pueblo Indian ceremonies and her skills as a hostess. She would, Stein promised Lawrence, take him everywhere, show him everything. But most important, he testified, Luhan "is the only educated, cultivated woman that I know of who has broken through the barrier between red and white and keeps it open in both directions." Finally, Mabel called upon Tony to help, although he hesitated because, she claimed, he like other Indians believed that writing about Indians would lessen their power. Nevertheless, Mabel convinced him to use his "magic" and in the fall of 1922, D. H. Lawrence and his wife, Frieda, arrived in New Mexico.[34]

Early correspondence between Lawrence and Luhan revealed several potential trouble spots in their relationship. First, Luhan discovered Lawrence despised psychoanalysis, therapy, and all forms of "conscious activity," things which fascinated her. She decided to overlook this. He also revealed a certain distrust of "dark people." If he came to the United States, Lawrence expected Indians would interest him as long as "one is sure that they are not jeering at one. I find all dark people have a fixed desire to jeer us." This was especially irritating, he went on, since he found little to admire in them. "They seem to be built round a gap, a hollow pit."[35] Lawrence's attitudes about race annoyed Luhan from their first meeting in Santa Fe, when she sensed Lawrence was not only conscious of Tony but also embarrassed by him. She believed that Frieda Lawrence "immediately saw Tony and me sexually, visualizing our relationship. I experienced her swift, female measurement of him, and how the shock of acceptance made her blink." Frieda later chastised Luhan for taking such an "old fashioned *moral* attitude" about Frieda's propensity to "see life from the sex center." Luhan, Frieda wrote, made thinking of people in sexual terms sound censorious when in fact it was the clue to people, the "ultimate thing that interests one *really*."[36]

Her disappointments with the Lawrences notwithstanding, Luhan was not inclined to abandon her purpose in bringing them to New Mexico. Early on she drafted Tony into escorting Lawrence to an Apache fiesta. Upon his return from that excursion, Lawrence told Luhan he wanted to write a novel based on her life, starting with her departure from New York and focusing on her "renunciation of the sick old world of art and artists." This was exactly what Luhan had been hoping for, although she claimed it would be a story not about herself, but about America:

> *it was for this I had called him from across the world—to give him the truth about America: the false, new, external America in the east, and the true, primordial undiscovered America that was preserved, living, in the Indian blood-stream.*[37]

Of course, it *would* be about Mabel, her vision of Indians and her experiences with Tony. The latter, she told Lawrence, was particularly important because Tony had "awakened [her] dormant heart." He taught her how to love. Yet somehow that was not enough. Tony communicated silently through the pores of his skin and by his intuition, but Mabel needed words.[38] Lawrence, she felt certain, could supply just the right words.

Alas, according to Luhan, Frieda would not allow it. She objected when Luhan invited Lawrence to work on her rooftop, outside her bedroom. Luhan countered that unless they worked together, in her home, they would not work at all. That ultimatum ended the work. As Luhan saw it, she and Frieda were competing for possession of Lawrence: his wife dominated his physical side; Luhan hoped to control the spiritual. When Frieda's influence predominated, Lawrence "would, in brilliant vituperative talk, sling mud at the whole inner cosmos, and at Taos, the Indians, the mystic life of the mountain, and the invisible, potent powers of the embodied spirit." At other times, defying his wife, Lawrence would talk about the power of consciousness and about the growth and triumphs of the soul. Luhan insisted she had hoped to "seduce his spirit" but not his body for she did not find him physically attractive. She wanted his soul, his will, his creative powers. Luhan needed Lawrence because she did not know how to use her own powers of perception. "I wanted Lawrence," she wrote, "to understand things for me. To take *my* experience, *my* material, *my* Taos, and to formulate it all into a magnificent creation."[39]

As it turned out, Lawrence had no interest in serving as Luhan's instrument for articulation. Her will to power drove him and Frieda away, fleeing to Luhan's little cottage on the Del Monte Ranch seventeen miles north of town. Rumors began to circulate that Lawrence was writing a nasty book about her. Bert Phillips, a Taos pioneer painter, sent a message to Lawrence's landlord that if the rumor was accurate, "a selected bunch from Taos would proceed up the mountain & horsewhip him!" Lawrence did, of course, write a short story, "The Woman Who Rode Away," inspired by Luhan's life. In it, a white woman sacrifices herself voluntarily to Indians who cut out her heart.[40] This story did not, however, sever the relationship and the Lawrences eventually renewed their friendship with Luhan and even returned to New Mexico in 1924.

Luhan, by now, realized that her plans for using Lawrence as a literary voice for this voiceless land would not materialize. She explained to Mary Austin that Lawrence was completely disconcerted by Indians when he discovered they were not at all like James Fenimore Cooper's Indian characters. Moreover, Lawrence believed they were evil, witchlike, and full of hate and opposition. Actually, Luhan went on, "It is D. H. who is evil at times, witchlike & full of hate! As for opposition!!! He dies of opposition." She reported to Leo Stein that Lawrence had been a dismal failure as both visitor and appreciator of "the whole thing." Lawrence, she concluded, "just didn't get it."[41]

Lawrence would disagree. Although superficially he did not particularly like Indians, he confessed to Luhan, he did deeply sympathize with them. What he particularly *opposed*, however, was Luhan's plans for them. "You can't 'save' them," he wrote from Mexico in 1923, harking back to Maurice Sterne's supplication. Politics, he believed, would only ruin them and so would Luhan with her "lust even for a Savior's power." John Collier, as well, with "his own White egoistic *benevolent* volition would, with your salvationist but poisonous white consciousness, destroy them." Their poking and prying into Indians was indecent. Finally, Lawrence admonished Luhan, "The only way to help the Indians is to *leave 'em alone*."[42]

Luhan, of course, would not be swayed. Next she lured California poet Robinson Jeffers to Taos, hoping he would become the literary channel for her vision of Indians. Luhan began working on Jeffers and found in Una, Jeffers's wife, an ally, for she liked Mabel and saw a New Mexico sojourn as a pleasant holiday for the Jeffers's sons. "Do bring Robin to do the Mexicans & the Indians! He *sees* things so," Luhan urged Una Jeffers. In the meantime, Luhan did not passively stand by. Instead, she wrote up her experiences with Lawrence in a manuscript addressed to Jeffers and eventually published it as *Lorenzo in Taos*. "Perhaps you are the one who will, after all, do what I wanted him to do: give a voice to this speechless land." Jeffers finally capitulated and after their first visit was nearly complete, Luhan reported to her son, "I believe [Jeffers] will return & do this country in poetry as it has never been done. Mary Austin says he is the 'appointed poet for New Mexico!'"[43]

The Jeffers family returned for a number of annual summer visits, but Robinson Jeffers never became the New Mexico poet Luhan hoped for.[44] In fact, he only wrote one poem about Indians. Una Jeffers, meanwhile, urged Luhan to stop looking for someone else to write about New Mexico and the Taos Pueblo and to do it herself. Interestingly, it was mostly women who urged Luhan to pick up pen and express her own vision. Jeffers pointed out that Luhan had already written an "unforgettable & true picture" of Tony in *Lorenzo*. Margery Toomer, writer Jean Toomer's wife and an author herself, also found the Indian parts of the Lawrence book particularly fascinating. "And I thought and have thought ever since," she wrote to Luhan, "'why doesn't *she* write the Indian book she wanted Lawrence and the others to write. She is the person. She has the conception, the appreciation and understanding—why doesn't *she* do it?"[45] Luhan's New York analyst, Dr. A. A. Brill, seconded her women friends' advice.

Actually, Luhan had been writing for some time. As early as 1916, she acknowledged a creative impulse in a letter to photographer Alfred Steiglitz, explaining that she had a compulsion "to add a mite more to the consciousness already in the world." When she wrote this, Luhan was dabbling in painting, but she eventually realized her abilities rested more with prose. During her New York years, she published a few articles in *The Masses, Mother Earth, The International*, and the New York *Evening Journal*. In New Mexico, she published several pieces in Spud Johnson's *Laughing Horse,* and in 1924, she told Mary Austin that such exposure brought her invitations to produce more work and that she liked to see her name in print. During the winter of 1925–26, Luhan began to write in earnest, composing the first volume of her memoirs. The encouragement of Una Jeffers, Margery Toomer, and even D. H. Lawrence provided the impetus to seek a publisher.[46]

In 1932, Alfred Knopf published her first book, *Lorenzo in Taos*. Harcourt, Brace and World followed that debut in quick succession with her four-volume autobiography: *Intimate Memories: Background* (1933), *European Experiences* (1935), *Movers and Shakers* (1936), and *Edge of Taos Desert: An Escape to Reality* (1937). She also published *Winter in Taos* in 1935. She wrote all the books, of course, from a post-Taos perspective, although Luhan attempted to recreate a sense of her life before Tony. She described herself, during her European years, as stupid, unhappy, heartless, and desperate. "How any of us have ever survived at all the system we inherited & were conditioned by, is more than I can understand." Luhan realized the difficulty of the task she assigned herself: "to give a picture of one's inner self." Yet she believed she had succeeded in taking off her mask, in showing her "actuality" as a "20th century *type*."[47] Reviewers did not necessarily agree.

If reviewers' frustrated her, so too did the task of translating Taos and Tony Lujan onto paper. In fact, she found the fourth volume of her memoirs the most difficult to complete. It was also the most important "for the other vols are senseless without this one which intends to show one can overcome heredity & environment—can change—can get a root—can *become* in fact!"[48] She elaborated on her writing dilemma to Carl Van Vechten:

> *The Tony book. How ever shall I be able to do it justice? To show the fatal undying charm & magnetism of those rare &* sterling *qualities—of integrity, goodness, heart? . . . And to show this without explanations, descriptions or interpretations but only by telling the words & the behavior—how difficult it will be—when Tony* says *&* does *so exist for me in* being *what he* is*!*[49]

In the meantime, Una Jeffers continued to encourage Luhan by telling her that she and Robin *did* understand what she was getting at, "what the Indian thing has meant to you." Anyone who knew her understood how Taos harmonized her life. Luhan's problem, Una explained, stemmed from trying to write about an aspect of her experience which was still evolving, not yet complete. The other autobiographical volumes dealt with finished aspects of Luhan's life, but her message about the magical aspects of Indian life "is a thing of emotion and not of intellect & until you come to an *end* out of it . . . it's fearfully difficult." Jeffers recommended that Luhan simply record her impressions as straightforwardly and objectively as possible.[50]

Finally, twenty years after she arrived in New Mexico, the "Tony book" came out. *Edge of Taos Desert* is Luhan's treatise on Indians: what they did for her and what she believed they could do for all people. It is also a critique of her time, her "epoch," as she puts it. As a solution she offers the adoption of Indians' sense of reality and relatedness to one another and to the earth. Whereas Maurice Sterne thought Pueblos had a "real Art of their own," Luhan believed it was "their life that seemed so real to me . . . Real, real, and deep as fate and full of wisdom and experience." A key element of its attraction was its essential incorporation of community, connectedness, and group consciousness. Luhan learned, through Indian examples, that the only way to experience true freedom was "to live as a group, and to be part and parcel of a living tribal organism, to share everything. . . . For certainly a shared misfortune must vanish when so divided, and joy pooled must gain immeasurably beyond the slight nervous spasms we know in our aloneness."[51] Leaving the artificial, alienating world of New York behind, she had longed to join the Indian life and regularly visited Taos Pueblo which, she claimed, was her real home.

In truth, Luhan was not especially welcomed there. The fact that Tony left a Pueblo wife to live with her did not endear her to the community. Furthermore, she was certainly aware of internal divisions within Taos Pueblo, including a rift between peyotists and those, including Tony, who opposed its use.[52] Her most direct connection with the Pueblo, of course, came through her relationship with Tony. And in marrying him she certainly came closer to joining her life with an individual Indian's, if not his community, than any other figure in this study. In fact, Tony became Mabel's sole entrée into the world she envisioned as Indian. She credited him with awakening in her dormant feelings and emotions and with teaching her to understand her relatedness to the earth, her surroundings, and other people. "Being with him liberated me, freed me from my world, made me *become* myself," she wrote in a comment that echoed Mary Austin's, George Wharton James's and Charles Fletcher Lummis's self-revelations in the Southwest.

Beyond the psychic and emotional attributes Tony provided, she also admired Indians' freedom from materialism. Mabel praised their supposedly simple life and claimed she wanted to emulate it. Here she quoted Tony providing him with the syntax Hollywood allowed its Indians:[53]

*Mabel Dodge Luhan built her home on the edge of Taos Pueblo, but she was never incorporated into the tribal community. Reproduced by permission of the Yale Collection of Western Literature, Beinecke Rare Book and Manuscript Library.*

> *White people have* things, *but God gave the Indians just what grows on the mountain . . . God gave white people things and Indians watch them go under them. You know. Wheel turning . . . So many things carry the wheel down, with the white people underneath. Pretty soon Indians come up again. Indians' turn next.*[54]

Mabel agreed white people allowed "all the accretions of our civilization" to weigh them down. Buildings, machines, inventions, collections of things suffocated people. They *were* going under.[55]

It was the spiritual aspects of Pueblo life, what Luhan called "the Indian cosmos," that most fascinated and attracted her. She experienced it whenever she was with Tony or in the Pueblo. This cosmos was difficult to define precisely, but Mabel gradually learned to respect its "inviolate unspoken mysteries" and to understand that her own culture was "losing certain values through the violations of our incorrigible and over-curious scientists." She believed these indefinable faculties gave Tony his dignity and poise. He seemed to easily bear the whole cosmic universe on his shoulders. This is what gave him "weight and balance . . . strength and fulness of being [which] was strikingly unlike the shifting demeanor of many white men who seem unballasted and empty and uncertain when they come hurrying along on their unconvincing errands."[56]

In the end, the most valuable lesson Mabel Dodge Luhan said she learned from Indians, and of course from Tony, was that love could overcome the conditioning of childhood and the legacies of heredity and environment. "I came to Taos," she concluded, "where I was offered and accepted a spiritual therapy that was cleansing, one that provided a difficult and painful method of curing me of my epoch and that finally rewarded me with a sense of reality."[57]

*Edge of Taos Desert* received a mixed reception from reviewers. Eastern reviewers tended to mock it; western reviewers did not. "Mary Austin used to say grumpily," Luhan wrote to friend Hutchins Hapgood, "the N.Y. critics never knew there was anything west of Broadway and it gets truer and truer!" When her publishers urged her to come east for a few days and have lunch with some of the reviewers, she refused. As she explained to Una Jeffers, "I want them to know me thro' my books—the point is there! After 100 years or so they will catch on!" Alas, many did not "catch on" with this book or with *Winter in Taos*. "They haven't even an idea of what I'm trying to do," she lamented. At least her friends (and eventually some critics) did understand and found the latter to be her best book. Una was even moved to write, "Perhaps I have never told you earnestly enough how very much I respect and admire your writing." Interestingly, the individual personalities which figure so prominently in her other books, play little role in *Winter in Taos*. Rather, it celebrates the harmony of Taos's natural and communal environment. Mabel feared that the absence of people made it not only quiet, but also dull. Yet she explained to writer Elsie S. Sergeant, "it *may* contain the slow readaption to the essential form of life so many have lost. I hope so."[58]

While acknowledging the Anglo and Mexican inhabitants of Taos's community, *Winter in Taos* again presented the Indians as the wisest. Ensconced at the base of their sacred mountain, they had learned the secrets of living. They knew best how to cope with the cyclical aspect of nature for they knew "they are themselves the earth and the rain and the sun and when the sun sets they feel the peace and rightness of it." While Anglos looked at Nature as something outside of themselves, Indians viewed themselves as a part of Nature. In addition to their connection with Nature, Indians also had it with one another. "Like a flock," she claimed, "a tribe is actuated with a single impulse, where the simple, major needs are concerned . . . they all move as one in a large rhythm of life in the winter."[59] In short, according to one recent critic, Taos became for Luhan what Walden Pond was to Thoreau: a place where she could "unify the opposing forces in her life."[60]

Luhan was not satisfied with her books. She found them too negative. She did not believe they effectively communicated what Taos and Tony meant to her. She felt unequal to the task, unable to muster the deep understanding it required.[61] So she turned to a different literary form, the novel. The result was a manuscript which Luhan entitled "The Water of Life." The setting is not New Mexico but rather an imaginary European town she called Trido. She claimed the characters were also imaginary although they represented contemporary, social types. The main female character, Gaza, sounds strikingly like Luhan. And although no Pueblo Indians played a part in the story, Luhan repeated her basic message about primitive or tribal people being the only ones whose "life-pattern has remained natural" and consequently the only ones who are happy.

Gaza is unhappy because she is separate, unsocial, solitary, and asexual. Her inability to love is not her fault but rather that of a "system that victimizes all of us" by emphasizing individual property and rights and thus destroys love. Tribes and ancient communal groups, however, never suffered from this affliction. What people needed to regain, she believed, was human relationships. They needed to relearn how to be individual and collective, simultaneously.[62]

Luhan encountered difficulties getting the novel published and so she considered another form of communication: the movies.[63] She first flirted with filmmaking when, in 1928, she helped Robert Flaherty, who wanted to make an Indian Pueblo picture, acquire financial backing for the project. Flaherty came out to Taos, intending to live there for one year before he touched a camera. But he gave up the venture, concluding that the camera could never capture the inner life of the Indians. In fact, he believed it could not be known by outsiders at all. Luhan was much less enthusiastic when Leonie Sterner arrived in Taos in 1933, with Collier's approval, to make a movie of Indian communal life. Apparently, Mary Austin also encouraged Sterner's ambitions, to which Luhan's response was: "what does she [Austin] know about Taos indian life? Nothing!" Luhan's reservations about Sterner's project included doubts about the character of the filmmaker who, she claimed, had been arrested on the Jemez reservation for "dissipating with indian boys." More important, she shared Flaherty's doubts about the viability of photographing Pueblo life, especially Taos Pueblo life. As she explained to Carl Van Vechten, Taos Pueblo people believed that they did not need to record ceremonies on film because they intended to practice and therefore preserve them perennially. Moreover, they resented the role of ethnographic curiosity and wanted to protect their ceremonies from "becoming an art delight without the great living nourishment of Being!"[64]

Luhan had doubts about cinema itself. She feared its artificiality and its impact on values. A friend, Frank Waters, who was writing scripts in Hollywood encouraged her to look beyond the movies' crudeness and vulgarity and to see them as a new, valid form of communication as well as art. Evidently, Mabel overcame her scruples, at least enough to compose a scenario and begin a filmscript that she entitled "Conquest." Set around 1500, the period of Spanish colonization of the Rio Grande, this was a movie that would have satisfied James *and* Lummis, for it allowed both the Spanish and the Pueblos to play heroic roles. Luhan conceived Part I as "Force of Arms" followed by Part II, "Force of Love." She envisioned an opening scene in an Indian village which portrayed their communal living and conveyed the peoples' dignity. The village peace would be shattered when the Pueblos spotted the Spanish. A battle begins, but Luhan, clueless about presenting warfare on film, threw up her hands and wrote on the manuscript, "Director, I cannot cope with this battle." She was much more comfortable describing the "Force of Love" section where two couples, one Spanish and the other Pueblo, along with a compassionate priest "with a powerful sex appeal," help reconcile European and Indian cultures.

Luhan's movie scenario ended with an epilogue. Twenty-five years later the village contained a small mission church in its center. Inside the church the camera would focus on a statue of St. Francis, who resembled the sexy priest, while the Pueblos engaged in a Harvest Dance before the saint. In short, Spanish and Indian now mingled together in a free and friendly fashion. The force of love overcame the force of war and all lived happily ever after. Perhaps to no one's great disappointment, Luhan never completed the script.[65]

Writing represented a central part of Luhan's life. Her voluminous correspondence, books, articles, and unpublished manuscripts all attest to that. Yet she once told Dorothy Brett that "Being, not doing, seems to me more important than anything else."[66] And certainly an important part of Being for Mabel in Taos was her connection with Tony Lujan. In both personal and public utterances, she presented him as the core of her Indian experience. *Edge of Taos Desert* makes clear his central role in her conversion. By marrying an Indian man, with all the challenges a cross-cultural, interracial partnership posed for them in their private relationship, as well as in the larger world, Luhan at the very least *attempted* to move closer to an "Indian reality."

The marriage attracted much attention, both because of Luhan's fame and for being mixed race. Even her supposedly sophisticated friends gossiped about it and succumbed to racist stereotypes. Carl Van Vechten sarcastically referred to Tony as the "chief" in correspondence with Gertrude Stein. Stein wrote to Van Vechten, "Not a word from Mabel at all. Lo, the poor Indian."[67] Mary Austin once rather cruelly told Luhan that among their friends Tony was "a joke, [although] a good natured and occasionally ribald joke." Over ten years after their wedding, the match still garnered comment. When Oliver LaFarge published a story in *Saturday Evening Post* about an Anglo woman's love affair with an Indian who rejected her after his baby died, Luhan received a sympathetic letter from a friend who assumed the Mabel-Tony liaison inspired the tale. Mabel doubted it, since she and Tony "have weathered 18 Hard Winters and no babies dying or other casualties." She went on to express her anger at those who continued to pry into her personal life. She thought her upcoming fifty-fifth birthday merited retirement from the curious, but she doubted gossip and speculation about the couple would ever end.[68]

Luhan apparently did not mind, however, when her friend Elizabeth Shepley Sergeant's biographical vignette, which appeared in the *Saturday Review of Literature,* featured Mabel's marriage to Tony, noting how she had departed from the social milieu of her background and created one of her own "in which racial taboos, even have been set aside." The relationship underscored Luhan's credentials as a cultural and social radical. However, in marrying a Pueblo man, Sergeant hastened to assure readers, Luhan had not embraced a primitive way of life and renounced a civilized one. She continued to run her household along the "canons of 'civilized society.'" Sergeant described Luhan as an adventuresome person and a "man's woman." She might appear to be a forerunner

*Tony Lujan became Mabel Dodge Luhan's primary conduit into Taos life and culture. They married in 1922. Reproduced by permission of the Yale Collection of Western Literature, Beinecke Rare Book and Manuscript Library.*

of American feminists, "the footloose, much-divorced lady, who puts individual expression, change and diversity before the old laws of hearth and home." But Tony, "the tall virile Indian, full of racial pride and power," was the kind of man "who could make a captious powerful woman . . . into a relatively stay-at-home wife." Through Tony, Sergeant claimed in a statement that neatly summarized Mabel's preferred view of her marriage, Luhan's attachment to home grew deeper. Out of place in the modern world, her relation with Tony provided the perfect place for an American antimodern woman. Her "primitive traits . . . which were disrupting in a more mental and mechanized world, here found real earth to grow in."[69]

Interestingly, Mabel did not see intermarriage between Anglos and Indians as a wise strategy for others. In fact, she feared the consequences of intermarriage for the perpetuation of Indian cultures. "Although I married an indian," she explained to John Collier, "I did not do so when we were both young & I don't believe in it for others." She feared in such marriages, the Indian's culture would be lost as he or she became absorbed into the Mexican or Anglo cultures. According to Mabel, Tony agreed and thought an especially dangerous combination was Indian and white for the latter "are destroyers."[70] And it was not necessarily easy for Anglos who committed themselves to such a match.

"What incomprehensible aloneness for the white woman Who crosses over into the Indian heart!" she wrote in *Lorenzo in Taos*.[71]

Yet she insisted that only with Tony could she be healthy and content. Mabel presented this same view of Tony in her personal correspondence. She informed Hutchins Hapgood that not only had she truly discarded the Anglo world, in favor of the Indian world, when she joined up with Tony, their lives were inextricably tied to one another . . . forever.[72] Not all her friends bought this view of the marriage. Luhan was especially sensitive to those who hinted she really *did not* leave her world behind but rather transported it with her to Taos, and that she never truly entered the Indian world. Frieda Lawrence, for one, questioned Luhan's conversion to things Indian, writing to her, "had Tony & the indians been *my* show I would gone Indian the whole hog." This infuriated Luhan. "Does she mean I should have gone to live in the Pueblo?" Mabel fumed to friend Dorothy Brett:

> *In the first place it has been Tony's* conscious wish *to go out in the world & live in it & develop himself up out of the tribe as an individual &* I have followed him. *Had* he wanted *to make his way* in the tribe *& shown any wish for me that way I would have followed him* there. . . . *How obtuse* [*Freida*] *is! Can you imagine me living in the Pueblo* or Tony either? *His whole* effort *is roused from life out in the world!*[73]

Ironically, Luhan did not see in this angry reaction any contradiction with many of her published works regarding the deep attractions of communal life. What she seemingly admitted here was that Tony preferred and even sought the outside world's opportunity for personal development. Also, by insisting that in making these choices Tony determined the contours of their marriage, Mabel ignored the complexity of their relationship and the fact that her will contributed to Tony's motivation to leave the Pueblo and her wealth provided him with the resources to do so. Tony did provide Mabel with love, some insight into Pueblo values and behavior, and perhaps even "a new sense of reality." At the same time, she most certainly provided Tony with the things of her world. Mabel most decidedly resided in the Anglo world, albeit on the edge of Taos Pueblo property. Tony seemed to go back and forth.[74]

Luhan was unable, however, to view their relationship as a blend or compromise between Anglo and Indian, so consistently did she insist that her husband dictated the values of the marriage. Only once did she drop her guard, revealing a completely different assessment of the relationship. It happened at a crisis point. Luhan met and became infatuated with African-American writer Jean Toomer. Not only was Toomer handsome, but he was also a disciple of the Russian mystic Gurdjieff, whose philosophy, according to one scholar, "combined a critique of Western civilization with a course of self-study that presumably led to total psychic harmony through mastery of the universal laws of 'cosmic consciousness.'" Toomer's charms and Gurdjieff's teachings appealed to Luhan. In 1925, she invited the writer out to Taos, offered her home as a potential Gurdjieff center in America, and even gave Toomer a $14,000 loan to lure the mystic to New Mexico. Toomer came to the Southwest, accepted the money, and initiated a serious crisis in Mabel's marriage. Her fascination with Gurdjieff and his attractive disciple crushed Tony.[75]

In a series of passionate letters to Toomer, Mabel revealed misgivings about Tony and the limits of that relationship. At one time, she explained, Tony had awakened her heart but now she was alarmed at her coldness toward him. The problem was she could not communicate consciously with him. Moreover, he bored her. She had suppressed this realization by occupying herself with other people, "always holding Tony before me like a banner or something that had to be accepted as a prior consideration in my life by anyone who wanted to come near at all to me." Now she realized that she had, quite simply, outgrown him. That realization brought with it a perhaps exaggerated sense of responsibility for Tony. Mabel blamed herself for taking him away from his wife, his community, "his pattern of life," and replacing those with "the soft things—of living." He no longer hunted, preferring the larder from Mabel's kitchen. He no longer walked, preferring to drive the car Mabel provided. She could not reproach him, however, because he was her product—"the product of my egotistical wishes during our first years together when I worked on him day & night—to separate him from his past & make him a present new born man for my own purposes." Tony, she decided in a devasting self-critique, was "the conquered—the subjugated . . . 'a spoiled indian.'"[76]

Meanwhile, she reported, Tony was so depressed that he talked of death. Alone in the world, he could not return to Taos Pueblo and had nowhere else to go. Mabel felt trapped. "I am caught in a net that I have woven around myself," Mabel concluded. "To break it & jump free is to repeat at one hundred per cent more ruthless a level the heartless & selfish escapes of the past: That is not the solution -but Oh! What a blind alley."[77] Even if she exaggerated her role in shaping Tony Luhan, there is no doubt that Mabel, at least momentarily, saw herself as a ruthless manipulator. Rather than becoming Indian through Tony, Mabel had de-Indianized Tony.

Toomer encouraged Mabel's interest but did not return her passion. Over time, it became clear that Gurdjieff was not going to establish a consciousness center in Taos nor was he going to repay the loan. Over time, Mabel's ardor for Toomer cooled, Mabel and Tony reconciled, and she never again saw herself as quite the demon she claimed to be in 1925.[78]

Mabel's dreary depiction of her marriage in these letters to Toomer, along with her confession of manipulating Tony, proved to be, in fact, unique. More typically, Luhan leaped to defend the marriage, as in her furious reaction to her son's suggestion that Tony irritated her because he hampered her in cities and was a burden. Mabel did not deny those things but went on to say that what Tony gave her in terms of comfort and security far outweighed such minor aggravations. True, Mabel no longer felt a sexual attraction to Tony, but the spiritual, psychic and "subtle form of love" between them was still strong. On another occasion she told Dorothy Brett, "Tony . . . year by year grows, develops & Goes On, seeming wiser & more mellow & always, to me, quite incalculable."[79]

In the end, the most accurate view of Mabel's relationship with Tony was the one she described to Toomer *and* the one she described to Brett. It was a marriage of genuine connection and genuine frustration. Mabel felt both deep affection for Tony's strengths and deep annoyance with his limitations. She did not flinch from acknowledging these different responses. For all Mabel's faults, one cannot deny her willingness to look at herself, and others, honestly. As a friend once put it, "Mabel, having no imagination, tells only the truth as she feels it."[80] Over the years, Mabel and Tony worked out a compromise, a marriage that, if far from perfect, worked. Mabel, of course, never did leave her world behind. She never could nor did she truly want to. What Mabel hoped to do was transform the world, not forsake it. Moreover, she tried very hard, through force of will and the lure of her Taos place, to bring her world of artists and writers to New Mexico. She took extended trips to California, New York, and eventually Mexico. She even temporarily revived her old salon in a Fifth Avenue apartment in 1940 and used that as a forum for Indian issues. Mabel had not forsaken her past, her compulsions, or her culture nearly as much as her books suggested.

At the same time, she participated—if only on the sidelines—in some aspects of Pueblo life. Once Tony gave a party outside Taos Pueblo for some visiting Kiowas. It was a "Present Dance," wherein the Kiowas received a flurry of gifts from the Pueblos. "Presently I saw Tony presenting one of our best old Mexico serapes to the chief! Ho Hum!," she wrote. Mabel had not completely overcome her "heredity" in acknowledging the value of that material object and flinching at its loss. Yet she acquiesced to Tony's way and said nothing about the gift. That night, while reading Thomas Mann on Freud, she heard the drum and singing from the pueblo. "Such odd extremes in one's life here! But very real, all of them."[81]

Just as Mabel did not leave her world behind, Tony did not sever his relationship with the Pueblo either, Mabel's claims to his being "alone" notwithstanding. On occasion he returned to Taos Pueblo to sleep with Candelaria, his former wife. He retained his position on the tribal council and remained influential in tribal matters, but his marriage to Mabel barred participation in kiva ceremonies. Even that changed in 1935, when he was invited back into Taos Pueblo ceremonial life. "This is my chance," he told Mabel and, although it meant giving up his beloved riding boots for moccasins, Tony welcomed the opportunity to have the pueblo once again "fold . . . him in their arms."[82] Mabel shared his enthusiasm, as she explained to Una Jeffers,

> *we both feel this is the thing to do. It is wonderful how they are bound together in a common belief, a* concern *about the elements that makes them feel they must all work together and unite their power to keep things* right. *And they*

> *may be doing more than white people know, for surely we don't* know *a thing really, only more and more* measurements *year by year, that don't* tell *us anything. What, on* earth, *do we* know?[83]

Mabel also claimed that if Tony wanted to be governor, they both could live in the Pueblo and inhabit the top room of his family compound. "[W]ouldn't that be fun?" she added.[84]

Tony Lujan did not become governor of Taos Pueblo, but by 1934, he was actively involved in encouraging the Pueblos and other Southwestern Indians, including the Hopi and the Jicarilla Apache, to support new Commissioner John Collier's Indian Reorganization Act (IRA). In a report he submitted to Collier, Lujan indicated he told the Hopi Collier was their friend. Whereas other commissioners tried to destroy ceremonial dances and Indian religion, Collier fought to save them. The IRA, Lujan urged them, represented Collier's effort to protect them.[85]

If Tony proved a constant ally for Commissioner Collier, Mabel proved more troublesome. Initially, she was euphoric about his appointment, telegraphing him: "GLORY BE . . . START NEW ERA NOW." Now they could work together, marshalling powerful, national forces not only to save Indians, but America as well. Alas, that was not to be. Mabel seemed to think that Collier had been appointed Commissioner of *Taos Pueblo* Indian Affairs. She inundated him with letters regarding local issues, ranging from conditions in the hospital, to a missing flute, to whether or not a Pueblo school assembly room could be used for basketball games. Finally, in 1936, Collier wrote in frustration to her, "I cannot possibly have the information to act on [such local issues]. . . . I wish you would take some occasion to get a total view of the Indian job and Pueblo job as they are now being attempted." This reaction infuriated Luhan but she did not stop plying him with more messages about not only specific, local issues but also with criticisms of Sophie Aberle, Collier's appointee as Superintendent of the Pueblos. Some Indians, and Luhan too, objected to a woman in that job. She believed Collier was "man enough to hear the truth and that you *should* hear it from someone," insisting her first loyalty in life was toward Indians and always would be. That such loyalty led her into opposition with Collier seemed crazy and, she concluded, what Collier needed was to spend more time in Indian country. Collier retorted that unless Luhan was willing to grant Collier a "minimum of intelligence upon my own part," her information about matters in New Mexico would prove useless.[86]

Luhan kept Una Jeffers informed of her battles with Collier. Not only was she unhappy with Aberle, but she also believed Collier was undermining genuine self-determination at Taos Pueblo by interfering with a tribal decision concerning peyote. Mabel interpreted Collier's attempts to persuade the tribal council to rescind fines levied against peyote users as an attack on Taos self-government. So, she jumped in, encouraging Anglo politicians in the area to consult with the Pueblo and inform them they had the right to run their community as they wished. In the meantime, Secretary of the Interior Harold Ickes informed the Pueblo they had to allow the minority group freedom to use peyote. Luhan was convinced this directive came out of Collier's instigation and was meant to punish the governor and the council for criticizing Aberle. She persevered and managed to obtain a hearing before some senators who visited New Mexico that summer. The hearing proved inconsequential and Luhan concluded the only hope for Indians was abolition of the Indian Bureau. No one, not even John Collier, could run it to the advantage of Indians.[87]

By this time, Luhan had expanded her quarrel with Collier, writing a letter to an editor about Aberle's supposed incompetence. She also corresponded with Harold Ickes, indicating she feared Collier would strike out at her through the Taos Pueblo for her opposition to Aberle. She offered to come to Washington to set Ickes straight about the facts but indicated that she would have to meet him at his home rather than his office for, if Collier knew she was talking to Ickes, he would strike back by harming the Pueblo. Ickes was not interested in Luhan's subterfuge and told her that if she had any allegations to make against Collier she should put them in writing.[88]

Mabel Dodge Luhan and John Collier did not communicate with one another for the next four years. In 1940, however, Luhan decided to reinaugurate her salon at One Fifth Avenue. She wanted Collier to speak at one of her "evenings," and she also wanted to introduce him to Frank Waters—"you see he too mutters to himself as I have for so long: 'The future of this continent lies with the indian americas.'!" Apparently, they patched up the friendship for Collier did address one of her "evenings," speaking about his plans for an Institute of Indian Affairs of the Inter-Americas. Collier even invited Luhan to serve on the organization's coordinating committee.[89] But Luhan's "evenings" were not the rage of 1940s New York that they had been in the pre-World War I days and they faded away.

Much had changed in the twenty-plus years since Luhan had left New York for New Mexico. As the world moved toward another global war, Mabel and Tony withdrew to Taos. She announced herself a pacifist and concluded "I cannot see that anything save a complete awakening & a change of heart can help the world." So, she ignored the war and its implications—until the war came to New Mexico. Not far from her Taos refuge, physicists developed the atomic bomb. By late August 1945, the secret was out and the bomb had ended the war. Now the scuttlebutt in northern New Mexico revolved around rumors that Los Alamos scientists were developing nonmilitary uses of atomic energy. Luhan confessed to Una Jeffers that she was scared. "Any minute we might be blown up. . . . I am very depressed about that whole thing anyway & when I heard it I felt it was the worst news I had heard in my long life time." Nothing in Luhan's experience prepared her for this. All she knew for certain was that man was "not sufficiently developed [*sic*] yet to be given this Knowledge!" Yet several months later she indicated, "We have stopped thinking of the atomic bomb! We are too busy coping."[90]

By this time Mabel Dodge Luhan was in her late sixties. She would live until 1962. Much of her correspondence from the 1940s focuses on declining health, both hers and Tony's. Her crusade to save the Indians—and the world—no longer consumed her. In 1941, she was hospitalized in Santa Barbara, California, and realized that financially it made sense to give up the Taos place, with its expensive upkeep and servants. But that was not really an option for them because Tony "has to live there & besides it is our home." She added, "I hope we can live there in partial peace till what is going to happen, happens. As it will!"[91]

Her letters to Carl Van Vechten chronicle her ailments, particularly her fading eyesight. She remained intellectually active, however, by devouring the books Van Vechten continued sending. Mabel especially loved J. D. Salinger's *Catcher In the Rye*. "I agree with every word the sixteen year old little character says about *everything*," she wrote Van Vechten, "& I bet a whole lot of kids nowadays feel the same way he did." If Mabel was flexible enough to identify with Salinger's youthful protagonist, she could also accept the inevitability of aging. Although all her friends were either sick or dead and her own vigor was fading, she told him, "nature is wonderful & sets up a mechanism that makes one accept *anything* so I am quite healthy & happy & peaceful. I don't know how. But it is so."[92]

Evidently, alcohol played some role in the Luhans' lives but in 1957, John Collier told Elizabeth Sergeant they were no longer drinking and, for the most part, were living wisely. Five years later, in January 1962, Collier, then living in nearby Ranchos de Taos, reported that Tony and Mabel were both very near the end. "Taos, the Pueblo, is as great as ever before." Two months later he repeated the same interesting juxtaposition. "Mabel & Tony Luhan have gone to pieces entirely. . . . The Pueblo Indians go on as grandly as ever before." In September, Mabel died. Collier acted as one of the numerous honorary pallbearers at her funeral at the Episcopal Church. It was a scorchingly hot day. A white guide led Tony in, but he seemed confused and was soon spirited away. Collier was uncertain about Tony's future but was convinced his mental and physical condition precluded his return to the Pueblo. Tony died one year later and was buried in the Indian graveyard within Taos Pueblo.[93]

As for Mabel, she was buried in the Kit Carson cemetery. Ten years before her death, the cemetery caretaker approached Luhan asking if she would like to buy a plot there, indicating the locals extended this invitation in recognition of her "old-timer" status and the fact that she had done much for the town of Taos. Luhan decided not to reveal her animosity toward Carson whom she, in contrast to Austin, deemed "one of the great indian killers." To be buried in Kit Carson's Park when he was famous for killing Indians and she was famous for saving them was, she told Carl Van Vechten, "quite odd!" Still, she decided to buy the plot and "so Kit Carson & I will be eternally connected!"[94] Her grave is located in a far corner of the cemetery, as far from Carson as possible.

In 1949, writer Frank Waters wrote to Luhan, "I sometimes wonder if you yourself realize what you have built up [at Taos]. Something so intangible that people ebb & return without knowing it is a center of gravity. And the same thing is happening out at the pueblo, and everywhere throughout the world. . . . Toward a new pattern, but still rooted in the old." If Luhan was disappointed that her plans to make her home a center for a new world order did not materialize, she could at least take solace in such words as Waters's. She also could feel delight in having encouraged Waters's works. She thought his book, *The Man Who Killed the Deer*, a novel inspired by Taos Pueblo, magnificent. At last she had found someone to give voice to the supposedly speechless land and the Indians of New Mexico. Forgetting her earlier fears about mixed bloods, Luhan told John Collier that Waters, whose father was an Oklahoma Indian, had been able "to integrate the two blood streams."[95]

It is difficult to assess Mabel's influence on Americans beyond that wide-ranging, important, influential, and truly remarkable coterie of friends, artists, and writers she hosted in New Mexico. And perhaps that collection of people she brought to Taos is enough to make a case for her significance. Still, others also felt the Luhan touch and heard her message. In 1939, for example, Luhan shared a fan letter she had received from a Des Moines, Iowa, banker's wife, with Alfred Steiglitz. "Somehow I have rather felt that you and Alfred Steiglitz," the Iowa housewife wrote, "are two Americans that speak to me. I find that you and he speak the same language . . . that of feeling. Isn't it strange how books bring one so close to each other. Thank you for your addition to my awareness of life."[96] This unsolicited voice from the hinterlands suggests, at the very least, people read Luhan's books and that some were moved by them.

By the 1940s, however, the cultural and political ferment Luhan, Collier, and others had generated in Taos of the twenties and thirties was waning. No one would deny that the Indian New Deal had halted some of the most disruptive and damaging aspects of forced acculturation, but World War II interrupted the momentum of Collier's reform. By decade's end, a new generation, with a different agenda, would halt the reform movement altogether and replace it with the termination policy, rejecting the fundamental assumptions of the Indian New Deal and attempting, once again, to hasten the extinction of tribal governments, reservations, and distinctive Indian cultures. It would take another twenty-five years or so for the policy pendulum to swing back in Collier's direction. It would take another generation, including some of the young people who shared Mabel's enthusiasm for *Catcher in the Rye,* as well as an emerging, articulate Indian leadership, to reassert the value of Indian cultures and call, once again, for their preservation. Mabel Dodge Luhan would have approved.

# CONCLUSION

MAPPING MIDDLEBROW PURVEYORS OF Indianness at the turn of the century entailed considerable frustrations. Absence of intellectual consistency within the authors' works posed one of them. Most of my sample lurched toward rethinking "the Indian" in fits and starts, humanizing Native Americans on one page and dehumanizing them on the next; giving Indians histories at one point, but denying them a future at another; using the language of race, while simultaneously undercutting its power and meaning; rooting their understandings in old concepts of primitivism or social evolutionism, while concurrently moving toward new ones such as cultural relativism.

Not only could individual writers prove maddeningly capricious, but also collectively their differences sometimes seemed more striking than their similarities. Because the writers worked autonomously and shared no school of thought or training, their idiosyncracies stand out. Each of them came to the subject of Indians independently, usually fleeing private demons, seeking private dreams, or searching for personal physical or psychic health. In addition, they brought disparate and extremely strong personalities to their Indian projects.

Often during the course of this project I have pondered the prospect of sitting them down together at a dinner table. I would cluster Luhan, Austin, James, and Wood together for they shared an artistic and aesthetic bent. McClintock, Grinnell, Linderman, Ickes, and Lummis would have much in common as amateur ethnographers. Austin, Lummis, and Linderman might enjoy grumbling about the chauvinism of eastern publishers while swapping Indian folk tales from various corners of the West. Grinnell and Lummis could chat about the Sequoyah League and their efforts to advise Theodore Roosevelt's Indian initiatives. Luhan and Austin might share complaints about Collier's inability to see policy matters their way.

On the other hand, there would be inevitable cross-table tensions. Lummis, of course, would have to be seated as far away as possible from James. Luhan, the effusive spiritualist, might find conversation with Grinnell, the sedate scientist, a bit strained. Would Linderman and Wood get in a heated political argument over labor, immigration, or foreign policy? How would Austin's feminism square with Linderman's hostility to women in power? Would Anna Ickes, the consummate politician, mediate? Imperious egos could certainly make a more unassuming character, such as McClintock's, shrink into silence. Austin's outspoken confidence in her authority on Indians might annoy or offend everyone.

Still, they shared interests and would find much to talk about. A deep and abiding passion in things they deemed "Indian" joined them as did a pronounced and growing unease with the modern world. All honored Indian cultures as worthy of study. Most believed them worthy of emulation. They all labored to humanize, sometimes individualize, Indian people in their works aimed at general audiences. Ironically, they praised Indians' sense of community while practicing irrepressible individualism and, sometimes, fierce egotism in their own lives. They claimed to find themselves, to experience personal regeneration, through connection with Indians. Simultaneously, the possibility for community and group life that tribal cultures supposedly offered proved equally attractive. Indians, they finally all believed, offered solace from crass, coarse, contemporary American life. Antimodern impulses, in short, bound them together in their dedication to these "premodern" cultures.

Their writings, then, cohere in various ways. To a certain extent, they represent a regional expression, albeit derived from transplanted Northeasterners and Midwesterners who assigned themselves the task of defining the West and its native occupants. Reimagining Indians largely developed out of western experiences, because that was the place where most Native Americans continued to live their lives and carry on their cultures, in spite of conquest and government policies designed to extinguish them. These writers hoped, therefore, for a cultural tilt in a western and Indian direction. This regional voice was most pronounced in the Southwest, that "strange corner of the country" where Lummis, James, Ickes, Austin, and Luhan all found inspiration and their life's work. But Montana-based Linderman shared their belief in the centrality of the West and Indians to American experience and culture. He also shared their common resentment of eastern command over the publishing world. New York controlled not only access to readers, but also tastes, topics, the very substance of "American culture." How to break through that East Coast chauvinism and stranglehold on the definition of America? Each tried and all expressed frustration with the effort.

These writers also believed, however, that in Indians they had found not a regional theme but a national one. Many of them began their careers by compiling collections of Native American tales, what Mary Austin defined as American folk culture. Such stories, songs, poetry, ritual, they maintained, served as the foundation of a truly American expression, distinctive from European ones. From this they expanded in various directions. Wood wrote his poetry, Grinnell his popular ethnographies, Linderman his Indian autobiographies, McClintock his opera, and Luhan her memoirs and screenplay. Whatever the genre, they all believed that Indians represented the essence of America, the bedrock of national culture, and a core component of American identity.

This turn-of-the-century cooptation of Indianness, of course, could cut several ways. Linderman's cultural nationalism rested in a nest of xenophobia regarding immigration, ethnic diversity, and feminism. Grinnell shared some of these concerns. Both men lamented the loss of a supposedly more heroic, virile frontier past. Austin's cultural nationalism worked in the opposite direction, promoting not only her country's distinctive aesthetic traditions but also women's roles in articulating them. Luhan, naturally, thought even more expansively. She believed adherence to Indian models of culture, and of living or being, would change the nation, and the world. Clearly, a shared concern about the state of national culture and life, as well as a tendency to look to Indians for solace, inspiration, or remedy, did not lead these writers to identical points of view.

Nevertheless, one is struck by the similarly prominent role their anxieties about modernity play in works supposedly devoted to articulating the wonders of Indian cultures. In nearly every instance, such unease or distaste propelled them into Native American orbits in the first place and an almost symbiotic relationship consequently developed between their understanding of Indianness and their concerns about contemporary life. Whether it was Grinnell's nostalgia for a fading past or Luhan's hope for the future, Indians proved exceedingly handy in demonstrating what had been lost or could still be reclaimed. Indianness offered, in fact, a most elastic and useful tool for these American cultural critics precisely because, to them, Indians represented the flip side of European-based American identity, life, and experience. Whenever Americans became too enthralled with the machinations of industrialization or the probing, prying inclinations of science to explain and then dispel the power of mystery, immersion in things Indian could reinstate some sense of balance. Whenever their countrymen became too consumed with the acquisition of material goods; too soft and flabby from a sedentary, urban existence; too lonely and alienated from one another, America's Indians provided prototypes for restoration of a simple, vigorous life and one of connection to others. If modern man needed models of virility, Indians obliged. If women needed examples of powerful women, Indians again proved useful.

Simultaneously, Indians represented what once had been, or yet could be, if only America's overpowering drive to conquer and contaminate could be reined in. Native Americans' cultures had sustained a great deal of damage over the centuries. Those in the Pacific Northwest, Northern Rockies, Plains, and California barely survived, or so it seemed to these late nineteenth-century observers. It was the Southwest's Pueblos who inspired the greatest hope that enough cultural fabric remained to first, protect; then, sustain; and finally, attempt to approximate. Increased awareness of the Pueblos' spiritual and artistic richness along with dedication to perpetuating their way of life would, in the end, save not only Indians but also all of America. Regeneration of individual tribe, country, and even world depended on commitment to such goals. Reconciliation between the best of the past and the worrisome present and future could somehow be made, these writers claimed, only by recognizing and reembracing the Indian within us all.

One can certainly find reasons to dismiss these authors' works, whether it is the lunacy of James, the narcissism of Wood and Luhan, the primitivism and romanticism of Austin and Wood, the boosterism of Lummis, the nostalgia of Grinnell, or the nativism of Linderman. At times their wishful yearnings projected onto unsuspecting Indian subjects are so pronounced it gives one pause in weighing the value of their ethnographic efforts. Can we trust James's discussion of Navajo blanket designs after his ridiculous treatise on nasal breathing, vegetarianism, and nudism? Can we believe anything Linderman writes about the Crow when his bitterness about the changing world colored his perspective on life? On many other matters we see these writers as mistaken, wrong-headed, simplistic. As it turns out, Indians did not vanish. They were never primitive, nor were they static.

But to discard these writers for these limitations would be to miss important clues not only into how some Americans simultaneously challenged and coped with modernity but also with how Americans' ideas about Indians worked themselves out at the turn of the century. For all their intellectual shortcomings, these people helped create new conceptions of Indians which, in turn, made a place for Native Americans—culturally and politically—in the twentieth century. In some respect, this group even helped create an audience for Indian writers who followed in the years to come.

As for policy, they pushed for reform. Most of these figures became politically active, at least temporarily. All of them disparaged the means, if not the ends, of forced acculturation. All hoped Indians would survive the onslaught, though Grinnell, Wood, and McClintock had their doubts. Until the advent of cultural radicals in the Southwest, these writers fell short of imagining and implementing a dramatically different policy. Yet in berating federal mismanagement of reservation resources, castigating off-reservation boarding schools, and demanding that the government stop interfering with Indian religious freedom, these people pushed beyond the status quo. Furthermore, once significant reform took hold from the Southwest, Wood, James, and Lummis enlisted in the cause that Luhan, Austin, and Ickes helped spearhead.

Finally, their published works endure. This is no small accomplishment. People still read them in reprinted editions. Their essential messages that Indians are human beings with families, individual personalities, vibrant cultures, artistic talents, histories, and religions of their own, continue to work their way into American consciousness. Grinnell's and Linderman's laymen ethnographies remain important sources for scholars. Cheyennes and Crows look to these works as well. In this respect, they help us understand the gradual dissemination and insinuation of concepts such as cultural relativism beyond the academy and into the American lexicon. None of the writers set out consciously to accomplish this, with the possible exception of Anna Ickes who, alone among them, brought to her work contact with anthropological theories and some academic training. Certainly, Grinnell remained too firmly steeped in nineteenth-century conventions concerning social evolution, cultural hierarchies, and progress to be linked to promulgation of such modern concepts. More often the messages of tolerance, acceptance of difference, and acknowledgment of the legitimacy of other cultures appeared as undercurrents, unstated and perhaps even startling to someone like Grinnell, had they been pointed out to him.

All of them, however, deliberately insisted on the fundamental humanity of Indian people—a message they agreed required articulation, argument, and emphasis. That point alone, during a period when some of the nation's most destructive notions about the supposedly scientific basis of racial difference and racial hierarchies held sway, must be underscored. True, acknowledgment of Indians as members of the family of man issued from whites who believed they controlled the membership rolls and dictated the qualifications. These qualifications reflected what the writers believed constituted the hallmarks of humanity: family life, certain forms of spiritual belief, and artistic expression. Nevertheless, some significant shift in "understanding" Indians is going on here. If it served to legitimate their own Anglo-American cultures by finding commonalities, it also challenged Anglo-American assumptions about supposed superiority by presenting Indians as equals and, in some respects, as betters. This may represent a muddled, halting baby step toward genuine acceptance of difference and a far cry from the more sophisticated concept of cultural relativism promulgated by academically trained anthropologists, but it is still a step. And certainly by the 1930s, in the works of Ickes and Luhan, that tentative step had transformed into a confident stride.

Taken altogether and viewed cumulatively, their works fostered growing acceptance of cultural diversity, tolerance, and even celebration of difference, within the nation as a whole. If they often fell short of consistently incorporating such ideals into their writings and their lives, they deserve at least some credit for starting the endeavor—one which Americans still have not completely mastered.

# NOTES

*Abbreviations*

CFLSWM—Charles Fletcher Lummis Papers, Braun Library, Southwest Museum, Los Angeles, California

CSSPL—Charles Scribner's Sons Papers, Princeton University Library, Princeton, New Jersey

ESBL—Elizabeth Shepley Sargent Papers, Beinecke Library, Yale University, New Haven, Connecticut

FBLMHS—Frank Bird Linderman Papers, Montana Historical Society, Helena, Montana

FBLMPI—Frank Bird Linderman Papers, Museum of the Plains Indian, Browning, Montana

FBLML—Frank Bird Linderman Papers, Mansfield Library, University of Montana, Missoula, Montana

GBGSL—George Bird Grinnell Papers, Sterling Library, Yale University, New Haven, Connecticut

GBGSWM—George Bird Grinnell Papers, Braun Library, Southwest Museum

GWJHL—George Wharton James Papers, Huntington Library, San Marino, California

GWJSWM—George Wharton James Papers, Braun Library, Southwest Museum

HFBL—Hapgood Family Papers, Beinecke Library

HILC—Harold Ickes Papers, Library of Congress, Washington, D.C.

JCSL—John Collier Papers, Sterling Library, Yale University

JTBL—Jean Toomer Papers, Beinecke Library

MAHL—Mary Austin Papers, Huntington Library

MDLBL—Mabel Dodge Luhan Papers, Beinecke Library

MSBL—Maurice Sterne Papers, Beinecke Library

RTPL—Ridgely Torrence Papers, Princeton University Library

SLHL—Sonya Levien Papers, Huntington Library

UJBL—Una Jeffers Papers, Bancroft Library, University of California, Berkeley, California

WCBL—C.E.S. Wood Papers, Bancroft Library

WCHL—C.E.S. Wood Papers, Huntington Library

WMBL—Walter McClintock Papers, Beinecke Library

WMSWM—Walter McClintock Papers, Braun Library, Southwest Museum

*Introduction*

1. Frederick E. Hoxie, *A Final Promise: The Campaign to Assimilate the Indians, 1880–1920* (Lincoln: University of Nebraska Press, 1984), 243, 244. For an example of how this works in a late twentieth-century Indian's life, see Delphine Red Shirt, *Bead on an Anthill: A Lakota Childhood* (Lincoln: University of Nebraska Press, 1998).

2. The phrase "war on homogeneity" comes from Hoxie, *A Final Promise*, 244.

3. Brian Dippie, *The Vanishing American: White Attitudes & U.S. Indian Policy* (Lawrence: University Press of Kansas, 1982). Originally published by Wesleyan University Press, 1982.

4. Karl Kroeber, "Native American Resistance and Renewal," in *American Indian Persistence and Resurgence*, ed. Karl Kroeber (Durham, N.C.: Duke University Press, 1994), 2.

5. For an overview of twentieth-century Indian affairs, see Donald L. Parman, *Indians, and the American West in the Twentieth Century* (Bloomington: Indiana University Press, 1994).

6. Ibid., 2. For a sampling of general histories concerning European and American attitudes toward American Indians, see Robert F. Berkhofer, Jr., *The White Man's Indian: Images of the American Indian From Columbus to the Present* (New York: Vintage Books, 1979), originally published by Alfred A. Knopf, 1978; Roy Harvey Pearce, *Savagism and Civilization: A Study of the Indian and the American Mind* (Baltimore: Johns Hopkins Press, 1953); John F. Moffitt and Santiago Sebastian, *O Brave New People: The European Invention of the American Indian* (Albuquerque: University of New Mexico Press, 1996), and E. Elizabeth Bird, ed., *Dressing in Feathers: The Construction of the Indian in American Popular Culture* (Boulder: Westview Press, 1996).

7. Alexandra Harmon, *Indians in the Making: Ethnic Relations and Indian Identities around Puget Sound* (Berkeley: University of California Press, 1998), 144.

8. See Susan Schekel, *The Insistence of the Indian: Race and Nationalism in Nineteenth-Century American Culture* (Princeton, N.J.: Princeton University Press, 1998); Philip J. Deloria, *Playing Indian* (New Haven: Yale University Press, 1998); Scott Vickers, *Native American Identities: From Stereotype to Archetype in Art and Literature* (Albuquerque: University of New Mexico Press, 1998).

9. Schekel, *The Insistence of the Indian*, 4.

10. Harmon, *Indians in the Making*, 144.

11. Lawrence W. Levine, "The Folklore of Industrial Society: Popular Culture and Its Audiences," *American Historical Review* 97 (1992): 1399. Or, as another historian put it, the ideas and practices associated with the way a society "defines certain truths about itself and the way it deploys social power [are] multiple, inconsistent and contradictory." See Gail Bederman, *Manliness and Civilization: A Cultural History of Gender and Race in the United States, 1880–1917* (Chicago: University of Chicago Press, 1995), 24. Bederman, in turn, acknowledges Michel Foucault, *The History of Sexuality: An Introduction*, Vol. 1 (New York: Vintage, 1978) and *Power and Knowledge: Selected Interviews and Other Writings*, trans. Colin Gordon (New York: Pantheon, 1972).

12. For some examples, see Hoxie, *A Final Promise*; Berkhofer, *The White Man's Indian*; Curtis M. Hinsley, Jr., *Savages and Scientists: The Smithsonian Institution and the Development of American Anthropology, 1846–1910* (Washington, D.C.: Smithsonian Institu-

tion Press, 1981); L. G. Moses, *The Indian Man: A Biography of James Mooney* (Urbana and Chicago: University of Illinois Press, 1984); and Robert Bieder, *Science Encounters the Indian, 1820–1880: The Early Years of American Ethnology* (Norman: University of Oklahoma Press, 1986).

13. L. G. Moses, *Wild West Shows and the Images of American Indians, 1883–1933* (Albuquerque: University of New Mexico Press, 1996), 272, 277. Moses maintains that these shows presented Indian participants "an opportunity . . . not so much to play a role but simply to be themselves." The shows celebrated their cultures and participation could be seen as a defiant act against marginalization.

14. Hoxie, *A Final Promise*, xi.

15. Ibid., 28–9, 42, 91–6, 112–29, 145, 236.

16. Kroeber, "Native American Resistance," 13.

17. Berkhofer, *The White Man's Indian*, 66; Hoxie, *A Final Promise*, 134–45. See also Richard Handler, "Boasian Anthropology and the Critique of American Culture," *American Quarterly* 42 (1990): 252–73.

18. For an analysis of the relationship between anthropological thought and modernism, see Desley Deacon, *Elsie Clews Parsons: Inventing Modern Life* (Chicago: University of Chicago Press, 1997), 97–110.

19. T. J. Jackson Lears, *No Place of Grace: Antimodernism and the Transformation of American Culture* (New York: Pantheon, 1981), xi, xvii, 4, 5. Other scholars who have made the connection between Indian enthusiasts and antimodernism include Deloria, *Playing Indian*; Leah Dilworth, *Imagining Indians in the Southwest: Persistent Visions of a Primitive Past* (Washington, D.C.: Smithsonian Institution Press, 1996); Margaret D. Jacobs, *Engendered Encounters: Feminism and Pueblo Cultures, 1878–1934* (Lincoln: University of Nebraska Press, 1999); and Carter Jones, "'Hope for the Race of Man': Indians, Intellectuals and the Regeneration of Modern America, 1917–1934" (Ph.D. dissertation, Brown University, 1991).

20. Dilworth emphasizes "primitivism" in her study of Southwestern cultural history, see *Imagining Indians*; David Shi's work on the "simple life" represents another way of looking at these turn-of-the-century cultural issues. Simple lifers hoped to evade the consequences of the modernizing world in a variety of ways, including an American Arts and Crafts revival and a Nature revival. See David Shi, *The Simple Life: Plain Living and High Thinking in American Culture* (New York: Oxford University Press, 1985).See also Roderick Nash, *Wilderness and the American Mind* (New Haven: Yale University Press, 1967).

21. Other nations in the Western Hemisphere experienced similar movements which exalted, at least culturally, their Indian occupants. This non-Indian doctrine of *indigenismo* found expression in Mexico and Peru, for instance, in the 1920s. See George J. Sanchez, *Becoming Mexican American: Ethnicity, Culture and Identity in Chicano Los Angeles, 1900–1945* (New York: Oxford University Press, 1993), 119–20; David Brading, "Manuel Gamio and Official Indigenismo in Mexico," *Bulletin of Latin America Research* 7:1 (1988): 75–89; and Henry E. Dobyns and Paul L. Doughty, *Peru: A Cultural History* (New York: Oxford University Press, 1976), 200, 222–23, 227, 230, 238, 247–48. For connections between American anthropologists and these developments, see Deacon, *Elsie Clews Parsons*, 309–48.

22. See Jacobs, *Engendered Encounters*.

23. James Clifford, *The Predicament of Culture: Twentieth Century Ethnograpy, Literature and Art* (Cambridge: Harvard University Press, 1988), 5, 14.

24. Ibid., 16.

25. Sally Price, *Primitive Art in Civilized Places* (Chicago: University of Chicago Press,

1989), 23. One of the areas where Westerners have issued such invitations is in the art world because, it is presumed, artistic sensitivity transcends cultural borders. Art is also perceived as a medium through which people everywhere address common problems. Critics thus deem primitive art as supposedly springing more directly from psychological and spontaneous drives. "Western enthusiasts of Primitive Art," according to Price, "have always argued that its authors are in particularly close touch with the 'fundamental, basic and essential drives of life'—drives that Civilized Man shared but 'buries' under a layer of learned behavior." Of course, no people are simple. All are complicated pattern-makers who live in the symbolic worlds they create. So the racist foundations of the belief that anyone is "primitive" or "simple" is fairly transparent. Price, 32.

26. Ibid., 33.

27. In fact, as historian Alexandra Harmon put it, especially by the turn of the century, Indian "self-definition was inseparable from ongoing dialogues with people who stood outside the Indian circle." Harmon, *Indians in the Making*, 157.

28. According to Phil Deloria, Indians also participated in "playing Indian" for white people at the turn of the century because "miming Indianness back at Americans" was a way to "redefine it." That they did so "indicates how little cultural capital Indian people possessed at the time." See Deloria, *Playing Indian*, 125.

29. See Frederick Hoxie, "Exploring a Cultural Borderland: Native American Journeys of Discovery in the Early Twentieth Century," *Journal of American History* 79 (1992): 969–95. After much deliberation, I chose not to include them here, however, because their concerns, orientations, and purposes were so distinctive from those of Anglo-American popularizers that, I concluded, they require their own book.

30. See Paula Gunn Allen, "Special Problems in Teaching Leslie Marmon Silko's *Ceremony*," in *Natives and Academics: Researching and Writing About American Indians*, ed. Devon Mihesuah (Lincoln: University of Nebraska Press, 1998), 61.

31. H. David Brumble, *American Indian Autobiography* (Berkeley: University of California Press, 1988), 72; Hoxie, "Exploring a Cultural Borderland," 976. Brumble explains that among many Indian cultures, it was a long-standing tradition for people to pay to learn from masters their visions, healing power, and history. Such information and knowledge, in fact, was considered "worth paying for."

32. Clifford, *The Predicament of Culture*, 7, 113.

33. Ibid., 59, 60, 249. See also Margot Liberty, "American Indians and American Anthropology," in *American Indian Intellectuals*, ed. Margot Liberty (St. Paul: West Publishing Co., 1978), 9.

34. Karl Kroeber makes a particularly strong case for the long-term value of earlier generations' work, arguing that "a special complex of anthropological data helped to provide grounding for the later resurgence of Indian self-awareness and self-assertiveness. There is almost no Native American, however alienated by American civilization from his tribal background, who cannot recover a considerable body of knowledge about his tribal roots not only from his people but also from ethnographic records of American anthropologists." See Kroeber, "Native American Resistance," 15.

35. Inevitably, readers will think of other non-Indians whose works I could have included such as Helen Hunt Jackson, James Willard Schultz, Lucullus McWhorter, James Mooney, Ernest Seton Thompson, Hamlin Garland, and Oliver LaFarge. Some of these authors fit the framework of this study better than others. Jackson, for instance, more neatly fits the assimilationist model.

36. To be sure, some academically trained anthropologists also wrote for popular audiences, but that was not their primary purpose. Popular writing served as an ancil-

lary activity to their professional productions, whereas the writers analyzed here aimed the vast majority of their works specifically and consistently to popular audiences. While professional anthropologists have received a good deal of scholarly attention, popularizers have been overlooked. In addition, some reformers were also authors. John Collier, for instance, wrote articles and books for general audiences, but he remains primarily significant for his involvement in policy reform and administration.

37. Levine, "The Folklore of Industrial Society," 1370, 1384.

38. For information on the connections between Luhan, Austin, and Collier, see Jones, "'Hope For the Race of Man.'"

39. Kenneth R. Philp, *John Collier's Crusade for Indian Reform, 1920–1954* (Tucson: University of Arizona Press, 1977), xiii, ix. Francis Paul Prucha made the second statement in the foreword to Philp's book. Berkhofer too emphasizes Collier's role in the transformation of policy, to the exclusion of others, in *The White Man's Indian*, 176–86. See also Lawrence C. Kelly, *The Assault on Assimilation: John Collier and the Origins of Indian Policy Reform* (Albuquerque: University of New Mexico Press, 1983).

40. David Shi argues that the "sense of social urgency that had energized turn-of-the-century [simple life] enthusiasts had dissipated by the 1920s." The same is not true of Indian enthusiasts. In fact, it was not until the 1920s that ideas of the preceding decades began to take hold and translate into significant reform. See Shi, *The Simple Life*, 222.

## *Chapter 2*

1. "Autobiographical Notes," Folder 1, Box 6, WCHL. In calling Erskine a "perfect Indian," the father evidently meant that the son would be silent if his feelings were hurt and that he never seemed to forgive.

2. For biographical information on Wood, see Edwin Bingham, "Experiment in Launching a Biography: Three Vignettes of Charles Erskine Scott Wood," *Huntington Library Quarterly* 35 (May, 1972): 221–39; Edwin Bingham, "Oregon's Romantic Rebels: John Reed and Charles Erskine Scott Wood," *Pacific Northwest Quarterly* 50 (July, 1959): 77–90; Erskine Wood, *Life of Charles Erskine Scott Wood*, (Portland: Erskine Wood, 1978); Edwin Bingham, *Charles Erskine Scott Wood* (Boise: Boise State University Western Writers Series 94, 1994); Edwin Bingham and Tim Barnes, ed. *Wood Works: The Life and Writings of Charles Erskine Scott Wood* (Corvallis: Oregon State University Press, 1997); and Robert Hamburger, *Two Rooms: The Life of Charles Erskine Scott Wood* (Lincoln: University of Nebraska Press, 1998).

3. "Autobiographical Notes," Folder 9, Box 6, WCHL. For an officer to establish a friendship of such warmth with an Indian man was truly unusual. See Sherry L. Smith, *The View From Officers' Row: Army Perceptions of Western Indians* (Tucson: University of Arizona Press, 1990), 42–54. According to Bingham and Barnes, it was not the adjutant general who refused Wood's request for a cavalry assignment, but rather another officer who declined Wood's offer to trade posts. See Bingham and Barnes, *Wood Works*, 6.

4. "Autobiographical Notes," Folders 9 & 38, Box 6, WCHL.

5. C.E.S. Wood to Department of the Interior, October 22, 1941, Folder 17, Box 238, WCHL. Wood wrote an extensive summary of his Alaskan adventure in this letter, the purpose of which was to request a map of the Alaskan Archipelago that he wanted to have while composing his autobiography. He wrote an earlier letter about these events to Lute Pease, February 22, 1928, Folder 57, Box 235, WCHL. Wood published an account of this trip, "Among the Thlinkits in Alaska," *Century Magazine* 24, no. 3 (1882): 323–39.

6. C.E.S. Wood to Lute Pease, February 22, 1928, Folder 57, Box 235; and "Autobiographical Notes," Folder 5, Box 5, WCHL. Wood made no mention of this relationship in his *Century Magazine* article about his Alaska adventure.

7. Wood to Pease, February 22, 1928, Folder 57, Box 235, WCHL.

8. Ibid.

9. For more on officers' sexual liaisons with Indian women, see Smith, *The View From Officers' Row*, 55–91. Wood eventually discussed his Alaskan sojourn with Frederick Schwatka, an Arctic explorer and gave him all his memoranda and notes about the region. When Schwatka embarked on his own expedition, Wood claimed he asked the explorer to find "the Chilcat Priness [*sic*] and explain to why it was I broke my solemn promise to return to her." Apparently, Schwatka did not follow through on this romantic request. See C.E.S. Wood to Department of the Interior, October 22, 1941, Folder 17, Box 238, WCHL.

10. June 19, June 21, 1877 diary, Box 26, WCHL.

11. July 23, 1877 diary, Box 26, WCHL.

12. June 27, 1877 diary, Box 26, WCHL.

13. July 17, 1887 diary, Box 26, WCHL.

14. This is the conclusion, for instance, of George Venn in "Chief Joseph's 'Surrender Speech' as a Literary Text,"*Oregon English* 20 (1998): 67–73, and Haruo Oaki, in "Chief Joseph's Words," *Idaho Yesterdays* 33 (1989): 16–21. Oaki finds the authenticity of the text questionable at best, writing, "Any citation of the long text as an example of American Indian oratory is unwarranted and is an outcome of citing only the last and unreliable accounts of C.E.S. Wood." No evidence to substantiate Wood's claims to the authenticity of the speech as Chief Joseph's words exists. Oaki, on the other hand, provides a convincing explanation of the evolution of the speech as the work of Wood. Bingham and Barnes also believe it is likely Wood's literary bent moved him to shape the surrender speech. See *Wood Works*, 9. For more on Wood and the Nez Perce War, see also Mark H. Brown, *The Flight of the Nez Perce* (New York: Capricorn Books, 1971); Merrill D. Beal, *"I Will Fight No More Forever": Chief Joseph and the Nez Perce War* (New York: Ballantine/Random House, 1971); and Bruce Hampton, *Children of Grace: The Nez Perce War of 1877* (New York: Macrae Books/Henry Holt, 1994).

15. Writing, in 1942, to Howard's son, Wood states that immediately after the Nez Perce Campaign, Howard sent him to Washington, D.C., where he reported to the adjutant general of the army. They discussed the surrender and when Wood showed him the only copy of the speech in existence, the adjutant general insisted on having it for his archives which already included speeches by other famous Indians such as Red Jacket and Logan. Wood reluctantly complied. Years later, when he returned to the nation's capital as a lawyer trying a case before the Supreme Court, he attempted to find the copy of the speech. Alas, the old adjutant general was no longer there and no one else knew anything about it. "That was the last I knew about Joseph's speech," Wood explained. C.E.S. Wood to Harry Stinson Howard, February 20, 1941, Folder 1, Box 234, WCHL.

16. For Erskine's account of this experience, see Erskine Wood, *Days With Chief Joseph* (Portland: Oregon Historical Society, 1973).

17. He wrote his fiancée, Nanny Moale Smith, for instance, that responsibility for the 1878 Bannock War rested with a small band of murderous Indian marauders. See C.E.S. Wood to Nanny, June 14, 1878, Box 243; for other examples, see "Bannock Indian Campaign Daily Journal, 1878," Folder 3, Box 26; telegram from C.E.S. Wood to *New York Times*, June 15, 1878, Folder 27, Box 235; 1879 diary, Box 26; all WCHL.

18. "Autobiographical fragment," dated January 13, 1944, Folder 3, Box 6, WCHL; Wood, *Life of Charles Erskine Scott Wood*, 47.

19. Bingham and Barnes, *Wood Works*, 13.

20. Bingham, "Oregon's Romantic Rebels," 81; Bingham, "Charles Erskine Scott Wood: Tiffany Radical?" paper presented at Western History Association Conference, Tacoma, Washington, 1989, 6.

21. Olin Warner to C.E.S. Wood, July 16, 1883, Folder 19; Warner to Wood, February 8, 1884, Folder 20; Warner to Wood, May 26, 1886, Folder 21; Warner to Wood, June 21, 1886, Folder 22; Oregon Historical Society to Mrs. William Maxwell Wood, October 3, 1977, Folder 30; Warner to Wood, September 1, 1893, Folder 29; Warner to Wood, March 11, 1894, Folder 30; C.E.S. Wood, "Shall We Move the Skidmore Fountain," ms. of article published in *The Spectator*, no date, Folder 31; all Box 214, WCHL.

22. September 20, 1887 and October 6, 1887 diary entries, Box 26, WCHL. Throughout the 1890s and beyond, Wood returned to this theme of Death. See July 11, August 3, and August 12, 1896 diary entries, Folder 11, Box 26; January 6, 1897 entry on the death of his brother David Abbott Wood, and December 20, 1897 entry on the death of another brother, Maxwell, Folder 1, Box 27, WCHL. C.E.S. and Nanny Wood also lost an infant, Katherine, when she was only several months old around this time.

23. January 1893 diary entry, Box 26, WCHL.

24. March 6, 1893 diary, Box 26, WCHL. In an address to the graduates of California's Menlo School, Wood indicated he sent Erskine to live with Joseph for more practical reasons: so he could learn "to live where another might starve" by learning to find edible wild foods, hunt and fish, etc.

25. Sara Bard Field, "Colonel Wood: 'Grand Old Rebel' Poet of Nature and Economic Bondage," *Saturday Review of Literature* 28 (March 24, 1945), 8.

26. August 2, 1898 diary entry, Folder 2, Box 27, WCHL.

27. "The Trooper," found in 1898 diary, Folder 3, Box 27, WCHL.

28. Untitled poem, 1899 diary, Folder 5, Box 27, WCHL.

29. "Battle Hymn of the Republic," dated March 14, 1899, Folder 4, Box 27, WCHL.

30. See Gail Bederman, *Manliness & Civilization: A Cultural History of Gender and Race in the United States, 1880–1917* (Chicago: University of Chicago Press, 1995).

31. "Private Stiles," dated February 9, 1899, Folder 5, Box 27, WCHL.

32. Wood, "Among the Thlinkits," 326, 338.

33. C.E.S. Wood, "Chief Joseph, the Nez Perce," *Century Magazine*, 28 (1884), 135–42. Wood later complained that the editor watered down his disgust over the injustices perpetrated against the Nez Perces, particularly regarding promises they could return to their own country after surrendering. See "When I was Stationed at West Point," c. 1938?, Folder 32, Box 74, WCHL.

34. C.E.S. Wood to Moorfield Storey, May 27, 1895, appeared in *Oregon Inn-Side News*, Vol. 1, No. 40 (Nov.–Dec. 1947), 5–6, Box 302, WCHL.

35. C.E.S. Wood, "What is Knowledge? What is Truth," circa 1910, 1–3, Folder 20, Box 74, WCHL.

36. Ibid. In a rare comparison with another racial group, Wood went on to claim that Uncle Phil, "a negro gardener" he knew from his youth, shared the Indian's elementary, uncomplicated approach to life. Uncle Phil was "happy in mere life, ignorant of all things, longing for no world greater than five miles away. . . . [He] lived his simple, ignorant, contented life and was each day happy in his living."

37. C.E.S. Wood, *A Book of Tales Being Some Myths of the North American Indians* (Portland: Attic Press, 1901), 1, 7, 21–2, 34–5, 66,68.

38. T. J. Jackson Lears demonstrates that antimodernists' interest in European fairy and folk tales stemmed, in part, from a belief that mystery could still exist in the mod-

ern world. See *No Place of Grace: Antimodernism and the Transformation of American Culture* (New York: Pantheon, 1981), 168–73.

39. Wood, *Book of Tales*, 100.

40. *A Book of Tales: Being Some Myths of the North American Indians*, Retold by Charles Erskine Scott Wood, One Time Lieutenant U.S. Army. (New York: The Vanguard Press, 1929). The reviews are quoted in Helena Kay, "Charles Erskine Scott Wood: His Life and Works" (M.A. thesis, University of Texas, 1937), 88.

41. Wood to Erskine, August 5, 1918, Folder 49, Box 242, WCHL. Wood's wife also recalled Indian visits to their Portland home, but she welcomed them with much less enthusiasm than her husband. When eight Indian leaders from various tribes visited Portland in 1889, Wood invited them to lunch. Nanny was not pleased, in part because she did not know what to feed them. But she was also "a bit taken back to go down to my parlor and see them lounging about on my divan and pillows." Perhaps to expect her to welcome them with open arms was too much to ask of a conventional woman with conventional nineteenth-century attitudes about race. Apparently, it was her husband's idea to send their son to live with the Nez Perce, and after he was gone, Nanny's friends "kept talking about the dangers that would result from contact with the Indians and seemed to think we were very foolish to let him remain there." She begged her husband to bring Erskine home and, with the help of an Indian agent, her will prevailed. This was just one of the many issues that illustrated the growing chasm between C.E.S. and Nanny Wood. She did not share her husband's politics, poetry, or philosophy. See Nanny Moale Wood, "Personal Recollections of Nanny Moale Wood," author's copy provided by Mary Wood, 11, 33–4, 35–6.

42. Wood diary, April 22, 1908, Folder 8, Box 27, WCHL.

43. Bingham and Barnes, *Wood Works*, 34.

44. Wood to Erskine, April 27, 1897, Folder marked "Before 1900," Box 7, WCBL.

45. Wood to Nan, January 30, 1907, Folder 27, Box 233, WCHL.

46. Ibid. For all his claims to unconventionality about marriage, Wood's advice to his children on such matters still owed a great deal to convention. Sounding a good deal like a Darwinian naturalist, he urged his children to pick mates with strong and healthy bodies so their children would have the same blessings. He told his daughters they must learn household duties because the most important things in life were food and shelter, and the household was the woman's greatest duty, next to having children. Wood clearly believed in biological determinism and its prescribed natural roles for women. Men provided food, women prepared it. He told his son Erskine that he could not marry, nor should he even engage in sexual intercourse, until he could provide financially for a wife and family. See Wood to Erskine, April 27, 1897, Folder marked "Before 1900," Box 7, WCBL; Wood to Lisa, no date, circa 1902, Folder 16, Box 237, WCHL; Wood to Nan, January 30, 1907, Folder 27, Box 233, WCHL.

47. Wood, "It was a beautiful wedding . . . ," n.d., Folder 19a, Box 8, WCHL. This description closely approximated the account of Indian courtship and marriage Sarah Winnemucca witnessed and shared with Wood in 1878. See Wood, "Private Journal, 1878," 32.

48. Wood to Max Hayek, July 4, 1926, Folder 65, Box 230, WCHL.

49. C.E.S. Wood, *The Poet in the Desert* (Portland, Oregon, n.p., 1915), 8–9, 31–2, 68, 89, 101.

50. C.E.S. Wood, *The Poet in the Desert* (Portland: F. W. Baltes and Company, 1918), 89, 90, 91.

51. Wood to Eunice Tietjens, October 2, 1915, Folder 8, Box 238, WCHL.

52. See Wood's introduction in *The Poet in the Desert* (New York: The Vanguard Press, 1929), n.p.

53. Wood, *The Poet in the Desert*, 1929 edition, 134-35.

54. Ibid., 145.

55. January 17, 1913 diary entry, Folder 1, Box 28, WCHL; Bingham, "Charles Erskine Scott Wood: A Tiffany Radical?", 9–10; and William Rose Benet's Introduction to Charles Erskine Scott Wood, *Collected Poems of Charles Erskine Scott Wood* (New York: The Vanguard Press, 1949).

56. C.E.S. Wood to Helena Kay, June 29, 1937, quoted in Kay, "Charles Erskine Scott Wood," 15.

57. Copies of these obituaries can be found in Folder 1, Box 309, WCHL. The Oregon governor bestowed the title "Colonel" upon Wood for his efforts to help organize the Oregon State Militia.

58. Mabel Dodge Luhan to Wood, January 11, 1933, Folder 64, Box 165, WCHL.

59. Wood to Franklin Lane, June 7, 1919, Folder 28, Box 234, WCHL.

60. Wood to Nan Wood Honeyman, March 8, 1937, Folder 51, Box 233; Wood to Mrs. Franklin D. Roosevelt, March 9, 1933, Folder 3, Box 236, WCHL. Wood apparently supported Franklin Roosevelt's presidency, at least for the first two terms. But the radical in him limited his hopes that Roosevelt would be able to address fundamental inequities which plagued the entire American system. "I like the flexibility of his economic programme," Wood wrote to his daughter who had been elected to Congress, "but of course I do not believe anything lasting and deep founded can be done under any form of the feudal system and all special privilege." And a few years later he told her, "I think Roosevelt will never lose the deserved praise for his conception of the under and over-privileged class and that the benefits must be more equally distributed. As he could not make a revolution—and was not a dictator he did the best he could to blaze a path." Wood to Nan Wood Honeyman, January 1, 1934, Folder 42, and February 4, 1938, Folder 54, Box 233, WCHL.

61. See Bingham and Barnes, *Wood Works*, for a summary assessment of Wood, 34–8.

## *Chapter 3*

1. Margot Liberty,"American Indians and American Anthropology," in *American Indian Intellectuals*, ed. Margot Liberty (St. Paul: West Publishing Co., 1978), 5.

2. George Bird Grinnell, "Memoirs," Folder 156, Series II, Box 34, 19, GBGSL.

3. Ibid., 11. Grinnell repeats this story, with some variation, on p. 19. Books also encouraged young Grinnell's sense of adventure, particularly Captain Mayne Reid's adventure stories for boys. See Edward Day Harris III, "Preserving a Vision of the American West: The Life of George Bird Grinnell" (Ph.D. dissertation, University of Texas, Austin, 1995), 30–1.

4. Reflecting the links between hunting and childhood which were so inextricably forged in Grinnell's mind, he later described Plains Indians who clung to the hunt as children. Only when they set aside the bow for the plow could he conceive of them as adults.

5. Ibid., 27, 29, 32, 33. For a published version of parts of these memoirs, see John F. Reiger, ed., *The Passing of the Great West: Selected Papers of George Bird Grinnell* (Norman: University of Oklahoma Press, 1984). This book was originally published in 1972.

6. Grinnell, "Memoirs," 33–7; Harris, "Preserving a Vision," 45–53.

7. Grinnell, "Memoirs," 37–9.

8. July 19 and July 24, 1870 diary, Manuscript #292, GBGSWM.

9. July 29, 1870 diary, GBGSWM; Harris, "Preserving A Vision," 79.

10. Grinnell, "Memoirs," 41–3.

11. Ibid., 45–7. See also George Bird Grinnell, *Pawnee Hero Stories and Folk Tales* (Lincoln: University of Nebraska Press, 1961), 273–302.

12. Grinnell, "Memoirs," 47–9.

13. Ibid.

14. Grinnell, "Memoirs," Folder 157, Series II, Box 34, 52, GBGSL.

15. August 23, 1874 diary, Manuscript #294, GBGSWM.

16. Grinnell, "Memoirs," Folder 157, 56-7; Harris, "Preserving a Vision," 146–47.

17. July 26, 1874 diary, Manuscript #293, GBGSWM; Grinnell, "Memoirs," 62–3. According to Harris, they released the old man several days after capturing him. Harris, "Preserving a Vision," 165.

18. For Grinnell's account of his 1875 trip to western Montana, see "Memoirs," 64–73.

19. Ibid., 77.

20. Ibid., 87.

21. Gail Bederman, *Manliness and Civilization: A Cultural History of Gender and Race in the United States, 1860–1917* (Chicago and London: University of Chicago Press, 1995), 4–6; E. Anthony Rotundo, "Learning about Manhood: Gender Ideals and the Middle-Class Family in Nineteenth Century America," in *Manliness and Morality: Middle-Class Masculinity in Britain and America, 1800–1940* ed. J. A. Mangan and James Walvin (New York: St. Martin's Press, 1987), 40, 42. See also Roderick Nash, *Wilderness and the American Mind* (New Haven: Yale University Press, 1967).

22. Harris, "Preserving A Vision," 240–42, 498–99, 292–315. For more on the link between manliness, hunting, sexual separation, and juvenile literature, see John M. MacKenzie, "The Imperial Pioneer and Hunter and the British Masculine Stereotype in Late Victorian and Edwardian Times," in Mangan and Walvin, eds., *Manliness and Morality*, 176–83.

23. Bederman, *Manliness and Civilization,* 26.

24. Ibid., 171–84.

25. Grinnell, "Memoirs," 98.

26. For information on Grinnell's growing disenchantment with hunting to kill and growing enthusiasm for conservation practices, see Harris, "Preserving A Vision," 242–43, 260–378.

27. Brian Dippie agrees with this assessment. He argues that Grinnell's shifting interest from natural history to ethnology typified many nineteenth-century anthropologists' experiences and that it represents another example of the deeply and long held American conception that Indians represented a vanishing race. See Brian Dippie, *The Vanishing American: White Attitudes & U.S. Indian Policy* (Lawrence: University Press of Kansas, 1982), 223–28.

28. Grinnell, "What We May Learn from the Indian," *Forest and Stream* 85 (March 1916): 845–46. For an analysis of how Grinnell projected his own progressive views of conservation onto Indians, see Richard Levine, "Indians, Conservation and George Bird Grinnell," *American Studies* 28 (Fall 1987): 41–55.

29. August 31 and September 8, 1885 diary entries, Manuscript #302, GBGSWM.

30. Grinnell to Mrs. Williams, May 3, 1888, letterpress book, Box 1, Series I, GBGSL.

31. Grinnell to Mr. Fred Pace, March 20, 1888; Grinnell to J.W. Schultz, May 24 and May 29, 1888; and Grinnell to Chief of the Bureau of Ethnology, April 2, 1888, all in letterpress book, Box 1, Series I, GBGSL.

32. For examples of how these relationships worked, see Ms. #139, 169, 10, 57, and 335, all GBGSWM; Harris, "Preserving A Vision," 543–47.

33. Harris, "Preserving A Vision," 514–17. See also James Mooney to Grinnell, Ms. #226 and "Acknowledgments of Grinnell's 'Pawnee Hero Stories,'" Ms. #236, both GBGSWM.

34. Thomas R. Wessel, "George Bird Grinnell," in *Historians of the American Frontier*, ed. John R. Wunder (Westport, CT: Greenwood Press, 1988), 283.

35. George Bird Grinnell, *Blackfoot Lodge Tales: The Story of a Prairie People* (Lincoln: University of Nebraska Press, 1962), xi–xiii; Harris, "Preserving A Vision," 381–86.

36. Grinnell, *Blackfoot Lodge Tales*, 180-81.

37. Ibid., 300.

38. August 8 and August 11, 1895 diary, Manuscript #325, GBGSWM.

39. August 18, 1895 diary, GBGSWM.

40. The notebooks repose in Los Angeles' Southwest Museum Library and remain rich sources of early twentieth-century Cheyenne testimony.

41. Harris, "Preserving A Vision," 541–48.

42. George Bird Grinnell, *The Fighting Cheyennes* (New York: Charles Scribner's Sons, 1915), x.

43. George Bird Grinnell, *The Cheyenne Indians: Their History and Ways of Life*, Volume I (Lincoln: University of Nebraska Press, 1972), v. This book was first published by Yale University Press in 1923.

44. T. J. Jackson Lears, *No Place of Grace: Antimodernism and the Transformation of American Culture* (New York: Pantheon Books, 1981), 98.

45. Robert J. Higgs, "Yale and the Heroic Ideal, Gotterdammering and Palnigenesis, 1865–1914," in Mangan and Walvin, eds., *Manliness and Morality*, 163.

46. Grinnell to Linderman, November 16, 1916, FBLML.

47. Grinnell, *The Cheyenne Indians* Vol. I, vi.

48. Ibid., 102.

49. Ibid., 128.

50. Grinnell, *The Cheyenne Indians* Vol. II, 193.

51. Harris, "Preserving A Vision," 551.

52. Ibid., 226–378.

53. Ibid., 397–405, 437–44, 461–63, 467–69, 476–85; William T. Hagan, *Theodore Roosevelt and Six Friends of the Indian* (Norman: University of Oklahoma Press, 1997), 140–41.

54. George Bird Grinnell, "Biographical Data," Folder 127, Box 32, Yale Series II, GBGSL; Grinnell, November 6 & 7, 1888 diary, Manuscript #307, GBGSWM; Harris, "Preserving A Vision," 391–97, 415–23.

55. George Bird Grinnell to Commissioner of Indian Affairs, November 20, 1888, letterpress book, Box 1, Series I, GBGSL. Apparently, this was not the first occasion when Grinnell involved himself in agency affairs. In this same letter he indicated that one or two years before he had provided Commissioner John D. C. Atkins with information which led to the removal of "Major Lincoln," Assiniboine agent at Fort Belknap.

56. These handwritten notes and a copy of Grinnell's *New York Times* letter can be found in Manuscript #79, "Papers and Correspondence as to M.D. Baldwin, Agent for the Blackfeet," GBGSWM.

57. Grinnell, September 9, 1889 diary, "Yellowstone Park with Haynes & Ashnola, B.C. with G.H. Gould," Manuscript #309, GBGSWM. Grinnell also took public credit (albeit well deserved) for the Lacey Act, which provided game protection in Yellowstone National Park and for assuring Blackfeet 320-acre allotments. See Harris, "Preserving A Vision," 372, 465.

58. Grinnell, "Yellowstone Park," Manuscript #309, GBGSWM.

59. Ibid.

60. A notation indicates that three letters arrived with presents from Indians and were published in the *New York Post*, July 31, 1889, Manuscript #390, GBGSWM.

61. Gerald A. Diettert, *Grinnell's Glacier: George Bird Grinnell and Glacier National Park* (Missoula, Mont.: Mountain Press Publishing Company, 1992), 57–64.

62. Quoted in Diettert, *Grinnell's Glacier*, 66. For a more generous view of Grinnell's role in these negotiations, see Harris, "Preserving A Vision," 452–57. Harris does not address Grinnell's hopes for a national park in this context.

63. For a transcript of the 1895 Blackfeet negotiation proceedings, see Senate Executive Document No. 118, 1st Session, 54th Congress; Diettert, *Grinnell's Glacier*, 67–71; and September 20, 1895 diary entry, Manuscript #325, GBGSWM. The transcript of the negotiations with the Assiniboines and Gros Ventres of Fort Belknap Reservation indicates Grinnell's comments did not carry the weight they had among the Blackfeet. In this case, most of the Assiniboines were willing to sell, but the Gros Ventres balked. Grinnell wrote in his diary: "the Gros Ventres are divided into two parties, young men vs. old men. The latter want to sell but the former—through pique—do not. They refused to be led by the old men." October 5, 1895, Manuscript #325, GBGSWM. Eventually, 190 of 334 male adults of the two tribes signed the agreement, a majority of 46 and so the Fort Belknap Reservation was reduced by about 40,000 acres in exchange for $360,000. Grinnell's role throughout the negotiations was to encourage the Fort Belknap Indians "to turn yourselves into white men; you can't be Indians any longer. If you stay Indians, then you will have to starve." He especially urged them to buy cattle with the proceeds of the sale. Senate Executive Document No. 117, 1st session, 54th Congress. To this day, some Gros Ventres remember George Bird Grinnell's role in this land cession with bitterness. Conversation with James Welch, June, 1991, Billings, Montana. For a critical account of Grinnell's role in these negotiations, see George N. Ruebelmann and William S. Hubbell, "Cultural Resource Assessment of the Little Rocky Mountains," Havre, Montana: Bureau of Land Management, Havre Resource Area Office, 1988, 17–8.

64. Grinnell to Secretary of the Interior, August 13, 1902, Manuscript #95, GBGSWM; J. C. Clifford to Grinnell, October 30, 1902, Manuscript #42, GBGSWM. Clifford gave Grinnell complete credit for the beef increase "and have told the Indians what you have done for them." More letters regarding the Northern Cheyenne beef issue can be found in both files. See also Hagan, *Theodore Roosevelt*, 142–43; Harris, "Preserving A Vision," 470–76.

65. Grinnell to Charles Fletcher Lummis, November 6, 1902, CFLSWM. In 1902, Lummis suggested Theodore Roosevelt replace Commissioner of Indian Affairs William A. Jones with Grinnell. See Hagan, *Theodore Roosevelt*, 122.

66. George Bird Grinnell to Ethan A. Hitchcock, July 1, 1901 and July 9, 1901, Manuscript #78, "Correspondence on the Blackfeet," GBGSWM; George Bird Grinnell's Report on the Standing Rock Reservation, Manuscript #26, GBGSWM. In this report Grinnell said the Sioux needed 100 head of cattle per man to become self-sufficient while they presently had 3 and one-half per man. At the same time, the government threatened to cut their rations. "To deprive such sick people of food is cruel. Many old people on this reservation are in a state of semi-starvation, because they deprive themselves of food in order that their young people may have a greater supply." See also Hagan, *Theodore Roosevelt*, 94–8. Grinnell did not leap at the chance to get involved more publically in cultural issues as correspondence with James Mooney in 1903 revealed. Mooney tried to enlist Grinnell's aid against the Southern Cheyenne reservation agent who accused Mooney and others of instigating the Sun Dance and hiring Indians to torture themselves. Grinnell apparently demurred from involvement in the contro-

versy. Mooney's letters to Grinnell on this topic are dated August 3, August 22, September 19, 1903. See Manuscript #45, "Notes and Correspondence on Various Indian Subjects," GBGSWM.

67. A copy of this article, dated May 11, 1921, can be found in Manuscript #150, GBGSWM.

68. Ibid.

69. Grinnell to Charles Fletcher Lummis, December 28, 1923, CFLSWM.

70. Grinnell to Mary Austin, August 18, 1924, MAHL. Reviews of his works reveal that other readers, besides Austin, appreciated Grinnell's efforts to shatter stereotypes. See Harris, "Preserving A Vision," 514, 533, 550. Grinnell's Indian interests focused solely on Rocky Mountain and Plains tribes. However, in 1919, he wandered into Mary Austin's Southwest, visiting Acoma Pueblo, as well as the Hopi and Navajo reservations. He found the Hopi agriculture "outstanding," but for the most part, Grinnell seemed uninterested in these people and made no comparisons between them and the groups he knew well. See Ms. #94, "Notes of Arizona and New Mexico trip—1919," GBGSWM.

71. See "Savage Lover," Manuscript #90, GBGSWM.

72. Grinnell, "The Indian," Manuscript #152, GBGSWM.

73. Grinnell, untitled piece in Manuscript #95, "Notes & Correspondence on Various Indian Subjects," GBGSWM.

74. For a critique of scholarship that ignores Indian oral history and testimony, see Devon A. Mihesuah, "Introduction," in Devon A. Mihesuah, ed., *Natives and Academics: Researching and Writing about American Indians* (Lincoln: University of Nebraska Press, 1998),1–22.

## *Chapter 4*

1. Walter McClintock, *Old Indian Trails* (Boston: Houghton Mifflin, 1992), 3.

2. Walter McClintock, unpublished autobiographical manuscript, Folder 40, Series II, WMBL.

3. Walter McClintock, typescript of 1895 trip, Folder 50, Series II, WMBL.

4. Walter McClintock, *The Old North Trail: Life, Legends & Religion of the Blackfeet Indians* (Lincoln: University of Nebraska Press, 1992), 20; McClintock, autobiography ms., Folder 40, Series II, WMBL.

5. Walter to Norman McClintock, October 22, 1896, Folder 40, and Walter to his mother, November 7, 1896, Folder 35, Series I, WMBL.

6. Walter McClintock to his father, November 11, 1896, Folder 41, Series I, WMBL.

7. Walter McClintock to his father, July 23, 1898, Folder 41. Series I, WMBL.

8. McClintock, autobiography ms., Folder 40, Series II, WMBL. See also McClintock, *The Old North Trail*, 26, and McClintock, *Old Indian Trails*, 35.

9. McClintock to his father, August 28, 1899, Folder 41, Series I, WMBL.

10. McClintock, *The Old North Trail*, 27.

11. Siyeh to Walter McClintock, December 14, 1898; December 1, 1899; undated letter circa 1900; January 4, 1900; March 6, 1900; May 6, 1901; all Folder 72, Series I, WMBL. In 1898, Maggie Wetzel reported to McClintock that she often hears from Grinnell. "During his last visit he did a great deal for our people. He had learned that the old men had signed a petition to employ a lawyer at Washington of no use at all. He explained their serious mistake and he went to Washington and had it thrown out entirely saving the Indians twenty-five thousand dollars." Maggie Wetzel to McClintock, January 1, 1898, Folder 80, Series I, WMBL.

12. Siyeh to McClintock, January 14, 1902, Folder 72, Series I, WMBL.

13. Walter McClintock to Siyeh, June 15, 1902, Folder 72, Series I, WMBL. There is no correspondence in the McClintock Papers with either Grinnell or the Bureau of Indian Affairs.

14. Jack Big Moon to McClintock, January 18, 1912, Folder 3, Series I, WMBL.

15. McClintock, "Notes on the Blackfeet Indians, 1903 Jul.," Folder 62, Series II, WMBL.

16. McClintock, "Notes on a Trip to the North Blackfoot Country, 1903 Sep.," Folder 63, Series II, WMBL. It is noteworthy that when McClintock published an account of this story, he did not acknowledge various versions.

17. Ibid.

18. Ibid.

19. McClintock, autobiography ms., "Origin of an Indian Opera," Folder 43, Series II, WMBL.

20. Ibid.

21. Ibid., Randolph Hartley to McClintock, November 4, 1907 and January 12, 1907, Folder 21, Series I, WMBL.

22. Oliver McClintock to William Sloan, October 19, 1905, Folder 47, Series I, WMBL; McClintock, autobiography ms., "Production of Pöia," Folder 44, Series II, WMBL; "Nevin's Indian Opera Scores Splendid Triumph," January 17, 1907, *Pittsburgh Dispatch* and "Triumphant Bow Is Made By Pöia," January 17, 1907, *Pittsburgh Gazette-Times*, both reviews found in Box 2, WMSWM.

23. J. I. Buchanan to Andrew Carnegie, April 15, 1907, Folder 61, Series I; McClintock autobiography ms., Folder 44, Series II, WMBL; and Theodore Roosevelt to McClintock, May 1, 1907, Box 2, WMSWM.

24. McClintock, autobiography ms., Folder 44, Series II, WMBL; copy of letter from Andrew Carnegie to Charlamagne Tower, May 16, 1907, in scrapbook, Box 1, WMSWM.

25. McClintock, "The American Grand Opera *Pöia* (Scarface)," Folder 51, Series II, WMBL.

26. McClintock to his mother, June 20, 1907, Folder 36, Series I, WMBL.

27. McClintock to his father, May 10, 1908, Folder 42, Series I, WMBL.

28. McClintock to his mother, April 4, 1909, Folder 38, Series I, WMBL. Yale did eventually grant him an honorary degree, but it was a Master's degree not a doctorate. For more on the professionalization of anthropology, see L. G. Moses, *The Indian Man: A Biography of James Mooney* (Chicago: University of Illinois Press, 1984), 226–27; Curtis Hinsley, Jr., *Savages and Scientists: The Smithsonian Institution and the Development of American Anthropology, 1846–1910* (Washington, D.C.: Smithsonian Institution Press, 1981).

29. McClintock to his mother, February 24, 1909, Folder 38, Series I, WMBL.

30. Copy of this review, dated April 25, 1910, can be found in scrapbook, Box 1, WMSWM.

31. "Greet 'Pöia' With Cheers and Hisses," *New York Times*, April 24, 1910, copy in scrapbook, Box 1, WMSWM.

32. "The Damning of 'Pöia,'" *Rochester New York The Post Express*, April 26, 1910, Box 2, WMSWM.

33. McClintock, "The American Grand Opera *Pöia*," Folder 51, Series II, WMBL.

34. John C. Symmes to McClintock, May 4, 1910, Folder 74; see also Eugenie von Huhn to McClintock, April 24, 1910 and August 25, 1910, Folder 27, Series I, WMBL.

35. Arthur Nevin to McClintock, April 26, 1910, Folder 57, Series I. For correspondence regarding Hartley's belief that McClintock was taking undue credit for the

opera's libretto, see Folder 6, Series I; for Mary Nevin's reaction, see Mary Lynham Nevin to McClintock, April 26, 1910, quoted in "American Grand Opera" ms., Folder 51, Series II, all WMBL.

36. Lillie de Hegermann-Lindencrone to McClintock, August 15, 1923, Folder 23, Series I, WMBL; Robert Nevin to McClintock, May 2, 1930, Folder 60 and McClintock to Robert Nevin, May 11, 1930, Folder 60, Series I, WMBL.

37. McClintock, *The Old North Trail*; McClintock, *Old Indian Trails*.

38. McClintock, *The Old North Trail*, xi, 25, 5.

39. Ibid., 18, 22. Apparently, J. G. Frazer, a Fellow of Trinity College, British Academy, Edinburgh Royal Society, encouraged McClintock to integrate stories of his personal travels and interactions with the Blackfeet into the book in order that "the book should appeal to a much wider circle than mere anthropologists." J. G. Frazer to Mr. Macmillan, no date, Folder 13, Series I, WMBL.

40. McClintock, *The Old North Trail*, 55, 411–12.

41. Ibid., 170, 311, 223, 398.

42. William Least Heat Moon, "Foreword," to McClintock, *Old Indian Trails*, xii.

43. In terms of "influence," it is likely that many more people have read his books than seen his photography collection, only a fraction of which appear in print.

44. For information on how McClintock went about securing these photographs, see "Notes on the Blackfeet Indians, 1903 Jul.," Folder 62, Series II; McClintock's autobiography ms., Chapter 17, p. 5, 9, 11, Folder 42, and Chapter 37, discarded pages, Folder 49, Series II, WMBL.

45. McClintock, *Old Indian Trails*, 240, 242.

46. McClintock, *The Old North Trail*, 393–94.

47. Ibid., 509.

48. Ibid., 509–12.

49. Oliver McClintock to Mr. Macmillan, June 1, 1909, Folder 46, Series I, WMBL.

50. Theodore Roosevelt to McClintock, January 14, 1911, Folder 67; Gifford Pinchot to McClintock, December 13, 1910, Folder 64; Clark Wissler to McClintock, December 8, 1910, Folder 83, all Series I, WMBL. The Grinnell review can be found in a scrapbook of articles and reviews regarding McClintock's work in Box 1, WMSWM.

51. Alice Jacobs to McClintock, no date, Folder 30, Series I, WMBL. Mrs. Jacobs wrote from Brighton, possibly England.

52. McClintock to Ferris Greenslet, December 15, 1922, Folder 26, Series I, WMBL; McClintock, *Old Indian Trails*, 3, 7. In this edition's foreword, William Least Heat Moon indicated that distribution problems with *The Old North Trail* convinced McClintock to write a new version for American audiences, p. xiii. In his letter to Greenslet, of Houghton Mifflin Company, McClintock indicated he had arranged to translate *The Old North Trail* into German, but the outbreak of war canceled that project.

53. Ibid., 24. For other examples of McClintock's greater willingness to write about mixed bloods and ranching, see 139–43, 149–52.

54. Ibid., 204. See also 154, 197.

55. Ibid., 159, 69, 77. As McClintock put it, "After my adoption, the women of Mad Wolf's family were hospitable and kind and treated me as a relative," 69.

56. Ibid., 316.

57. Pearl Wetzel Hagerty to McClintock, November 7 [?], 1930, Folder 20, Series I, WMBL.

58. Pearl Wetzel Hagerty to McClintock, December [no day], 1930, Folder 20, Series I, WMBL. Mrs. Hagerty, the mother of two and apparently widowed, was interested in renewing her friendship with McClintock but he did not reciprocate. In 1932, Pearl tried

to find him during his visit to Glacier National Park, but McClintock had already checked out. "I wanted to see you," she wrote, "and see if you didn't want a good housekeeper. Some one to mend your socks, and look after you when you are feeble. The pioneer girl you tell about on page 26 of your book has changed very little and I think for the better . . . Are you such a confirmed bachelor that you have no time for women?" Pearl Wetzel Hagerty to McClintock, July [no day], 1932, Folder 20, Series I, WMBL. This was the last letter from Mrs. Hagerty in McClintock's files.

59. The texts of these lectures can be found in Ms. #533, Folder 2, WMSWM. For an example of the letter McClintock sent out soliciting lecture dates, see McClintock to Academy of Natural Sciences, April 23, 1934, Folder 1, Series I, WMBL.

60. Walter McClintock, "Statement of the Coloring of Blackfoot Indian Pictures," Box 1, WMSWM; another copy of this statement can be found in Folder 70, Series II, WMBL.

61. Clark Wissler to McClintock, April 18, 1929; May 6, 1930; and June 25, 1930; Folder 83, Series I, WMBL. In a later letter Wissler invited McClintock to arrange a program together regarding contact between Blackfeet and whites. It is not clear if anything came of this invitation. Wissler to McClintock, September 30, 1932, Folder 83, Series I, WMBL.

62. John Quillin Tilson, *Sixty Years After: Being a History of the Class of Eighteen Ninety One Yale College* (New Haven: Yale University, 1951), 112–13; Howard Lamar to author, January 9, 1995, in author's possession; telephone interview with Archibald Hanna, January 24, 1995. Lamar presented a slightly different version of how McClintock earned the nickname "Old Beaver Bundle." He said it came about because McClintock always carried his glass slides in sturdy leather boxes lined with beaver fur.

63. Tilson, 113; "The Southwest Museum announced the appointment of Walter McClintock as Research Fellow in Ethnology, July 31, 1927," brochure, Box 1, WMSWM.

64. Walter McClintock, "The Tragedy of the Blackfoot," *Southwest Museum Papers*, Number 3 (Los Angeles: Southwest Museum, 1930), 44.

65. Ibid., 45.

66. Ibid., 45, 51.

67. Jan Cohn, *Improbable Fiction: The Life of Mary Roberts Rinehart* (Pittsburgh: University of Pittsburgh Press, 1980); Sybil Downing and Jane Valentine Barker, *Crown of Life: The Story of Mary Roberts Rinehart* (Niwot, Colorado: Roberts Rinehart Publishers, 1992). See also Mary Roberts Rinehart, *My Story* (New York: Rinehart & Company, Inc., 1948), 29. The first edition of this autobiography was published in 1931.

68. Cohn, *Improbable Fiction*, 94. In 1983, Roberts Rinehart, Inc. Publishers reprinted *Through Glacier Park in 1915*.

69. Rinehart, *My Story*, 202.

70. Ibid., 202–03.

71. Ibid., 204–05. Rinehart's involvement with the Blackfeet did lead to at least some correspondence with George Bird Grinnell. Apparently, in the summer of 1916, she returned to Glacier National Park, but Grinnell failed to see her, writing that too many people wanted to speak with her and so "it seemed quite hopeless to get a word with you." George Bird Grinnell to Mary Roberts Rinehart, August 5, 1916, Ms. #171, GBGSWM.

72. Mary Roberts Rinehart, *Tenting Tonight: A Chronicle of Sport and Adventure in Glacier Park and the Cascade Mountains* (Boston: Houghton Mifflin Company, 1918), 97. Among the Blackfeet she identified as "chiefs" were Two Guns, White Calf, Medicine Owl, Curly Bear, Big Spring, Bird Plume, Wolf Plume, Bird Rattler, Bill Shute, Stabs-by-Mistake, Eagle Child, and Many Tail-Feathers.

73. Ibid., 98.

74. Mary Roberts Rinehart, *The Out Trail* (New York: George H. Doran Company, 1923), 97, 107.

75. Ibid., 147. She added, "His towns are the same. He is the same. Only—he has remained a vassal."

## Chapter 5

1. The term "endangered authenticities" comes from James Clifford, *The Predicament of Culture: Twentieth Century Ethnography, Literature and Art* (Cambridge: Harvard University Press, 1988).

2. Frank B. Linderman, *Montana Adventure: The Recollections of Frank B. Linderman*, ed. H. G. Merriam (Lincoln: University of Nebraska Press, 1968), 162–63. He made the same comment in his preface to *Plenty-coups: Chief of the Crows* (Lincoln: University of Nebraska Press, 1962), viii. This book was originally published as *American: The Life Story of a Great Indian, PlentyCoups, Chief of the Crows* (New York: The John Day Company, 1930).

3. Frank Linderman to Manette Swetland, June 9, 1933, Folder No. 1/1, Frank Linderman Small Collection #74, FBLMHS; Roland Baumann, Oberlin College Archivist to author, September 27, 1994; and Linderman, *Montana Adventure*, 2.

4. Frank Linderman, "Autobiographical Statement," Scrapbook VI, FBLML; Linderman, *Montana Adventure*, 6–8.

5. Linderman, "Autobiographical Statement," Scrapbook VI, FBLML.

6. Linderman, *Montana Adventure*, 20–1, 24.

7. Ibid., 42. For another version of this story, see Linderman's grandson's account, James Beale Waller, "Frank Bird Linderman," FBLMHS.

8. Ibid., 24–7.

9. Ibid,, 28–30.

10. Linderman, "Autobiographical Statement," 2; Linderman to Dear Medicine-woman, May 31, 1935, FBLMHS; Linderman to Jane Wall, August 17, 1911, FBLMHS; and Linderman, *Montana Adventure*, 64.

11. Linderman, *Montana Adventure*, 67.

12. Linderman, *Montana Adventure*, 94, 97, 106. For negative accounts of Italian, Welsh, and Irish immigrant miners, see *Montana Adventure*, 89, 92–3, 97–8.

13. Ibid., 99–100.

14. Ibid., 109-11, 118-34.

15. Ibid., 137–38, 144.

16. Ibid., 140–41.

17. Frank Linderman to Roberts, March 12, 1918, quoted in Celeste River, "A Mountain in His Memory: Frank Bird Linderman, His Role in Acquiring the Rocky Boy Indian Reservation for the Montana Chippewa and Cree, and the Importance of That Experience in the Development of His Literary Career" (M.A. thesis, University of Montana, 1990), 50. For evidence that Linderman saw himself as a Chippewa family member, see Linderman to Cato Sells, June 10, 1916, FBLMPI. In this letter Linderman indicates he is Big Rock's "adopted 'younger brother.' This probably means nothing to you, but a great deal to the old man." It also meant a great deal to Linderman.

18. River, "A Mountain in His Memory," 18–9; C.M. Russell to Senator Henry L. Myers, January 11, 1913, FBLMPI.

19. Quoted in River, "A Mountain in His Memory," 35–6.

20. Ibid., 28.

21. River, "A Mountain in His Memory," 83, 189. For examples of Grinnell's reactions to Linderman's pleas for help, see George Bird Grinnell to Frank Bird Linderman, February 20, 1912; March 15, 1912; January 23, 1913; and March 17, 1916, FBLMPI.

22. Linderman to Cato Sells, February 21, 1916; George Bird Grinnell to Linderman, March 17, 1916; and Linderman to Grinnell, March 24, 1916; FBLMPI. In a letter Linderman composed but did not send to Sells, he was more militant, even radical regarding reasons why the Cree and Chippewa deserved their reservation. See notes for this letter dated March 6, 1916, typewritten copy in Scrapbook VI, FBLML.

23. Linderman, *Montana Adventure*, 157–61; Big Rock to "My dear Brother" (Linderman), July 16, 1916, FBLMPI; Linderman to Rossiter, December 1916, quoted in River, "A Mountain in His Memory," 199. Linderman himself explained it this way: "'Injuns, whites, niggers and all come to my camp and I sometimes wish I had been born with more guts and less sentiment."

24. Frank B. Linderman, *Indian Why Stories: Sparks From War Eagle's Lodge-Fire* (New York: Charles Scribner's Sons, 1915), xvi, vii, viii-ix.

25. H. G. Merriam, "The Life and Work of Frank B. Linderman," in Linderman, *Montana Adventure*, 209; River, "A Mountain in His Memory," 104–12; Charles Scribner's Sons to Frank Linderman, June 22, 1914; Linderman to Scribner's, June 14, 1915; Linderman to Scribner's July 2, 1915; all in Folder 12, Box 4; and Charles Scribner's Sons to O. M. Lanstrum, March 1, 1915; Scribner's Sons to O. M. Lanstrum, June 9, 1915; and Scribner's advertisement for *Indian Why Stories*, Folder 14, Box 5, all FBLML. According to H. G. Merriam, Linderman first submitted the manuscript to the Curtis Publishing Company, who declined to publish it but passed it along to the Century Publishing Company. Merriam did not indicate Century's reaction and simply noted Scribner's eventually took it. H. G. Merriam, "Sign-Talker with Straight Tongue," *Montana, the Magazine of Western History* (Summer 1962): 2.

26. Linderman to Grinnell, May 6, 1915; Grinnell to Linderman, May 24, 1915; Grinnell to Linderman, November 25, 1915; and Grinnell to Linderman, February 23, 1916, all in Folder 10, Box 2, FBLML. In this last letter Grinnell reminded Linderman, once again, that Indian books would not bring him much money: "I should be very sorry if I had to depend for bread and butter solely on what I get from my books."

27. Linderman, *Montana Adventure*, 144–48; Frank Bird Linderman, *Recollections of Charley Russell* (Norman: University of Oklahoma Press, 1963), 50–1; Linderman to Scribner's, August 21, 1919 and September 6, 1919, CSSPL.

28. Verne Linderman, "As We Remember Mr. Russell," in Linderman, *Recollections of Charley Russell*, 131–32; Russell to Linderman, September 22, 1919 and November 11, 1919, Folder 6, Box 4, FBLML. For correspondence between Linderman and Scribner's over these incidents, see Scribner's to Linderman, April 4, 1919; Linderman to Scribner's, September 16, 1919; Scribner's to Linderman, September 26, 1919, November 21, 1919, and January 24, 1920, all in Folder 14, Box 4, FBLML. See also Linderman to Scribner's, January 11, January 23, April 8, June 9, August 2, September 1, September 11, and December 28, 1919; Scribner's to Linderman, April 18, June 4, June 16, 1919, all CSSPL. Although the Linderman-Russell friendship was damaged, they lived near one another when they wintered in Santa Barbara, California, in the 1920s, and the friendship was patched up before Russell died in 1926.

29. Frank B. Linderman, *On a Passing Frontier: Sketches from the Northwest* (New York: Charles Scribner's Sons, 1920), 38, 124.

30. The former consisted of stories Linderman created, rather than collected. Scribner's worried that publishing such a work might cast doubt on the authenticity of his earlier books. Linderman shared their concern but eventually convinced them to pro-

ceed since the work would not have Indians in it. See Linderman to Scribner's, January 23, March 4, June 24, July 12, 1919; Scribner's to Linderman, July 8 and November 21, 1919, all CSSPL.

31. Howard Miller to Frank Linderman, March 5, 1921; Linderman to Miller, March 9, 1921; Folder 15, Box 4, FBLML; Scribner's to Linderman, January 24 and February 19, 1920; Linderman to Scribner's, January 29, February 24, April 8, May 29, 1920, CSSPL. For more on Linderman's opinions of Nancy Russell, see Linderman to Van de Water, November 8, 1931, Folder 33, Box 4 and Van de Water to Linderman, December 20, 1931, Folder 32, Box 4, FBLML.

32. Linderman to Howard Miller, March 29, 1921, Folder 15, Box 4, FBLML.

33. Linderman, *Montana Adventure*, 72–3.

34. Linderman to Scribner's, September 4, 1926 and June 21, 1927; Scribner's to Linderman, January 24 and August 19, 1927, CSSPL.

35. Linderman, *Montana Adventure*, 181–84; James J. Sladen to Linderman, April 25, 1927, Folder 20, Box 4, FBLML. Linderman, *American*. For more on Plenty Coups, see Frederick E. Hoxie, *Parading through History: The Making of the Crow Nation in American, 1805–1935* (New York: Cambridge University Press, 1995).

36. Clifford, *The Predicament of Culture*, 42, 43, 45.

37. H. David Brumble, *American Indian Autobiography* (Berkeley: University of California Press, 1988), 11–2, 22–3, 84–7. For discussion of problems with well-meaning versions of Indian accounts, see Raymond J. DeMallie, "'These Have No Ears': Narrative and the Historical Method," *Ethnohistory* (Fall 1993): 518–23; and Elizabeth Cook Lynn, "American Indian Intellectualism and the New Indian Story," in *Natives and Academics: Researching and Writing about American Indians*, ed. Devon Mihesuah (Lincoln: University of Nebraska Press, 1998), 111–38.

38. Linderman, *American*, vii. His modesty here was perhaps feigned. Linderman, in a jab possibly meant for Mary Roberts Rinehart, complained about instant experts who wrote about Indians after a few weeks in national parks. See *American*, vii.

39. Linderman, *American*, n.p.

40. For examples of Linderman's belief that he was telling the truth about the West, see Linderman to H. M. Hebden, March 8, 1921, Folder 22, Box 2; Linderman to Harry R. Cunningham, June 28, 1922, Folder 42, Box 3; the "queers it with publishers" quote comes from Linderman to Roger Burlingame, December 21, 1923, Folder 17, Box 4; Linderman to Elmer Green, June 12, 1929, Folder 10, Box 5; Linderman to Caspar Hodgson, August 23, 1929, Folder 11, Box 5; all FBLML; Linderman, *Montana Adventure*, 183. Linderman also believed non-Indians who married Indian women and thus "into a tribe" proved unreliable as sources of authentic information. "I've never yet found such a man who knew anything about the people with whom he lived," Linderman to Lew Callaway, December 18, 1935, Folder 20, Box 1, FBLML.

41. Merriam, "Sign-Talker," 16, 18; Robert Lowie's review of *American* can be found in *American Anthropologist* (1932): 532–33. Lowie's review is quoted in Merriam, "The Life and Work of Frank B. Linderman," 212. For the University of Chicago plan, see Merriam, "The Life and Work of . . . Linderman," 208; Earl Newsom to Frank Linderman, May 23, 1930; Linderman to Newsom, June 7, 1930; Newsom to Linderman, July 28, 1930; Newsom to Linderman, September 29, 1930; and Newsom to Linderman, December 11, 1930; all in Folder 37, Box 1, FBLML.

42. James Oppenheim to Linderman, December 12, 1930, Folder 47, Box 3, FBLML.

43. Linderman to Hermann Hagedorn, no date, Folder 18, Box 2, FBLML.

44. Frank B. Linderman, *Pretty-shield: Medicine Woman of the Crows* (Lincoln: University of Nebraska Press, 1972), 2, 24. For an analysis of this book see Christine Colasurdo,

" 'Tell Me a Woman's Story': The Question of Gender in the Construction of *Waheenee, Pretty-shield*, and *Papago Woman*," *American Indian Quarterly* (Summer 1997): 391–96.

45. Linderman to "Frau" (his wife), March 23 and March 25, 1931, Folder 11, Box 3, FBLML.

46. Linderman, *Pretty-shield*, 16, 38, 167, 168.

47. Ibid., 202, 227–31.

48. Linderman to Hermann Hagedorn, November 8, 1931, Folder 18, Box 2; Richard Walsh to Linderman, October 23, 1931, and November 28, 1931, Folder 38, Box 1, FBLML.

49. Hugh Scott to Mr. Walsh, October 12, 1932, Folder 38, Box 1, FBLML; Robert Lowie's review of *Red Mother* is in *American Anthropologist* (1934): 125–26; Merriam, "The Life and Work of Frank B. Linderman," 206, 212; Linderman to Mrs. Henrietta Crockett, September 22, 1934, Folder 34, Box 3; and Linderman to Harry Turney-High, October 10, 1934, Folder 29, Box 4, FBLML. For more on the Pretty-shield error regarding Sitting-heifer, see Linderman to Harry [Turney-High], August 7, 1934, Folder 29, Box 4; Henrietta Crockett to Linderman, November 10, 1934; and Crockett to Linderman, May 9, 1934, all Folder 34, Box 3, FBLML; and Linderman to Mrs. Coates, November 14, 1934, Small Collection #74, FBLMHS.

50. Mary Brace Kimball to Linderman, July 16, 1930, Folder 3, Box 3; Frank Van de Water to Linderman, October 29, 1931, November 22, 1932 and February 26, 1933, Folder 32, Box 4; and Walter Campbell to Linderman, October 14, 1932, Folder 35, Box 1, all FBLML.

51. Oliver LaFarge's comments are quoted in Linderman to Hermann Hagedorn, July 10, 1930, Folder 18, Box 2; Linderman to O. J. McGillis, November 17, 1935 and McGillis to Linderman, November 22, 1935, Folder 9, Box 2; all FBLML. It is possible that cronyism played some role in other writers' estimations of Linderman's books. In the letter cited above, Vestal told Linderman he was "counting on [him] for a good review of my *Sitting Bull* . . . You will no doubt recall your promise when *American* came out." Linderman told Van de Water that he reviewed *Sitting Bull* because Vestal asked him to, "though I didn'y [*sic*] want to." Vestal "makes breaks that gag me" so Linderman's review was "not a very hot one." Vestal's errors in this book and his Kit Carson book display his ignorance. "[N]o man can possibly know the idiom of this land unless he has lived the life he portrays here," he explained. Van de Water privately told Linderman that he thought Vestal's *Sitting Bull* to be "a dull, not particularly scrupulous or intelligent piece of special pleading, muddy in style and credulous in the extreme. It's pewter, badly done and your Indian books have the clear, authentic ring of pure silver. Which isn't in the least hyperbole but sober fact." Linderman to Van de Water, "Mch" 4, 1933, Folder 33, Box 4 and Van de Water to Linderman, February 26, 1933, Folder 32, Box 4, FBLML.

52. Henrietta Crockett to Linderman, May 9, 1934, Folder 34, Box 3, FBLML.

53. For information of how Linderman was hailed as a Montana man of letters see copy of an Introduction made at an affair at St. Ignatius, September 27, 1935, Folder 16, Box 1, FBLML; and untitled ms., which summarizes Linderman's literary accomplishments, by Grace Stone Coates, Small Collection #74, FBLMHS. Linderman to Frank Van de Water, December 16, 1932, Folder 33, Box 4; Hermann Hagedorn to Linderman, August 15, 1935, Folder 19, Box 2, FBLML. Linderman's nativism also spilled over to antisemitism. See his comments on "kike editors" in Linderman to Hagedorn, June 15, 1928, Folder 16, Box 2; Linderman to Van de Water, June 4, 1932, Folder 33, Box 4, FBLML.

54. Linderman, *Montana Adventure*, 163; Linderman to Dad, September 2, 1916 and Linderman to Theodore Gibson, September 2, 1916, Folder 8, Box 6, FBLML. See also Linderman to Percy Raban, September 2, 1916, Folder 8, Box 6, FBLML. In *Montana Ad-*

*venture* Linderman touched briefly on what was obviously a painful episode and hinted at his theory that Rankin's election was a fad, noting that "her political planet faded into an ordinary star." She was not reelected in 1918.

55. Linderman to Grinnell, October 4, 1916, Folder 10, Box 2, FBLML.

56. Linderman to Theodore Gibson, September 2, 1916, Folder 8, Box 6; Grinnell to Linderman, September 15, 1916, Folder 10, Box 2, FBLML.

57. Linderman, *Montana Adventure*, 163–64; Linderman to Henry Cabot Lodge, December 28, 1918, Folder 9, Box 6; Linderman to Gertrude Atherton, March 9, 1922, Folder 4, Box 1; Linderman to Senator Henry Myers, March 23, 1922, Folder 41, Box 3; Linderman to P.A. Morrison, April 29, 1922, Folder 38, Box 3; John Lindquist to Linderman, August 30, 1924, Folder 11, Box 6, all FBLML. For another example of this kind of "fan letter" heavily laced with masculine imagery, see Lew Sarrett to Linderman, January 3, 1923, Folder 9, Box 4, FBLML, wherein Sarrett writes, "would to God that more writing men had the humanness and the virility you have. I'm sick of the emasculated poseurs I see around here; of the two for a nickel pseudo literati . . . Give my very best regards to your family of true, refined sweet women . . . how rare in this generation!" One of Linderman's big supporters was B.K. Baghdigian, founder and director of the Counsel Bureau, which according to his letterhead was "Established to Promote Americanization and a Better Understanding of Americanism." See B. K. Baghdigian to Linderman, January 6, 1925 and March 3, 1925, Folder 7, Box 1, FBLML.

58. Fred Gabriel to Linderman, August 4, 1921, Folder 14, Box 2, FBLML. The titles reveal the deep strains of antimodernism in Linderman's work. According to Jackson Lears, antimodernists especially feared anarchists, immigrants, strikers, tramps, and criminals. Linderman would have added feminists to the list. See T. J. Jackson Lears, *No Place of Grace: Antimodernism and the Transformation of American Culture* (New York: Pantheon, 1981), 102.

59. Frank Linderman to Hon. Jos. M. Dixon, no date, Folder 44, Box 1; Samuel McKelvie to Ray Wilbur, March 29, 1929, Folder 22, Box 3; and William H. Murgittroyd to Linderman, April 9, 1929, Folder 40, Box 3, all FBLML.

60. See, for example, Linderman to Van de Water, December 18, 1932, Folder 33, Box 4, FBLML.

61. Linderman to Rossiter, circa 1912, quoted in River, "A Mountain in His Memory," 60.

62. Linderman to Hermann Hagedorn, November 24, 1928, Folder 16, Box 2, FBLML; Linderman to Scott Leavitt, November 11, 1931, Microfilm Roll #1, File 17, FBLMPI; River, "A Mountain in His Memory," 223.

63. Linderman, *Montana Adventure*, 181–83.

64. Linderman to Cato Sells, June 10, 1916 and Cato Sells to Linderman, July 7, 1916, microfilm copies, FBLMPI. See also River, "A Mountain in His Memory," 136–41. For a discussion of federal interference with Indian dancing, see Margaret D. Jacobs, *Engendered Encounters: Feminists and Pueblo Cultures, 1879–1934* (Lincoln: University of Nebraska Press, 1999), 106–48.

65. Evan Jones to Linderman, June 10, 1925, microfilm copy, FBLMPI.

66. John D. Keeley to Linderman, May 21, 1925 and Evan Jones to Linderman, June 10, 1925, microfilm copies, FBLML.

67. Linderman to Hermann Hagedorn, September 9, 1933, Folder 19, Box 2; Linderman to Van de Water, September 18, 1933, Folder 33, Box 4, FBLML.

68. Linderman to John Collier, January 31, 1934, microfilm copy, FBLMPI.

69. John Collier to Linderman, May 19, 1934; Collier to Linderman, March 27, 1935;

and Linderman to Business Council (Four-Souls, Joe Corcoran, Malcolm Mitchell, John Parker, and Jim Courchare), March 18, 1934; all microfilm copies, FBLMPI. See also Linderman to Mrs. Coates, June 27, 1934, Small Collection #74, FBLMHS.

70. George W. Blodgett to Linderman, March 14, 1937; Blodgett to Linderman, December 30, 1937; Linderman to Blodgett, January 6, 1938, all in Folder 11, Box 1, FBLML.

71. Linderman to Fritz and Eleanor (Van de Water), December 16, 1932; and Linderman to Fritz and Eleanor, June 20, 1932, Folder 33, Box 4, FBLML. For an interesting discussion of Linderman's visit to New York City and the attractions an eastern life held out for him as a writer, see Hermann Hagedorn, "Frank Linderman As I Knew Him," *Frontier and Midland*, Vol. 19, No. 3 (Spring 1939): 144–45.

*Chapter 6*

1. Edwin R. Bingham, *Charles F. Lummis, Editor of the Southwest* (San Marino, Calif.: Huntington Library, 1955), 9–10.

2. Charles Fletcher Lummis, "As I Remember," autobiography, quoted in Turbese Lummis Fiske and Keith Lummis, *Charles F. Lummis: The Man and His West* (Norman: University of Oklahoma Press, 1975), 20–1.

3. This represents an alternative interpretation to Frederick Hoxie's claim that Lummis and Grinnell believed "conquest of the West represented the triumph of Anglo-Saxon civilization over unbending barbarism." See Frederick E. Hoxie, *A Final Promise: The Campaign to Assimilate the Indians, 1880–1920* (Lincoln: University of Nebraska Press, 1984), 101.

4. Kevin Starr, *Inventing the Dream: California Through the Progressive Era* (New York: Oxford University Press, 1985), 76. For a view which emphasizes Lummis's harsher racial judgments, see Fred Hoxie, *A Final Promise*, 99–101.

5. "The Indians' Charles Fletcher Lummis," *American Indian Life*, Vol. 23, No. 14, (May 1929), 8.

6. For biographical information on Lummis, see Fiske and Lummis, *Charles F. Lummis*; Dudley Gordon, *Charles F. Lummis*, (Los Angeles: Cultural Assets Press, 1972); Bingham, *Charles F. Lummis*; and Robert J. Fleming, *Charles F. Lummis* (Boise: Boise State University Western Writers Series, No. 50, 1981).

7. Lummis to David Starr Jordan, February 16, 1916, David Starr Jordan File, CFLSWM.

8. "As I Remember," CFLSWM; see also Starr, *Inventing the Dream*, 81, 92–3.

9. Quoted in Patrick T. Houlihan and Betsy E. Houlihan, *Lummis in the Pueblos* (Flagstaff, Ariz.: Northland Press, 1986), 87.

10. Quoted in James W. Byrkit, *Charles Lummis: Letters from the Southwest* (Tucson: University of Arizona Press, 1989), 19–20. This volume contains Lummis's letters back to the Chillicothe, Ohio, *Leader*.

11. Quoted in Byrkit, *Charles Lummis*, 96–7; 112–13; and 118.

12. Ibid., 119–20, 124.

13. Ibid., 131-35, 192.

14. Ibid., 217, 227–36, 261.

15. Quoted in Fiske and Lummis, *Charles F. Lummis*, 37.

16. Quoted in Dan L. Thrapp, ed., *Dateline Fort Bowie: Charles Fletcher Lummis Reports on an Indian War* (Norman: University of Oklahoma Press, 1979), 17, 48, 26–7, 68, 65. See also Charles F. Lummis, *General Crook and the Apache Wars*, ed. Turbese Lummis Fiske (Flagstaff, Ariz.: Northland Press, 1966).

17. "Man-Who-Yawns," in *A Bronco Pegasus* (Boston: Houghton Mifflin, 1928), 35–43.

(Excerpts from *A Bronco Pegasus* by Charles Fletcher Lummis. Copyright, 1928, by Houghton Mifflin Company. Copyright © renewed 1956 by Turbese Lummis Fiske. Reprinted by permission of Houghton Mifflin Company. All rights reserved.) For an earlier example of Lummis's movement toward this point of view, see Charles F. Lummis, *The Land of Poco Tiempo* (New York: Charles Scribner's Sons, 1906), 157–214.

18. See Bingham, *Charles F. Lummis,* 11–19; Fiske and Lummis, *Charles F. Lummis,* 39–74.

19. Houlihan and Houlihan, *Lummis in the Pueblos,* 8; Fiske and Lummis, *Charles F. Lummis,* 49.

20. Fiske and Lummis, *Charles F. Lummis,* 50.

21. Ibid., 51.

22. Quoted in William T. Hagan, *Theodore Roosevelt and Six Friends of the Indian* (Norman: University of Oklahoma Press, 1997), 55.

23. Quoted in Houlihan and Houlihan, *Lummis in the Pueblos,* 87, 88, 144.

24. "As I Remember," CFLSWM, n. p.

25. Starr, *Inventing the Dream,* 84; Charles Fletcher Lummis to Dorothea, February 23, 1903; Lummis to C. Hart Merriam, October 27, 1909, CFLSWM; Lummis's description of Amado is quoted in Fiske and Lummis, *Charles F. Lummis,* 101.

26. Lummis to Mr. Brownell, March 25, 1892, CSSPL.

27. Charles Fletcher Lummis, *A New Mexico David and Other Stories and Sketches of the Southwest* (New York: Scribner's, 1891), n.p.

28. Lummis to Washington Matthews, February 6, 1900, CFLSWM. For Lummis's lengthiest statement on the need for popularizers (particularly of archaeology), see "Humanizing the Sciences of Man" (Washington: Government Printing Office, 1917). For an interesting example of Lummis's stinging criticism of others over technical points (in this case, regarding the Spanish language), see Mary Austin to Lummis, November 6, 1904, CFLSWM and his response, Lummis to Mary Austin, November 24, 1904, MAHL. In the chapter that follows, I'll examine Lummis's particularly vitriolic attacks on George Wharton James.

29. Lummis, *A New Mexico David,* 55, 40, 41, 43, 63, 67.

30. Ibid., 149, 174, 175.

31. Ibid., 115, 54.

32. Ibid., 174.

33. See Fleming, *Charles F. Lummis,* 24.

34. Lummis, *A Tramp Across the Continent* (New York: Charles Scribner's Sons, 1892), xii, 52, 75, 71–2. See also Lummis, *Some Strange Corners of Our Country* (Tucson: University of Arizona Press, 1989), 255–61. This is a reprint of the original edition. For more on Lummis's campaign against bigotry, see Bingham, *Charles F. Lummis,* 33, 97–8, 102, 103. Lummis's own assessment of *A Tramp* was that it was his "least worthy work—a boy's careless flippancy." He feared its popular reception would limit sales of his "more important & more dignified because more earnest & more instructive work." See Lummis to Mr. Brownell, May 17, 1892, CSSPL.

35. Lummis, *Land of Poco Tiempo,* 29–30, 46, 88–9, 111.

36. Lummis, *Tramp,* 97, 94–5, 96. For an elaboration on this theme, see Charles Fletcher Lummis, *The Spanish Pioneers* (Chicago: A.C. McClurg and Company, 1893), 23–4, 26, 39, 40–1, 53, 60–2, 92, 149–50. See also *Land of Poco Tiempo,* 67–8.

37. Ibid., 144. See also 162–63.

38. Lummis, *Some Strange Corners,* 5; in *The Land of Poco Tiempo* Lummis moderated this view considerably, although he still referred to Pueblo traditional beliefs as "pagan."

39. Lummis, *The Spanish Pioneers*, 11, 18.

40. Lummis, "As I Remember," CFLSWM, n.p.

41. Ibid.

42. Charles Fletcher Lummis, *The Home of Ramona* (Los Angeles: Charles F. Lummis & Co., 1888), n.p.

43. For Lummis's early articles on Spanish topics, see *In The Land of Sunshine*, Vol. 2, Nos. 2, 3, & 5; for information on The Landmarks Club, see "In the Lion's Den," Vol. 4, No. 1 (December 1895), p. 43 and every "In the Lion's Den" thereafter, until Lummis left the editorship of the magazine. See also Bingham, *Charles F. Lummis*, 103–11, 51–78, 134–91.

44. Horatio N. Rust, "A Fiesta at Warner's Ranch," *Land of Sunshine*, Vol. 10, No. 5 (April 1899), 230.

45. Charles F. Lummis, "My Brother's Keeper," Part I, *Land of Sunshine*, Vol. 11, No. 3 (August 1899), 139–47.

46. Lummis, "My Brother's Keeper," Vol. 11, No. 4 (September 1899), 212; Vol. 12, No. 2 (January 1900), 92; Vol. 12, No. 3 (Febuary 1900), 178–80.

47. "My Brother's Keeper," Vol. 11, No. 5 (October 1899), 264; Vol. 11, No. 6 (November 1899), 334–35; "In the Lion's Den," Vol. 12, No. 5 (April 1900), 319.

48. "The Sequoyah League," Vol. 16, No. 4 (April 1902), 413; "In the Lion's Den," Vol. 15, No.1 (July 1901), 50–51.

49. Lummis to George Bird Grinnell, December 12, 1901 and January 1, 1902, and Lummis to C. Hart Merriam, January 25, 1902, CFLSWM.

50. Lummis to Grinnell, December 12, 1901, CFLSWM.

51. Ibid.

52. Bingham, *Charles F. Lummis*, 113–23; Lummis quoted in Fiske and Lummis, *Charles F. Lummis*, 117; Lummis to Grinnell, April 1, 1903, CFLSWM. For George Bird Grinnell's comments on the Warner's Ranch case, see also correspondence from Grinnell to Lummis, December 24, 1901 and March 21, 1902, CFLSWM. See also Hagan, *Theodore Roosevelt*, 120–28.

53. Lummis to C. Hart Merriam, April 11, 1902; Lummis to Ethan Allen Hitchcock, August 24, 1903; Ethan Allen Hitchcock to Lummis, September 10, 1903, CFLSWM; Bingham, *Charles F. Lummis*, 128–30; Hagan, *Theodore Roosevelt*, 129–38.

54. Lummis to C. Hart Merriam, April 11, 1902; March 11, 1903; and April 10, 1903, CFLSWM. See also Lummis, "As I Remember," 7–9, CFLSWM.

55. Hagan, *Theodore Roosevelt*, 123, 190, 122.

56. Lummis to Grinnell, November 13, 1902; Grinnell to Lummis, November 22, 1902; Lummis to Grinnell, November 29, 1902; Lummis to Grinnell, April 1, 1903; Lummis to C. Hart Merriam, April 20, 1903; CFLSWM; Hagan, *Theodore Roosevelt*, 177–78. Lummis told Merriam that he doubted Grinnell could manage congressmen, senators, lessees, and the secretary of the interior, because "he could not manage me."

57. "Sequoyah League Form Letter," 1922, Sequoyah League Box, CFLSWM. Lummis's comment, "Now here is what we have been looking for a long time," appeared in letters to Major George Pradt, Mr. and Mrs. Kenneth Chapman, and Lorenzo Hubbell.

58. John Collier to Lummis, September 21, 1922; Lummis to C. Hart Merriam, July 8, 1923; Lummis to David Starr Jordan, July 8, 1923; CFLSWM.

59. John Collier to Mrs. Katherine Edison, June 11, 1924, in folder marked "John Collier, 1924–26," CFLSWM.

60. Fiske and Lummis, *Charles F. Lummis*, 215.

61. Lummis to Edgar L. Hewett, January 7, 1927; Lummis to Collier, January 19, 1927; Lummis to Collier, August 7, 1927; Lummis to "My dear Friends of the Pueblos of

New Mexico," November 5, 1927; Lummis to Antonio Abieta, November 25, 1927; CFLSWM.

62. Lummis to Edgar L. Hewett, October 8, 1927, CFLSWM.

63. Lummis to Edgar L. Hewett, December 17, 1927; and January 12, 1928, CFLSWM.

64. Lummis to Hewett, September 12, 1925, CFLSWM.

65. "Man-Who-Yawns," in *A Bronco Pegasus* (Boston: Houghton Mifflin, 1928), 35–43.

66. "The Prose Of It," following the "Man-Who-Yawns," in *A Bronco Pegasus*, 43–8.

67. "Santiago Naranjo," in *A Bronco Pegasus*, 31.

68. Lummis, *Flowers of Our Lost Romance* (Boston: Houghton Mifflin, 1929), xi–xv, 11.

69. A copy of this epitaph can be found in CFLSWM.

70. Starr, *Inventing the Dream*, 125; Bingham, *Charles F. Lummis*, 35; Byrkit, *Letters From the Southwest*, xlviii, xvii.

71. Collier, "The Indians' Charles Fletcher Lummis," 23. For an earlier Collier poem on Lummis, see "A Thought of Charles F. Lummis. In the New Mexico Desert," by John Collier, dated September 16, 1922, copy in "John Collier" file, CFLSWM.

72. Edgar L. Hewett, *Lummis the Inimitable* (Santa Fe, N.M.: Archaeological Institute of America, 1944), 1.

## *Chapter 7*

1. Letter from Charles Fletcher Lummis to Washington Matthews, January 18, 1900, CFLSWM.

2. Lummis to Matthews, November 27, 1900, CFLSWM. James's plagiarized piece appeared in London's *Wide World Magazine* in September 1900, 516–23. For a view of Lummis's early marriage, see Edwin Bingham, *Charles Fletcher Lummis* (San Marino, Calif.: Huntington Library, 1958), 212.

3. Washington Matthews to Charles Fletcher Lummis, December 7, 1900, CFLSWM.

4. Matthews to Lummis, March 3, 1901, CFLSWM; see also Charles F. Lummis, "Untruthful James," *The Land of Sunshine* (April 1901), 215.

5. Peter Wild, *George Wharton James* (Boise, Idaho: Boise State University Western Writers Series, 93, 1990), 27.

6. George Wharton James, *Indian Blankets and Their Makers* (Chicago: A.C. McClurg & Co., 1914), viii–ix. In his *Indians of the Painted Desert* book, James acknowledged "all the writers of the United States Bureau of Ethnology and the Smithsonian Institution," listing some by name such as Fewkes, Matthews, Hodge, and Cushing. In what seems like overkill he added, "To those who know the persistency and conscientiousness of my labors in my chosen field, and the pains I take both by observation and from the works of authorities to gain accurate knowledge, and my *over*-willingness to acknowledge by pen and voice those to whom I am indebted, it will not be necessary to state that I have endeavored to make this book a standard. If I have failed to give credit where it is due, I do so now with an open heart." See James, *Indians of the Painted Desert Region: Hopis, Navahoes, Wallapais, Havasupais* (Boston: Little, Brown, and Company, 1903), xx. James eventually answered Lummis in a 1920 book, *Singing Through Life With God*. See Roger Joseph Bourdon, "George Wharton James, Interpreter of the Southwest" (Ph.D. dissertation, University of California, Los Angeles, 1964), 146–47.

7. George Wharton James to Lummis, May 25, 1907, CFLSWM; Bourdon, "George Wharton James," 148. No evidence of a Lummis response to James's request is apparent in the James Papers. In print, James never failed to give Lummis's own work recogni-

tion. See, for example, George Wharton James, *New Mexico: The Land of the Delight Makers* (Boston: Page Co., 1920), 359–60.

8. Bourdon, "George Wharton James," 48; Stephen G. Maurer, "In the Heart of the Great Freedom: George Wharton James and the Desert Southwest," *Masterkey* 60 (Summer 1986), 4–5.

9. For more biographical information on James see Wild, *George Wharton James*.

10. Bourdon, "George Wharton James," 62.

11. Wild, 11–8; Bourdon, 50–62, 65, 132. Wild doubts James's wife's more scandalous accusations, finding no evidence of the most unseemly charges. In spring 1892, the Methodist Conference issued a statement indicating that they believed James innocent of the charges his former wife levied against him, but they did not restore him to his pulpit. For more on James's introduction to and interactions with Indians, see Paul R. Arreola, "George Wharton James and the Indians," *Masterkey* 60 (Summer 1986), 11–18.

12. Bourdon, "George Wharton James," 91; Enrique Cortes, "George Wharton James: Advocate for the Golden State," *Masterkey* 60 (Summer 1986), 19.

13. Wild, *George Wharton James*, 38–9.

14. James, *New Mexico*, vi–vii.

15. Wild, *George Wharton James*, 34; Bourdon also agrees this is James's finest work, 122. Patricia Nelson Limerick was less enamored with James's prose, commenting that "nearly every sentence could have been composed by committee." Patricia Nelson Limerick, *Desert Passages: Encounters with the American Deserts* (Albuquerque: University of New Mexico Press, 1985), 125. James simultaneously disparaged commercialism and promoted it, particularly in his own commercial enterprises. At the conclusion of his Indian blankets book, he listed several reliable dealers, including himself. See *Indian Blankets*, 202, 208. He concluded a book on Indian baskets with a series of advertisements for major western traders and included a lengthy description of his museum sales room in his book, *Picturesque Southern California*. See Bourdon, "George Wharton James," 138.

16. Although he did not acknowledge any personal culpability, James did note that the presence of photographers at the Hopi Snake Dance brought about some changes there. The tribe began to place regulations on photographers, assigning their own police the job of keeping photographers in line. In past years he had been able to photograph the priests vomiting the emetic they had consumed. But now they got as far away from the cameras as possible. "It cannot be said that the changes are to the advantage of the photographer," James wrote. "They render his work less certain and effective, and it will not be long before one can write a learned and accurate paper from the standpoint of scientific ethnology on 'the change in religious ceremonies owing to the camera.'" James, "The Snake Dance of the Hopis," *Camera Craft* VI (November 1902), 10.

17. George Wharton James, *Through Ramona's Country* (Boston: Little, Brown, and Company, 1909), 269–70.

18. James, untitled manuscript fragment, #60, Carton 3, GWJSWM.

19. James, *Painted Desert*, 104; George Wharton James, "Photographing Indian Babies," *Camera Craft* VI (December 1902), 58–9, 145.

20. George Wharton James, "The Study of Indian Faces," *Camera Craft* VII (December 1903), 14.

21. Ibid., 16, 17.

22. James, *New Mexico*, 68–9. For a contrasting view of a Carlisle student account of a returning student to Acoma Pueblo, the young man displays contempt for his pueblo's ceremonies and is seriously punished. The man "informed us that he had

s in conformity with the ancient habits of his peo- vert suspicion from himself was by being, as we d vigorous dancer in the throng." George Whar- *ces and Peoples* (Chicago: A. Flanagan Company,

3–4; George Wharton James, *In & Around the Colorado River in Arizona* (Boston: Little, Brown,

other Navajo woman did not hesitate to chastise er skirt in a "more feminine" way for his photo- skirt alone. See *Painted Desert,* 229.

*Basketry*, (Pasadena, Calif.: privately published, 1901), 196.

27. James, "Indian Basketry," Folder 14, Box 5, GWJHL, no page.

28. Ibid., no page.

29. James, *Indian Basketry,* 216.

30. James, *Indian Blankets*, 122. This book, like the one on baskets, offers a hodgepodge of information about Indian blankets, including some information on Zuni, Pueblo, and Chimayo blankets but focusing mostly on Navajo. James provides information on blankets' origins, artistic merits, and symbolism, along with practical information on how to clean them and where to buy them.

31. Ibid., 145.

32. Perhaps Barbara Babcock had James in mind when she argued that Indian women's crafts had value to tourists "because they embody a synchronic essentialism . . . something of a bourgeois dream of an alternative redemptive life, as well as an imagistic transformation of an unmanageable native into a manageable one." See Barbara A. Babcock, "A New Mexico Rebecca: Imagining Pueblo Women," *Journal of the Southwest* 32 (Winter 1990), 400–37.

33. James, *Indian Blankets*, 80.

34. Ibid., 185; *New Mexico*, 210.

35. James, *Indian Blankets*, 45.

36. James, *New Mexico*, 195. James made his most emphatic case for religious toleration regarding Mormonism, but he also believed it appropriate regarding Indian religions. See George Wharton James, *Utah: The Land of Blossoming Valleys* (Boston: Page Company, 1922), viii. At the same time, James could not completely rid himself of old patterns of thought which categorized such religions as primitive or relied on models of social evolution to explain cultural differences. See *Indian Basketry*, 11, 13, 230–31; *New Mexico*, 201; and *Little Journey*, 151. For examples of James's cultural relativism, see James *In and Out of the Old Missions of California,* (Boston: Little, Brown, and Company; 1905), 55, and *New Mexico*, 97. In the latter, he reminds readers of New England's bout with witchcraft.

37. James, *Painted Desert*, 151.

38. James, *Through Ramona's*, 190

39. James, *Through Ramona's*, 84–6.

40. George Wharton James, *What the White Race May Learn from the Indian* (Chicago: Forbes & Company, 1908), 11–2.

41. Wild, *George Wharton James*, 29–30.

42. James, *What the White Race May Learn*, 39–41. James advised, "emulate the Indian. Breathe through your nose"; but he added, "do not use it as an organ of speech."

He also advocated deep breathing as a way to increase lung cap[...] James pointed to the Hopi as models of deep breathing. Ibid., 41, [...]

43. Ibid., 38, 54–5, 94, 59. Outdoor exercise also brought good po[...] white boys slouching and shambling along the streets I wish with a g[...] could have them put under the training of some of my wild Indian friends[...] soon brace up," 87.

44. Ibid., 54, 56, 57, 67, 68–9.

45. Ibid., 107–09, 113, 118.

46. Ibid., 177, 179–80, 194–95, 198–99. See also *New Mexico*, 198.

47. Ibid., 121–27, 145–46, 165–66.

48. Ibid., 216

49. Ibid., 204, 207–09, 222–27, 233–34, 256–57.

50. Ibid., 50–1, 230–31, 246, 249.

51. Ibid., 268. In 1917, James republished this book under the new title, *The Indians' Secrets of Health Or What the White Race May Learn from the Indian* (Pasadena, Calif.: The Radiant Life Press, 1917). The second edition added a brief foreword and a chapter called "The Mentality of the Indian." According to James, "Many hundreds have spoken and written to me of the great helpfulness of this book. Hence it did not seem wise to let it die," 12. In other works James also promoted the basic idea that whites could learn valuable lessons from Indians. See James, *Through Ramona's*, 267–68.

52. James, *In and Out*, 1–2.

53. Ibid., 44, 53–4, 68, 73, 75; *Through Ramona's*, 362–63.

54. *In and Out*, 295, 145–46, 139, 98–99; *Through Ramona's*, 362–63, 288–89.

55. *Through Ramona's*, 290, 349, 273–74.

56. *New Mexico*, xvi; *Indian Blankets*, 14

57. *Indian Blankets*, 14

58. Ibid., 33. Of course, James was not completely consistent here either. He says the story of Spanish reconquest is one of "great bravery," 33.

59. Ibid., 25, 152–53, 369.

60. *Through Ramona's*, 60, 44; *In and Out*, 293.

61. *Through Ramona's*, 3–5; *In and Out*, 295–97; and *What the White Race May Learn*, 16–7, 26.

62. For an exception regarding California Indians, see Bourdon, "George Wharton James," 333–40.

63. *Painted Desert*, 135–36, 174; *Indian Blankets*, 180-81; *Through Ramona's*, 232–33; *In and Out*, 307.

64. *Indian Basketry*, 229.

65. James, "Comment on This Message," typed, undated ms., File #36, Carton 2, GWJSWM.

66. George Wharton James, "The Pueblo Indians of New Mexico," #61, Carton 3, GWJSWM. It is interesting, and frustrating, that in this piece James asserted that the Spanish friars handled the Pueblos wisely and made little effort to alter their way of life or thinking.

67. Limerick, *Desert Passages*, 123–24.

68. Bourdon, "George Wharton James," vi. James claimed he sold 10,000 copies of *Indian Basketry* within ten months and that it continued to sell well for many years. Ibid., 133.

69. May S. Wood to George Wharton James, February 7, 1910, File #8, Carton 1, GWJSWM.

*Chapter 8*

1. Mabel Dodge Luhan will be examined in a separate chapter. For more on women and men, artists and anthropologists who were drawn to the Southwest at this period, see Margaret D. Jacobs, *Engendered Encounters: Feminism and Pueblo Culture, 1879–1934* (Lincoln: University of Nebraska Press, 1999); Desley Deacon, *Elsie Clews Parsons: Inventing Modern Life* (Chicago: University of Chicago Press, 1997); Arrell Morgan Gibson, *The Santa Fe and Taos Colonies: Age of the Muses, 1900–1942* (Norman: University of Oklahoma Press, 1983); Barbara A. Babcock and Nancy J. Parezo, *Daughters of the Desert: Women Anthropologists and the Native American Southwest: Persistent Visions of a Primitive Past* (Washington, D.C.: Smithsonian Institution Press, 1996); and Carter Jones, "'Hope for the Race of Man': Indians, Intellectuals and the Regeneration of Modern America, 1917–1934," (Ph.D. dissertation, Brown University, 1991).

2. Actually, both Austin and Luhan helped spark Collier's interest in Indians. Mary Austin certainly discussed "Indians" with John Collier during their New York City days. Mabel Dodge Luhan is generally credited with bringing Collier to New Mexico and introducing him to the Taos Pueblo. From that point forward, Collier became increasingly involved in Indian affairs and reform.

3. See Esther Lanigan Stineman, *Mary Austin: Song of a Maverick* (New York: Yale University Press, 1989); Augusta Fink, *I-Mary: A Biography of Mary Austin* (Tucson: University of Arizona Press, 1983).

4. Stineman, *Mary Austin*, 27.

5. Mary Austin, *Earth Horizon, Autobiography* (Albuquerque: University of New Mexico Press, 1989), 14, 16, 17. This book was originally published in 1932 by Houghton Mifflin Company.

6. Ibid., 3, 188.

7. Ibid., 188, 197.

8. Ibid., 198.

9. Stineman, *Mary Austin*, 3, 4, 29.

10. This essay was recently reprinted in Esther F. Lanigan, ed., *A Mary Austin Reader* (Tucson: University of Arizona Press, 1996), 23–8.

11. Austin, *Earth Horizon*, 228.

12. Mary Austin, *The American Rhythm: Studies and Reexpressions of Amerindian Songs* (Boston: Houghton Mifflin Co., 1930), 38. This book was originally published in 1923.

13. Austin, *Earth Horizon*, 267.

14. Austin, *The American Rhythm*, 41.

15. Austin, *Earth Horizon*, 234–35.

16. Ibid., 237, 246–47.

17. Ibid., 283, 289.

18. Ibid., 266-67.

19. Stineman, *Mary Austin*, 64–5.

20. Lummis to Austin, November 24, 1904, MAHL.

21. Austin, *Earth Horizon*, 292.

22. Although eventually estranged from Lummis himself, she remained friends with Lummis's wives and dedicated her first book, *The Land of Little Rain*, to Eve Lummis. In the end, Austin concluded about Lummis, "It always seemed to me that poor Charles allowed himself to be diverted to the unimportant ends rather to any main purpose of his life, and perhaps that is the worst I shall have to say of him." See Mary Austin to Eve Lummis DeKalb, July 19, 1929; Austin to DeKalb, August 14, 1929, MAHL.

23. Mary Austin, *The Land of Little Rain* (Albuquerque: University of New Mexico Press, 1974), 59, 62, 97, 98. This book was originally published in 1903 by Houghton Mifflin.

24. Ibid., 103, 109, 106.

25. Ibid., 106.

26. Ibid.

27. Ibid., 109, 110, 111.

28. Leah Dilworth, *Imagining Indians in the Southwest* (Washington, D.C.: Smithsonian Institution Press), 199.

29. Mary Austin, *The Land of Journeys' Ending* (Tucson: University of Arizona Press, 1985), 80, 71, 259–60. This book was originally published in 1924 by the Century Company.

30. Austin, *Earth Horizon*, 283; see also Stineman, *Mary Austin*, 61.

31. "Preface" to First Edition of "The Arrow Maker," ms., MAHL.

32. Austin, *Earth Horizon*, 346–48. Not only did Mary place African-Americans below Indians in her cultural hierarchy, but within the Indian subgroup some proved more advanced than others. She described the "Papa-Ootam" as grouped with the "culturally superior Pimas," for instance. See *Land of Journeys' Ending*, 163.

33. Austin, *Land of Journeys' Ending*, 191–92, 195, 237.

34. Ibid., 196.

35. Ibid., 196–97.

36. Ibid., 197.

37. Ibid., 221–22.

38. Ibid., 221. For some reason, Kit Carson's role in this tragic episode earned him no scorn from Austin. See the Mabel Dodge Luhan chapter for an alternative, and much more negative, assessment of Carson.

39. Ibid., 238.

40. Ibid., 244.

41. Ibid., 244–45.

42. Ibid., 245, 246.

43. Austin, *Earth Horizon*, 362, 367–38.

44. Austin, *The American Rhythm*, 42, 19. For an extended analysis of this book ,see Dilworth, *Imagining Indians*, 173–210.

45. Ibid., 20. Dilworth makes the interesting point that while artists and writers such as Austin made much of Indians' supposed group mindedness, they still expected the individual artist to become cultural leaders. "The modernist turn to the Indian did not represent the success of the community but was a way for artists to claim authority in their own communities, which seemed to be increasingly engulfed by a mass culture they could not control." See Dilworth, *Imagining Indians*, 199.

46. Austin, *Land of Journeys' Ending*, 263–64, 265; Austin, *Earth Horizon*, 368.

47. Mary Austin to Mabel Dodge Luhan, November 9, no year; Austin to Luhan, June 26, 1922; and Austin to Luhan, September 15, no year (probably 1926); all MDLBL.

48. Austin to Luhan, September 15, no year, MDLBL. If such victories proved rare, Austin nevertheless took full credit for them. She wrote Luhan, "few publishers in New York will undertake any Indian book without consulting me." Austin to Luhan, January 2, no year, MDLBL. On another occasion, she lashed out at Walter Lippmann, condemning him for "an impudently ignorant comment . . . I have written a protest against Mr. Lippmann's attempting to speak for all America, and I wish you would drop them a line. The attitude of the New Republic is becoming insufferable, but the truth is that there is a lot of jealousy in Manhattan against the inde-

pendent art movements which originate elsewhere," Austin to Luhan, December 12, 1920, MDLBL.

49. Austin, "Preface to the First Edition," in *The Arrow-Maker: A Drama in Three Acts* (New York: AMS Press, 1969), xi, xii. This is a reprint of the 1915 edition.

50. Stineman, *Mary Austin*, 114.

51. Ibid., 129–30. For a most detailed account of the Luhan, Collier, Austin partnership on these cultural and political issues, see Jones, "'Hope for the Race.'"

52. Jones, "'Hope for the Race,'" 193.

53. Ibid., 210; Austin to Luhan, January 1, [1923], MDLBL.

54. Austin to Luhan, no date [1923], MDLBL. See Jones, "Hope for the Race," for elaboration of a speech Austin gave at Washington's National Popular Government Leagues in January 1923, as part of the anti-Bursum Bill campaign, 211–14.

55. Austin to Luhan, January 1, [1923]; Austin to Luhan, February 1, [1923], MDLBL.

56. Jones, "'Hope for the Race,'" 233.

57. Ibid., 289–90.

58. Ibid., 291–98.

59. Austin to Collier, May 16, 1930, Reel 1, JCSL.

60. Collier to Austin, May 21, 1930, JCSL. For more on conflicts between Collier and Austin, see Tomas Amalio Salinas, "Pearl Chase, John Collier, and Indian Reform Through the New Deal: Native American Affairs in California and the West," 1880–1937" (Ph.D. dissertation, University of California, Santa Barbara, 1995), 181–213.

61. Robert Fay Schrader, *The Indian Arts and Crafts Board: An Aspect of the New Deal Policy* (Albuquerque: University of New Mexico Press, 1983).

62. John Collier, *From Every Zenith: A Memoir and Some Essays on Life and Thought* (Denver: Sage Books, 1963), 155.

63. Austin to Luhan, April, 1929, MDLBL.

64. Luhan to Una Jeffers, no date, [1935], MDLBL.

65. "Mrs. Ickes Equals Husband's Energy," no author, no newspaper, no date. Story found in Ickes Family Scrapbook, 1934–5, Container 531, HILC.

66. "'Wife's Place Is With Husband,'" no author, no date, no newspaper, Ickes Family Scrapbook, 1918–35, Container 530, HILC.

67. "Interior Secretary's Wife Acclaims Tribal Fete as Season Peak," no author, no date, no newspaper, copy in Ickes Family Scrapbook, Container 531, HILC.

68. J. Leonard Bates, "Anna Wilmarth Thompson Ickes," in *Notable American Women, 1607–1950*, Volume II, ed. Edward T. James, (Cambridge: Belknap Press of Harvard University Press, 1974), 251.

69. Ibid., 251. No biography of Anna Ickes exists but some information on her can be found in T. H. Watkins, *Righteous Pilgrim: The Life and Times of Harold L. Ickes, 1874–1952* (New York: Henry Holt, 1990).

70. Anna to Harold Ickes, September 14, 1925; Harold to Anna, no date, 1925 file, Box 27, HILC.

71. See Watkins, *Righteous Pilgrim*.

72. Bates, "Anna . . . Ickes," 252.

73. Anna Wilmarth Ickes, *Mesa Land: The History and Romance of the Southwest* (Boston: Houghton Mifflin Company, 1933), 1, v.

74. Ibid., 216, vi.

75. Ibid., 143.

76. Ibid., 76, 141, 183–84.

77. Ibid., 6, 8.

78. This phrase is Dilworth's, *Imagining Indians*, 206.

79. Ickes, *Mesa Land*, 24, 35.

80. Ibid., 127–28.

81. Ibid., 164, 165, 147–49, 51-53, 68, 158–59, 58, 69, 62.

82. Anna Ickes to Mary Austin, February 7, 1934, MAHL; a copy of *The Washington Star* review can be found in Ickes Family Scrapbook, 1918–35, Container 530, HILC.

83. Ickes, *Mesa Land*, 202, 205, 206.

84. Collier to Anna Ickes, February 16, 1927; Collier to Anna Ickes, February 24, 1928; Anna Ickes to Collier, July 31, 1928, all Reel #3, JCSL.

85. Quoted in "Mrs. Ickes Equals Husband's Energy," no author, no newspaper, no date, in Ickes Family Scrapbook, 1934–5, Container 531, HILC.

86. For correspondence regarding the Navajo, see Anna Ickes to Collier, June 13, 1933; Collier to Anna Ickes, June 16, 1933; Anna Ickes to Collier, June 24, 1933; for correspondence regarding personnel issues, see Anna Ickes to John Collier, October 14, 1933; Collier to Ickes, October 17, 1933; and letter regarding Indian Reorganization Act, Collier to Anna Ickes, February 26, 1934, all Reel 14, JCSL. For Ickes's comment on policy, see *Mesa Land*, 5.

87. "Indian Affairs Revision Urged at Conference," January 7, 1934, no author, no newspaper, in Ickes Family Scrapbook, 1934–5, HILC; Anna Ickes to Mary Austin, February 7, 1934 and February 11, 1934, MAHL.

88. Quoted in unidentified article, no date, no newspaper, Container 531; "Archaeology, Snakes, Politics Are All Hobbies of Mrs. Ickes," *Indianapolis Star*, May 18 [no year], Ickes Family Scrapbook, 1918–35, Container 530, HILC.

89. Emma Perley Lincoln, "Mrs. Ickes Packs Navajo Jewelry Box for Customary Trip to New Mexico," *Washington Post*, no date, Ickes Family Scrapbook, 1918–35, Container 530, HILC. For other articles on Anna's trips to New Mexico, see "Mrs. Ickes Off Aug. 5 For Trip to Desert Indians," Container 530; and "Mrs. Ickes At Summer Home" and "Secretary's Wife Is Studying Lore of Indian Tribes," Ickes Family Scrapbook, 1934–35, Container 531, HILC.

90. "Despite Brilliant Career in Public Life Mrs. Ickes Disagrees With Feminists," no author, no newspaper, no date, Ickes Family Scrapbook, 1918–35, Container 530, HILC. The article concluded with the comforting message that Anna's "keen interest in public affairs has never lessened Mrs. Ickes' interest in her home, and in speaking of the various phases of her activities, she seems to enjoy most talking of her children."

91. "At First White House Masquerade," no date, no author, no newspaper, Ickes Family Scrapbook, 1918–35, Container 530, HILC.

## *Chapter 9*

1. Mabel Dodge Luhan to Carl Van Vechten, December 18, 1913; Luhan to Van Vechten, "Saturday," no year, MDLBL. Luhan added in this second letter, "I am the only western looking woman in the West. Others look like horrific imitations of Broadway. All women spit here."

2. Christopher Lasch, *The New Radicalism in America, 1889–1963: The Intellectual As a Social Type* (New York: Alfred A. Knopf, 1965), 107. Lasch describes her as "another rich and restless woman, a footnote in the cultural history of Bohemia . . . a marginal figure in literary as in social history." Lasch maintains that Luhan's memoirs struck contemporaries as hopelessly out-of-date. "At a time when political involvement was the fashion among intellectuals, Mrs. Luhan's painstaking investigations of the intricacies of personal intercourse could hardly have commanded a following . . . her continuing indifference to the great issues of the day forfeited her chance for a reputation."

3. Mabel Dodge Luhan, *Edge of Taos Desert: An Escape to Reality* (Albuquerque: University of New Mexico Press, 1987), 295. This book was originally published in 1937 by Harcourt, Brace and Company. Carter Jones, "'Hope for the Race of Man': Indians, Intellectuals and the Regeneration of Modern America, 1917–1934" (Ph.D. dissertation, Brown University, 1991).

4. Lois Palken Rudnick, *Mabel Dodge Luhan: New Woman, New Worlds* (Albuquerque: University of New Mexico Press, 1984), 88, 90.

5. Luhan explained to Sterne her view of the artist's wife was to be "the soil for the man's spiritual seed. She is the warmth that his work ripens in. She is the *will* for his creative impulse to feed on. Therefore she has only her life thro' her man." Mabel to Maurice, [1917], Folder 62, Box 3, MSBL.

6. Mabel Dodge Luhan to Maurice Sterne, no date, Folder 65, Box 3, MSBL. A copy of the September 26, 1917, *New York City Herald* clipping about the marriage can be found in the Maurice Sterne correspondence to Luhan, MDLBL. Sterne's choice of words was painfully appropriate. Luhan controlled the purse-strings in the family and was not above reminding him of this once the marriage faced a crisis in Taos. Their correspondence immediately after the wedding, and Sterne's departure, indicates they meant to reassure one another that they did the right thing. See Luhan to Sterne, August 6, 1917; Sterne to Luhan, August 25, 1917, MDLBL. In his published autobiography, Sterne indicates he married Luhan as much for her money as for sexual desire and that he told her this at the time. See Maurice Sterne, *Shadow and Light: The Life, Friends and Opinions of Maurice Sterne*, ed. Charlotte Leon Mayerson (New York: Harcourt Brace & World Inc. 1965), 123. For Mabel's view of the marriage, see *Movers and Shakers* (Albuquerque: University of New Mexico Press, 1980), 524–30. This book was originally published by Harcourt, Brace and Company, 1936.

7. Sterne, *Shadow and Light*, 98, 99, 103, 105, 132. Luhan took up Sterne's enthusiasm for the Balinese, encouraging *The New Republic*'s Ridgley Torrence to examine Sterne's photographs of Bali in order to write a play about it. "I never imagined that there was anywhere a life so beautiful in its externals as well as in its interior significance as expressed by the[ir] rituals and ceremonies," she wrote in language that anticipated her reaction to the Pueblos. Clearly, Luhan's understanding of Bali rested solely on Sterne's testimony. Eventually, the Balinese's supposed attributes would shift to American Indians, first for Sterne—then for Luhan. See Mabel to Torrence, no date [1915], Series II, Box 43, RTPL.

8. Maurice Sterne to Luhan, November 10, 1917; November 14, 1917; November 16, 1917; November 18, 1917; and November 22, 1917; MDLBL.

9. Sterne to Luhan, November 30, 1917, MDLBL.

10. Ibid.

11. Ibid.

12. Luhan to Neith Hapgood, no date, Folder 155, Box 5, HFBL; Luhan to Sterne, December 12, 1917, Folder 61, Box 3, MSBL.

13. Luhan to Sterne, December 4, 1917, Folder 61, Box 3, MDLBL.

14. T. J. Jackson Lears, *No Place of Grace: Antimodernism and the Transformation of American Culture* (New York: Pantheon Books, 1981), 169, 177, 179.

15. Luhan to Sterne, November 24, 1917, Folder 62, Box 3, MSBL; Luhan, *Edge of Taos Desert*, 201. When Mabel married Tony, she changed the spelling of her new last name to "Luhan," believing that would encourage her non-Spanish speaking friends to pronounce her name correctly. Here I will retain "Lujan" when writing about Tony, however.

16. Luhan to Sterne, December 4, 1917, Folder 61, Box 3, MSBL.

17. Luhan to Neith Hapgood, April 21, [no date, but context indicates 1918], Folder 154, Box 5, HFBL.

18. Luhan, *Edge of Taos Desert,* 95, 102, 162, 176, 216, 296. Christopher Lasch's reading of Luhan is interesting. He found her self-absorbed and self-indulgent. He argues that she saw sex as the highest form of love and describes her as "a pioneer in the cult of orgasm." Her Taos conversion was merely a "biological outlet for her energies." In what seems like an almost willful misreading of Luhan's autobiography, Lasch also focuses almost totally on her relationship with D. H. Lawrence rather than with Tony. See Lasch, *New Radicalism,* 109, 118. 119.

19. Maurice Sterne, autobiobraphical fragment, Folder 197, Box 8, MSBL.

20. Sterne, *Shadow and Light,* 140–44.

21. Maurice Sterne, ms. autobiographical fragments, Folders 196, 197, and 198, Box 8, MSBL.

22. Luhan to Sterne, March 2, no year, Folder 62, Box 3; Luhan to Sterne, no date, Folder 63, Box 2; March 21, no year, Folder 63, Box 3; March 26, no year, Folder 63, Box 3, MSBL.

23. Luhan to Neith Hapgood, no date [1919], Folder 154; Luhan to Neith Hapgood, August 10, 1919, Folder 152, Box 5, HFBL.

24. Lois Palken Rudnick, *Utopian Vistas: The Mabel Dodge Luhan House and the American Counterculture* (Albuquerque: University of New Mexico Press, 1996), 7–10, 21–183. For a visitor's point of view, see Miriam Hapgood DeWitt, *Taos: A Memory* (Albuquerque: University of New Mexico Press, 1992).

25. Luhan to Sterne, no date, Folder 63, Box 3; Luhan to Sterne, no date, Folder 65, Box 3; MSBL; Sterne to Luhan, no date, MDLBL.

26. Rudnick, *Mabel Dodge Luhan,* 172.

27. Ibid., 172–75.

28. "The Indian Speaks," Za/Luhan/27, copy in MDLBL.

29. Luhan to Leo Stein, December 27, 1922, MDLBL. For a copy of the letter Luhan sent to all the Pueblos, see Luhan to Pueblos, November 3, 1922, Reel 5, JCSL.

30. Luhan to Collier November 21, 1922; Collier to Luhan, November 26, 1922, Reel 3, JCSL.

31. Luhan, *Edge of Taos Desert,* 322, 328; Luhan to Stella Atwood, no date, Reel 3, JCSL.

32. Stella Atwood to Luhan, December 2, 1922, MDLBL. Actually, Luhan was not at all sure she would feel the same about Navajos, writing in her book, *Lorenzo in Taos,* that they were "different" people who looked at you with "dry-eyed, molten, black glances from haughty, metal-hot eyes . . . They feel separate and they seem to like it." See Mabel Dodge Luhan, *Lorenzo in Taos* (New York: Alfred A. Knopf, 1932), 259.

33. Luhan to Leo Stein, December 27, no year, MDLBL.

34. Luhan, *Lorenzo in Taos,* 12, 6, 20, 35.

35. Ibid., 13–4, 19.

36. Luhan, *Lorenzo in Taos,* 37; Frieda Lawrence to Mabel, August 17, 1930, MDLBL. Frieda told Mabel that she despised Dorothy Brett, a mutual friend, "for her antagonism to the phallic mystery, that I live by." Maurice Sterne said that Mabel, deep down, was "a very respectable bourgeoise . . . she always had middle-class scruples about her misdemeanors *against convention*. That is why her love affairs eventually had to be sanctified. She had to pay her debt to society by marriage, like a good Buffalo Christian." Sterne, *Shadow and Light,* 124.

37. Luhan, *Lorenzo in Taos,* 52.

38. Ibid., 48, 60, 63–4.

39. Ibid., 66, 70, 76. For Christopher Lasch's interpretation of these events see Lasch, *The New Radicalism*, 131–40.

40. Luhan to Van Vechten, March 16, no year; Luhan to Leo Stein, no year, MDLBL.

41. Luhan to Mary Austin, November 28, no year, MAHL; Luhan to Leo Stein, November 27, no year, MDLBL; and Luhan, *Lorenzo in Taos*, 253. Mabel believed that Lawrence, in the few essays he wrote about New Mexico, did capture some fragments of the Indian cosmos. Also she claimed he took all he learned from Tony about Indians and transposed Taos to Mexico in *The Plumed Serpent*. "What I wanted him to do for Taos, he did do," she wrote, "but he gave it away to the mother country of Montezuma." *Lorenzo in Taos*, 253, 114.

42. Quoted in Luhan, *Lorenzo in Taos*, 343–44, 120, 128, 151.

43. Luhan to Dorothy Brett, no date, MDLBL; Luhan to Una Jeffers, 1930, Folder 1, Box 1, UJBL; Luhan, *Lorenzo in Taos*, 252, 280–81; Luhan to John Evans, June 17, no year, Folder 12, Box 2, UJBL.

44. Una would eventually have reason to regret the Mabel connection. In 1938, Luhan encouraged another woman guest to carry on an affair with Robinson Jeffers, believing this would inspire him in his work. Upon learning this, Una tried to commit suicide in Luhan's bathroom. Luckily, she was not successful. See Rudnick, *Mabel Dodge Luhan*, 298–99.

45. Una Jeffers to Luhan, April 13, 1931; Una Jeffers to Luhan, February 4, 1932; Margery Toomer to Luhan, April 16, 1932; MDLBL.

46. Luhan to Alfred Steiglitz, September 14, 1916, MDLBL; Luhan to Mary Austin, January 20, 1924, Box 95, MAHL; Jane Nelson, *Mabel Dodge Luhan* (Boise: Boise State University Press, 1982), 7–9. Luhan informed Carl Van Vechten that D. H. Lawrence encouraged her to bequeath her memoirs to the Academe Francaise and they would publish them. "He has read most all the 2nd (Italian) vol. & likes it very much." Luhan to Carl Van Vechten, November 3, no year, MDLBL.

47. Luhan to Leo Stein, November 30, 1935?, MDLBL; Luhan to Hutchins Hapgood, November 5, no year, Folder 150, Box 5, HFBL.

48. Luhan to Hutchins Hapgood, December 25, no year, Folder 150, Box 5, HFBL.

49. Luhan to Carl Van Vechten, April 8, no year, MDLBL.

50. Una Jeffers to Luhan, October 25, 1933; Jeffers to Luhan, December 11, 1933, MDLBL.

51. Luhan, *Edge of Taos Desert*, 101, 110.

52. For Luhan's interpretation of the peyote conflict within Taos Pueblo, see Luhan to John Collier, March 8, 1934, JCSL.

53. It is extremely difficult to grasp a sense of Tony apart from Mabel's construction of him. He was illiterate, thus his letters to others always went through the mediation of either Mabel or friend and artist Dorothy Brett. When Mabel gives him a voice in her published works, he sounded stilted and stereotypical even though she meant to present him as wise, profound, and as the key to her new found sense of "reality."

54. Luhan, *Edge of Taos Desert*, 197.

55. Ibid, 197.

56. Ibid., 280–81, 284.

57. Ibid., 298.

58. Rudnick, *Mabel Dodge Luhan*, 259; Luhan to Hutchins Hapgood, no date, Folder 150, Box 5, HFBL; Luhan to Una Jeffers, no date, Folder 6 & Folder 7, Box 1, UJBL; Luhan to Elizabeth S. Sargeant, February 22, 1935?, Folder 118, Box 5, ESBL; Una Jeffers to Luhan, August 21, 1934 and November 1, 1934, MDLBL. In the latter, Jeffers told Luhan, "'Winter in Taos' is enchanting as writing. I think its the best thing you've done.

Robin likes it tremendously." More recently, critic Jane Nelson deemed *Winter in Taos* "unquestionably the finest of her six books published in the 1930s." See Nelson, *Mabel Dodge Luhan*, 18.

59. Mabel Dodge Luhan, *Winter in Taos* (Taos, New Mexico: Las Palomas de Taos, 1987), 54, 195–96. This book was originally published by Harcourt, Brace, and Company, Inc. in 1935.

60. Nelson, *Mabel Dodge Luhan*, 19.

61. Luhan considered seeking help from Carl Jung to break through her limitations but, while he came to Taos in 1925, they never met for Luhan was in New York at the time. Luhan to Hutchins Hapgood, November 4, 1937, Folder 149, Box 5, HFBL; Rudnick, *Mabel Dodge Luhan*, 185–86.

62. Luhan, "Water of Life," ms. MDLBL, 2, 257, 259, 260, 284. For another example of Luhan's interpretation of the value of "group life" and one more obviously based on Taos Pueblo, see "The Whole is Greater than the Part," Za/Luhan/72, undated, MDLBL.

63. Luhan to Hutchins Hapgood, February 24, 1938?, Folder 149, Box 5, HFBL. Publishers instead clamored for more autobiography. She wrote a new volume for *Intimate Memories* in 1947, but vowed it would never be published because it contained too much secret anthropological material. Its publication would betray both her husband and the Pueblo. It remains sealed to this day, in the Beinecke Library. See Luhan to Sonya Levien, August 10, 1947, Box 4, SLHL.

64. Luhan to Carl Van Vechten, April 16, 1928, MDLBL; Luhan to Elizabeth Sergeant, [1933], Folder 118, Box 5, ESBL; Luhan to Carl Van Vechten, October 11, 1950, MDLBL.

65. Frank Waters to Luhan, no date, MDLBL; "Conquest," the scenario and several versions of Part I's script can be found in Za/Luhan/17, MDLBL.

66. Luhan to Dorothy Brett, no date, MDLBL.

67. Both are quoted in Patricia R. Everett, *A History of Having a Great Many Times Not Continued To Be Friends* (Albuquerque: University of New Mexico Press, 1996), 253.

68. Austin to Luhan, undated letter; Luhan to Dorothy Brett, February 24, 1934, both MDLBL.

69. Elizabeth Shepley Sergeant, "Sphinx of Taos Desert," *Saturday Review of Literature*, copy found in Folder 285, Box 12, ESBL.

70. Luhan to John Collier, November 30, 1933, JCSL. Perhaps we should not be surprised to learn that Luhan was not always consistent about the issue of intermarriage. A 1932 interview with Mabel that appeared in *The Denver Post* quotes her as saying, "the races may amalgamate and the Indians be the ones to save our race. A wealth of artistic sentiment will be blended in the new blood infusion with the white race." Quoted in Rudnick, *Mabel Dodge Luhan*, 182.

71. Luhan, *Lorenzo in Taos*, 235–37.

72. Luhan to Hutchins Hapgood, January 14, no year, Folder 149, Box 5, HFBL.

73. Luhan to Dorothy Brett, February 23, no year, MDLBL.

74. In *Edge of Taos Desert*, Mabel asks Tony if they each can truly leave their own people in order to be together. Tony answered, "'Perhaps we help more when we go back, leavin' for a little while.'" Although this was not the answer she expected, she "found out later . . . his answer answered my question." See *Edge of Taos Desert*, 222.

75. Rudnick, *Mabel Dodge Luhan*, 225–30.

76. Luhan to Jean Toomer, no date, Folder 159, Box 5, JTBL.

77. Ibid.

78. Tony was not beyond extramarital affairs himself. Mabel wrote to Dorothy Brett

about his love affair with Marian Shevky in the late 1920s: "If Tony & Marion could only go off for 6 months somewhere & get it out of their systems it might work out—this way keeps everyone upset all the time." Luhan to Dorothy Brett, April 22, no year, MDLBL.

79. Luhan to Una Jeffers, no date, Folder 8, Box 2, UJBL; Luhan to Dorothy Brett, no date, MDLBL.

80. Quoted in "A Bird's Eye View of Mabel by Adrian," included in a letter from Luhan to Una Jeffers, September 16, 1936 [?], Folder 7, Box 1, UJBL.

81. Luhan to Carl Hoven, no date, Box 4, SLHL.

82. Rudnick, *Mabel Dodge Luhan*, 155; Luhan to John Collier, February 3, 1935, and February 16, 1935, JCSL; Luhan to Elizabeth S. Sergeant, February 22, 1935, Folder 118, Box 5, ESBL.

83. Luhan to Una Jeffers, no date, Folder 6, Box 1, UJBL.

84. Luhan to Una Jeffers, February 16, 1935, Folder 6, Box 1, UJBL.

85. Tony Lujan to John Collier, December 9, 1934, JCSL.

86. Luhan to Collier, April 13, 1933; August 18, 1933; September 24, 1933; Collier to Luhan, October 6, 1933; Luhan to Lucy Collier, February 20, 1936; John Collier to Luhan, February 25, 1936; Luhan to Collier, February 28, 1936; Collier to Luhan, March 6, 1936; Luhan to Collier, March 10, 1936; and Collier to Luhan, March 14, 1936; all letters are in JCSL.

87. Luhan to Una Jeffers, three undated letters circa June 1936, Folder 7, Box 1; Luhan to Una Jeffers, March 5, 1937, Folder 8, Box 2; Luhan to Una Jeffers, no date, Folder 10, Box 2, all UJBL.

88. Luhan to Collier, May 12, 1936; Luhan to Harold Ickes, June 15, 1936; Ickes to Luhan, no date; all JCSL.

89. Luhan to Collier, January 7, 1940; Luhan to Collier, "Thursday," no year, JCSL; Luhan to Dorothy Brett, no date, MDLBL.

90. Luhan to Hutch & Neith Hapgood, August 5, 1941, Folder 149, Box 5, HFBL; Luhan to Dorothy Brett, no date, MDLBL; Luhan to Brett, December 29, no year, MDLBL; Una Jeffers to Luhan, May 29, 1940, MDLBL; Luhan to Jeffers, August 26, 1945 and November 24, 1945, Folder 9, Box 2, UJBL.

91. Luhan to Dorothy Brett, March 20, 1941, MDLBL.

92. Luhan to Van Vechten, November 16, 1951; July 10, 1952; and February 5, 1953, MDLBL.

93. John Collier to Elizabeth Sergeant, March 25, 1957; Collier to Sergeant, January 5, 1962; Collier to Sergeant, March 15, 1962; and September 4, 1962; Folder 30, Box 1, ESBL; Rudnick, *Mabel Dodge Luhan*, 330.

94. Luhan to Carl Van Vechten, August 22, 1951, MDLBL.

95. Frank Waters to Luhan, June 5, 1949, MDLBL; Luhan to Sonya Levien, June 23, no year, Box 4, SLHL; Luhan to Collier, January 1, 1940, JCSL.

96. This is included in a letter Luhan sent Alfred Steiglitz, February 15, 1939, MDLBL.

# INDEX